Houghton Mifflin
Reading

Teacher's Edition
Grade 5
Expeditions

Theme 1 — Back to School
Nature's Fury
Focus on **Tall Tales**

Theme 2 — **Give It All You've Got**
Focus on **Poetry**

Theme 3 — **Voices of the Revolution**

Theme 4 — **Person to Person**
Focus on **Plays**

Theme 5 — **One Land, Many Trails**
Focus on **Autobiography**

▶ **Theme 6** — **Animal Encounters**

Senior Authors J. David Cooper, John J. Pikulski

Authors Kathryn H. Au, David J. Chard, Gilbert G. Garcia, Claude N. Goldenberg, Phyllis C. Hunter, Marjorie Y. Lipson, Shane Templeton, Sheila W. Valencia, MaryEllen Vogt

Consultants Linda H. Butler, Linnea C. Ehri, Carla B. Ford

HOUGHTON MIFFLIN   BOSTON

LITERATURE REVIEWERS

Consultants: **Dr. Adela Artola Allen,** Associate Dean, Graduate College, Associate Vice President for Inter-American Relations, University of Arizona, Tucson, AZ; **Dr. Manley Begay,** Co-director of the Harvard Project on American Indian Economic Development, Director of the National Executive Education Program for Native Americans, Harvard University, John F. Kennedy School of Government, Cambridge, MA; **Dr. Nicholas Kannellos,** Director, Arte Publico Press, Director, Recovering the U.S. Hispanic Literacy Heritage Project, University of Houston, TX; **Mildred Lee,** author and former head of Library Services for Sonoma County, Santa Rosa, CA; **Dr. Barbara Moy,** Director of the Office of Communication Arts, Detroit Public Schools, MI; **Norma Naranjo,** Clark County School District, Las Vegas, NV; **Dr. Arlette Ingram Willis,** Associate Professor, Department of Curriculum and Instruction, Division of Language and Literacy, University of Illinois at Urbana-Champaign, IL

Teachers: Midge Anuson, Ridge Hall Lutheran School, Rodona Beach, CA; **Sue Hooks,** Lebanon Road Elementary School, Charlotte, NC; **Anatia Gayle Mills,** Cranberry-Prosperity School, Beckley, WV; **Tom Torres,** Elaine Wynn Elementary School, Las Vegas, NV; **Celeste Watts,** Meadow Hill Magnet Elementary School, Newburgh, NY

PROGRAM REVIEWERS

Linda Bayer, Jonesboro, GA; **Sheri Blair,** Warner Robins, GA; **Faye Blake,** Jacksonville, FL; **Suzi Boyett,** Sarasota, FL; **Carol Brockhouse,** Madison Schools, Wayne Westland Schools, MI; **Patti Brustad,** Sarasota, FL; **Jan Buckelew,** Venice, FL; **Maureen Carlton,** Barstow, CA; **Karen Cedar,** Gold River, CA; **Karen Ciraulo,** Folsom, CA; **Marcia M. Clark,** Griffin, GA; **Kim S. Coady,** Covington, GA; **Eva Jean Conway,** Valley View School District, IL; **Marilyn Crownover,** Tustin, CA; **Carol Daley,** Sioux Falls, SD; **Jennifer Davison,** West Palm Beach, FL; **Lynne M. DiNardo,** Covington, GA; **Kathy Dover,** Lake City, GA; **Cheryl Dultz,** Citrus Heights, CA; **Debbie Friedman,** Fort Lauderdale, FL; **Anne Gaitor,** Lakeland, GA; **Rebecca S. Gillette,** Saint Marys, GA; **Buffy C. Gray,** Peachtree City, GA; **Merry Guest,** Homestead, FL; **Jo Nan Holbrook,** Lakeland, GA; **Beth Holguin,** San Jose, CA; **Coleen Howard-Whals,** St. Petersburg, FL; **Beverly Hurst,** Jacksonville, FL; **Debra Jackson,** St. Petersburg, FL; **Vickie Jordan,** Centerville, GA; **Cheryl Kellogg,** Panama City, FL; **Karen Landers,** Talladega County, AL; **Barb LeFerrier,** Port Orchard, WA; **Sandi Maness,** Modesto, CA; **Ileana Masud,** Miami, FL; **David Miller,** Cooper City, FL; **Muriel Miller,** Simi Valley, CA; **Walsetta W. Miller,** Macon, GA; **Jean Nielson,** Simi Valley, CA; **Sue Patton,** Brea, CA; **Debbie Peale,** Miami, FL; **Loretta Piggee,** Gary, IN; **Jennifer Rader,** Huntington, CA; **April Raiford,** Columbus, GA; **Cheryl Remash,** Manchester, NH; **Francis Rivera,** Orlando, FL; **Marina Rodriguez,** Hialeah, FL; **Marilynn Rose,** MI; **Kathy Scholtz,** Amesbury, MA; **Kimberly Moulton Schorr,** Columbus, GA; **Linda Schrum,** Orlando, FL; **Sharon Searcy,** Mandarin, FL; **Melba Sims,** Orlando, FL; **Judy Smith,** Titusville, FL; **Bea Tamo,** Huntington, CA; **Dottie Thompson,** Jefferson County, AL; **Dana Vassar,** Winston-Salem, NC; **Beverly Wakefield,** Tarpon Springs, FL; **Joy Walls,** Winston-Salem, NC; **Elaine Warwick,** Williamson County, TN; **Audrey N. Watkins,** Atlanta, GA; **Marti Watson,** Sarasota, FL

Supervisors: Judy Artz, Butler County, OH; **James Bennett,** Elkhart, IN; **Kay Buckner-Seal,** Wayne County, MI; **Charlotte Carr,** Seattle, WA; **Sister Marion Christi,** Archdiocese of Philadelphia, PA; **Alvina Crouse,** Denver, CO; **Peggy DeLapp,** Minneapolis, MN; **Carol Erlandson,** Wayne Township Schools, IN; **Brenda Feeney,** North Kansas City School District, MO; **Winnie Huebsch,** Sheboygan, WI; **Brenda Mickey,** Winston-Salem, NC; **Audrey Miller,** Camden, NJ; **JoAnne Piccolo,** Westminster, CO; **Sarah Rentz,** Baton Rouge, LA; **Kathy Sullivan,** Omaha, NE; **Rosie Washington,** Gary, IN; **Theresa Wishart,** Knox County Public Schools, TN

English Language Learners Reviewers: Maria Arevalos, Pomona, CA; **Lucy Blood,** NV; **Manuel Brenes,** Kalamazoo, MI; **Delight Diehn,** AZ; **Susan Dunlap,** Richmond, CA; **Tim Fornier,** Grand Rapids, MI; **Connie Jimenez,** Los Angeles, CA; **Diane Bonilla Lether,** Pasadena, CA; **Anna Lugo,** Chicago, IL; **Marcos Martel,** Hayward, CA; **Carolyn Mason,** Yakima, WA; **Jackie Pinson,** Moorpark, CA; **Jenaro Rivas,** NJ; **Jerilyn Smith,** Salinas, CA; **Noemi Velazquez,** Jersey City, NJ; **JoAnna Veloz,** NJ; **Dr. Santiago Veve,** Las Vegas, NV

CREDITS

Cover
Cover photography Nick Vedros, Vedros & Associates.

Photography
Theme Opener © Frans Lanting/Minden Pictures. **599B** Jon Triffo/Triffo Online Magazine. **625S** (cover) © Wolfgang Kaehler, www.wkaehlerphoto.com. **625T** © Wolfgang Kaehler, www.wkaehlerphoto.com. **645** Heidi Powers/Morgan-Cain & Associates. **647BB** Photo 24/Brand X Pictures/PictureQuest. **670** Hemera Technologies, Inc. **M12** David Bowman/U.S. Fish and Wildlife Service. **M14** Steve Allen/Brand X Pictures/PictureQuest. **R3** © Marty Snyderman/CORBIS. **R7** © Getty Images.

Illustration
All kid art by Morgan-Cain & Associates.

ACKNOWLEDGMENTS

Grateful acknowledgment is made for permission to reprint copyrighted material as follows:

Theme 6
"Fun Around the Globe," by Donna O'Meara from *Faces* Magazine, May 1999 issue: Nunavut. Copyright © 1999 by Cobblestone Publishing, 30 Grove Street, Suite C, Peterborough, NH 03458. All rights reserved. Reprinted by permission of Carus Publishing Company.

"Giving Wildlife a Second Chance," by Connie Goldsmith from *Cricket* Magazine, May 1999 issue, Vol. 26, No. 9. Copyright © 1999 by Connie Goldsmith. Reprinted by permission of *Cricket* Magazine.

STUDENT WRITING MODEL FEATURE

Special thanks to the following teachers whose students' compositions appear as Student Writing Models: **Cindy Cheatwood,** Florida; **Diana Davis,** North Carolina; **Kathy Driscoll,** Massachusetts; **Linda Evers,** Florida; **Heidi Harrison,** Michigan; **Eileen Hoffman,** Massachusetts; **Julia Kraftsow,** Florida; **Bonnie Lewison,** Florida; **Kanetha McCord,** Michigan

Animal Encounters

Theme **6**

Animal Encounters

C O N T E N T S

The Grizzly Bear Family Book

Nonfiction

Below Level   *On Level*   *Above Level*   *Language Support*

Nonfiction

Below Level *On Level* *Above Level* *Language Support*

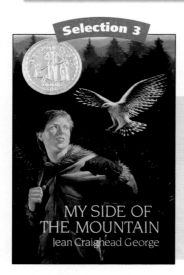

Realistic Fiction

Below Level *On Level* *Above Level* *Language Support*

Theme Wrap-Up
Monitoring Student Progress

Nonfiction

Fiction

Assessing Student Progress

Leveled Theme Paperbacks

Leveled Bibliography

BOOKS FOR INDEPENDENT READING AND FLUENCY BUILDING

 To build vocabulary and fluency, choose books from this list for students to read outside class. Suggest that students read for at least thirty minutes a day, either independently or with an adult who provides modeling and guidance.

Key

 Science

 Social Studies

 Multicultural

 Music

 Math

 Classic

 Art

 Career

Classroom Bookshelf

WELL BELOW LEVEL

Orcas Around Me: My Alaskan Summer
by Deborah Page
Whitman 1997 (40p)
Taiga, who lives aboard an Alaskan fishing boat, encounters many sea animals.

The Way Home
by Nan Parson Rossiter
Dutton 1999 (32p)
A father and son take care of an injured Canada goose and her mate, who finally fly south.

 Dolphins: What They Can Teach Us
by Mary Cerullo
Dutton 1999 (48p)
The author discusses dolphin behavior, including dolphins' interactions with humans.

 Tooth and Claw: Animal Adventures in the Wild
by Ted Lewin
Harper 2003 (64p)
Lewin relates and illustrates his sometimes-dangerous adventures photographing wildlife.

 Baby Whale Rescue: The True Story of J. J.
by Caroline Arnold
BridgeWater 1999
A stranded baby whale is rescued, nursed back to health, and returned to the ocean.

BELOW LEVEL

 The Leopard Family Book
by Jonathan Scott
North-South 1999 (56p)
The author explains how the leopard is able to survive in the wild.

 Hippos in the Night: Autobiographical Adventures in Africa
by Christina Allen
Harper 2003 (128p)
Wildlife biologist Allen travels through East Africa to study disappearing animals.

 Hawk Highway in the Sky
by Caroline Arnold
Harcourt 1997 (48p)
Members of the HawkWatch International Project study the migration patterns of raptors in Nevada's Goshute Mountains.

 Sea Otter Rescue
by Roland Smith
Dutton 1999 (64p) paper
After a disastrous oil spill, a team of animal rescue experts rushes to the aid of sea otters.

ON LEVEL

 Swimming with Sharks
by Twig C. George
Harper 1999 (128p)
On a visit to the Florida Keys, Sarah develops an interest in sharks and studies them with her marine-biologist grandfather.

Dolphin Freedom
by Wayne Grover
Greenwillow 1999 (112p)
Grover and his friends Amos and Jack rescue a family of dolphins from poachers who plan to sell them to marine parks.

 Wild Horses I Have Known
by Hope Ryden
Clarion 1999 (90p)
The author studies the wild mustangs along the Wyoming-Montana border.

 Project UltraSwan
by Elinor Osborn
Houghton 2002 (64p)
Scientists teach trumpeter swans, once nearly extinct, how to live in their former habitat and to relearn their migration routes.

Once a Wolf
by Stephen R. Swinburne
Houghton 1999 (48p)
Wildlife biologists work to bring the gray wolf back to Yellowstone National Park.

Elephant Woman
by Laurence Pringle
Simon 1997 (48p)
Cynthia Moss studies elephants in Africa's Amboseli National Park.

The House of Wings
by Betsy Byars
Penguin 1982 (142p)
Caring for an injured crane helps bring a boy and his grandfather closer.

The Snake Scientist
by Sy Montgomery
Houghton 1999 (48p)
Dr. Robert Mason has studied Canada's fascinating red-sided garter snake for fifteen years.

Misty of Chincoteague
by Marguerite Henry
Simon 1988 (172p) also paper
A brother and sister have their hearts set on owning Phantom, the wildest mare on Chincoteague Island, and her newborn foal, Misty.

Back to the Wild
by Dorothy Hinshaw Patent
Harcourt 1997 (48p)
Many endangered animals are born in captivity and released to the wild.

My Season with the Penguins: An Antarctic Journal
by Sophie Webb
Houghton 2000 (48p)
Webb, a biologist and an artist, went to Antarctica for two months to study and draw penguins.

Journey of the Red Wolf
by Roland Smith
Cobblehill 1997 (64p)
Nearly extinct in the 1960s, the red wolf has been saved.

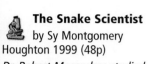
ABOVE LEVEL

Frightful's Mountain
by Jean Craighead George
Dutton 1999 (258p)
Frightful, Sam's falcon from My Side of the Mountain, must now try to survive in the wilderness.

One Wing's Gift: Rescuing Alaska's Wild Birds
by Joan Harris
Alaska Northwest 2002 (64p)
After the Exxon Valdez oil spill, One Wing, a badly injured bald eagle, recovers and becomes a blood donor to other injured birds.

Julie of the Wolves
by Jean Craighead George
Harper 1972 (180p) also paper
When Julie becomes lost on the Alaskan tundra, she is protected by a pack of wolves.

Platero y yo/Platero and I
by Juan Ramón Jiménez
Houghton 1994 (64p)
The Spanish classic about the journeys of a poet and his donkey.

BOOKS FOR TEACHER READ ALOUD

Ten True Animal Rescues
by Jean Betancourt
Scholastic 1998 (64p)
In these true stories, animals save the lives of their owners or of complete strangers.

Mr. Popper's Penguins
by Richard and Florence Atwater
Little 1938 (152p) also paper
In this humorous classic, Mr. Popper's life changes dramatically when a crate of penguins arrives at his door.

Technology

Computer Software Resources

- **Get Set for Reading CD-ROM**
  Animal Encounters
  Provides background building, vocabulary support, and selection summaries in English and Spanish

- **Spelling Spree!® CD-ROM**
  Provides interactive spelling and proofreading practice

- **Wacky Web Tales® floppy disk**
  Helps students create humorous stories and review parts of speech

Video Cassettes

- **My Side of the Mountain** by Jean Craighead George. *Filmic Archives*
- **Fly Away Home.** *Media Basics*
- **The Black Stallion** by Walter Farley. *Media Basics*

Audio

- **My Side of the Mountain** by Jean Craighead George. *Recorded Books*
- **Julie of the Wolves** by Jean Craighead George. *HarperAudio*
- **The Summer of the Swans** by Betsy Byars. *Recorded Books*
- **Lassie Come-Home** by Eric Knight. *HarperAudio*
- **A Dolphin Named Bob** by Twig C. George. *Recorded Books*
- **The Music of Dolphins** by Karen Hesse. *Listening Library*
- **Misty of Chincoteague** by Marguerite Henry. *Recorded Books*

Technology Resources addresses are on page R31.

Education Place®

www.eduplace.com *Log on to Education Place for more activities relating to* Animal Encounters, *including vocabulary support—*
  e • **Glossary**
  e • **WordGame**

Book Adventure®

www.bookadventure.org *This Internet reading incentive program provides thousands of titles for students to read.*

Accelerated Reader® Universal CD-ROM

This popular CD-ROM provides practice quizzes for Anthology selections and for many popular children's books.

Theme Skills Overview

	Selection 1	Selection 2
Pacing Approximately 4–6 weeks	**The Grizzly Bear Family Book** Nonfiction pp. 595A–623R	**The Golden Lion Tamarin Comes Home** Nonfiction pp. 625I–647R
Reading **Comprehension** **Information and Study Skills** **Leveled Readers** • Fluency Practice • Independent Reading	**Guiding Comprehension** **Making Generalizations** T **Evaluate** **Poetry Link** How to Compare Poems Preparing a Report **Leveled Readers** *The Hyrax of Top-Knot Island* *The Bald Eagle Is Back* *The Return of Wild Whoopers* *The Hyrax: An Interesting Puzzle* Lessons and Leveled Practice	**Guiding Comprehension** **Topic, Main Idea, and Supporting Details** T **Monitor/Clarify** T **Technology Link** How to Read a Technology Article Evaluating the Effects of Media **Leveled Readers** *Saving Sea Turtles* *The Emerald Cathedral: Inside a Tropical Rain Forest* *Invaders!* *Protecting Sea Turtles* Lessons and Leveled Practice
Word Work **Decoding** **Phonics Review** **Vocabulary** **Spelling**	**Prefixes *com-/con-*, *en-*, *ex-*, *pre-*, *pro*** T **The /k/ and /kw/ Sounds** **Using Context** T Prefixes *com-/con-*, *en-*, *ex-*, *pre-*, *pro* T	**Three-Syllable Words** T **Consonant Alternations** **Pronunciations in a Dictionary** T Three-Syllable Words T
Writing and Oral Language **Writing** **Grammar** **Listening/Speaking/Viewing**	**Writing an Opinion Paragraph** Avoiding Double Negatives T Contractions; Negatives T Planning a Multimedia Presentation	**Writing a Compare/Contrast Essay** Combining Sentences with Prepositional Phrases T Prepositions T Giving Directions
Cross-Curricular Activities	Responding: Math, Health and Safety, Internet Classroom Management Activities	Responding: Science, Listening and Speaking, Internet Classroom Management Activities

T Skill tested on Theme Skills Test and/or Integrated Theme Test

Target Skills

Comprehension
Vocabulary
Phonics/Decoding
Fluency

Selection 3	**Monitoring Student Progress**

Selection 3

My Side of the Mountain
Realistic Fiction
pp. 647S–671R

Monitoring Student Progress

Check Your Progress
Interrupted Journey
Nonfiction

The Rabbit's Judgment
Fiction
pp. M1–M43

Guiding Comprehension

 Drawing Conclusions T

Summarize

Career Link
How to Categorize Information

Completing Applications and Forms T

Leveled Readers

Kat the Curious
Brinker's Isle
The Observations of Emma Boyle
Curious Kat

Lessons and Leveled Practice

Guiding Comprehension

Theme Connections

Comprehension Skills Review T

Monitor/Clarify T

Taking Tests: Writing an Opinion Essay

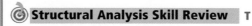

Connecting Leveled Readers

Suffixes *-ent, -ant, -able, -ible* T

Vowel Alternations

Run-on Dictionary Entries T

-ent, -ant; -able, -ible T

Structural Analysis Skill Review T

Vocabulary Skills Review T

Spelling Skills Review T

Writing an Answer to an Essay Question

Placing Prepositional Phrases Correctly

Object Pronouns T

Viewing for Information and Details

Writing Skills Review

Grammar Skills Review T

Responding: Social Studies, Viewing, Internet

Classroom Management Activities

Cross-Curricular Activities

Classroom Management Activities

Combination Classrooms

See the **Combination Classroom Planning Guide** for lesson planning and management support.

Writing Process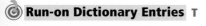

Reading-Writing Workshop: Persuasive Essay
- Student Writing Model
- Writing Process Instruction
- Writing Traits Focus

Additional Theme Resources

- Leveled Theme Paperbacks Lessons
- Reteaching Lessons
- Challenge/Extension Activities

Technology

Education Place
www.eduplace.com

Log on to Education Place for more activities relating to *Animal Encounters*.

Lesson Planner CD-ROM
Customize your planning for *Animal Encounters* with the Lesson Planner CD-ROM.

Cross-Curricular Activities

Independent Activities

Assign these activities at any time during the theme while you work with small groups.

Additional Independent Activities

- Challenge/Extension Activities, Theme Resources, pp. R9, R11, R13

- Theme 6 Assignment Cards 1–13, Teacher's Resource Blackline Masters, pp. 89–93

- Cross-Curricular Activities, pp. 598A–598B, 625Q–625R, 647AA–647BB, M6–M7

- Language Center, pp. 623M–632N, 647M–647N, 671M–671N

- **Classroom Management Handbook,** Activity Masters CM6-1–CM6-12

- **Challenge Handbook,** Activity Masters CH6-1–CH6-6

Look for these activities and more in the Classroom Management Kit.

Math

Massive Meals

Pairs	⏱ **20 minutes**
Objective	Write math word problems.

Write word problems about how much large animals eat.

- The chart below shows how much bears, elephants, giraffes, and lions eat per day.

AWESOME AMOUNTS

Animal	Pounds of Food per Day
Bear	90
Elephant	125
Giraffe	75
Lion	80

- Use the chart to write word problems that ask

  – how much each animal eats in a week or year

  – how much more (or less) one animal eats than another

- Try your math problems out on the other members of your group.

Art

Caption Classics

🧍 **Singles**	⏱ **30 minutes**
Objective	Write photo captions.
Materials	Reference sources, construction paper, art materials

It's true—a picture is sometimes worth a thousand words. However, captions can add helpful information to pictures.

- Use an encyclopedia or other reference source to find three photographs of wild animals. Note the text caption that accompanies each picture.

- Draw a picture of the animal in the photo and mount it on construction paper.

- Write an original caption for each picture.

A male Bengal tiger rests in a field in India.

Consider copying and laminating these activities for use in centers.

Science

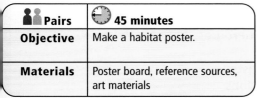
Habitat Histories

Pairs	🕐 45 minutes
Objective	Make a habitat poster.
Materials	Poster board, reference sources, art materials

The selections in this theme focus on three habitats: the North American Arctic, South American rain forest, and North American forest. With a partner, make a poster that displays facts about one habitat.

- Use an encyclopedia, the Internet, or other reference source to find out about your habitat, including:
  1) where it is found,
  2) what the climate is like,
  3) what kinds of animals and plants grow there, and
  4) how these plants and animals have adapted to this habitat.

- Display key facts on your poster. Include one or two illustrations.

Media

Get the Picture

👥 Groups	🕐 30 minutes
Objective	Compare and contrast types of media.
Materials	Writing materials

Many television programs and books focus on wild animals. With a partner, compare and contrast these two types of media.

- First, copy the chart below onto a sheet of paper. Think about any television shows about animals you have watched, and the books about animals you have read.

- Then evaluate the types of information each type of media gives and fill out the chart.

Type of Media	Television	Books
Information Given		
Advantages		
Disadvantages		

Writing

Sound Off

👤 Singles	🕐 35 minutes
Objective	Write an opinion essay.

When humans and wild animals co-exist, there are bound to be problems.

- Write a one-page opinion essay about one of these topics:
  - Should growing communities be allowed to spread into wildlife areas?
  - Is it okay for countries to cut down rain forests to make room for crop fields?
  - Should people be allowed to keep wild animals as pets?

- Follow the format below to write your essay.

I. Introduction
  A. State your opinion.
  B. Introduce main arguments.
II. Argument #1
  A. State main idea.
  B. Give supporting details.
III. (For other arguments, repeat format in section II.)
IV. Conclusion

Planning for Assessment

During instruction in Theme 6 . . .

1 SCREENING AND DIAGNOSIS

Screening
- Baseline Group Test

Diagnosis
- Leveled Reading Passages Assessment Kit
- Phonics/Decoding Screening Test
- Lexia Quick Phonics Assessment CD-ROM

2 MONITORING PROGRESS

ONGOING INFORMAL ASSESSMENT
- Guiding Comprehension questions
- Literature Discussion groups
- Comprehension Checks
- Fluency Practice
- Monitoring Student Progress boxes
- Writing Samples
- Observation Checklists
- Skill lesson applications

END-OF-THEME REVIEW AND TEST PREPARATION
- Monitoring Student Progress
- Assessing Student Progress

FORMAL ASSESSMENT
- Selection Tests
- Integrated Theme Tests
- Theme Skills Tests
- Fluency Assessment
- Reading-Writing Workshop

3 END-OF-YEAR ASSESSMENT

Additional opportunities for monitoring students' yearly progress at the end of the year:
- Administer the **Benchmark Progress Tests**, a measure of students' reading and narrative and expository writing levels compared to a national sample.
- Review student performance in the **Integrated Theme Tests**, Themes 1–6, using the Integrated Theme Test Class Record form in the *Teacher's Assessment Handbook*.
- Compare the performance of students reading below level, on passages in the **Leveled Reading Passages Assessment Kit** and/or the **Oral Reading Record** for **Below-Level Leveled Readers** since the beginning of the school year. You may want to use the variety of oral reading checklist forms in the *Teacher's Assessment Handbook*.

4 MANAGING AND REPORTING

 **Technology**   Record each student's performance on the **Learner Profile® CD-ROM**.

National Test Correlation
Documenting Adequate Yearly Progress

SKILLS for *Animal Encounters*	ITBS	Terra Nova (CTBS)	CAT	SAT	MAT
Comprehension Strategies and Skills					
• Strategies: Monitor/Clarify, Evaluate, Summarize*	O	O	O	O	O
• Skills: Making Generalizations, Topic, Main Idea, Supporting Details, Drawing Conclusions, Fact and Opinion*, Making Judgments*, Following Directions*, Compare/Contrast*	O	O	O	O	O
Structural Analysis					
• Prefixes *com-, con-, en-, ex-, pre-, pro-*	O	O	O	O	
• Words with *-ent, -ant, -able, -ible*	O	O	O	O	
• Three-Syllable Words					
Vocabulary/Dictionary					
• Using Context	O	O	O	O	O
• Idioms and Run-on Entries					
• Variations in Pronunciation					
Information and Study Skills					
• Completing Applications and Forms					
Spelling					
• Prefixes *com-, con-, en-, ex-, pre-, pro-*	O	O	O	O	O
• Words with *-ent, -ant, -able, -ible*	O	O	O	O	O
• Three-Syllable Words					
Grammar					
• Contractions with *not*	O				O
• Negatives	O		O		
• Object Pronouns in Prepositional Phrases	O	O	O		
• Prepositional Phrases	O		O		
• Prepositions	O		O		
Writing					
• Formats: Opinion, Compare/Contrast Essay, Answer to an Essay Question	O	O		O	O
• Avoiding Double Negatives	O		O		
• Combining Sentences with Prepositional Phrases	O	O	O	O	
• Reading-Writing Workshop: Persuasive Essay	O	O		O	O

*These skills are taught, but not tested, in this theme.

KEY

ITBS Iowa Tests of Basic Skills

Terra Nova (CTBS) Comprehensive Tests of Basic Skills

CAT California Achievement Tests

SAT Stanford Achievement Tests

MAT Metropolitan Achievement Tests

Launching the Theme

Theme **6**

Animal Encounters

The great hurrah about wild animals is that they exist at all, and the greater hurrah is the actual moment of seeing them.

— *Annie Dillard*
from Pilgrim at Tinker Creek

594

595

Introducing the Theme: Discussion Options

Read aloud the theme title and excerpt on Anthology page 595. Ask:

1 What wild animals have you seen in their natural environment? (Sample answer: squirrels, birds, raccoons, rabbits)

2 What are some different reasons why people come in contact with wild animals? (Sample answer: to study them, to rescue them, to try to help them)

3 What are some dangers people may face around wild animals? How should people stay safe? (Sample answer: Wild animals sometimes bite or defend themselves when they are afraid. People should keep their distance and try not to startle the animals.)

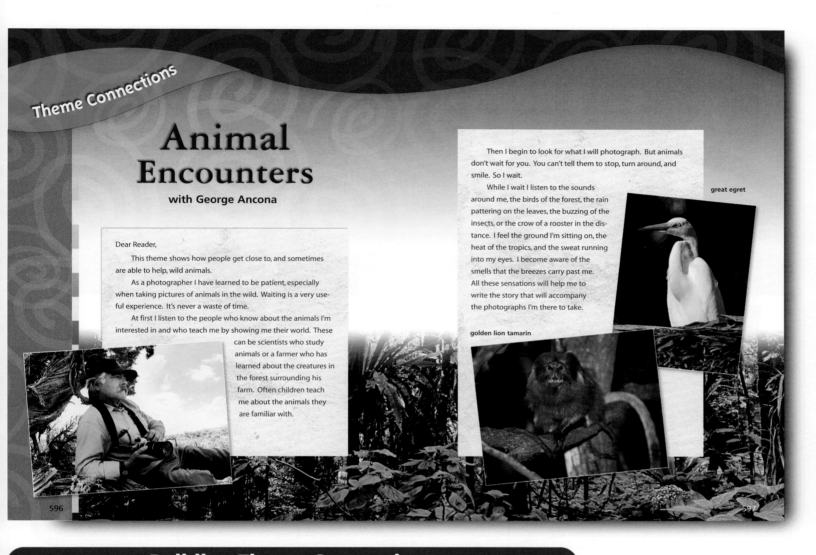

Animal Encounters

with George Ancona

Dear Reader,

This theme shows how people get close to, and sometimes are able to help, wild animals.

As a photographer I have learned to be patient, especially when taking pictures of animals in the wild. Waiting is a very useful experience. It's never a waste of time.

At first I listen to the people who know about the animals I'm interested in and who teach me by showing me their world. These can be scientists who study animals or a farmer who has learned about the creatures in the forest surrounding his farm. Often children teach me about the animals they are familiar with.

Then I begin to look for what I will photograph. But animals don't wait for you. You can't tell them to stop, turn around, and smile. So I wait.

While I wait I listen to the sounds around me, the birds of the forest, the rain pattering on the leaves, the buzzing of the insects, or the crow of a rooster in the distance. I feel the ground I'm sitting on, the heat of the tropics, and the sweat running into my eyes. I become aware of the smells that the breezes carry past me. All these sensations will help me to write the story that will accompany the photographs I'm there to take.

great egret

golden lion tamarin

596

597

Building Theme Connections

Ask volunteers to read aloud the author's letter on Anthology pages 596–598. Tell students that George Ancona wrote and illustrated *The Golden Lion Tamarin Comes Home,* a selection they will read in this theme. (See Teacher's Edition page 628 for more information on George Ancona.)
Use the following questions to prompt discussion:

1 What is your favorite wild animal? Why? (Sample answer: lions, because they are respected by other animals)

2 How is patience very useful to a nature photographer? (Waiting patiently can help the photographer get a better picture.)

3 What would you focus on while you waited for an animal to appear? (Sample answer: I would listen to the rain and look at the plants around me.)

4 What wild animals are found where you live? (Sample answer: There are skunks and squirrels around the neighborhood.)

Your Animal Encounters

Take a minute to remember encounters you have had with animals. Think about how your experiences were like or different from those of George Ancona.

Each of the selections in this theme, shown below, gives its own meaning to the title *Animal Encounters*. As you read, think about how the animals and the people in each selection were changed by the encounter.

red panda

Sometimes days will pass and no animals appear. One never knows when something will happen. If what I am looking for doesn't appear, often the unexpected will astonish me.

Then, holding my breath, I begin to take pictures and hope that my camera is working. When that moment ends I am happy.

I think, *I got it, I hope*, since I won't know until the film is developed. Then I have the pictures for my book.

You will see moments like that in this theme, when people and animals discover each other. And as a reader, you will also take part in that discovery.

Yours truly,

George Ancona

common marmoset

Internet

To learn about the authors in this theme, visit Education Place. **www.eduplace.com/kids**

598

599

Home Connection

Send home the theme letter for *Animal Encounters* to introduce the theme and suggest home activities. (See the **Teacher's Resource Blackline Masters**.)

For other suggestions relating to *Animal Encounters*, see **Home/Community Connections**.

Building Theme Connections, *continued*

Read aloud the first paragraph on Anthology page 599.

- Have students brainstorm ideas, images, and words they associate with the wild. Record their thoughts.

- Discuss how students' ideas would compare with George Ancona's ideas.

Have students finish reading Anthology page 599.

- Explain that the books pictured there are the selections students will read in the theme *Animal Encounters*.

- Ask students to predict what kind of animal encounters will occur in the selections. Have the students explain their predictions. (Answers will vary.)

- Allow students time to look ahead at the selections and illustrations. Have them revise their original predictions as necessary.

Making Selection Connections

Introduce Selection Connections in the Practice Book.

• Preview the **Graphic Organizers** on **Practice Book** pages 199–200. Read aloud the directions, column heads, and selection titles. Explain that when they finish reading each selection, students will add to the chart to deepen their understanding of the theme *Animal Encounters*.

Classroom Management

At any time during the theme, you can assign the independent cross-curricular activities on Teacher's Edition pages 594I–594J while you give differentiated instruction to small groups. For additional independent activities related to specific selections, see the Teacher's Edition pages listed below.

• Week 1: pages 598A–598B, 623M–623N

• Week 2: pages 625Q–625R, 647M–647N

• Week 3: pages 647AA–647BB, 671M–671N

• Week 4: pages M6–M7, M24–M25, M26–M27, M42–M43

Monitoring Student Progress

Monitoring Progress

Throughout the theme, monitor your students' progress by using the following program features in the Teacher's Edition:

• Guiding Comprehension questions

• Literature discussion groups

• Skill lesson applications

• Monitoring Student Progress boxes

Wrapping Up and Reviewing the Theme

Use the two selections and support material in **Monitoring Student Progress** on pages M1–M46 to review theme skills, connect and compare theme literature, and prepare students for the Integrated Theme Test and the Theme Skills Test as well as for standardized tests measuring adequate yearly progress.

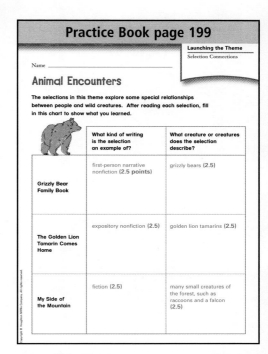

Practice Book page 199

Launching the Theme
Selection Connections

Name _____

Animal Encounters

The selections in this theme explore some special relationships between people and wild creatures. After reading each selection, fill in this chart to show what you learned.

	What kind of writing is the selection an example of?	What creature or creatures does the selection describe?
Grizzly Bear Family Book	first-person narrative nonfiction **(2.5 points)**	grizzly bears **(2.5)**
The Golden Lion Tamarin Comes Home	expository nonfiction **(2.5)**	golden lion tamarins **(2.5)**
My Side of the Mountain	fiction **(2.5)**	many small creatures of the forest, such as raccoons and a falcon **(2.5)**

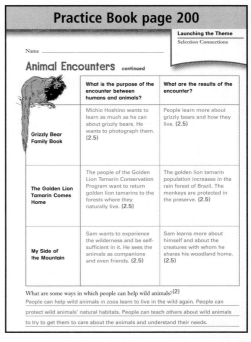

Practice Book page 200

Launching the Theme
Selection Connections

Name _____

Animal Encounters continued

	What is the purpose of the encounter between humans and animals?	What are the results of the encounter?
Grizzly Bear Family Book	Michio Hoshino wants to learn as much as he can about grizzly bears. He wants to photograph them. **(2.5)**	People learn more about grizzly bears and how they live. **(2.5)**
The Golden Lion Tamarin Comes Home	The people of the Golden Lion Tamarin Conservation Program want to return golden lion tamarins to the forests where they naturally live. **(2.5)**	The golden lion tamarin population increases in the rain forest of Brazil. The monkeys are protected in the preserve. **(2.5)**
My Side of the Mountain	Sam wants to experience the wilderness and be self-sufficient in it. He sees the animals as companions and even friends. **(2.5)**	Sam learns more about himself and about the creatures with whom he shares his woodland home. **(2.5)**

What are some ways in which people can help wild animals? **(2)**
People can help wild animals in zoos learn to live in the wild again. People can protect wild animals' natural habitats. People can teach others about wild animals to try to get them to care about the animals and understand their needs.

Lesson Overview

Literature

The Grizzly Bear Family Book

Michio Hoshino

Selection Summary

Photographer Michio Hoshino spends nearly a year in the Alaskan wilderness capturing the lives of grizzly bears.

1 Background and Vocabulary

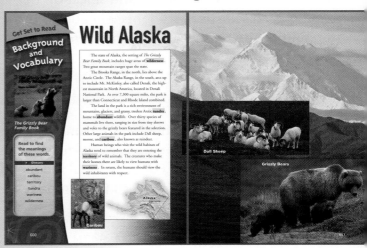

2 Main Selection

The Grizzly Bear Family Book
Genre: Nonfiction

3 Poetry Link

Instructional Support

Planning and Practice

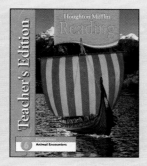

- Planning and classroom management
- Reading instruction
- Skill lessons
- Materials for reaching all learners

- Independent practice for skills

- Newsletters
- Selection Summaries
- Assignment Cards
- Observation Checklists
- Selection Tests

- Transparencies
- Strategy Posters
- Blackline Masters

Reaching All Learners

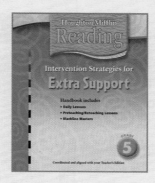

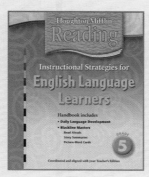

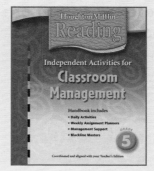

Coordinated lessons, activities, and projects for additional reading instruction

For
- Classroom Teacher
- Extended Day
- Pull Out
- Resource Teacher

Technology

Audio Selection

The Grizzly Bear Family Book

Get Set for Reading CD-ROM
- Background building
- Vocabulary support
- Selection Summary in English and Spanish

Accelerated Reader
- Practice quizzes for the selection

www.eduplace.com

Log on to Education Place for more activities related to the selection.

e• **Glossary**
e• **WordGame**

Leveled Books for Reaching All Learners

Leveled Readers and Leveled Practice

- Independent reading for building fluency
- Topic, comprehension strategy, and vocabulary linked to main selection
- Lessons in Teacher's Edition, pages 623O–623R
- Leveled practice for every book

Technology

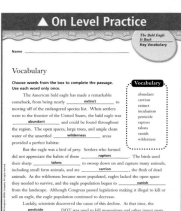

Leveled Readers
Audio available

Book Adventure

- Practice quizzes for the Leveled Theme Paperbacks

www.eduplace.com

Log on to Education Place® for activities related to the Leveled Theme Paperbacks.

● BELOW LEVEL

The HYRAX of Top-Knot Island
by Robin Bernard ✦ photography by Jerry Lesser

▲ ON LEVEL

The Bald Eagle Is Back
by Mary Kay Carson

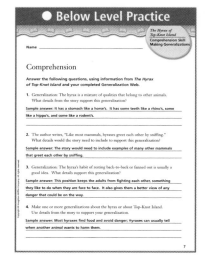

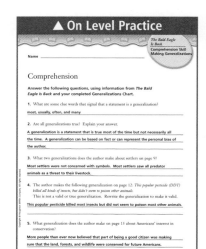

■ ABOVE LEVEL

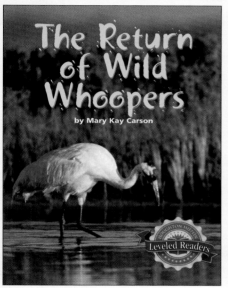

◆ LANGUAGE SUPPORT

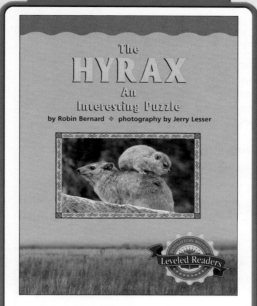

Leveled Theme Paperbacks

- Extended independent reading in theme-related trade books
- Lessons in Teacher's Edition, pages R2–R7

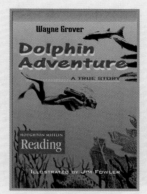

Below Level

On Level

Challenge

■ Above Level Practice

The Return of Wild Whoopers
Key Vocabulary

Name _____

Vocabulary

Write each word from the box in the correct category.

Words That Describe People Who Help the Whooper
conservationists
biologists

Words That Relate to the Whooper's Habitat
wetland
territory

Words That Describe the Whooper's Characteristics
endangered
aquatic

Words That Relate to the Whooper as an Egg and a Young Bird
viable
imprinted

Now choose 4 of the vocabulary words and use them to write a paragraph about the whooping crane. Answers will vary.

Vocabulary
aquatic
biologists
conservationists
endangered
imprinted
territory
viable
wetland

◆ Language Support Practice

The Hyrax An Interesting Puzzle
Build Background

Name _____

Build Background

Draw a line from the name of each animal to the picture of where it lives. Then write one thing you know about each animal on the lines below.

horse

bird

whale

dog

■ Above Level Practice

The Return of Wild Whoopers
Comprehension Skill
Making Generalizations

Name _____

Comprehension

Answer the following questions, using information from *The Return of Wild Whoopers* and your completed Generalizations Chart.

1. What are some clue words that signal that a statement is a generalization?
most, usually, often, and many

2. What two generalizations does the author make about whooping cranes on page 6?
   A. Most cranes fly less than 465 miles in a day.
   B. Through all that time, whooping cranes have survived all the enormous changes the centuries have brought.

3. How would you recognize an invalid generalization?
An invalid generalization is one that is not based on fact.

4. Why do you think that recognizing generalizations is a useful reading skill?
Sample answer: Recognizing generalizations helps me separate facts from general statements.

◆ Language Support Practice

The Hyrax An Interesting Puzzle
Key Vocabulary

Name _____

Vocabulary

Choose the word from the box that best completes each sentence.

1. There are two big _____boulders_____ on top of the mountain.

2. My cat has some _____habits_____ that I like and other ones that I don't like.

3. My sister _____whistles_____ to our dog to tell it to come in the house.

4. The mouse went to _____sniff_____ the cheese, then ate it.

5. Some animals defend their _____territory_____, other animals run away.

6. Elephants and hyraxes are both _____mammals_____.

Vocabulary
boulders
habits
mammals
sniff
territory
whistles

Daily Lesson Plans

T Skill tested on Theme Skills Test
and/or Integrated Theme Test

	DAY 1	**DAY 2**
50–60 minutes ## Reading **Comprehension** **Leveled Readers** • Fluency Practice • Independent Reading	**Teacher Read Aloud,** 599A–599B *Intown Animals* Building Background, 600 **Key Vocabulary,** 601 abundant dominance tundra aggressive subservience wariness carcass territory wilderness caribou **Reading the Selection,** 602–617 **Comprehension Skill,** 602 Making Generalizations **T** **Comprehension Strategy,** 602 Evaluate **Leveled Readers** *The Hyrax of Top-Knot Island* *The Bald Eagle Is Back* *The Return of Wild Whoopers* *The Hyrax: An Interesting Puzzle* Lessons and Leveled Practice, 623O–623R	**Reading the Selection,** 602–617 Comprehension Check, 617 Responding, 618 Think About the Selection **Comprehension Skill Preview,** 615 Making Generalizations **T** **Leveled Readers** *The Hyrax of Top-Knot Island* *The Bald Eagle Is Back* *The Return of Wild Whoopers* *The Hyrax: An Interesting Puzzle* Lessons and Leveled Practice, 623O–623R
20–30 minutes ## Word Work **Phonics/Decoding** **Vocabulary** **Spelling**	**Phonics/Decoding,** 603 Phonics/Decoding Strategy **Vocabulary,** 602–617 Selection Vocabulary **Spelling,** 623E Prefixes *com-, con-, en-, ex-, pre-, pro-* **T**	**Structural Analysis,** 623C Prefixes *com-, con-, en-, ex-, pre-, pro-* **T** **Vocabulary,** 602–617 Selection Vocabulary **Spelling,** 623E Prefixes *com-, con-, en-, ex-, pre-, pro-* Review and Practice **T**
20–30 minutes ## Writing and Oral Language **Writing** **Grammar** **Listening/Speaking/Viewing**	**Writing,** 623K Prewriting an Opinion Paragraph **T** **Grammar,** 623I Contractions with *not* **T** **Daily Language Practice** 1. "The city will perpose to open a skating rink" said Mrs. Evans. (propose; rink,") 2. Jared and Mara they have pledged to clean up the park this weekend. (Jared and Mara have) **Listening/Speaking/Viewing,** 599A–599B, 609 Teacher Read Aloud, Stop and Think	**Writing,** 623K Drafting an Opinion Paragraph **Grammar,** 623I Contractions with *not* Practice **T** **Daily Language Practice** 3. "My consirn is for your safety." explained the lifeguard. (concern; safety,") 4. "Hasn't Alex used that same escuse before," asked Tina. (excuse; before?") **Listening/Speaking/Viewing,** 617, 618 Wrapping Up, Responding

  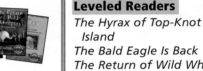

Target Skills of the Week

Comprehension	Evaluate; Making Generalizations
Vocabulary	Using Context
Phonics/Decoding	Prefixes *com-, con-, en-, ex-, pre-, pro-*
Fluency	Leveled Readers

DAY 3

Rereading the Selection

Rereading for Writer's Craft, 605
Voice

Comprehension Skill, 623A–623B
Making Generalizations **T**

Leveled Readers

The Hyrax of Top-Knot Island
The Bald Eagle Is Back
The Return of Wild Whoopers
The Hyrax: An Interesting Puzzle

Lessons and Leveled Practice, 623O–623R

Phonics Review, 623D
The /k/ and /kw/ Sounds

Vocabulary, 623G
Using Context **T**

Spelling, 623F
Vocabulary: Word Extensions; Prefixes
com-, con-, en-, ex-, pre-, pro- Practice **T**

Writing, 623L
Revising an Opinion Paragraph

Grammar, 623J
Negatives **T**

Daily Language Practice
5. Anita she will inclose a check with her soccer team application. (Anita will enclose)
6. The newspaper article didn't never conpare the two candidates. (didn't compare)

DAY 4

Reading the Poetry Link, 620–623
"Three Poems"

Skill: How to Compare Poems
Rereading for Writer's Craft, 622
Imagery and Figurative Language

Comprehension Skill Review, 611
Topic, Main Idea, and Supporting Details

Leveled Readers

The Hyrax of Top-Knot Island
The Bald Eagle Is Back
The Return of Wild Whoopers
The Hyrax: An Interesting Puzzle

Lessons and Leveled Practice, 623O–623R

Phonics/Decoding, 620–623
Apply Phonics/Decoding Strategy to Link

Vocabulary, 623M
Language Center: Building Vocabulary

Spelling, 623F
Prefixes Game, Proofreading **T**

Writing, 623L
Proofreading an Opinion Paragraph
Avoiding Double Negatives **T**

Grammar, 623J
Negatives Practice **T**

Daily Language Practice
7. You should measure twice and cut once" said Mr. Daniel. ("You; once,")
8. Bett explained, "we don't ixchange presents on Valentine's Day." ("We; exchange)

Listening/Speaking/Viewing, 623
Discuss the Link

DAY 5

Rereading for Fluency, 607

Responding Activities, 618–619
Write About Bears
Cross-Curricular Activities

Information and Study Skills, 623H
Preparing a Report

Comprehension Skill Review, 613
Fact and Opinion

Leveled Readers

The Hyrax of Top-Knot Island
The Bald Eagle Is Back
The Return of Wild Whoopers
The Hyrax: An Interesting Puzzle

Lessons and Leveled Practice, 623O–623R

Structural Analysis, 623M
Language Center: Word Cut-Ups

Vocabulary, 623M
Language Center: Vocabulary Game

Spelling, 623F
Test: Prefixes *com-, con-, en-, ex-, pre-, pro-* **T**

Writing, 623L
Publishing an Opinion Paragraph

Grammar, 623J, 623N
Adjective or Adverb?
Language Center: Adverbs in Action

Daily Language Practice
9. Since the accident, Pablo hasn't never been able to axtend the little finger on his right hand. (hasn't ever) or (has never; extend)
10. "If you want to go on the field trip," explained Mrs. Tam, you will need an adult's concent." ("you; consent.")

Listening/Speaking/Viewing, 623N
Language Center: Planning a Multimedia Presentation

Managing Flexible Groups

Leveled Instruction and Leveled Practice

	DAY 1	**DAY 2**
WHOLE CLASS	• Teacher Read Aloud (TE pp. 599A–599B) • Building Background, Introducing Vocabulary (TE pp. 600–601) • Comprehension Strategy: Introduce (TE p. 602) • Comprehension Skill: Introduce (TE p. 602) • Purpose Setting (TE p. 603) **After reading first half of *The Grizzly Bear Family*** • Stop and Think (TE p. 609)	**After reading *The Grizzly Bear Family Book*** • Wrapping Up (TE p. 617) • Comprehension Check (Practice Book p. 203) • Responding: Think About the Selection (TE p. 618) • Comprehension Skill: Preview (TE p. 615)
SMALL GROUPS **Extra Support**	**TEACHER-LED** • Preview *The Grizzly Bear Family Book* to Stop and Think (TE pp. 602–609). • Support reading with Extra Support/ Intervention notes (TE pp. 603, 605, 607, 608, 613, 616).	**Partner or Individual Work** • Reread first half of *The Grizzly Bear Family Book* (TE pp. 602–609). • Preview, read second half (TE pp. 610–617). • Comprehension Check (Practice Book p. 203)
Challenge	**Individual Work** • Begin "Wildlife Photography Exhibit" (Challenge Handbook p. 48). • Extend reading with Challenge Note (TE p. 616).	**Individual Work** • Continue work on activity (Challenge Handbook p. 48).
English Language Learners	**TEACHER-LED** • Preview vocabulary and *The Grizzly Bear Family Book* to Stop and Think (TE pp. 601–609). • Support reading with English Language Learners notes (TE pp. 600, 606, 608, 612, 615).	**TEACHER-LED** • Review first half of *The Grizzly Bear Family Book* (TE pp. 602–609). ✔ • Preview, read second half (TE pp. 610–617). • Begin Comprehension Check together (Practice Book p. 203).

Independent Activities

- Get Set for Reading CD-Rom
- Journals: selection notes, questions
- Complete, review Practice Book (pp. 201–205) and Leveled Readers Practice Blackline Masters (TE pp. 623O–623R).
- Assignment Cards (Teacher's Resource Blackline Masters pp. 89–90)
- Leveled Readers (TE pp. 623O–623R), Leveled Theme Paperbacks (TE pp. R2–R7), or book from Leveled Bibliography (TE pp. 594E–594F)

✔ Opportunity to informally assess oral reading rate

Rereading: Lesson on Writer's Craft (TE p. 605)

Comprehension Skill: Main lesson (TE pp. 623A–623B)

- Reading the Poetry Link (TE pp. 620–623): Skill lesson (TE p. 620)
- Rereading the Link: Writer's Craft Lesson (TE p. 622)
- Comprehension Skill: First Comprehension Review lesson (TE p. 611)

- Responding: Select from Activities (TE pp. 618–619)
- Information and Study Skills (TE p. 623H)
- Comprehension Skill: Second Comprehension Review lesson (TE p. 613)

TEACHER-LED

Reread, review Comprehension check (Practice Book p. 203).

Preview Leveled Reader: Below Level (TE p. 623O), or read book from Leveled Bibliography (TE pp. 594E–594F). ✔

Partner or Individual Work

- Reread Poetry Link (TE pp. 620–623).
- Complete Leveled Reader: Below Level (TE p. 623O), or read book from Leveled Bibliography (TE pp. 594E–594F).

TEACHER-LED

- Comprehension Skill: Reteaching lesson (TE p. R8)
- Preview, begin Leveled Theme Paperback: Below Level (TE pp. R2–R3), or read book from Leveled Bibliography (TE pp. 594E–594F). ✔

TEACHER-LED

- Teacher check-in: Assess progress (Challenge Handbook p. 48).
- Preview Leveled Reader: Above Level (TE p. 623Q), or read book from Leveled Bibliography (TE pp. 594E–594F). ✔

Individual Work

- Complete activity (Challenge Handbook p. 48).
- Complete Leveled Reader: Above Level (TE p. 623Q), or read book from Leveled Bibliography (TE pp. 594E–594F).

TEACHER-LED

- Evaluate activity and plan format for sharing (Challenge Handbook p. 48).
- Read Leveled Theme Paperback: Above Level (TE pp. R6–R7), or read book from Leveled Bibliography (TE pp. 594E–594F). ✔

Partner or Individual Work

- Complete Comprehension Check (Practice Book p. 203).
- Begin Leveled Reader: Language Support (TE p. 623R), or read book from Leveled Bibliography (TE pp. 594E–594F).

TEACHER-LED

- Reread the Poetry Link (TE pp. 620–623) ✔ and review Link Skill (TE p. 620).
- Complete Leveled Reader: Language Support (TE p. 623R), or read book from Leveled Bibliography (TE pp. 594E–594F). ✔

Partner or Individual Work

- Preview, read book from Leveled Bibliography (TE pp. 594E–594F).

- Responding activities (TE pp. 618–619)
- Language Center activities (TE pp. 623M–623N)
- **Fluency Practice:** Reread *The Grizzly Bear Family Book*. ✔
- Activities relating to *The Grizzly Bear Family Book* at Education Place www.eduplace.com

Turn the page for more independent activities.

Classroom Management

Independent Activities

Assign these activities while you work with small groups.

Differentiated Instruction for Small Groups

- **Handbook for English Language Learners**, pp. 208–217

- **Extra Support Handbook**, pp. 204–213

Independent Activities

- Language Center, pp. 623M–623N

- Challenge/Extension Activities, Resources, pp. R9, R15

- **Classroom Management Handbook**, Activity Masters CM6-1–CM6-4

- **Challenge Handbook**, Challenge Masters CH6-1–CH6-2

Look for more activities in the Classroom Management Kit.

Science

Perpetual Daylight

 Pairs	⏱ **40 minutes**
Objective	Create a diagram explaining Arctic sunlight.
Materials	Research, writing, and art materials

Why does the sun shine 24 hours a day during Alaskan summers? Find out, and then diagram your findings.

- With a partner, use an encyclopedia, a science textbook, or another reference source to research Arctic sunlight. Then answer the questions below.

- Make a diagram showing Earth's angle in relation to the sun.

- Remember to include labels and a title.

What months of the year are considered "summer" in Alaska?

During this time, what are the relative positions of the sun and the earth?

How does Earth's rotation and the tilt of its axis affect how the sun reaches Alaska?

Media

Worth a Thousand Words?

 Groups	⏱ **30 minutes**
Objective	Write an evaluation of a photograph.
Materials	Anthology, writing materials

How do Michio Hoshino's photographs add to his written observations of grizzly bears? Evaluate one of his photographs. Then share your findings with your group.

- Choose a photograph from the selection that interests you.

- Think about these questions:
  - Why did this photograph get your attention?
  - How well does this photo go with the written information about grizzly bears or Alaska in the text?
  - What information can you get from the photograph that you can't get from the text?
  - Why do you think Michio Hoshino decided to include this photo?

- Write a paragraph explaining your answers to these questions.

- Share your findings with other members of your group.

Consider copying and laminating these activities for use in centers.

Geography

Mapping Alaska

👤 Singles	🕐 40 minutes
Objective	Make a map of Alaska.
Materials	Atlas, art materials

What are the major features of Alaska? Make a map highlighting them.

- In an atlas, find a map of Alaska and copy or trace it. Use the atlas to locate Alaska's major cities, rivers, ports, and oil fields. Then find land formations, such as mountains and tundra. See if you can locate the places named in *The Grizzly Bear Family Book*.

  Mark these places on your map. Create a key and include a scale copied from the atlas. Use colored pencils to highlight your map.

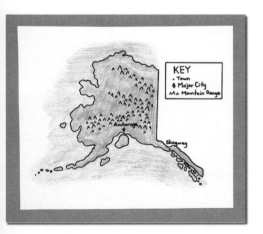

Poetry

Animal Encounter

👤 Singles	🕐 25 minutes
Objective	Write a poem.

Write a poem about an encounter with a wild animal.

- You've probably seen wild animals more often than you think. For example, you may have seen:
  - a squirrel running across a fence
  - a deer crossing the road
  - geese waddling down to a river
  - a frog beside a pond
- Choose an encounter, then freewrite for five minutes to prompt your memory. Jot down descriptive images, smells, sounds, and feelings.
- Look over your notes for details that can be used in your poem. After you write a draft, read it aloud to a classmate.

Science

Bear versus Bear

👥 Pairs	🕐 30 minutes
Objective	Create a chart about bears.
Materials	Encyclopedia, writing materials

When is a bear not a grizzly? When it's a polar bear—or any other member of the bear family. Make a chart that shows the various types of bears.

- With a partner, use an encyclopedia to find out about different kinds of bears. Takes notes on the elements listed in the chart below.
- Copy the chart, then complete it with information from your notes.

The Bear Essentials

Type of Bear	Where They Live	Physical Features	What They Eat
Brown Bear (includes Grizzly)			
American Black Bear			
Asiatic Black Bear			
Polar Bear			
Sun Bear			
Sloth Bear			
Spectacled Bear			

Listening Comprehension

- Listen to identify and evaluate generalizations.

Building Background

Tell students that you will read aloud a selection about wild animals in cities.

- Ask students to tell about any encounters they have had with wild animals in cities (not including pets or zoo animals).

Fluency Modeling

Explain that as you read aloud, you will be modeling fluent oral reading. Ask students to listen carefully to your phrasing and your expression, or tone of voice and emphasis.

COMPREHENSION SKILL

Making Generalizations

Explain that generalizations

- are statements that are usually true
- may include signal words such as *most*, *usually*, and *often*
- may be valid (based on facts) or invalid

Purpose Setting Read the selection aloud, asking students to listen for any generalizations. Then use the Guiding Comprehension questions to assess students' understanding. Reread for clarification as needed.

Teacher Read Aloud

Intown Animals
by Carolyn J. Gard

As cities stretch into the countryside around them, wild animals move into town. The peregrine falcon has moved to the city! It joins other country animals that have lost their natural homes to new neighborhoods and shopping malls.

Twenty-five years ago, peregrine falcons were a dying breed. DDT, a chemical that was used to poison insects, also harmed animals. DDT caused falcons to lay eggs with shells so thin that the eggs broke when the falcons nested.

In 1972, the United States banned the use of DDT, and scientists began trying to rebuild the falcon population. Eggs taken from falcons were hatched in laboratories. Once the chicks were old enough, they were returned to

1 the wild. But in the wild, the young falcons were often killed by great horned owls.

Scientists at the Tyson Research Center near St. Louis, Missouri, developed the Raptor Project to help the peregrine falcon. Project scientists knew the birds liked to nest in high places. Why not use skyscrapers in cities for nesting places? Scientists placed falcon chicks in nesting boxes on the ledges of skyscrapers. The young birds had all that they needed: food, water, shelter, and best of all, no great horned owls.

At last, two grown falcons from the Raptor Project laid several eggs in one of the project's nesting boxes. But only one egg hatched. The chick needed company. So, Walter Crawford, the project director, crawled out onto a three-foot-wide ledge, 30 stories high, and put a lab-bred chick in the nest!

2 Many other wild animals have also moved into cities. Red-tailed hawks nest on apartment buildings. Canada geese like golf courses. Red foxes hunt rats and mice in cities. Raccoons tip over trash cans to find food.

These animals can cause problems. In one city, an opossum chased a car down a driveway. In some eastern cities, deer eat flower and vegetable gardens. In the West, roaming pets may become prey for mountain lions. Bears, too, may come into a yard to eat berries.

Although wild animals may look cute, they can carry diseases such as rabies. Health experts say to stay away from wild animals, especially if they appear to be acting strangely.

Other problems come up when people feed wild animals. When they are fed, the animals lose fear of people, and they may attack when they don't get the food they expect.

Enjoy the wildlife around you. But remember that it is just that—wild!

CRITICAL THINKING
Guiding Comprehension

1 MAKING GENERALIZATIONS Is the sentence *But in the wild, the young falcons were often killed by great horned owls* a generalization? How can you tell? (Yes. The signal word *often* is used. The facts can be checked.)

2 MAKING GENERALIZATIONS What facts support the generalization that many other wild animals have also moved into cities? (Red-tailed hawks nest on buildings, geese like golf courses, red foxes hunt rodents in cities, and raccoons find food in trash cans.)

3 MAKING GENERALIZATIONS When the author says that deer in eastern cities eat gardens, does she mean that this is true of all deer? (No, her generalization is true of many deer.)

Discussion Options

Personal Response Have students discuss what they think is most surprising about the information in the selection.

⭐ **Connecting/Comparing** Ask students why they think this selection is in the theme *Animal Encounters*.

REACHING ALL LEARNERS
English Language Learners

Language Development

Help students recognize compound words used in the selection, such as *countryside, skyscrapers, driveway,* and *wildlife.* Explain that a compound word is made from two or more smaller words. Ask volunteers to suggest other compound words they know, such as *backpack, homework,* or *notebook.* Then have partners write "word equations" for each compound, and use each one in a sentence. For example:

wild + life = wildlife
We read about wildlife in cities.

Building Background

Key Concept: The Alaskan Wilderness

Tell students that *The Grizzly Bear Family Book* describes an author's encounters with animals while observing and photographing bears in the Alaska wilderness. Point out on the map the location of the Brooks and Alaska Mountain ranges as well as Denali National Park. Then use "Wild Alaska" on Anthology pages 600–601 to build background and introduce Key Vocabulary.

- Ask volunteers to read aloud "Wild Alaska."

- Have students use the text, photographs, and captions to discuss Alaska. Use details in the last paragraph to discuss the challenges of photographing grizzly bears there.

Get Set to Read

Background and Vocabulary

The Grizzly Bear Family Book

Read to find the meanings of these words.

e ● Glossary

abundant

caribou

territory

tundra

wariness

wilderness

600

Wild Alaska

The state of Alaska, the setting of *The Grizzly Bear Family Book*, includes huge areas of **wilderness**. Two great mountain ranges span the state.

The Brooks Range, in the north, lies above the Arctic Circle. The Alaska Range, in the south, arcs up to include Mt. McKinley, also called Denali, the highest mountain in North America, located in Denali National Park. At over 7,300 square miles, the park is larger than Connecticut and Rhode Island combined.

The land in the park is a rich environment of mountains, glaciers, and grassy, treeless Arctic **tundra**, home to **abundant** wildlife. Over thirty species of mammals live there, ranging in size from tiny shrews and voles to the grizzly bears featured in the selection. Other large animals in the park include Dall sheep, moose, and **caribou**, also known as reindeer.

Human beings who visit the wild habitats of Alaska need to remember that they are entering the **territory** of wild animals. The creatures who make their homes there are likely to view humans with **wariness**. In return, the humans should view the wild inhabitants with respect.

Caribou

Alaska
Denali National Park
Brooks Range
Alaska Range

English Language Learners

Supporting Comprehension

Beginning/Preproduction Have students listen to the article and view the photographs. Then name each type of animal shown, and ask students to point out each animal as it is named.

Early Production and Speech Emergence Have students repeat the Key Vocabulary words after you. Use selection illustrations to help students understand *caribou, tundra,* and *wilderness.* Explain *territory,* and mime the meaning of the remaining words.

Intermediate and Advanced Fluency Have students work in small groups to read and then restate in their own words facts about the Alaskan wilderness.

all Sheep

Grizzly Bears

601

Introducing Vocabulary

Key Vocabulary

These words support the Key Concept and appear in the selection.

abundant plentiful

aggressive ready and quick to fight

carcass the dead body of an animal

caribou a type of Arctic deer

dominance the condition of having the most control

subservience willingness to yield to others' power

territory an area inhabited by an animal or animal group and defended against intruders

tundra a treeless Arctic region where the subsoil is permanently frozen and where only low shrubs, lichens, and mosses can grow

wariness the state of being on one's guard

wilderness any unsettled region in its natural state

e • Glossary
e • WordGame

See Vocabulary notes on pages 606, 608, 610, 612, 614, and 616 for additional words to preview.

Transparency 6–1

Words About Wilderness

Welcome to Denali National Park

We hope you enjoy your visit to this beautiful and unspoiled wilderness. These tips will help you have a safe and pleasant stay.

Tips for Wilderness Travelers

1. You are likely to see abundant wildlife, including moose, Dall sheep, grizzly bears, and herds of caribou. Many small creatures live in the grasses of the tundra, including ground squirrels and shrews. So keep your binoculars and your camera handy.

2. Please remember that grizzly bears make this land their home. When hiking in bear territory, be careful. A certain amount of wariness will help prevent unpleasant encounters with grizzlies. If you see a bear cub, stay away! Mother grizzlies become aggressive when their cubs are approached. If you see a bear eating the dead carcass of an animal, steer clear! Bears are very protective of their food.

3. You might be lucky enough to see an encounter between two wild animals. Such encounters can be violent and frightening. Often when wild animals meet, they fight for dominance. Fortunately, these battles are usually short, and they seldom result in serious injury. The loser shows subservience by leaving the area. If you see such an encounter, keep your distance. Don't make any sudden moves. Just stand back and observe nature in action.

Practice Book page 201

Name _____

Creatures of the Far North

Answer each question with a word from the word box.

Vocabulary
carcass
caribou
aggressive
dominance
subservience
tundra
wilderness
abundant
territory
wariness

1. Which word names a grazing animal that lives in the Arctic?
   caribou **(1 point)**

2. Which word names the frozen land near the Arctic Ocean?
   tundra **(1)**

3. Which word names land that has not been developed?
   wilderness **(1)**

4. Which word names the body of an animal that has died?
   carcass **(1)**

5. Which word is a synonym for *cautiousness*?
   wariness **(1)**

6. Which word names the region that a predator such as a bobcat or a grizzly bear ranges across to find food?
   territory **(1)**

7. Which word is an adjective that means "likely to attack"?
   aggressive **(1)**

8. Which word is an adjective that means "plentiful"?
   abundant **(1)**

9. Which word means "the state of controlling others"?
   dominance **(1)**

10. Which word means "the state of being willing to yield to others"?
    subservience **(1)**

Display Transparency 6–1.

- Model how to figure out the meaning of *wilderness* from context clues.

- Ask students to use context clues to figure out the remaining Key Vocabulary words. Have students explain how they figured out the meaning of each word.

- Have students look for these words as they read and use them in discussion.

COMPREHENSION STRATEGY
Evaluate

Teacher Modeling Ask a student to read aloud the Strategy Focus. Explain that to evaluate means to decide what to think or feel about an author's writing, ideas, or information. Ask students to read page 603. Then model the strategy.

Think Aloud *From the first page I learn that the author, Michio Hoshino, spends more than half of each year in the Alaskan wilderness. As I read on, I'll evaluate whether his connection to the land helps the story he tells.*

✓ Test Prep Explain that reading tests often have multiple-choice questions that ask about generalizations. Caution students that the answer choices may all sound true. Tell them to choose the answer that is best supported by details in the test passage.

COMPREHENSION SKILL
Making Generalizations

Introduce the Graphic Organizer.
Remind students that generalizations are broad statements that are true most of the time. They can describe items, people, or situations. Explain that a Generalizations Chart can help students focus on an author's generalizations. Students will fill out the chart on **Practice Book** page 202.

- Display **Transparency 6–2.** Have students read Anthology page 605.

- Model how to write the first generalization on the chart. Monitor students' work.

Selection I

The Grizzly Bear Family Book

Michio Hoshino

Strategy Focus

The author of this selection spent a year photographing grizzly bears. As you read, **evaluate** how his personal involvement enhances the story he tells.

602

Transparency 6–2

ANIMAL ENCOUNTERS The Grizzly Bear Family Book
Graphic Organizer Generalizations Chart

ANNOTATED VERSION

Detective Work

Page	Clue	Generalization
605	how people see bears	People have a fearful image of bears.
607	what all living things do	All living things, including humans, depend on each other for survival.
608	how grizzlies act toward each other during most of the year	Grizzlies avoid contact with other bears during most of the year.
608	which bears command the best fishing spots	Stronger, more aggressive males usually get the best fishing spots.
609	the tolerance of mother bears	Mother bears are usually tolerant of the cubs of others.
610	bears selecting salmon	Bears can probably smell the difference between male and female fish.
612	bears and soapberries	Bears seem to like soapberries best.
614	bears pursuing people	Very few bears are interested in pursuing people.
615	how hunters kill bears	A high-powered rifle was fired from a distance.
616	how people treat nature	People continue to tame and subjugate nature.

TRANSPARENCY 6–2
TEACHER'S EDITION PAGES 602 AND 623A

Practice Book page 202

The Grizzly Bear Family Book

Name _____

Graphic Organizer
Generalizations Chart

Detective Work

What generalizations does the author make about bears, about people, and about the wilderness in this selection? As you read, look for generalizations on the pages listed below. Use the clues to help you recognize them. Write each generalization you find.

Page	Clue	Generalization
605	how people see bears	People have a fearful image of bears. (1)
607	what all living things do	All living things, including humans, depend on each other for survival. (1)
608	how grizzlies act toward each other during most of the year	Grizzlies avoid contact with other bears during most of the year. (1)
608	which bears command the best fishing spots	Stronger, more aggressive males usually get the best fishing spots. (1)
609	the tolerance of mother bears	Mother bears are usually tolerant of the cubs of others. (1)
610	bears selecting salmon	Bears can probably smell the difference between male and female fish. (1)
612	bears and soapberries	Bears seem to like soapberries best. (1)
614	bears pursuing people	Very few bears are interested in pursuing people. (1)
615	how hunters kill bears	A high-powered rifle was fired from a distance. (1)
616	how people treat nature	People continue to tame and subjugate nature. (1)

Imagine meeting a grizzly bear in the wild. Not at the zoo, not in a book, but out in the open — a chance encounter with the real thing. Just you and the bear, face to face.

It happened to me once, when I was camping near Mount McKinley in Alaska. For more than half of each year, I hike through the mountains and plains of Alaska, the Great Land, with my tent on my back, taking pictures of the land which has attracted me since my teens.

Around four o'clock one morning I was awakened by something brushing against my tent. Wondering what it was, I rubbed my eyes and opened the tent flap. There, right in front of me, was a bear's face. I was startled, but the bear must have been even more surprised. It took one look at me and clumped hastily away.

I had never before been so close to a bear. And I knew that I wanted to use my camera to record one year in the lives of the Alaskan grizzlies.

603

Purpose Setting

- Remind students that the selection is set in the Alaskan wilderness.

- Have students preview the selection by looking at the illustrations. Ask them to predict what they might learn about grizzly bears from this first-person account.

- As they read, have students evaluate how well the author uses his experience to help his writing.

- Ask students to look for generalizations about bears, people, and the wilderness.

- You may wish to preview with students the Responding questions on Anthology page 618.

Journal ▸ Students can record their evaluations of the author's writing.

STRATEGY REVIEW

Phonics/Decoding

Remind students to use the Phonics/Decoding Strategy as they read.

Modeling Write the following text from *The Grizzly Bear Family Book* on the board: *Sedges—grasses that grow in wetlands— are particularly important...* Point to *Sedges.*

Think Aloud *This word begins with* s. *Then I see a sound pattern I recognize —edge. When I blend these two sounds and add the plural ending* -s, *I get* SEHJ-ehz, *but what does it mean? I see a definition set off by dashes—grasses that grow in wetlands. That makes sense in the sentence.*

Extra Support/Intervention

Selection Preview

pages 602–605 These photographs show wild grizzly bears in Alaska. What can you learn from these pictures about how grizzlies look, where they live, and how they act?

pages 606–610 The bears are thinner than usual when they first come out of the den in the spring. Why do you think they are so thin? What do you think the bears like to eat?

pages 611–613 How does the Alaskan wilderness change after summer passes? What might the bears do and eat during autumn?

pages 614–616 Why do you think the author included these pictures? What do they tell you about the Alaskan wilderness and the author's experiences there?

CRITICAL THINKING

Guiding Comprehension

❶ NOTING DETAILS How does the tundra change with the arrival of spring? (The air warms, snow melts, flowers grow, and the bears wake from hibernation.)

❷ COMPARE AND CONTRAST In what ways do grizzly bears act similar to humans? (They play, enjoy themselves, and enjoy life; Like human mothers, mother bears hug cubs and show love and affection.)

COMPREHENSION STRATEGY

Evaluate

Teacher/Student Modeling Model using the Evaluate strategy to decide how well the author's personal involvement helps his writing. Offer these prompts:

- How does the author's experience help him write an informative description of the bears? (He uses firsthand knowledge to write about them.)

- In what other ways does his experience help his writing? (He was able to take photographs that show readers some of what he saw.)

Have students read page 605 and point out details that could only be described by a writer who had spent time with grizzlies. (Sample answers: details about the games and the love the mother and cub shared, and the author's own reactions)

     In midwinter the temperature here may fall to fifty degrees below zero. During this harsh time, a grizzly bear will sleep in a snug underground den, the entrance covered by a blanket of snow.

     While the mother bear sleeps, her tiny cubs are born. They nurse and snuggle next to her until longer days and warmer temperatures signal the arrival of spring.

     One day in April, as I hiked through the mountains called the Alaska Range, I noticed fresh bear tracks on the snowy slope. Following them with my binoculars, I spotted a mother bear and her cub walking through the snow.

     The cold, biting wind was already giving way to spring breezes. When the bears come out of their dens, it's a sure sign that the long winter is over.

604

ASSIGNMENT CARD 3

Grizzly Bear Calendar

Noting Details

Use facts from the selection to create a grizzly bear calendar that shows what grizzlies do in spring, summer, fall, and winter. For each season, include details about what the grizzlies eat (or don't eat); how they get food; what their appearance is like; and the way they interact with other bears.

Theme 6: Animal Encounters

Teacher's Resource BLM page 90

As the snow melts and shrinks into patches of crusty ice, wildflowers push their faces towards the sky. In the far north, the flowers are very small. But each blossom possesses tremendous strength. I am moved when I come upon these tiny shapes, living their lives to the fullest extent. **1**

In early spring, grizzly bears also enjoy life to its fullest. Once I watched as a mother and her cub played tag on a slope across from me. The mother chased her cub across the grassy hillside. When she caught the youngster, she took it in her arms and hugged it to her gently, and they began to roll down the slope together. They seemed to be having such a wonderful time, I couldn't help but burst out laughing. **2**

A nursing bear will often lie on her back and offer milk to her cub. If she has two, she will cradle one in each arm. I'm not sure that nursing tires her out, but afterwards the mother often spread-eagles on the ground, sound asleep.

People have such fearful images of bears. But is the affection and care of a human mother for her children so different from the love and tenderness the mother bear shows her cubs?

605

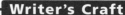

Writer's Craft

Voice

Review

- Remind students that voice is an author's own way of expressing ideas. It gives readers the sense that the writing comes from that author alone.

- Voice is expressed through
  - first-person "I"
  - anecdotes that share the author's personal experience
  - expressions of feelings or beliefs that convey the author's point of view
  - rhetorical questions that engage the reader

Practice/Apply

- Point out the rhetorical question at the end of page 605 as an example of voice.

- Ask students how this question affects the reader's experience. (It makes readers feel that the author is talking directly to them; It makes them think about an important issue.)

- Have students list examples of writing that shows the author's personal voice. (Sample answers, page 613: *Were they coming at me on purpose, or did they not realize I was there?*; *I was so excited, I thought my heart would burst.*)

Extra Support/Intervention

Strategy Modeling: Evaluate

Use this example to model the strategy.

On page 605, the author describes how he watched a mother and her cub play tag. He writes, They seemed to be having such a wonderful time, I couldn't help but burst out laughing. *I think the author's personal interest in grizzlies allows him to enjoy and write about them in a special way.*

CRITICAL THINKING
Guiding Comprehension

❸ MAKING INFERENCES What do you think the bears look for first when they emerge from their winter dens? Why? (food; Because they have not eaten for months, they are thin, and mothers have cubs to feed.)

❹ TOPIC, MAIN IDEA, AND DETAILS The author writes on page 607 that animals giving birth in the spring must keep constant watch over their newborns to protect them. What supporting detail does he give? (A grizzly tries to attack a young moose, whose mother fights off the bear.)

❺ MAKING GENERALIZATIONS The author says that all living things depend on each other for survival. How is this statement true for humans? (Families depend on each other; Communities work together; Farmers grow food for all.)

❸ Grizzlies just emerging from their winter dens are as thin as they will be all year. They have not eaten for months, and in the snow-covered landscape, their first meal may be the carcass of a moose or caribou that did not survive the winter. Near the sea, bears may find a beached whale, or a dead sea lion or walrus.

After the snow melts and the earth turns green, bears begin to eat roots and grasses. Sedges — grasses that grow in wetlands — are particularly important, because they grow rapidly in the early spring and are rich in protein.

606

English Language Learners

Supporting Comprehension

Point out that the selection mentions many animals other than bears. As they read, encourage students to list the names of these animals. Have them pay particular attention to pages 606 (moose, caribou, whale, sea lion, walrus) and 607 (squirrel, wolves, Dall sheep). If possible, show pictures of the animals.

Vocabulary

carcass the dead body of an animal

caribou a type of Arctic deer

wilderness any unsettled region in its natural state

Arctic ground squirrels are a popular food for bears, but it takes real work to catch one. An 850-pound bear chasing a 2-pound squirrel is a truly comical sight. When the squirrel dives into its hole, the bear begins digging furiously with its front paws. But there may be many holes, all connected underground. Sometimes the squirrel will pop out of a hole behind the bear and watch it dig away.

Of course, many squirrels do get caught and eaten by bears. Scientists at Denali National Park in Alaska found that each grizzly bear eats about 400 ground squirrels a year.

Caribou, wolves, Dall sheep, moose, and many other animals give birth in the spring. They must keep constant watch over their new-borns to protect them from danger. ❹

One June afternoon I was sitting on a mountain slope looking down at a moose with her two young calves. For some reason the moose was uneasy, her ears pulled far back to the sides. A bear suddenly appeared from the bushes and rushed towards the calves.

The moose turned to confront the powerful bear. The bear stopped and the two faced off, staring at each other intently. A moment later the moose charged. The startled bear took off, with the moose close behind.

The moose had risked her life to protect her calves. And the bear retreated rather than risk being injured by the slashing hooves of the determined cow.

The bear will try again, of course, and next time it may be successful. But I have come to understand that when a bear catches a moose calf, it is not a sad event. The bear may have cubs of her own who will share in the meal. There will be new moose calves and new bear cubs next year, and life in the wilderness will go on. In nature, all living things, including humans, depend on other lives for their existence. ❺

607

Fluency Practice

Rereading for Fluency Have students choose a favorite part of the story to reread to a partner, or suggest that they read page 607. Encourage students to read expressively.

Extra Support/Intervention

Strategy Modeling: Phonics/Decoding

Model the strategy for *comical*.

KAHM-ih-kuhl

I'll try breaking this word into parts to see how it is pronounced. I can try dividing the first part after the vowel: KOH-mihk-uhl. *This isn't a word I know. Next I'll try dividing it after the m:* KAHM-ih-kuhl. *It means "funny." It makes sense in the sentence.*

CRITICAL THINKING
Guiding Comprehension

❻ CAUSE AND EFFECT How does the social behavior of grizzly bears change in June, when the salmon swim upstream? Why? (During most of the year, the bears avoid each other, but at this time they feed side by side; There are many fish, so the bears crowd into the streams.)

❼ MAKING INFERENCES A mother bear is usually tolerant of cubs that are not her own. What does this tell you about mother grizzlies? (Their instincts tell them that the cubs of others are not a threat.)

As summer nears, the daylight hours lengthen quickly until the nights are completely gone.

Imagine having no night at all. The sun moves around the sky in a big circle, always staying just above the horizon. Without a watch, it's hard to know when one day ends and the next begins. You may forget what day of the week it is, and even what month. And all the while, the sun's energy feeds the trees, grasses, and shrubs of the Alaskan wilderness.

❻ In June salmon swim upstream in Alaska's rivers and streams, and bears are drawn to choice fishing spots. Grizzlies avoid contact with other bears during most of the year, but fishing season brings them shoulder to shoulder along the streams. With food temporarily abundant, they seem to tolerate one another more, but first a dominance order — an understanding of who bosses whom — must be established.

The stronger, more aggressive bears, usually males, command the best places. When a new bear joins a group, a brief struggle for dominance is often the result. Bears avoid fighting if at all possible, but two bears of nearly equal strength may wage a fierce battle. When two bears who have already fought meet again, the loser will automatically give up its place to the victor, avoiding another fight.

608

Vocabulary

abundant plentiful

dominance the condition of having the most control

aggressive bold; ready and quick to fight

subservience the state of being willing to yield to others' power

tolerant able to allow the presence of something unusual without resistance

REACHING ALL LEARNERS

Extra Support/ Intervention	English Language Learners

Review (pages 603–609)

Before students who need extra support join the whole class for Stop and Think on page 609, have them

- check predictions
- take turns modeling Evaluate and other strategies they used
- help you add to **Transparency 6–2**
- check and revise their Generalizations Chart on **Practice Book** page 202, and use it to summarize

Language Development

Point to your shoulder and explain that *shoulder to shoulder* on page 608 means "close together."

- Ask pairs of volunteers to position themselves and demonstrate the meaning of this phrase.
- Repeat the process with *face to face* on page 603.
- Mime for students the meaning of *side to side* from *wagging their heads from side to side* on page 613.

Bears use body language to express dominance or subservience within the temporary community at the river. By observing bears as they fish, I have learned some useful clues about the safest way to behave around bears in the wild.

One time I watched a mother bear with one cub, and another mother with two cubs, approach a river. While the mothers fished for salmon in the river, the cubs waited on the riverbank. Curiosity drew all three cubs together. Suddenly the mother of the two cubs rushed up the bank. Would she kill the stranger? But the mother bear simply sniffed the cub that was not her own. Then the mother of the single cub realized what was happening, and charged out of the water to defend her young. Again it seemed as if there might be trouble. The cubs looked on nervously, staying near their mothers. In the end, the two families parted peacefully. Mother bears are usually quite tolerant of the cubs of others, even to the point of adopting strays and orphans.

609

Stop and Think

Critical Thinking Questions

1. **SUMMARIZE** How would you describe grizzly bears, based on what you have learned so far? (They are strong, resourceful, wild, somewhat aggressive, and playful; Mother bears are loving.)

2. **MAKING JUDGMENTS** Do you think the rewards of Hoshino's job are worth the risks he takes? Why or why not? (Answers will vary.)

Strategies in Action

Have students take turns modeling Evaluate and other strategies they used.

Discussion Options

You may wish to bring the entire class together to do one or more of the activities below.

- **Review Predictions/Purpose** Discuss students' predictions about grizzlies, what they learned, and any details that are different from what they predicted.

- **Share Group Discussions** Have students share their literature discussions.

- **Summarize** Help students use their Generalizations Charts to summarize the story so far.

ASSIGNMENT CARD 2

Literature Discussion

Discuss your own questions and the following questions with a group of your classmates:

- How does the author seem to feel about grizzly bears and the Alaskan wilderness? Find specific passages that support your answer.

- The author has organized the selection carefully. He starts by describing the bears in early spring, and goes on to describe their behavior throughout the other seasons. Do you think this is a good way to organize the selection? Explain.

- Do you think you would enjoy photographing grizzly bears in the Alaskan wilderness? Why or why not?

Theme 6: Animal Encounters

Teacher's Resource BLM page 89

Monitoring Student Progress

If . . .	Then . . .
students have successfully completed the Extra Support activities on page 608,	have them read the rest of the selection cooperatively or independently.

CRITICAL THINKING
Guiding Comprehension

8 **FACT AND OPINION** Read the first paragraph on page 610. Does it state facts or opinions? How can you tell? (facts; They can be proven.)

9 **CAUSE AND EFFECT** Why does the bears' temporary society break up when the salmon run ends? (The bears leave the streams to search for other food sources alone.)

8   I was surprised the first time I saw a bear catch a salmon, hold it briefly as if examining it, and then release it in the river. When salmon are rare, grizzlies will hungrily devour every one they catch. But at the height of the salmon season, a bear may capture ten salmon an hour and can afford to be selective. Sometimes bears just eat the head and eggs, discarding the rest. The uneaten portion of the fish doesn't go to waste, however, because gulls swarm nearby, ready to grab the leftovers.

    When a bear catches a salmon with its paws and mouth, it can probably smell the difference between a male fish and a female fish. The bear I saw catching and releasing salmon may have been selecting only the female fish with their delicious eggs.

610

Vocabulary

selective choosy

territory an area inhabited by an animal or animal group and defended against intruders

bugling a noise similar to the noise a bugle makes

First-year cubs wait on the riverbank for their mothers to bring freshly caught salmon. By their second year, cubs wade in to fish for themselves. Although rarely successful at first, they learn by watching and imitating their mothers.

With the end of the salmon run, the bears' temporary society breaks up, each bear returning to its own mountain territory, where autumn food sources are now maturing.

The bugling of sandhill cranes sweeping south in great ragged Vs announces autumn across Alaska. The animals of the Arctic grow lovely, thick winter coats. Moose and caribou antlers are now very large. Aspen and birch forests turn golden, and the tundra blazes red.

Blueberry, cranberry, and crowberry bushes blanket the ground, offering a rich harvest for bears.

611

Topic, Main Idea, and Details

Review

- Remind students that the topic is the subject of a selection or paragraph.

- The main idea is the most important point about the topic. It may be directly stated or unstated.

- Details support the main idea.

Practice

- Have students read page 610 and the first paragraph on page 611. Ask them to identify the topic of these sections. (bears catching salmon)

- Then ask students to identify the main idea of the first paragraph on page 611. (Gradually, cubs learn to fish for themselves.)

Apply

- Have students work in pairs to reread pages 608–611.

- Ask them to list other main ideas and supporting details that have to do with bears feeding on salmon.

Review Skill Trace	
Teach	Theme 2, p. 229A
Reteach	Theme 2, p. R14
▶ Review	p. 611; Theme 1, p. 89; Theme 3, p. 273

ASSIGNMENT CARD 4

A Bear Tale

Outline

Write an outline for a fiction story about the life of one particular grizzly bear. Use facts and details from the selection, as well as your own imagination, to help you. Here are some questions you might want to consider as you plan the story.

- male or female?
- its name?
- favorite hibernation spot?
- favorite foods?

- encounters with humans?
- fights for dominance?
- favorite "grizzly games"?

Theme 6: Animal Encounters

Teacher's Resource BLM page 90

CRITICAL THINKING
Guiding Comprehension

10 **NOTING DETAILS** How does the author help readers picture how grizzly bears eat berries on page 612? (He describes them as *engrossed in berry picking* and able to *gently* strip berries off branches.)

11 **WRITER'S CRAFT** Why do you think the author included the story of his encounter with the two young bears? (to add interest and suspense)

12 **MAKING JUDGMENTS** The author writes using a mix of facts about bears and personal experiences. Do you like this way of presenting information? Why or why not? (Answers will vary.)

COMPREHENSION STRATEGY
Evaluate

Student Modeling Ask students to evaluate how the author's personal experience helps his description of the grizzly bears preparing for winter. If necessary, offer this prompt:

• How might the author have described the bears differently if he had not seen them himself?

Vocabulary

engrossed completely occupied

tundra a treeless Arctic region where the subsoil is permanently frozen and where only low shrubs, lichens, and mosses can grow

---

10 "Don't bump heads with a bear when you go blueberry picking!" This frequently heard advice is no joke in Alaska. Both humans and bears become so engrossed in berry picking that they scarcely take a moment to lift their heads and look around. While you probably won't actually bump heads with a bear, it's wise to check your surroundings now and then.

Bears seem to like soapberries best of all. Wondering how they taste, I picked a ripe red one and popped it in my mouth. It didn't taste very good to me, but then I don't like fish heads, either.

It's wonderful to observe a huge bear holding a thin soapberry branch, gently stripping it of the delicate fruit.

As the days shorten, bears must put on a large store of fat to take them through winter. Berries are high in sugar, and the autumn feast can be critical to a bear's survival. With their shiny coats rippling as they move across the tundra, grizzlies consume an enormous amount of berries.

How many berries would you guess a grizzly can eat in one day? The bears in Denali National Park eat berries for twenty hours a day in late summer, hardly stopping to sleep. One bear may consume 200,000 berries in a single day! Bear droppings at this time of year consist mainly of partially digested berries. From the seeds in these droppings new bushes will grow to feed a new generation of bears.

612

English Language Learners

Supporting Comprehension

Pause and have students discuss what they have read about how bears behave. Encourage students to look at the pictures as a guide. Ask: What do bears do in winter? in spring? in summer? Why do bears sometimes fight? What do they eat?

One autumn day as I was hiking through the Brooks Range near the Arctic Circle, I suddenly noticed two bears running towards me from a riverbank. Were they coming at me on purpose, or did they not realize I was there? They appeared to be siblings, just old enough to leave their mother's care, but already powerful. Closer and closer they came, loping gracefully. My heart beat like a drum. When they were about twenty yards away, I raised my arms and shouted, "*Stop!*"

The two bears skidded to a halt as if in complete surprise. They stood up on their hind legs, wagging their heads from side to side, sniffing the air. I was so excited, I thought my heart would burst.

Then, as if they had finally become aware of my existence, they turned and raced off in the direction they'd come from. It had been a pretty frightening experience for me, but it must have been equally startling for the bears.

11

12

613

Extra Support/Intervention

Strategy Modeling: Evaluate

Use this example to model the strategy.

On page 613, the author describes the two bears loping gracefully, *skidding to a stop, and* wagging their heads from side to side, sniffing the air. *Only a person who spent time observing grizzlies would notice these details. I think the author's experience has helped him write about grizzlies in a vivid way.*

Fact and Opinion

Review

- Remind students that a fact is a statement that can be proven.
- An opinion is a statement of belief, feeling, or preference.

Practice

- Read aloud the following sentences from page 612.
- Have students identify each as fact or opinion.
  - *While you probably won't actually bump heads with a bear, it's wise to check your surroundings now and then.* (opinion)
  - *Bear droppings at this time of year consist mainly of partially digested berries.* (fact)

Apply

- Ask pairs of students to reread page 607.
- Have them list facts and opinions in a chart like the one below.

Fact	Opinion
Each grizzly bear eats about 400 ground squirrels a year.	An 850-pound bear chasing a 2-pound squirrel is truly a comical sight.

Review Skill Trace	
Teach	Theme 2, p. 157A
Reteach	Theme 2, p. R8
▶ Review	p. 613; Theme 1, p. 65

CRITICAL THINKING
Guiding Comprehension

13 **DRAWING CONCLUSIONS** Why do you think Michio Hoshino had trouble sleeping after his encounter with the two bears? (He felt nervous because he realized that he might have gotten hurt.)

14 **MAKING INFERENCES** What does the author mean when he says that *wariness forces upon us a valuable sense of humility* on page 614? (Meeting a powerful animal reminds us that we are not always in control.)

15 **AUTHOR'S VIEWPOINT** What opinion does the author seem to have of trophy hunters? Why? (a low opinion; He thinks they pretend to be *heroic* when they really shot a peaceful bear from a safe distance.)

13 That night I couldn't fall asleep. The two grizzlies might be close by. Very few bears are interested in pursuing people, but still I felt somewhat uneasy. Unable to sleep, I thought about bears, about people, and about Alaska.

If there wasn't a single bear in all of Alaska, I could hike through the mountains with complete peace of mind. I could camp without worry. But what a dull place Alaska would be!

Here people share the land with bears. There is a certain wariness **14** between people and bears. And that wariness forces upon us a valuable sense of humility.

People continue to tame and subjugate nature. But when we visit the few remaining scraps of wilderness where bears roam free, we can still feel an instinctive fear. How precious that feeling is. And how precious these places, and these bears, are.

614

Vocabulary

wariness the state of being on one's guard

humility the quality of being meek or modest

subjugate to bring under control; conquer

instinctive in a way that is inborn or naturally present at birth

Trophy hunters from the lower United States and from Europe come to Alaska to shoot grizzlies. They smile for the camera and stand, gun in hand, over the body of a dead bear. They hang their trophy on the wall — the head of a bear with its fangs bared, as if it was killed while attacking the heroic hunter. In truth, a high-powered rifle was fired from a great distance at a bear that was peacefully eating berries. **15**

Just imagine: You're alone and unarmed on the Arctic plain with a bear. You and the bear feel the same breeze pass over your faces. You — a human being — are on an equal footing with the bear.

How wonderful that would be. No matter how many books you read, no matter how much television you watch, there is no substitute for experiencing nature firsthand. If you cannot meet a bear in the wild, then you must try to imagine it — for even if you only imagine it, the feeling can be real. And it is the feeling that is important.

English Language Learners

Language Development

Have students locate the word *unarmed* in the second paragraph on page 615. Point out that the word *armed* means "having a weapon." Remind students that the prefix *un-* means "not." Ask them what *unarmed* means. Then point out the words *uneasy* and *unable* in the first paragraph on page 614 and *uneaten* on page 610. Help students understand what these words mean.

Comprehension Preview

TARGET SKILL

Making Generalizations

Teach

- A generalization is a broad statement, based on fact, that is usually true.

- Words such as *most, all, always, generally, often, many, usually, few,* and *never* often signal generalizations.

Practice

- Read aloud this sentence: *There is a certain wariness between people and bears.*

- Ask if students think every person who encounters a bear feels wariness, and why. (probably not; Some people don't realize how powerful bears are.)

- Have students rewrite the generalization to make it valid, or true. (Sample answer: There is often a certain wariness between people and bears.)

Apply

- Have students identify each generalization below as valid or invalid.

- Then have them rewrite invalid generalizations to make them valid.

  – Most bears avoid fighting, if at all possible. (valid)

  – People do not appreciate the wilderness. (invalid; change to "Some people…")

  – Stronger, more aggressive bears, usually males, command the best fishing spots. (valid)

Target Skill Trace	
Preview; Teach	p. 599A, p. 602, p. 615; p. 623A
Reteach	p. R8
Review	p. 639; Theme 3, p. 277

Reading the Selection 615

CRITICAL THINKING

Guiding Comprehension

16 NOTING DETAILS How does the tundra region change as winter approaches? (The days shorten, the aurora dances in the sky, the first snow falls, and the bears return to their dens.)

17 DRAWING CONCLUSIONS How did Michio Hoshino's life and death reflect his love of the wilderness? (He worked as a wildlife photographer; He died in the wilderness, probably studying bears or other wildlife.)

Today's snowfall marks the advent of winter. The daylight hours are shorter now. The aurora dances in the clear night sky. A mother bear and her half-grown cubs trace footprints in the new snow as they climb up the mountain to their den. The cubs will spend the long winter with their mother snug beneath the snow.

The snow continues to fall, and finally the tracks are gone. Alaska, the Great Land, settles down for a quiet winter sleep.

616

Vocabulary

advent the arrival of a new person, thing, or event

aurora a brilliant display of lights visible in the night sky, chiefly in the polar regions

REACHING ALL LEARNERS

| Extra Support/ Intervention | On Level | Challenge |

Selection Review

Before students join in Wrapping Up on page 617, have them

- review and discuss the accuracy of their predictions
- take turns modeling the reading strategies they used
- help you complete **Transparency 6–2**
- complete their Generalizations Charts and summarize the whole selection

Literature Discussion

Have small groups of students discuss the selection, using their own questions. Then have students discuss the Responding questions on Anthology page 618.

Meet the Author/Photographer

Michio Hoshino

Michio Hoshino grew up in Tokyo, Japan. When he was a young man he saw a picture of a remote Inuit village in a book. He sent a letter to the village's mayor, who invited him to Alaska to spend the summer living with a family in the village. He accepted.

Hoshino was fascinated by the Alaskan wilderness, and his photographs of the state's wildlife were published in many books, and in magazines including *National Geographic* and *Smithsonian*. In addition, Hoshino wrote several books, including *Grizzly*, an award-winning book of bear photography.

17

After a career of almost twenty years as a wildlife photographer, Hoshino's life was cut short. In the early morning of August 8th, 1996, he was pulled from his tent and killed by a brown bear at a camp in a wildlife refuge in Siberia. Witnesses said the bear had begun behaving aggressively towards human beings as a result of being given food by visitors to the refuge.

Internet

Learn more about Michio Hoshino by visiting Education Place. **www.eduplace.com/kids**

617

Practice Book page 203

Wrapping Up

Critical Thinking Questions

1. **COMPARE AND CONTRAST** How is this selection different from an encyclopedia article about grizzly bears? (includes author's feelings and point of view; may not be as complete as an encyclopedia)

2. **MAKING JUDGMENTS** Should more people take the author's advice and experience the wilderness firsthand? Why? (Sample answer: no, because more people in the wilderness might spoil it)

Strategies in Action

Have students tell how and where they used the Evaluate strategy.

Discussion Options

Bring the entire class together to do one or more of the activities below.

Review Predictions/Purpose Discuss students' predictions of what they would learn from a firsthand account of grizzlies.

Share Group Discussions Have students discuss what they learned about grizzlies and the Alaska wilderness.

Summarize Ask students to summarize the selection using their Generalizations Chart.

Comprehension Check

Use **Practice Book** page 203 to assess students' comprehension of the selection.

Monitoring Student Progress

If . . .	Then . . .
students score 7 or below on **Practice Book** page 203,	have them work in small groups to reread key selection pages to clarify understanding.

Reading the Selection **617**

Responding

Think About the Selection

Have students discuss or write their answers. Sample answers are provided; accept reasonable responses.

1. **CONNECTING TO PERSONAL EXPERIENCE** Answers will vary.

2. **AUTHOR'S PURPOSE** to make people see bears in a more positive way

3. **AUTHOR'S PURPOSE** to help readers appreciate and care about the wild habitat necessary for the bears' survival

4. **MAKING JUDGMENTS** Sample answers: yes, because all living things need food; no, because the moose calf dies

5. **MAKING GENERALIZATIONS** Most bears like to play but live alone or with their cubs; Females make good mothers; Bears eat fish, game, and berries.

6. **EXPRESSING PERSONAL OPINIONS** Answers will vary.

7. **Connecting/Comparing** Alike— Both love the animals' natural habitats and understand their behavior; Different—Hoshino's purpose is to photograph the bears, but Lemmons's is to capture the mustangs.

Think About the Selection

1. A surprise encounter caused the author to want to learn more about grizzlies. Would you have had the same reaction? Explain.

2. Why do you think the author compares bear mothers to human mothers on page 605?

3. Why do you think the author includes so much information about the grizzly bears' habitat?

4. The author writes on page 607: ". . . when a bear catches a moose calf, it is not a sad event." Do you agree? Why or why not?

5. Based on the selection, what generalizations can you make about bears? Think about their family life, growth, and feeding habits.

6. Has reading this selection changed your feelings about bears? Why or why not?

7. **Connecting/Comparing** Compare the relationship of Michio Hoshino and the bears he photographs with that of Bob Lemmons and the horses he rounds up in *Black Cowboy, Wild Horses*.

Describing

Write About Bears

Choose two photographs of grizzly bears from the selection. Write a paragraph about each photograph. Describe the setting and season, how fully grown the bears are, and what the bears are doing.

Tips

- Include a topic sentence in each paragraph.
- Make each paragraph more interesting by using differe[nt] sentence types and lengths[.]

618

English Language Learners

Supporting Comprehension

Beginning/Preproduction Have students draw a scene showing grizzlies in their natural habitats. Then help them describe what they have drawn.

Early Production and Speech Emergence Have students look at the pictures in the selection. Ask students to describe the bears' habitat.

Intermediate and Advanced Fluency Read aloud the sentence *Imagine meeting a grizzly bear in the wild* on page 603. Ask students to describe how they might react, using *If* and *would* in their response. Offer this prompt: If I met a bear face to face, I would feel frightened.

Math

Make a Graph

Make a list of all the animals mentioned in the selection. Then take a poll of your class or school. Find out how many people have seen each kind of animal the author mentions. Create a graph that shows the results.

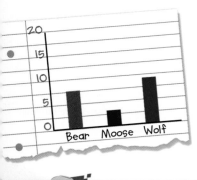

Health and Safety

Make a Safety Poster

Humans in bear territory need to be educated about grizzlies, for both their own and the bears' protection. Use information from the selection about bear behavior to make a safety poster especially for people who pick wild berries or people who fish for salmon.

Go on a Web Field Trip

Connect to Education Place and explore a part of the world where grizzlies roam.

www.eduplace.com/kids

619

Additional Responses

Personal Response Invite students to share their personal responses to *The Grizzly Bear Family Book.*

Journal ▶ Ask students to write in their journals about how they might feel being close enough to observe a grizzly and other wild animals in the wilderness.

Selection Connections Remind students to add to **Practice Book** pages 199 and 200.

Practice Book page 199

Launching the Theme
Selection Connections

Name _____

Animal Encounters

The selections in this theme explore some special relationships between people and wild creatures. After reading each selection, fill in this chart to show what you learned.

	What kind of writing is the selection an example of?	What creature or creatures does the selection describe?
Grizzly Bear Family Book	first-person narrative nonfiction **(2.5 points)**	grizzly bears **(2.5)**
The Golden Lion Tamarin Comes Home	expository nonfiction **(2.5)**	golden lion tamarins **(2.5)**
My Side of the Mountain	fiction **(2.5)**	many small creatures of the forest, such as raccoons and a falcon **(2.5)**

Practice Book page 200

Launching the Theme
Selection Connections

Name _____

Animal Encounters continued

	What is the purpose of the encounter between humans and animals?	What are the results of the encounter?
Grizzly Bear Family Book	Michio Hoshino wants to learn as much as he can about grizzly bears. He wants to photograph them. **(2.5)**	People learn more about grizzly bears and how they live. **(2.5)**
The Golden Lion Tamarin Comes Home	The people of the Golden Lion Tamarin Conservation Program want to return golden lion tamarins to the forests where they naturally live. **(2.5)**	The golden lion tamarin population increases in the rain forest of Brazil. The monkeys are protected in the preserve. **(2.5)**
My Side of the Mountain	Sam wants to experience the wilderness and be self-sufficient in it. He sees the animals as companions and even friends. **(2.5)**	Sam learns more about himself and about the creatures with whom he shares his woodland home. **(2.5)**

What are some ways in which people can help wild animals? **(2)**
People can help wild animals in zoos learn to live in the wild again. People can protect wild animals' natural habitats. People can teach others about wild animals to try to get them to care about the animals and understand their needs.

Monitoring Student Progress

End-of-Selection Assessment

Selection Test Use the test on page 149 in the **Teacher's Resource Blackline Masters** to assess selection comprehension and vocabulary.

Student Self-Assessment Have students assess their reading with additional questions such as

- Which parts of this selection were difficult for me? Why?
- What strategies helped me understand the story?
- Would I recommend this story to my friends? Why?

Responding 619

Poetry Link

Skill: How to Compare Poems

- **Introduce** the three poems about animal encounters written by Joseph Bruchac.

- **Discuss** the Skill Lesson on Anthology page 620. If necessary, clarify that *images in the poems* in the first bullet refers to pictures that come to mind when reading.

- **Model** reading a poem. Read aloud "Above Jackson Pond" on page 620.

- **Explain** that using a Comparison Chart like the one below will help students compare the three poems. Tell students that *theme* refers to the poem's message.

- **Set a purpose** for reading. Tell students to read the poems and complete their own charts to compare the subjects, moods, sounds, rhythms, and other elements of the poems.

Title	Subject	Theme
"Above Jackson Pond"	an eagle flying	the earth as a gift
"Raccoons on the Shore at Paradox Lake"	young raccoons by a lake at night	the wonder of nature and living things
"A Thousand Geese"	geese flying during fall	remembering what is important in life

Vocabulary

updraft a current of air that flows upward

sentinel guard

Poetry Link

Skill: How to Compare Poems

When you read two or more poems together, ask these questions:

- What is the **subject** of each poem? How are the subjects or images in the poems alike or different?

- What is the **mood** of each poem? Light and funny? Dark and serious? How are the moods alike or different?

- How are the **sounds** and **rhythms** alike or different?

- If the poems are by the same poet, what **elements** (subject, sound, images, mood) tell you that the same person wrote them?

620

Three Poems by Joseph Bruchac

Above Jackson Pond

Long-winged, it circled
slow as a heron
yet shoulders broader in flight.

Seeking an updraft
to lift it higher,
it flapped wings
darker than clouds,
tail fanned, catching light.

An Eagle.

I whistled its way
and on my third whistle
it folded wings,
dove and rolled in answer
before flying on
past the tallest pines
which sentinel
the hill above Jackson Pond.

Valleys widen with green,
with the flow of spring,
rivers and lakes
veins pulsing the heart
of the land
held under those wide wings.

Thinking now of that great bir
praising its return,
my own vision opens
to see this earth
more gift than we humans
can give.

621

Extra Support/Intervention

Reading Poetry

Remind students that when they read poetry, they should read on past the end of each line to try to find the complete thought. Ask students to read aloud part of one poem to demonstrate their understanding.

Writer's Craft

Imagery and Figurative Language

Teach

- Explain that poets often use ordinary words in inventive ways to make their language fresh and vivid.

- Point out that one way they do this is to compare one thing to another to create an image or set a mood.

Practice/Apply

- Read aloud the second line of "Raccoons on the Shore at Paradox Lake." Point out that the poet uses the adjective *grey* as a verb, *greyed*.

- Ask students what the author achieved by using *grey* in this way. (created a picture in the reader's mind of lake shore mist)

- Then ask why the poet compares the raccoon to a cork in the second stanza. (to create a vivid and funny image of how it looked as it popped up)

- Have students list other examples of how the poet used words in unusual and vivid ways.

Vocabulary

greyed made gray by dusk

basswood a linden tree

wake the visible track of waves behind a boat

sumacs any of various shrubs or small trees having feathery leaves

sustain to support the spirits of; to keep alive

Raccoons on the Shore at Paradox Lake

From the lake shore
greyed in by trails of mist
from the warm evening water
bright eyes flash at me
in the beam of the lantern
as I lift my paddle
and let the boat drift.

Six small raccoons, cubs of this year.
One curious one edges too close
and, nudged by a brother or a sister,
splashes off the dock,
comes up like a cork
and scrambles back onto the land.

They watch me,
until the canoe bumps in
to the dock, then after
a quick glance at each other,
they scoot to the base
of the big basswood tree
and hand over hand
up to its thin branches
which arch over water.

Their small paws
break free twigs
which rain about me
as a sudden wind
cuts across the lake,
cutting through the low
grey clouds above me,
so that there,
above their lifting heads I see
the shoulder of the mountain
and then, just before the mist
closes in again, high above
on the night trail of the Milky Way.

There, too, beyond Great Bear
and The Hunter
are the Northern Lights,
the ones my old people
called the spirits who dance.
They ripple the edge of the sky.

Stars reflect around me
in the lake's dark mirror
and between the shapes of the dancing stars
and that rippling form of my canoe cutting its wake
across the stars, I see again
those small raccoons,
looking up and down
in wonder.

622

English Language Learners

Language Development

Read aloud the title "A Thousand Geese" on page 623.

- Explain that geese are birds that fly south for the winter—they migrate.

- Ask if the word *geese* is singular or plural. (plural) Point out that the singular form is *goose*.

- Tell students that plural forms of certain words are formed by internal spelling changes rather than by adding -s or -es.

A Thousand Geese

Geese have flown over
for twelve days now.
I've counted each flock
lying on my back
at the edge of the old field
where sumacs edge in.

All that they carry
is all that they are.
They travel far
in need of nothing
but fair weather,
food and a safe place to rest,
their wide wings linking
winter and spring.

As the last flight passes
they take with them
my weariness
which had no reason
yet held me back
from doing the real work
half of my life.

Now, like those geese,
today all I seek
is warmth enough,
food and light enough
to sustain myself and
those whose lives
are close to mine
as we journey
the seasons.

623

Wrapping Up

Critical Thinking Questions

Have students use their Comparison Charts and the poems to answer these questions.

1. **AUTHOR'S VIEWPOINT** What can you infer about the poet's viewpoint from these poems? (He believes that it is important to value and learn from nature.)

2. **MAKING INFERENCES** What do you think the poet is saying in the last stanza of "Above Jackson Pond"? (The earth gives more to humans than humans can ever give back.)

3. **DRAWING CONCLUSIONS** Why do you think the poet admires the birds he sees in "A Thousand Geese"? (because they lead a simpler life than he does)

4. **COMPARE AND CONTRAST** How is Joseph Bruchac's view of nature similar to Michio Hoshino's view? (Both seem to love and respect everything, large and small, in the natural world.)

The Grizzly Bear Family Book

Challenge

Writing Poetry

Have students write their own poems about places, animals, or events in nature that seem particularly powerful or beautiful to them. Encourage them to use similes, metaphors, and figurative language to create unusual and vivid images.

REACHING ALL LEARNERS

Poetry Link 623

OBJECTIVES

- Identify words that often signal generalizations.
- Analyze and evaluate the validity of generalizations.
- Make generalizations based on story events and their own experiences.
- Learn academic language: *generalization*.

Target Skill Trace

Preview; Teach	p. 599A; p. 602; p. 615; p. 623A
Reteach	p. R8
Review	pp. M32–M33; p. 639; Theme 3, p. 277
See	*Extra Support Handbook*, pp. 206–207; pp. 212–213

Transparency 6–2

Detective Work

Page	Clue	Generalization
605	how people see bears	People have a fearful image of bears.
607	what all living things do	All living things, including humans, depend on each other for survival.
608	how grizzlies act toward each other during most of the year	Grizzlies avoid contact with other bears during most of the year.
608	which bears command the best fishing spots	Stronger, more aggressive males usually get the best fishing spots.
609	the tolerance of mother bears	Mother bears are usually tolerant of the cubs of others.
610	bears selecting salmon	Bears can probably smell the difference between male and female fish.
612	bears and soapberries	Bears seem to like soapberries best.
614	bears pursuing people	Very few bears are interested in pursuing people.
615	how hunters kill bears	A high-powered rifle was fired from a distance.
616	how people treat nature	People continue to tame and subjugate nature.

Practice Book page 202

The Grizzly Bear Family Book
Graphic Organizer Generalizations Chart

Name _____

Detective Work

What generalizations does the author make about bears, about people, and about the wilderness in this selection? As you read, look for generalizations on the pages listed below. Use the clues to help you recognize them. Write each generalization you find.

Page	Clue	Generalization
605	how people see bears	People have a fearful image of bears. (1)
607	what all living things do	All living things, including humans, depend on each other for survival. (1)
608	how grizzlies act toward each other during most of the year	Grizzlies avoid contact with other bears during most of the year. (1)
608	which bears command the best fishing spots	Stronger, more aggressive males usually get the best fishing spots. (1)
609	the tolerance of mother bears	Mother bears are usually tolerant of the cubs of others. (1)
610	bears selecting salmon	Bears can probably smell the difference between male and female fish. (1)
612	bears and soapberries	Bears seem to like soapberries best. (1)
614	bears pursuing people	Very few bears are interested in pursuing people. (1)
615	how hunters kill bears	A high-powered rifle was fired from a distance. (1)
616	how people treat nature	People continue to tame and subjugate nature. (1)

COMPREHENSION: Making Generalizations

TARGET SKILL

❶ Teach

Review generalizations. Remind students that a generalization is a statement that is true for most but not all of the subjects or circumstances it describes.

- Words such as *most, usually,* and *often* can signal a generalization.
- An overgeneralization is not valid because it is too broad or does not follow logically from facts.
- To decide whether a generalization is valid, readers can decide whether it is based on enough examples or whether it is supported by their own experience.

Display **Transparency 6–2** and review generalizations in *The Grizzly Bear Family Book*. (Sample answers are shown.) Students may refer to the selection and to **Practice Book** page 202.

Model evaluating a generalization. Use the last item on **Transparency 6–2** as an example of a possible overgeneralization.

Think Aloud
The author makes this generalization: People continue to tame and subjugate nature. *I know this statement is true of some people, such as the trophy hunters the author describes. But I also know it's not true of all people. For example, the author doesn't tame and subjugate nature. I think he is making an overgeneralization. Saying "People" might suggest that he means everyone.*

❷ Guided Practice

Have students evaluate and write generalizations. Have students work individually, then discuss their evaluations and generalizations as a class.

- Tell students to use **Practice Book** page 202, evaluate the other generalizations they found, and determine whether each is valid.
- Ask each student to write a generalization about the wilderness, about grizzly bears, or about people who study grizzly bears in the wild.

❸ Apply

Assign Practice Book pages 204–205. Also have students apply this skill as they read their **Leveled Readers** for this week. You may also select books from the Leveled Bibliography for this theme (pages 594E–594F).

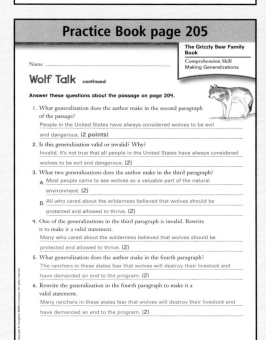

Test Prep Tell students that questions on reading tests usually focus on important details only. Remind students that being able to distinguish more important from less important details will help them do better on reading tests.

Leveled Readers and Leveled Practice

Students at all levels apply the comprehension skill as they read their Leveled Readers. See lessons on pages 623O–623R.

● BELOW LEVEL ▲ ON LEVEL ■ ABOVE LEVEL ◆ LANGUAGE SUPPORT

Reading Traits

As students develop the ability to make generalizations, they are learning to "read between the lines" of a selection. This comprehension skill supports the reading trait **Developing Interpretations**.

Practice Book page 204

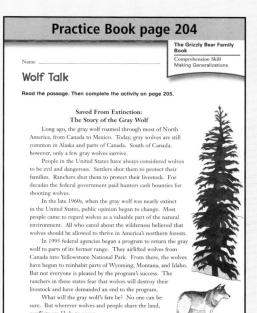

The Grizzly Bear Family Book
Comprehension Skill
Making Generalizations

Name _____

Wolf Talk

Read the passage. Then complete the activity on page 205.

Saved From Extinction: The Story of the Gray Wolf

Long ago, the gray wolf roamed through most of North America, from Canada to Mexico. Today, gray wolves are still common in Alaska and parts of Canada. South of Canada, however, only a few gray wolves survive.

People in the United States have always considered wolves to be evil and dangerous. Settlers shot them to protect their families. Ranchers shot them to protect their livestock. For decades the federal government paid hunters cash bounties for shooting wolves.

In the late 1960s, when the gray wolf was nearly extinct in the United States, public opinion began to change. Most people came to regard wolves as a valuable part of the natural environment. All who cared about the wilderness believed that wolves should be allowed to thrive in America's northern forests.

In 1995 federal agencies began a program to return the gray wolf to parts of its former range. They airlifted wolves from Canada into Yellowstone National Park. From there, the wolves have begun to reinhabit parts of Wyoming, Montana, and Idaho. But not everyone is pleased by the program's success. The ranchers in these states fear that wolves will destroy their livestock and have demanded an end to the program.

What will the gray wolf's fate be? No one can be sure. But wherever wolves and people share the land, conflicts are likely to occur.

Practice Book page 205

The Grizzly Bear Family Book
Comprehension Skill
Making Generalizations

Name _____

Wolf Talk continued

Answer these questions about the passage on page 204.

1. What generalization does the author make in the second paragraph of the passage?
   People in the United States have always considered wolves to be evil and dangerous. **(2 points)**

2. Is this generalization valid or invalid? Why?
   Invalid. It's not true that all people in the United States have always considered wolves to be evil and dangerous. **(2)**

3. What two generalizations does the author make in the third paragraph?
   A. Most people came to see wolves as a valuable part of the natural environment. **(2)**
   B. All who cared about the wilderness believed that wolves should be protected and allowed to thrive. **(2)**

4. One of the generalizations in the third paragraph is invalid. Rewrite it to make it a valid statement.
   Many who cared about the wilderness believed that wolves should be protected and allowed to thrive. **(2)**

5. What generalization does the author make in the fourth paragraph?
   The ranchers in these states fear that wolves will destroy their livestock and have demanded an end to the program. **(2)**

6. Rewrite the generalization in the fourth paragraph to make it a valid statement.
   Many ranchers in these states fear that wolves will destroy their livestock and have demanded an end to the program. **(2)**

Monitoring Student Progress

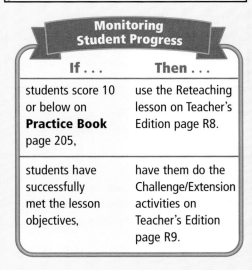

If . . .	Then . . .
students score 10 or below on **Practice Book** page 205,	use the Reteaching lesson on Teacher's Edition page R8.
students have successfully met the lesson objectives,	have them do the Challenge/Extension activities on Teacher's Edition page R9.

Comprehension Skills 623B

OBJECTIVES

- Read words that have the prefixes *com-, con-, en-, ex-, pre-,* and *pro-.*
- Use the Phonics/Decoding Strategy to decode longer words.

Target Skill Trace

Teach	p. 623C
Reteach	p. R14
Review	pp. M34–M35
See	*Handbook for English Language Learners,* p. 209; *Extra Support Handbook,* pp. 204–205; pp. 208–209

Practice Book page 206

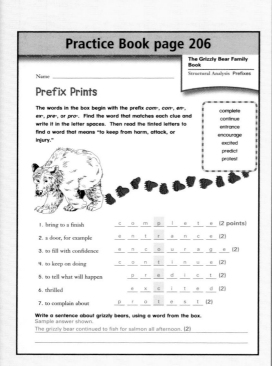

The Grizzly Bear Family Book

Structural Analysis Prefixes

Name _____

Prefix Prints

The words in the box begin with the prefix *com-, con-, en-, ex-, pre-,* or *pro-.* Find the word that matches each clue and write it in the letter spaces. Then read the tinted letters to find a word that means "to keep from harm, attack, or injury."

complete
continue
entrance
encourage
excited
predict
protest

1. bring to a finish   c o m p l e t e   (2 points)
2. a door, for example   e n t r a n c e   (2)
3. to fill with confidence   e n c o u r a g e   (2)
4. to keep on doing   c o n t i n u e   (2)
5. to tell what will happen   p r e d i c t   (2)
6. thrilled   e x c i t e d   (2)
7. to complain about   p r o t e s t   (2)

Write a sentence about grizzly bears, using a word from the box. Sample answer shown.
The grizzly bear continued to fish for salmon all afternoon. (2)

Monitoring Student Progress

If . . .	Then . . .
students score 12 or below on **Practice Book** page 206,	use the Reteaching lesson on Teacher's Edition page R14.

STRUCTURAL ANALYSIS/ VOCABULARY: More Prefixes

❶ Teach

Introduce prefixes. Explain that a prefix is a word part that comes before a base word or root and changes its meaning.

Explain the prefix *con-*. Write *The moose turned to <u>confront</u> the bear.*

- Explain that the prefix *con-* means "with."
- Define the base word *front* as "the part that faces forward."
- Tell students that *confront* means "to come face to face with."

Explain the prefix *ex-*. Write *Grizzlies depend on salmon and other nourishing foods for their <u>existence</u>.*

- Circle the prefix *ex-*. Note that in some words the base word or root may not be familiar apart from the prefix.
- Point out how recognizing *ex-* does help students break the word into syllables: *ex/is/tence.*

Introduce other prefixes. Write other prefixes and sample words: *com- (computer); en- (enforce); pre- (preserve);* and *pro- (proceed).*

Model the Phonics/Decoding Strategy. Write *Grizzlies avoid <u>contact</u> with other bears.* Then model decoding *contact.*

> **Think Aloud** *I'm not sure how to read this word. I see the prefix con-. I've seen the base word* tact *before. I'll try reading the two syllables together:* KAHN-takt. *I recognize this word, and it makes sense in the sentence.*

❷ Guided Practice

Have students use prefixes. Display the phrases below. Have students use prefixes to decode and define each underlined word, consulting a dictionary, if necessary. Have students share their work with the class.

a chance <u>encounter</u>   <u>protect</u> them from danger
all <u>connected</u> underground   <u>premature</u> snowfall
<u>command</u> the best places

❸ Apply

Assign Practice Book page 206.

PHONICS REVIEW:
The /k/ and /kw/ Sounds

OBJECTIVES
- Read words that have the /k/ and /kw/ sounds.
- Use the Phonics/Decoding Strategy to decode longer words.

❶ Teach

Review the /k/ and /kw/ sounds. Tell students that recognizing the letter patterns can help them decode many new words.

- The letters *k, c, ck,* or *ch* can stand for the /k/ sound.
- The letters *qu* or *kw* can stand for the /kw/ sound.

Model the Phonics/Decoding Strategy. Write *As summer nears, the daylight hours lengthen* quickly *until the nights are completely gone.* Then model how to decode *quickly.*

Think Aloud *I see the letters* qu *at the beginning of the underlined word. I know that these letters stand for the /kw/ sound. I also see the letters* ck *in the middle of the word. If these letters stand for the /k/ sound, the first syllable is* kwihk. *When I add the* -ly *ending, I say* KWIHK-lee. *That makes sense in the sentence.*

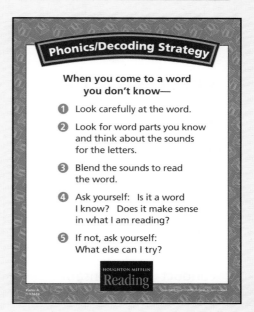

Phonics/Decoding Strategy

When you come to a word you don't know—

❶ Look carefully at the word.

❷ Look for word parts you know and think about the sounds for the letters.

❸ Blend the sounds to read the word.

❹ Ask yourself: Is it a word I know? Does it make sense in what I am reading?

❺ If not, ask yourself: What else can I try?

HOUGHTON MIFFLIN
Reading

❷ Guided Practice

Have students identify the /k/ and /kw/ sounds. Display these sentences. Have partners circle the letters in each underlined word that stand for the /k/ or /kw/ sound, pronounce the word, and check to see if it makes sense in the sentence. Call on volunteers to model at the board.

1. He <u>quietly</u> watched the bear.
2. A bear may <u>capture</u> ten salmon an hour.
3. His hands were <u>aching</u> because of the water's <u>coldness</u>.
4. The two bears awkwardly <u>skidded</u> to a halt.

❸ Apply

Have students decode words with the /k/ and /kw/ sounds. Ask students to decode these words from *The Grizzly Bear Family Book* and discuss their meanings.

blanket	p. 604	Arctic	p. 607	riverbank	p. 608
carcass	p. 606	squirrel	p. 607	critical	p. 612
caribou	p. 606	comical	p. 607	equally	p. 613

SPELLING: More Prefixes

OBJECTIVES

- Write Spelling Words that have prefixes.

SPELLING WORDS

Basic

propose	extend
convince	prefix
concern	engage
enforce	pronoun
compare	consist*
excuse	enclose
conduct	consent
preserve	proverb
contain	complete*
excite*	exchange

Review	Challenge
compose	enactment
exact	procedure
enjoy*	confront*
common	preamble
expert	concise

*Forms of these words appear in the literature.

Extra Support/Intervention

Basic Word List You may want to use only the left column of Basic Words with students who need extra support.

Challenge

Challenge Word Practice Have students write each Challenge Word and another word that they associate with it. Ask them to write a sentence using both words.

DAY 1 — INSTRUCTION

More Prefixes

Pretest Use the Day 5 Test sentences.

Teach Write _compare_, _convince_, _enforce_, _excite_, _preserve_, and _propose_ on the board.

- Tell students that the underlined word parts are prefixes, word parts added to the beginning of a base word or word root to add meaning.

- Point to _compare_; explain that _com-_ is a form of the prefix _con-_, and that _com-_ is used before the letter _p_.

- Tell the class that finding familiar prefixes can help them focus on the spelling of the base word or word root in new words.

- Erase the board. Write _com-_, _con-_, _en-_, _ex-_, _pre-_, and _pro-_ as column heads. Have students say each Basic Word. Ask them to identify the word's prefix, and write the word in the appropriate column.

Practice/Homework Assign **Practice Book** page 279.

Practice Book page 279

Take-Home Word List	Take-Home Word List	Take-Home Word List
Animal Encounters Reading-Writing Workshop	**Grizzly Bear Family Book**	**One Land, Many Trails Spelling Review**
Look for familiar spelling patterns in these words to help you remember their spellings.	**More Words with Prefixes** compare convince excite enforce preserve propose	
Spelling Words	**Spelling Words**	**Spelling Words**
1. heard 9. build	1. propose 11. extend	1. unable 16. voyage
2. your 10. family	2. convince 12. prefix	2. correction 17. pleasure
3. you're 11. can't	3. concern 13. engage	3. native 18. countries
4. field 12. cannot	4. enforce 14. pronoun	4. distance 19. happiness
5. buy 13. didn't	5. compare 15. consist	5. spinach 20. furniture
6. friend 14. haven't	6. excuse 16. enclose	6. vulture 21. promotion
7. guess 15. don't	7. conduct 17. consent	7. curtain 22. react
8. cousin	8. preserve 18. proverb	8. dirtier 23. solid
	9. contain 19. complete	9. spied 24. notice
	10. excite 20. exchange	10. treasure 25. destroy
		11. discover 26. mountain
		12. inspect 27. adventure
		13. tension 28. busier
		14. language 29. pitied
		15. respond 30. scariest
Challenge Words	**Challenge Words**	**See the back for Challenge Words.**
1. truly	1. enactment	
2. benefited	2. procedure	
3. height	3. confront	
4. believe	4. preamble	
5. received	5. concise	
My Study List Add your own spelling words on the back.→	**My Study List** Add your own spelling words on the back.→	**My Study List** Add your own spelling words on the back.→

Take-Home Word List

DAY 2 — REVIEW & PRACTICE

Reviewing the Principle

Go over the spelling principle of words with prefixes with students.

Practice/Homework Assign **Practice Book** page 207.

Practice Book page 207

Name _____

The Grizzly Bear Family Book
Spelling: More Words with Prefixes

More Words with Prefixes

Com-, con-, en-, ex-, pre-, and _pro-_ are prefixes. Because you know how to spell the prefix, pay special attention to the spelling of the base word or the word root. Spell the word by parts.

compare convince enforce
excite preserve propose

Write each Spelling Word under its prefix.
Order of answers for each category may vary.

com-, con-

convince (1 point)	contain (1)
concern (1)	consist (1)
compare (1)	consent (1)
conduct (1)	complete (1)

en-, ex-

enforce (1)	engage (1)
excuse (1)	enclose (1)
excite (1)	exchange (1)
extend (1)	

pre-, pro-

propose (1)	pronoun (1)
preserve (1)	proverb (1)
prefix (1)	

Spelling Words
1. propose
2. convince
3. concern
4. enforce
5. compare
6. excuse
7. conduct
8. preserve
9. contain
10. excite
11. extend
12. prefix
13. engage
14. pronoun
15. consist
16. enclose
17. consent
18. proverb
19. complete
20. exchange

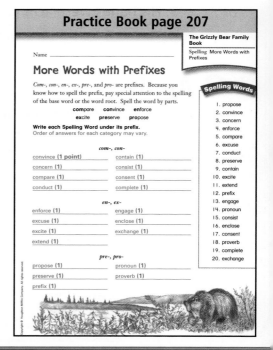

DAY 3 VOCABULARY

Word Extensions

List the Basic Words on the board.

• Beside *consist*, write the word *inconsistent*. Point out that *inconsistent* is a new word formed by adding a prefix and a suffix to *consist*.

• Challenge students to build more new words by adding prefixes, suffixes, and endings to the Basic Words. (Responses will vary.)

• Have students use each Basic Word from the board orally in a sentence. (Sentences will vary.)

Practice/Homework For spelling practice, assign **Practice Book** page 208.

Practice Book page 208

Name _____

The Grizzly Bear Family Book

Spelling More Words with Prefixes

Spelling Spree

Alphabet Puzzler Write the Spelling Word that fits alphabetically between the two words in each group.

1. prong, _____, proof
2. company, _____, compass
3. enchant, _____, encore
4. contact, _____, contest
5. prefer, _____, preheat
6. convert, _____, convoy
7. consider, _____, consonant
8. express, _____, extinct

1. pronoun (1 point)
2. compare (1)
3. enclose (1)
4. contain (1)
5. prefix (1)
6. convince (1)
7. consist (1)
8. extend (1)

The Third Word Write the Spelling Word that belongs in each group.

9. trade, swap, _____
10. suggest, recommend, _____
11. agree, grant, _____
12. saying, phrase, _____
13. save, protect, _____
14. thrill, energize, _____
15. whole, total, _____

I really (like, fancy, enjoy) books about bears!

9. exchange (1)
10. propose (1)
11. consent (1)
12. proverb (1)
13. preserve (1)
14. excite (1)
15. complete (1)

Spelling Words
1. propose
2. convince
3. concern
4. enforce
5. compare
6. excuse
7. conduct
8. preserve
9. contain
10. excite
11. extend
12. prefix
13. engage
14. pronoun
15. consist
16. enclose
17. consent
18. proverb
19. complete
20. exchange

DAY 4 PROOFREADING

Game: Prefix Bingo

Ask students to form groups of 4: 3 players and 1 announcer. Provide the announcer with a list of Basic and Review Words. Tell each player to make a game card divided into 16 boxes and to label a corner of each box randomly with one of these prefixes: *com-, con-, en-, ex-, pre-, pro-*. (Players should leave room in each box for writing a Basic or Review Word.)

• To play, the announcer reads a list word, and players write it in a box containing the appropriate prefix.

• The first player to write 4 correctly spelled words in a row across, down, or diagonally wins.

Practice/Homework For proofreading and writing practice, assign **Practice Book** page 209.

Practice Book page 209

Name _____

The Grizzly Bear Family Book

Spelling More Words with Prefixes

Proofreading and Writing

Proofreading Circle the five misspelled words in these park rules. Then write each word correctly.

PARK RULES

While in the park, please conduct yourself as follows:

1. If you see a bear, do not try to ingage it. Instead, leave it in peace. Trust us! You don't want a bear to concirn itself with you.

2. If you come across a bear, *never* turn and run. It will excite the bear, who will then run after you. There is no way to outrun a bear!

3. Do not feed any park animals. There is no excuse for breaking this rule. We will enforse it strictly.

1. conduct (1 point)
2. engage (1)
3. concern (1)
4. excuse (1)
5. enforce (1)

Write an Essay The author of this selection knew and respected grizzlies, but he was killed by one. Does this change your thinking about bears?

On a separate piece of paper, write a short essay stating your reaction to Michio Hoshino's fate. Use Spelling Words from the list. Responses will vary. (5)

Spelling Words
1. propose
2. convince
3. concern
4. enforce
5. compare
6. excuse
7. conduct
8. preserve
9. contain
10. excite
11. extend
12. prefix
13. engage
14. pronoun
15. consist
16. enclose
17. consent
18. proverb
19. complete
20. exchange

DAY 5 ASSESSMENT

Spelling Test

Say each underlined word, read the sentence, and then repeat the word. Have students write only the underlined word.

Basic Words

1. Roberto will **propose** a new law.
2. Can Maria **convince** you to vote for her?
3. Did Dad show **concern** about the problem?
4. The police **enforce** the laws.
5. Let's **compare** your notes with mine.
6. Please **excuse** me for being late.
7. Who will **conduct** the meeting?
8. Some laws try to **preserve** wildlife.
9. What does the box **contain**?
10. Do not **excite** the baby.
11. We need to **extend** the road by two miles.
12. The word *extend* has the **prefix** ex-.
13. Did the army **engage** in battle?
14. The word *you* is a **pronoun**.
15. What does the mixture **consist** of?
16. A fence will **enclose** the yard.
17. Did they **consent** to your plan?
18. A **proverb** is a short saying.
19. Is that set of dishes **complete**?
20. We should **exchange** addresses.

Challenge Words

21. They voted for the **enactment** of the law.
22. Follow the **procedure** given in the guide.
23. I will **confront** him about the problem.
24. Read the **preamble** slowly.
25. Her report was short and **concise**.

Target Skill Trace

Teach	p. 623G
Review	pp. M36–M37
Extend	Challenge/Extension Activities, p. R15
See	*Handbook for English Language Learners*, p. 213

Transparency 6–3

ANIMAL ENCOUNTERS The Grizzly Bear Family Book
Vocabulary Skill Using Context Clues
ANNOTATED VERSION

Using Context Clues

When salmon are rare, grizzlies will hungrily <u>devour</u> every one they catch. (page 610)

The <u>bugling</u> of sandhill cranes sweeping south in great ragged Vs announces autumn across Alaska. (page 611)

Blueberry, blackberry, and <u>crowberry</u> bushes blanket the ground, offering a rich harvest for bears. (page 611)

As the days shorten, bears must put on a large <u>store</u> of fat to take them through winter. (page 612)

People continue to tame and <u>subjugate</u> nature. (page 614)

Today's snowfall marks the <u>advent</u> of winter. (page 616)

TRANSPARENCY 6–3
TEACHER'S EDITION PAGE 623G
Copyright © Houghton Mifflin Company. All rights reserved.

Monitoring Student Progress

If . . .	Then . . .
students score 8 or below on **Practice Book** page 210,	have them work with partners to correct the items they missed.

TARGET SKILL VOCABULARY: Using Context

❶ Teach

Explain context. A word's context consists of the words and sentences surrounding it. Context clues can help readers figure out a word's meaning.

Display Transparency 6–3. Explain how context can help readers figure out the meaning of the underlined word in the first sentence.

- The word's position in the sentence, after the adverb *hungrily*, shows that it is probably a verb.
- The word *hungrily* shows that the action has to do with eating.
- The word *salmon* and the phrase *every one they catch* are other clues.
- Together, these clues suggest that *devour* means "eat."

Model how to use context clues. Use the following sentences from page 610 to model using context to figure out the meaning of *discarding*. *Sometimes bears just eat the head and eggs, <u>discarding</u> the rest. The uneaten portion of the fish doesn't go to waste, however, because gulls swarm nearby, ready to grab the leftovers.*

Think Aloud Discarding *is probably a verb because it ends with* -ing*. The words* just eat the head and eggs *and* The uneaten portion *provide another clue.* Gulls swarm nearby, ready to grab the leftovers *tells me that what the bears don't eat is floating in the water.* Discarding *must mean "throwing away."*

❷ Guided Practice

Give students practice using context clues.

- Have students use context clues to figure out the meaning of the remaining underlined words on **Transparency 6–3.**
- Ask students to identify the context clues they found in each sentence or passage.

❸ Apply

Assign Practice Book page 210.

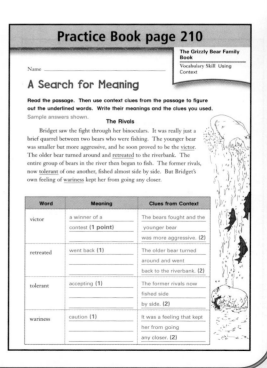

Practice Book page 210

The Grizzly Bear Family Book
Vocabulary Skill Using Context

Name _____

A Search for Meaning

Read the passage. Then use context clues from the passage to figure out the underlined words. Write their meanings and the clues you used.
Sample answers shown.

The Rivals

Bridget saw the fight through her binoculars. It was really just a brief quarrel between two bears who were fishing. The younger bear was smaller but more aggressive, and he soon proved to be the <u>victor</u>. The older bear turned around and <u>retreated</u> to the riverbank. The entire group of bears in the river then began to fish. The former rivals, now <u>tolerant</u> of one another, fished almost side by side. But Bridget's own feeling of <u>wariness</u> kept her from going any closer.

Word	Meaning	Clues from Context
victor	a winner of a contest (1 point)	The bears fought and the younger bear was more aggressive. (2)
retreated	went back (1)	The older bear turned around and went back to the riverbank. (2)
tolerant	accepting (1)	The former rivals now fished side by side. (2)
wariness	caution (1)	It was a feeling that kept her from going any closer. (2)

STUDY SKILL: Preparing a Report

OBJECTIVES

- Describe the types of information shown by various kinds of graphic aids.
- Create graphic aids using facts from texts.
- Include graphic aids in a written report.

❶ Teach

Introduce graphic aids.

- Graphic aids make information easy to understand at a glance.
- **Maps** can show the location of places such as national parks. They can also show the distribution of wildlife, population, resources, or other elements.
- **Tables** and **charts** show comparisons and relationships.
- **Graphs** show numeric information.
- **Time lines** visually show when events took place.
- **Diagrams, photographs,** and **illustrations** can show readers how places and features look.

Model how to use graphic aids in a report about grizzly bears.

Think Aloud *If I were writing a report about Alaskan grizzlies, I would try to include a number of graphic aids. I might include a map that shows the location and features of Denali National Park. I could use a graph to show how the Alaskan grizzly bear population has changed over time. A cutaway diagram could show what the inside of a grizzly bear's den is like. I could include a table that compares bear populations in Alaska, Montana, and Wyoming.*

❷ Practice/Apply

Give students practice in selecting graphic aids for reports.

- Ask pairs of students to list other ways in which graphic aids might have been used in *The Grizzly Bear Family Book*. For example:
  - **maps** (to show the grizzlies' habitat)
  - **tables** (to show how habits and food change with the seasons)
  - **graphs** (to give statistics on food consumed by cubs and adults)
  - **time lines** (to show the development of grizzlies from infancy to adulthood)
  - **Venn diagrams** (to compare grizzlies with other bears)
- Have students research another large North American animal, and use written information about that animal to create two graphic aids.

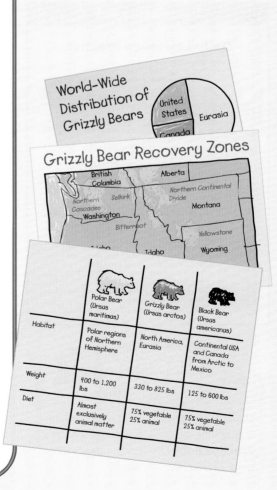

World-Wide Distribution of Grizzly Bears

Grizzly Bear Recovery Zones

	Polar Bear (Ursus maritimus)	Grizzly Bear (Ursus arctos)	Black Bear (Ursus americanus)
Habitat	Polar regions of Northern Hemisphere	North America, Eurasia	Continental USA and Canada from Arctic to Mexico
Weight	400 to 1,200 lbs	330 to 825 lbs	125 to 600 lbs
Diet	Almost exclusively animal matter	75% vegetable 25% animal	75% vegetable 25% animal

INFORMATION & STUDY SKILLS

The Grizzly Bear Family Book

GRAMMAR: Contractions; Negatives

OBJECTIVES

- Identify and write contractions with *not*.
- Identify double negatives and use negatives in sentences correctly.
- Proofread and correct sentences with grammar and spelling errors.
- Use adjectives and adverbs correctly to improve writing.
- Learn academic language: *negatives*.

DAY 1 INSTRUCTION

Contractions with *not*

Teach Remind students that they have already learned about contractions formed by combining pronouns and verbs. Go over the following rules:

- You can combine some verbs with the word *not* to make contractions.
- An apostrophe (') takes the place of the letter or letters dropped to shorten the word.

- Display the example sentences at the top of **Transparency 6–5.** Point out that *hasn't* is a contraction formed by combining the verb *has* with the word *not*. Go through the chart of contractions with students.

- Ask volunteers to underline the words with *not* that can be written as contractions in Sentences 1–6. Have them write the contraction for each set of words they underlined.

Daily Language Practice

Have students correct Sentences 1 and 2 on **Transparency 6–4.**

DAY 2 PRACTICE

Independent Work

Practice/Homework Assign **Practice Book** page 211.

Daily Language Practice

Have students correct Sentences 2 and 3 on **Transparency 6–4.**

Transparency 6–4

Daily Language Practice

Correct two sentences each day.
Answers may vary.

1. "The city will perpose to open a skating rink" said Mrs. Evans.
   "The city will propose to open a skating rink," said Mrs. Evans.

2. Jared and Mara they have pledged to clean up the park this weekend.
   Jared and Mara have pledged to clean up the park this weekend.

3. "My consirn is for your safety." explained the lifeguard.
   "My concern is for your safety," explained the lifeguard.

4. "Hasn't Alex used that same escuse before," asked Tina.
   "Hasn't Alex used that same excuse before?" asked Tina.

5. Anita she will inclose a check with her soccer team application.
   Anita will enclose a check with her soccer team application.

6. The newspaper article didn't never conpare the two candidates.
   The newspaper article didn't compare the two candidates.

7. You should measure twice and cut once" said Mr. Daniel.
   "You should measure twice and cut once," said Mr. Daniel.

8. Bett explained, "we don't ixchange presents on Valentine's Day."
   Bett explained, "We don't exchange presents on Valentine's Day."

9. Since the accident, Pablo hasn't never been able to extend the little finger on his right hand.
   Since the accident, Pablo hasn't ever been able to extend the little finger on his right hand.

10. "If you want to go on the field trip," explained Mrs. Tam, you will need an adult's concent."
    "If you want to go on the field trip," explained Mrs. Tam, "you will need an adult's consent."

TRANSPARENCY 6–4 TEACHER'S EDITION PAGE 623I

ANIMAL ENCOUNTERS The Grizzly Bear Family Book
Grammar Skill Contractions, Negatives
Spelling Skill More Words with Prefixes
ANNOTATED VERSION

Monitoring Student Progress

If . . .	Then . . .
students score 7 or below on **Practice Book** page 211 or 212,	use the Reteaching lessons on Teacher's Edition pages R20 and R21.

Transparency 6–5

Contractions with *not*

Noli has not hiked in the wilderness before.
Noli hasn't hiked in the wilderness before.

1. She is not sure how to purify river water for drinking.
   isn't

2. The instructions do not explain the process clearly.
   don't

3. Hikers should not drink river water without purifying it.
   shouldn't

4. We are not taking any chances.   aren't

5. Noli will not have a problem once we show her how to use her filter properly.   won't

6. Boris did not bring a filter, so we will share our water with him.   didn't

Contractions formed with *not*

is not	isn't
are not	aren't
was not	wasn't
will not	won't
has not	hasn't
cannot	can't
did not	didn't
have not	haven't
could not	couldn't
must not	mustn't

TRANSPARENCY 6-5 TEACHER'S EDITION PAGE 623I

ANIMAL ENCOUNTERS The Grizzly Bear Family Book
Grammar Skill Contractions with not

Practice Book page 211

The Grizzly Bear Family Book
Grammar Skill Contractions with *not*

Name _____

Contraction Action

Contractions with *not* You can combine some verbs with the word *not* to make a **contraction**. An apostrophe takes the place of the letter or letters dropped to shorten the word.

In sentences 1–5, underline the word combination with *not* that can be written as a contraction. Then write the contraction on the line. For sentences 6–10, underline the contraction. On the line, write the words that make up the contraction.

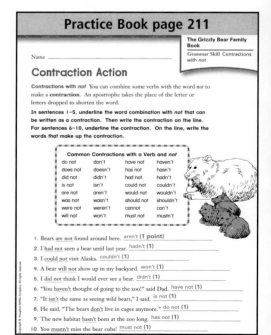

Common Contractions with a Verb and *not*			
do not	don't	have not	haven't
does not	doesn't	has not	hasn't
did not	didn't	had not	hadn't
is not	isn't	could not	couldn't
are not	aren't	would not	wouldn't
was not	wasn't	should not	shouldn't
were not	weren't	cannot	can't
will not	won't	must not	mustn't

1. Bears are not found around here.   aren't (1 point)
2. I had not seen a bear until last year.   hadn't (1)
3. I could not visit Alaska.   couldn't (1)
4. A bear will not show up in my backyard.   won't (1)
5. I did not think I would ever see a bear.   didn't (1)
6. "You haven't thought of going to the zoo!" said Dad.   have not (1)
7. "It isn't the same as seeing wild bears," I said.   is not (1)
8. He said, "The bears don't live in cages anymore."   do not (1)
9. The new habitat hasn't been at the zoo long.   has not (1)
10. You mustn't miss the bear cubs!   must not (1)

Copyright © Houghton Mifflin Company. All rights reserved.

Negatives

Teach Go over the following:

- A negative is a word that means "no" or "not."
- Do not use double negatives in sentences.

Display **Transparency 6–6,** and read aloud the example sentence at the top.

Point out the two negatives *won't* and *no*. Remind students that the contraction *won't* is made up of the words *will* and *not*.

Ask students how the sentence can be corrected. (Use one negative, not both.)

Have volunteers underline the word or words in parentheses that correctly complete each numbered sentence.

Daily Language Practice
Have students correct Sentences 5 and 6 on **Transparency 6–4**.

Independent Work

Practice/Homework Assign **Practice Book** page 212.

Daily Language Practice
Have students correct Sentences 7 and 8 on **Transparency 6–4**.

Adjective or Adverb?

Teach Tell students that a good writer is careful to use an adverb, not an adjective, to tell *how much* or *to what extent* about an adjective.

- Model correcting a sentence in which an adjective was used where an adverb should have been used:
  - You are a real good friend.
  - *Corrected:* You are a <u>really</u> good friend.

- Have students proofread a piece of their own writing for correct use of adjectives and adverbs.

Practice/Homework Assign **Practice Book** page 213.

Daily Language Practice
Have students correct Sentences 9 and 10 on **Transparency 6–4**.

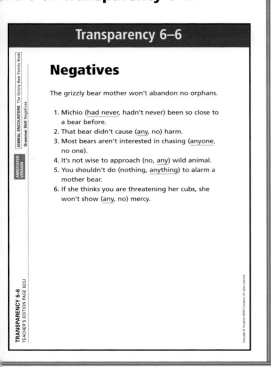

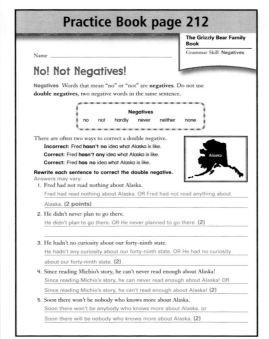

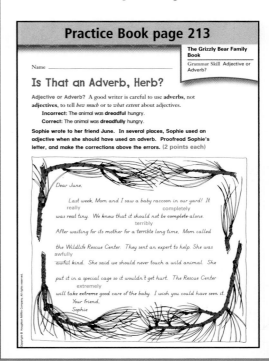

GRAMMAR

The Grizzly Bear Family Book

WRITING: Opinion Paragraph

OBJECTIVES

- Identify the characteristics of a good opinion paragraph.
- Analyze and evaluate an opinion paragraph.
- Write an opinion paragraph.
- Avoid and correct double negatives.

Writing Traits

Voice As students are writing their drafts on Day 2, remind them that a good opinion paragraph clearly shows the voice of the person who wrote it.

- The writer's personality in writing shows the thoughts and feelings of a real person.
- A strong, personal voice helps communicate an opinion in a convincing way.

DAY 1 PREWRITING

Introducing the Format

Define an opinion.

- An opinion is a belief that may or may not have facts to support it.
- Opinions are highly personal and vary from person to person.
- Opinions are often written for the purpose of persuading others.

Start students thinking about opinion paragraphs.

- Remind students of how the author of *The Grizzly Bear Family Book* expressed and supported his opinions about grizzlies and their importance.
- Ask partners to discuss whether or not grizzlies should be kept in zoos, and list at least two reasons to support their opinion.
- Have students save their notes.

DAY 2 DRAFTING

Discussing the Model

Display Transparency 6–7. Ask:

- What opinion is the writer expressing? (More land should be set aside for wildlife.)
- In which sentence does the writer express this opinion? (the first one)
- What does the writer include in the body of the paragraph? (reasons why the writer believes this is the right thing to do)
- How does the writer end the paragraph? (by restating the opinion)

Display Transparency 6–8, and discuss the guidelines.

Have students draft an opinion paragraph.

- Have students write an opinion paragraph about whether or not they believe grizzlies should be kept in zoos. Have them use their notes from Day 1.
- Assign **Practice Book** page 214 to help students focus on the topic and organize their writing.
- Provide support as needed.
- See Writing Traits on this page.

Transparency 6–7

Writing a Paragraph of Opinion

In order to protect and preserve wildlife, more land should be set aside in all parts of the world. First of all, many species have become endangered or threatened because of the loss of habitat or overhunting. Protecting wilderness lands from development would help to stop the loss of habitat for wildlife. Also, in those areas where wildlife habitat has already been lost to farms and towns, some of the land could be restored as wildlife habitat. Finally, the hunting of wildlife should be carefully controlled, since it not only deprives animals of the possibility of living out their lives but can also deplete animal populations. After all, in most places, the animals were there long before the humans were. For these reasons, it is my strong opinion that more wilderness preserves are needed.

Transparency 6–8

Guidelines for Writing a Paragraph of Opinion

- Begin your paragraph with a strong statement of your opinion.
- In the body of the paragraph, give several reasons for your opinion.
- Include both facts and examples to support your opinion.
- End your paragraph with a concluding sentence that restates your opinion.

Practice Book page 214

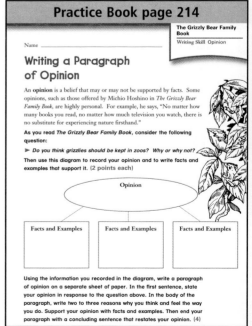

The Grizzly Bear Family Book

Writing Skill Opinion

Name _____

Writing a Paragraph of Opinion

An **opinion** is a belief that may or may not be supported by facts. Some opinions, such as those offered by Michio Hoshino in *The Grizzly Bear Family Book*, are highly personal. For example, he says, "No matter how many books you read, no matter how much television you watch, there is no substitute for experiencing nature firsthand."

As you read *The Grizzly Bear Family Book*, consider the following question:

▶ *Do you think grizzlies should be kept in zoos? Why or why not?*

Then use this diagram to record your opinion and to write facts and examples that support it. (2 points each)

Opinion

| Facts and Examples | Facts and Examples | Facts and Examples |

Using the information you recorded in the diagram, write a paragraph of opinion on a separate sheet of paper. In the first sentence, state your opinion in response to the question above. In the body of the paragraph, write two to three reasons why you think and feel the way you do. Support your opinion with facts and examples. Then end your paragraph with a concluding sentence that restates your opinion. (4)

DAY 3 REVISING

Evaluating to Revise

Display Transparency 6–8 again.

- Ask students to use the guidelines to decide how to make their writing better. Encourage students to turn each point into a question: Did I…?

- Students may work with a partner in a writing conference.

- Ask students to revise any parts of their writing that still need work.

DAY 4 PROOFREADING

Improving Writing: Avoiding Double Negatives

Review double negatives.

- The words *no, not, none,* and *nothing* are called negatives.

- Two negatives should not be used within a single phrase.

Display Transparency 6–9.

- Ask a volunteer to read Example A aloud and underline the double negatives. (*not, no*)

- Demonstrate that the double negative can be corrected by changing either one of the negatives to a positive.

- Have volunteers read Examples B and C aloud, underline the double negatives, and suggest sentences to correct them.

Assign Practice Book page 215.

- Students can use the proofreading checklist on **Practice Book** page 287 and the chart of proofreading marks on **Practice Book** page 288 to help them proofread their opinion paragraphs.

- Have students review their opinion paragraphs, correcting double negatives and proofreading for other errors.

DAY 5 PUBLISHING

Sharing Opinion Paragraphs

Consider these publishing options.

- Ask students to read their opinion paragraphs or some other piece of writing from the Author's Chair.

- Invite students to mail their opinion paragraphs to a zoo along with a cover letter asking for the zookeeper's opinion.

Portfolio Opportunity

Save students' opinion paragraphs as samples of their writing development.

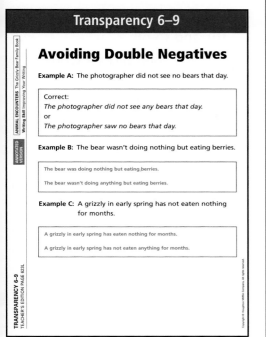

Transparency 6–9

Avoiding Double Negatives

Example A: The photographer did not see no bears that day.

> Correct:
> *The photographer did not see any bears that day.*
> or
> *The photographer saw no bears that day.*

Example B: The bear wasn't doing nothing but eating berries.

> The bear was doing nothing but eating berries.
>
> The bear wasn't doing anything but eating berries.

Example C: A grizzly in early spring has not eaten nothing for months.

> A grizzly in early spring has eaten nothing for months.
>
> A grizzly in early spring has not eaten anything for months.

TRANSPARENCY 6–9
TEACHER'S EDITION PAGE 623L

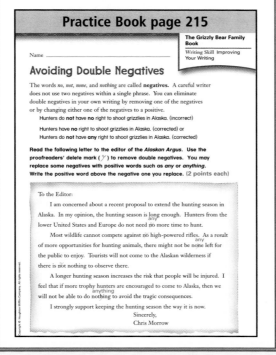

Practice Book page 215

The Grizzly Bear Family Book
Writing Skill Improving Your Writing

Name _____

Avoiding Double Negatives

The words *no, not, none,* and *nothing* are called **negatives.** A careful writer does not use two negatives within a single phrase. You can eliminate double negatives in your own writing by removing one of the negatives or by changing either one of the negatives to a positive.

> Hunters do **not** have **no** right to shoot grizzlies in Alaska. (incorrect)
>
> Hunters have **no** right to shoot grizzlies in Alaska. (corrected) or
> Hunters do **not** have **any** right to shoot grizzlies in Alaska. (corrected)

Read the following letter to the editor of the *Alaskan Argus*. Use the proofreaders' delete mark ( ) to remove double negatives. You may replace some negatives with positive words such as *any* or *anything*. Write the positive word above the negative one you replace. (2 points each)

To the Editor:

I am concerned about a recent proposal to extend the hunting season in Alaska. In my opinion, the hunting season is long enough. Hunters from the lower United States and Europe do not need no more time to hunt.

Most wildlife cannot compete against no high-powered rifles. As a result of more opportunities for hunting animals, there might not be none left for the public to enjoy. Tourists will not come to the Alaskan wilderness if there is not nothing to observe there.

A longer hunting season increases the risk that people will be injured. I feel that if more trophy hunters are encouraged to come to Alaska, then we will not be able to do nothing to avoid the tragic consequences.

I strongly support keeping the hunting season the way it is now.

Sincerely,
Chris Morrow

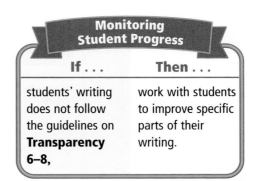

Monitoring Student Progress

If . . .	Then . . .
students' writing does not follow the guidelines on **Transparency 6–8,**	work with students to improve specific parts of their writing.

Language Center

VOCABULARY

Building Vocabulary

👤 Singles	🕐 20 minutes
Objective	Write a chart of seasonal words.
Materials	Dictionary, science textbook

In *The Grizzly Bear Family Book,* the author studies grizzlies during the long summer days. The longest day of summer is called the *summer solstice.* Write a chart with information about this and other words related to the seasons.

- Use a dictionary or science textbook to find words related to the seasons, such as *winter solstice, vernal equinox,* and *autumnal equinox.*

- Create a chart that includes information about the definition and origins of each word.

Words Related to Seasonal Change			
Word	Definition	When It Occurs	Word Origins
summer solstice	Time of year when sun seems to stand still at its high point at the tropic of Cancer	June 21	from Latin *solstitium: sol,* sun + *sistere,* to stand

STRUCTURAL ANALYSIS/SPELLING

Word Cut-Ups

👥 Pairs	🕐 30 minutes
Objective	Match prefixes and base words.
Materials	Activity Master 6–1, six index cards, scissors

A prefix comes at the beginning of a word to change its meaning. Recognizing a prefix can help you to figure out the meaning of a word or to break an unfamiliar word into syllables. Work with a partner to match prefixes and word roots.

- On separate index cards, write the following prefixes:

  com-, con- = with

  en- = in, into, within

  ex- = out of, away from

  pre-, pro- = before, earlier

- Cut out the words and word roots on Activity Master 6–1.

- Sort the word roots by matching them with the appropriate prefix. (HINT: Two of the roots can take two different prefixes. Can you find these?)

- Write each complete word on the back of the index card with its prefix.

VOCABULARY

Vocabulary Game

👥👥 Groups	🕐 40 minutes
Objective	Play an Arctic Word Game.
Materials	Activity Master 6–2, scissors, basket

Play the following Arctic Word Game.

- Cut out each strip on Activity Master 6–2.

- Fold each strip, place it in a basket, and mix the strips.

- Player 1 draws a word strip. Then Player 1 must give a clue about the word or its meaning.

- Player 2 must guess the word. If Player 2 can't guess the word, then Player 3 gets to try, and so on.

- Player 2 then picks a word and repeats the process.

- Continue playing until all word strips have been used.

> **This word describes when there is a huge amount of something.**

> **Abundant!**

Consider copying and laminating these activities for use in centers.

VIEWING

Planning a Multimedia Presentaion

👥 Pairs	🕐 40 minutes	
Objective	Plan a multimedia presentation.	
Materials	Reference sources	

Michio Hoshino used both text and images to describe his encounters with grizzlies. With a partner, plan a multimedia presentation about another wild animal.

- Use a reference source such as an encyclopedia or the Internet to learn about another animal.

- Take notes on key information about the animal, such as its appearance, habitat, and behavior.

- Decide which media format would be most effective for sharing different types of information. For example, how could you use photographs, video, or sound effects?

- Write out a plan for your multimedia presentation. Include reasons why you chose to use each type of media.

GRAMMAR

Adverbs in Action

👤 Singles	🕐 25 minutes	
Objective	Check your writing for adverbs.	
Materials	Student writing samples	

Adverbs are words that modify verbs, adjectives, or other adverbs. They give information about time, place, manner, or degree. Using adverbs can help you make your writing more vivid.

- Review a piece of your own writing to see where you have used adverbs.

- Identify sentences that you might want to make more exciting or descriptive. Brainstorm adverbs that you might use.

- Rewrite the sentences to include appropriate adverbs. Then compare your new sentences with the original sentences. What new information or effect do the adverbs help you express?

Adverbs

completely	frantically
extremely	loudly
quickly	happily
daily	carefully

The Grizzly Bear Family Book

The Hyrax of Top-Knot Island

Summary *Robin Bernard tells about her summer on the African plains observing small animals called hyraxes. These animals live on boulder "islands" called* kopjes, *one of which is referred to as "Top-Knot." She discusses the habits of these hard-to-classify mammals and the other creatures in their habitat. By remaining close to these animals for a summer, Bernard was able to study them closely and provides an interesting portrait of these unfamiliar creatures.*

Vocabulary

Introduce the Key Vocabulary and ask students to complete the BLM.

topknot a knot of hair on top of the head, *p. 3*

boulders large rounded rocks, *p. 3*

greenery leaves of green plants, *p. 10*

fanned out spread out in a fan shape, *p. 17*

dens cavelike homes of wild animals, *p. 18*

● BELOW LEVEL

Building Background and Vocabulary

Have students share what they know about how small animals survive in the wild. Preview the story with students, using the story vocabulary when possible.

◉ Comprehension Skill: Making Generalizations

Have students read the Strategy Focus on the book flap. Remind students to use the strategy and to make generalizations as they read the book. (See the Leveled Readers Teacher's Guide for **Vocabulary and Comprehension Practice Masters.**)

Responding

Have partners discuss how to answer the questions on the inside back cover.

Think About the Selection Sample answers:

1. It is an island of boulders surrounded by land, not water.
2. She spent a whole summer living close to them and studying them.
3. The hyraxes find protection in the spaces between the boulders.
4. The leopard knew that the impalas were big enough for a feast, rather than just the snack he could have made out of the hyraxes.

Making Connections Responses will vary.

◉ Building Fluency

Model Read aloud page 11, emphasizing the exclamation. Explain that sentences that end in exclamation points should be read with great feeling.

Practice Have partners look for other sentences in the story that end in exclamation points. Have them take turns reading aloud the sentences they find until they are able to read them accurately and with appropriate expression. Direct students to pages 12 and 18 if they have difficulty finding other exclamations.

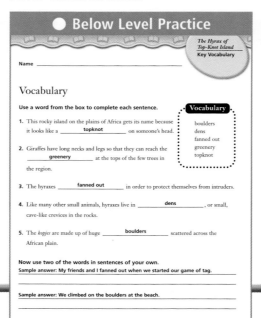

The Bald Eagle Is Back

Summary The Bald Eagle Is Back *describes the bald eagle's near destruction and then comeback in the United States. Thanks to a ban on DDT, and the enactment of the Endangered Species Act of 1973, the bald eagle began a slow recovery.*

Vocabulary

Introduce the Key Vocabulary and ask students to complete the BLM.

talons claws, *p. 3*

carrion decaying or dead flesh, *p. 5*

wilderness* any unsettled region in its natural state, *p. 5*

raptors birds of prey, *p. 5*

abundant* more than enough, plentiful, *p. 9*

extinct no longer existing, *p. 10*

vanish disappear, *p. 11*

pesticide a chemical used to destroy pests, *p. 12*

incubation to warm and hatch by body heat, *p. 13*

*Forms of these words are Anthology Key Vocabulary words.

▲ ON LEVEL

Building Background and Vocabulary

Have students share what they know about endangered species. Preview the story with students, using the story vocabulary when possible.

Comprehension Skill: Making Generalizations

Have students read the Strategy Focus on the book flap. Remind students to use the strategy and to make generalizations as they read the book. (See the Leveled Readers Teacher's Guide for **Vocabulary and Comprehension Practice Masters**.)

Responding

Have partners discuss how to answer the questions on the inside back cover.

Think About the Selection Sample answers:

1. An endangered species is a kind of plant or animal that is in danger of becoming extinct, or dying out. Bald eagles became endangered because of DDT interfering with their reproduction, habitat loss, and being hunted.

2. If birds were killed off by dangerous chemicals, spring would be without birdsong.

3. Responses will vary.

4. Responses will vary.

Making Connections Responses will vary.

Building Fluency

Model Read aloud page 4. Point out that the word *represented* is hyphenated. Sometimes words are broken up between syllables and hyphenated at the end of a line because the whole word won't fit, but it should still be read as one word.

Practice Students can find other examples of words that are divided in the same way as the model. Then have them practice reading each divided word as one word, without pausing between syllables.

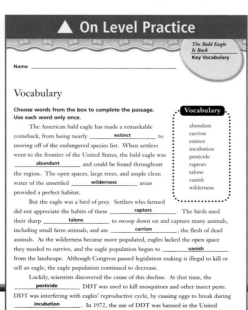

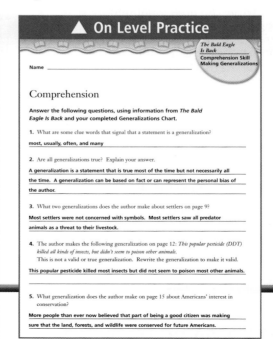

LEVELED READERS

The Return of Wild Whoopers

Summary *The nonfiction selection* The Return of Wild Whoopers *focuses on the movement to save the nearly extinct whooping crane.*

Vocabulary

Introduce the Key Vocabulary and ask students to complete the BLM.

endangered threatened with extinction, *p. 4*

wetland area containing high soil moisture, such as a marsh or swamp, *p. 6*

territory* an area inhabited by an animal or animal group, *p. 7*

conservationists people who protect natural resources, *p. 8*

biologists people who study living things, *p. 11*

viable capable of living or growing, *p. 13*

aquatic growing in, living in, or frequenting water, *p. 16*

imprinted marked or influenced by, *p. 17*

*Forms of these words are Anthology Key Vocabulary words.

■ ABOVE LEVEL

Building Background and Vocabulary

Have students share what they know about the growth and habits of birds and endangered species. Preview the story with students, using the story vocabulary when possible.

Comprehension Skill: Making Generalizations

Have students read the Strategy Focus on the book flap. Remind students to use the strategy and to make generalizations as they read the book. (See the Leveled Readers Teacher's Guide for **Vocabulary and Comprehension Practice Masters**.)

Responding

Have partners discuss how to answer the questions on the inside back cover.

Think About the Selection Sample answers:

1. loss of their wetland and prairie habitat and being hunted
2. The young whooping cranes raised by sandhill cranes imprinted on their foster parents. They saw themselves as sandhill cranes, and when they matured, they didn't choose other whoopers for breeding partners.
3. Responses will vary.
4. Responses will vary.

Making Connections Responses will vary.

Building Fluency

Model Read aloud pages 3 and 4. Point out the heading and explain that headings tell about the paragraphs that follow them.

Practice Have students find and read aloud each heading in the story. Then they can read the paragraphs that follow the heading and explain why the heading is appropriate.

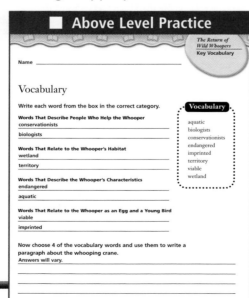

**The Hyrax:
An Interesting Puzzle**

Summary *The author takes readers on a visit to Top-Knot Island and describes the life and habitat of a very unusual creature — the hyrax.*

Vocabulary

Introduce the Key Vocabulary and ask students to complete the BLM.

boulders large rounded rocks, *p. 3*

mammals warm-blooded animals that give birth to live young rather than hatching them from eggs, *p. 6*

whistles makes a clear, high-pitched sound by pushing air through the teeth or lips, *p. 8*

habits ways of acting learned through repetition, *p. 14*

territory* an area inhabited by an animal or animal group and defended against intruders, *p. 15*

sniff to smell something, *p. 16*

*Forms of these words are Anthology Key Vocabulary words.

◆ LANGUAGE SUPPORT

Building Background and Vocabulary

Have students who have been to a zoo tell about the animals they have seen. Discuss where those animals live in the wild. Distribute the **Build Background Practice Master**. Have partners complete the page.

Comprehension Skill: Making Generalizations

Have students read the Strategy Focus on the book flap. Remind students to use the strategy and to make generalizations as they read the book. (See the Leveled Readers Teacher's Guide for **Build Background, Vocabulary, and Graphic Organizer Masters.**)

Responding

Have partners discuss the questions on the inside back cover.

Think About the Selection Sample answers:

1. It does not have water around it.

2. It has food, water, and places to hide from dangerous animals. It also has shady places where it can keep cool.

3. A guard hyrax whistles when a predator is near; a hyrax hides near rocks; its color and size make it hard to see.

4. Responses will vary.

Making Connections Responses will vary.

Building Fluency

Model Read aloud pages 12–13 as students follow along in their books. Explain that the word *I* shows that the author is telling about his or her own experience.

Practice Have students read the pages aloud three times until they can read with accuracy and expression.

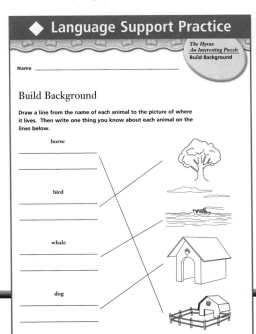

◆ Language Support Practice

*The Hyrax
An Interesting Puzzle*
Build Background

Name _____

Build Background

Draw a line from the name of each animal to the picture of where it lives. Then write one thing you know about each animal on the lines below.

horse
_____

bird
_____

whale
_____

dog
_____

◆ Language Support Practice

*The Hyrax
An Interesting Puzzle*
Key Vocabulary

Name _____

Vocabulary

Choose the word from the box that best completes each sentence.

Vocabulary
boulders
habits
mammals
sniff
territory
whistles

1. There are two big ___**boulders**___ on top of the mountain.

2. My cat has some ___**habits**___ that I like and other ones that I don't like.

3. My sister ___**whistles**___ to our dog to tell it to come in the house.

4. The mouse went to ___**sniff**___ the cheese, then ate it.

5. Some animals defend their ___**territory**___, other animals run away.

6. Elephants and hyraxes are both ___**mammals**___.

Reading-Writing Workshop

Persuasive Essay

In the Reading-Writing Workshop for Theme 6, *Animal Encounters,* students read Michiala's persuasive essay, "Why People Should Get a Dog," on Anthology pages 624–625. Then they follow the five steps of the writing process to write a persuasive essay.

Meet the Author

Michiala L.
Grade: five
State: Massachusetts
Hobbies: playing softball, making friendship bracelets, listening to music, and riding her bike
What she wants to be when she grows up: a veterinarian

Theme Skill Trace

Writing
- Avoiding Double Negatives, 623L
- Combining Sentences with Prepositional Phrases, 647L
- Placing Prepositional Phrases Correctly, 671L

Grammar
- Adjective or Adverb? 623J
- Expanding Sentences with Prepositional Phrases, 647J
- Using the Correct Pronoun in a Compound Structure, 671J

Spelling
- More Words with Prefixes, 623E
- Three-Syllable Words, 647E
- Words with *-ent, -ant, -able, -ible*, 671E

Pacing the Workshop

Here is a suggestion for how you might pace the workshop within one week or on five separate days across the theme.

DAY 1 — PREWRITING

Students
- read the student model, 624–625
- choose a topic for their persuasive essay, 625A
- organize and plan their essay, 625B
- answer possible objections, 625C

Spelling Frequently Misspelled Words, 625F; *Practice Book,* 279

DAY 2 — DRAFTING

Students
- brainstorm facts and details to support their reasons, 625D
- draft their persuasive essay, 625D

Spelling *Practice Book,* 218

Focus on Writing Traits: Persuasive Essay

The workshop for this theme focuses on the traits of ideas and organization. However, students should think about all of the writing traits during the writing process.

IDEAS It is often easier for students to think of convincing reasons if they can talk about them during prewriting.

- Ask students to tell their goal and each reason that supports the goal. Praise convincing reasons. Ask questions about weak or unrelated reasons.

- Have students discuss their goal and reasons with a partner. Partners can identify convincing reasons and ask questions about unconvincing ones.

ORGANIZATION Your students will write better paragraphs if you help them group each reason with the details that support it.

- Have students circle each reason with a different color.

- Have them underline the details that support this reason, using a corresponding color.

- Encourage them to check their work by rereading each detail and asking, Does this detail really tell more about this reason?

Tips for Teaching the Writing Traits

- Teach one trait at a time.

- Discuss examples of the traits in the literature students are reading.

- Encourage students to talk about the traits during a writing conference.

- Encourage students to revise their writing for one trait at a time.

DAY 3 REVISING

Students

- evaluate their persuasive essay, 625E

- revise their persuasive essay, 625E

- have a writing conference, 625E

Spelling *Practice Book,* 219

DAY 4 PROOFREADING

Students

- proofread their persuasive essay, 625E

- improve their writing by correcting run-on sentences, 625E

- correct frequently misspelled words in their essay, 625F

Spelling *Practice Book,* 220

DAY 5 PUBLISHING

Students

 publish their persuasive essay, 625G

- reflect on their writing experience, 625G

Spelling Assessment, 625F

Persuasive Essay

Discussing the Guidelines

Display **Transparency RWW6–1,** and discuss what makes a great persuasive essay.

- Remember that students should think about all the writing traits as they write: ideas, organization, voice, word choice, sentence fluency, conventions, and presentation.

Discussing the Model

Have students read the Student Writing Model on Anthology pages 624–625.

- Discuss with students what the writer did to make her persuasive essay interesting to read.

- Use the Reading As a Writer questions on the next page.

A Persuasive Essay

The purpose of a persuasive essay is to convince the reader to think or act in a particular way. Use this student's writing as a model when you write a persuasive essay of your own.

Why People Should Get a Dog

> A good persuasive essay usually states the **goal** in the **introduction.**

> The persuasive goal should be supported by **strong reasons.**

I think people should get dogs because they are good companions. I also think pets, especially dogs, help you and improve your life. Some people say their dogs changed their lives because when you take care of a dog you need to learn to be unselfish. People also say dogs help them communicate better. When you have a dog, you have to try to find out what it wants, and that can help you find out how to talk to other people.

An important thing about getting a dog is to find one that suits you. When I had my dog Simba, he was my best friend. He was my favorite mammal to be with besides my mom. He always made my family and me laugh. Sometimes he got all mixed up and ran into the wall. When we played music, he tried to sing. I loved him very much. I could tell him anything in the world as if he was my best friend.

624

Transparency RWW6–1

TRANSPARENCY RWW 6–1
TEACHER'S EDITION PAGE 624

ANNOTATED VERSION   ANIMAL ENCOUNTERS   Reading-Writing Workshop   Persuasive Essay

What Makes a Great Persuasive Essay?

In a **persuasive essay,** the writer tries to persuade his or her readers to think or act in a particular way.

Follow these guidelines when you write your persuasive essay.

- Start by telling your goal, what you want your audience to think or do.
- Support your goal with reasons that will convince your audience.
- Support your reasons with facts and details.
- Answer objections that your audience might have.
- Order your reasons from most to least important or from least to most important.
- Use positive, confident language that shows you care about your goal.
- End by summing up your reasons and restating your goal.

Dogs help you because your personality is one of the many important parts of your life, and dogs help improve it. My dog helped me improve my personality by making me be more open because it wasn't always about me. He also improved my knowledge because I did not know dogs needed so many things to be satisfied. I had to learn how to react to him and find out when to feed him and what he liked to eat.

> It's important to state **facts** and give **examples**.

Some people say that dogs need too much care. You have to feed them and take them for walks. My dog Simba was worth any work I had to do because he was my friend.

> A good persuasive essay **answers objections**.

I think everyone should have a dog because they may improve your life. Simba and every other pet I had taught me a valuable lesson I will need to know later in life. By getting a dog, you too can learn a valuable lesson or two.

> The **conclusion** should bring the essay to a satisfactory close.

Meet the Author

Michiala L.

Grade: five
State: Massachusetts
Hobbies: playing softball, making friendship bracelets, listening to music, and riding her bike
What she wants to be when she grows up: a veterinarian

625

Reading As a Writer

1. What does Michiala want her audience to do? (get a dog)

2. What reasons does the writer give to support her goal? (Sample answer: Dogs are good companions; dogs improve your personality; dogs help you communicate better.)

3. In the third paragraph, Michiala says dogs help improve your personality. What examples does she give to support this reason? (Michiala's dog made her more open and more responsive to the needs of others.)

4. What objection does the writer address in the fourth paragraph? How does she respond to this objection? (Objection: Dogs are too much trouble. Response: Dogs are worth the trouble because of what they give back.)

5. Does the writer build a convincing case? How successfully did she persuade you that her point of view is correct? (Answers will vary.)

Choosing a Topic

1 **Tell students they are going to write their own persuasive essay.** Tell them that they will start by choosing a goal, what they want their audience to think or do. Tell students to brainstorm at least three ideas for their own persuasive essay. Offer the following sentence starters if students are having trouble thinking of topics.

- My principal should change _____.
- My city or town should fix the _____.
- My parents should allow me to _____.
- Kids my age should stop _____.

2 **Have students answer these questions** as they choose a topic, either in a writing journal or on a sheet of paper.

- Who will be your audience: your classmates? your parents? a leader in your city or town?
- What is your purpose: to persuade someone to change a rule? to take up a hobby? to allow you to do something?
- How will you publish your research report: make it into a flier or poster? deliver it as a speech? send it to a newspaper?

3 **Have students discuss their list of goals with a partner** and decide which goal they want to write about. Encourage them to choose a goal that they feel strongly about. Then review these tips with students.

Tips for Getting Started with a Topic

- Think about whether your goal will make sense to your audience. Is it reasonable? Can they do what you are asking?

- Begin to brainstorm reasons to support your goal. Think about which reasons your audience would find most convincing.

- Tell your goal to a partner. Have your partner think of objections to your goal. Try to answer each objection with convincing reasons.

Organizing and Planning

① Discuss reasons in a persuasive essay. Explain that a goal or opinion should be supported by at least three important reasons. Help students understand the characteristics of an important reason.

- It is easy to support with facts and examples.
- It is accurate. It does not exaggerate the truth.
- It will convince the writer's audience.

② Display Transparency RWW6–2. Explain that a Target Diagram can be used to compare and rank reasons in order of importance. Go over the categories. Then use the sample answers below to model comparing and ranking reasons.

- **Bull's-eye:** Reason is easy to support, accurate, and convincing.
- **Not bad:** Reason is less convincing but still worth including.
- **On the edge:** Reason is hard to support, inaccurate, or unconvincing.

③ Distribute copies of Transparency RWW6–2 to the class. Tell students to use the Target Diagram to brainstorm reasons to support their goal. Encourage them to replace the "on the edge" reasons.

Writing Traits

ORGANIZATION Have students put a star beside their three most persuasive reasons. Then have them number the reasons from most to least important or from least to most important.

Transparency RWW6–2

Target Diagram

Opinion

Bull's-eye
Not bad
On the edge

Bull's-eye

Not bad

On the edge

Stating Reasons and Answering Objections

Writing Traits

IDEAS Remind students that their reasons should explain why their audience should think or act a certain way. Ask, What will your audience say if they disagree with you? Explain that students should think about possible objections.

1 **Explain answering objections.** Tell students that they should introduce and answer possible objections. Discuss the examples below.

> **Goal or Opinion** Fifth-graders need lockers.
>
> **Possible Objection** Why can't students just carry backpacks?
>
> **Objection Answered** Students could use backpacks. However, when you weigh ninety pounds, it's tough to carry gym clothes, four textbooks, lunch, and a thermos on your back.

2 **Display Transparency RWW6–3,** and discuss reasons and objections.

- Explain that each numbered statement tells what readers should think or do.

- Explain that each pair of lettered statements (a and b, c and d, and so on) either shows a reason that supports an opinion or raises an objection to it.

- Discuss the first pair of statements under 1 (a and b). Ask, Which is a reason that supports the opinion? (a) Which is an objection? (b)

- Have volunteers suggest possible answers to the objection. (Sample answer: If you make a shopping list, you won't end up buying things you don't need.)

- Have students complete the rest of the transparency.

3 **Have students analyze their own goal and reasons.** Tell them to work with a partner to think of possible objections for their own topics.

- Ask them to think of new reasons or facts to answer objections.

- Have them add any new reasons or facts to their Target Diagram.

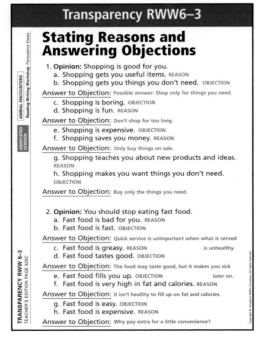

Transparency RWW6–3

Stating Reasons and Answering Objections

1. **Opinion:** Shopping is good for you.
   a. Shopping gets you useful items. REASON
   b. Shopping gets you things you don't need. OBJECTION

Answer to Objection: Possible answer: Shop only for things you need.
   c. Shopping is boring. OBJECTION
   d. Shopping is fun. REASON

Answer to Objection: Don't shop for too long.
   e. Shopping is expensive. OBJECTION
   f. Shopping saves you money. REASON

Answer to Objection: Only buy things on sale.
   g. Shopping teaches you about new products and ideas. REASON
   h. Shopping makes you want things you don't need. OBJECTION

Answer to Objection: Buy only the things you need.

2. **Opinion:** You should stop eating fast food.
   a. Fast food is bad for you. REASON
   b. Fast food is fast. OBJECTION

Answer to Objection: Quick service is unimportant when what is served is unhealthy.
   c. Fast food is greasy. REASON
   d. Fast food tastes good. OBJECTION

Answer to Objection: The food may taste good, but it makes you sick later on.
   e. Fast food fills you up. OBJECTION
   f. Fast food is very high in fat and calories. REASON

Answer to Objection: It isn't healthy to fill up on fat and calories.
   g. Fast food is easy. OBJECTION
   h. Fast food is expensive. REASON

Answer to Objection: Why pay extra for a little convenience?

Using Supporting Facts and Details

1 **Discuss using facts and details.** Tell students that good writers include facts and details in their persuasive essay to support their reasons. Explain that supporting facts and details should be accurate.

2 **Model using facts and details to support a reason.** Use this example.

> **Reason** Lockers reduce back injuries.
>
> **Facts and Details** Our school reported fewer back injuries after they installed lockers. My cousin swears that her posture improved after her school got lockers.

3 **Display Transparency RWW6–4.** Ask a volunteer to read aloud the topic and Reason 1.

- Point out the box of details. Ask, Which of these details support Reason 1? (Answers will vary. Sample answers: a, d, k)

- Then have students complete the rest of the transparency on their own.

4 **Have students draft their persuasive essay.**

- Tell students to write an introduction that states their goal.

- Remind students to group each reason in a separate paragraph, along with the facts and details that support it.

- Tell them to leave out any details that don't support a reason.

- Encourage students to sound confident and positive, using persuasive words and phrases, such as *certainly, surely, definitely,* and *without a doubt.*

- Ask them to vary their sentences by writing questions or exclamations as well as statements.

- Tell them to sum up their reasons and restate their goal in the conclusion.

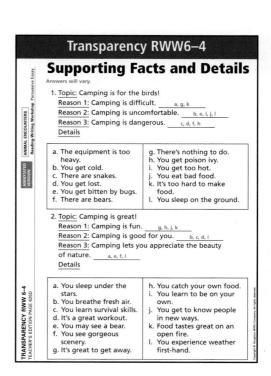

Transparency RWW6–4

Supporting Facts and Details

Answers will vary.

ANIMAL ENCOUNTERS
Reading-Writing Workshop Persuasive Essay

ANNOTATED VERSION

1. Topic: Camping is for the birds!
   Reason 1: Camping is difficult.   a, g, k
   Reason 2: Camping is uncomfortable.   b, e, i, j, l
   Reason 3: Camping is dangerous.   c, d, f, h
   Details

a. The equipment is too heavy.	g. There's nothing to do.
b. You get cold.	h. You get poison ivy.
c. There are snakes.	i. You get too hot.
d. You get lost.	j. You eat bad food.
e. You get bitten by bugs.	k. It's too hard to make food.
f. There are bears.	l. You sleep on the ground.

2. Topic: Camping is great!
   Reason 1: Camping is fun.   g, h, j, k
   Reason 2: Camping is good for you.   b, c, d, i
   Reason 3: Camping lets you appreciate the beauty of nature.   a, e, f, l
   Details

a. You sleep under the stars.	h. You catch your own food.
b. You breathe fresh air.	i. You learn to be on your own.
c. You learn survival skills.	j. You get to know people in new ways.
d. It's a great workout.	k. Food tastes great on an open fire.
e. You may see a bear.	l. You experience weather first-hand.
f. You see gorgeous scenery.	
g. It's great to get away.	

TRANSPARENCY RWW 6–4
TEACHER'S EDITION PAGE 625D

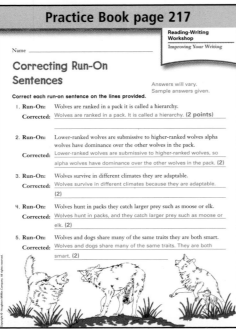

Practice Book page 216

Name _____

Revising Your Persuasive Essay

Reread your persuasive essay. Put a checkmark in the box for each sentence that describes your paper. Use this page to help you revise.

Rings the Bell
- ☐ My introduction clearly tells my goal.
- ☐ I supported my goal with at least three important reasons. Facts and details support reasons. I answered objections.
- ☐ My voice is confident. I used persuasive words.
- ☐ My paper is organized in paragraphs. My conclusion is strong.
- ☐ My sentences flow well. There are almost no mistakes.

Getting Stronger
- ☐ I did not tell my goal clearly in the introduction.
- ☐ I need more reasons, facts, and details. I did not answer objections.
- ☐ More persuasive words would make my voice more confident.
- ☐ Some paragraphs are disorganized. My conclusion is weak.
- ☐ Some sentences are choppy. There are some mistakes.

Try Harder
- ☐ My goal is not clear. The introduction is missing.
- ☐ There are almost no reasons. There are few facts and details.
- ☐ I don't sound like I care about this goal. Word choice is weak.
- ☐ My paper has only one paragraph. I didn't write a conclusion.
- ☐ Most sentences are choppy. There are many mistakes.

Practice Book page 217

Name _____

Correcting Run-On Sentences

Answers will vary. Sample answers given.

Correct each run-on sentence on the lines provided.

1. **Run-On:** Wolves are ranked in a pack it is called a hierarchy.
   Corrected: Wolves are ranked in a pack. It is called a hierarchy. **(2 points)**

2. **Run-On:** Lower-ranked wolves are submissive to higher-ranked wolves alpha wolves have dominance over the other wolves in the pack.
   Corrected: Lower-ranked wolves are submissive to higher-ranked wolves, so alpha wolves have dominance over the other wolves in the pack. **(2)**

3. **Run-On:** Wolves survive in different climates they are adaptable.
   Corrected: Wolves survive in different climates because they are adaptable. **(2)**

4. **Run-On:** Wolves hunt in packs they catch larger prey such as moose or elk.
   Corrected: Wolves hunt in packs, and they catch larger prey such as moose or elk. **(2)**

5. **Run-On:** Wolves and dogs share many of the same traits they are both smart.
   Corrected: Wolves and dogs share many of the same traits. They are both smart. **(2)**

Transparency RWW6–5

Correcting Run-On Sentences

1. **Run-On:** I think Thomas Jefferson's influence on the United States was huge he had a vision of what America's future would be like.
   Corrected: I think Thomas Jefferson's influence on the United States was huge. He had a vision of what America's future would be like.

2. **Run-On:** Alexander Hamilton had a different vision of America he thought we would live in a country based on industry.
   Corrected: Alexander Hamilton had a different vision of America. He thought we would live in a country based on industry.

3. **Run-On:** Jefferson saw the United States as a farming society the leaders of this society would be citizen farmers.
   Corrected: Jefferson saw the United States as a farming society. The leaders of this society would be citizen farmers.

4. **Run-On:** Jefferson and Hamilton were rivals in 1801 Jefferson became president and went on to have a distinguished career.
   Corrected: Jefferson and Hamilton were rivals. In 1801 Jefferson became president and went on to have a distinguished career.

5. **Run-On:** Hamilton never rose to be elected to a high office in 1803 Hamilton was killed in a duel with Aaron Burr.
   Corrected: Hamilton never rose to be elected to a high office. In 1803 Hamilton was killed in a duel with Aaron Burr.

6. **Run-On:** Hamilton's vision of the country prevailed we have become an industrial country, not a farming country.
   Corrected: Hamilton's vision of the country prevailed. We have become an industrial country, not a farming country.

Revising

Have students use **Practice Book** page 216 to help them evaluate and then revise their persuasive essay. Students should also discuss their drafts in a writing conference. (See the Conference Master on page R30. Discuss the sample thoughts and questions before students have their conferences.) Remind students to keep in mind their listeners' comments and questions when they revise.

Proofreading

Have students proofread their papers to correct capitalization, punctuation, spelling, and usage. Students can use the proofreading checklist and proof-reading marks on **Practice Book** pages 287–288.

Improving Writing: Correcting Run-On Sentences

Explain that a run-on sentence keeps going, or "runs on," even after a complete thought has been expressed. Point out that run-on sentences are confusing for readers because they can't tell where one thought ends and another begins.

Go over the following options for correcting run-on sentences. Remind students to change capitalization and punctuation as needed.

- Create two or more sentences. Write each thought as a separate sentence.
- Use a conjunction such as *and, but, so,* or *or* to divide the parts of the run-on sentence into a compound sentence.

Display **Transparency RWW6–5.**

- Discuss the first run-on sentence and the corrected version.
- Then have students complete the rest of the transparency on a separate sheet of paper.

Assign **Practice Book** page 217. Then have students look at their persuasive essay to see how they can improve it by correcting run-on sentences.

READING-WRITING WORKSHOP

Frequently Misspelled Words

Write the Spelling Words on the board, or distribute the list on **Practice Book** page 279. Help students identify the part of the word likely to be misspelled.

Spelling Pretest/Test

Basic Words

1. Have you **heard** a buffalo snort?
2. What is **your** favorite wild animal?
3. If **you're** quiet, it won't run away.
4. A moose stood in the **field**.
5. I want to **buy** a bird feeder.
6. My **friend** saw a fox in the woods.
7. I can't **guess** what a turtle eats.
8. Once my **cousin** saw a bear.
9. Beavers **build** dams from sticks.
10. That **family** of lions is asleep.
11. I **can't** wait to go on a safari!
12. Those baby birds **cannot** fly.
13. I **didn't** have enough film.
14. I **haven't** ever seen a beehive.
15. Deer **don't** hibernate in winter.

Challenge Words

16. I **truly** love wild animals.
17. The money **benefited** the zoo.
18. The giraffe's **height** surprised us.
19. We couldn't **believe** our eyes!
20. I **received** postcards from Africa.

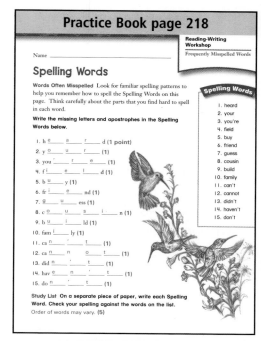

Practice Book page 218

Reading-Writing Workshop
Frequently Misspelled Words

Name _____

Spelling Words

Words Often Misspelled Look for familiar spelling patterns to help you remember how to spell the Spelling Words on this page. Think carefully about the parts that you find hard to spell in each word.

Write the missing letters and apostrophes in the Spelling Words below.

1. h e a r d (1 point)
2. y o u r (1)
3. you ' r e (1)
4. f i e l d (1)
5. b u y (1)
6. fr i e nd (1)
7. g u ess (1)
8. c o u s i n (1)
9. b u i ld (1)
10. fam i ly (1)
11. ca n ' t (1)
12. ca n n o t (1)
13. did n ' t (1)
14. hav n ' t (1)
15. do n ' t (1)

Study List On a separate piece of paper, write each Spelling Word. Check your spelling against the words on the list.
Order of words may vary. (5)

Spelling Words
1. heard
2. your
3. you're
4. field
5. buy
6. friend
7. guess
8. cousin
9. build
10. family
11. can't
12. cannot
13. didn't
14. haven't
15. don't

Practice Book page 219

Reading-Writing Workshop
Frequently Misspelled Words

Name _____

Spelling Spree

Alphabet Puzzler Write the Spelling Word that fits alphabetically between the two words in each group.

1. fried, _____, frighten
2. head, _____, heart
3. donation, _____, doom
4. familiar, _____, famous
5. guard, _____, guest
6. fiddle, _____, filed
7. button, _____, buzz
8. court, _____, cover

1. friend (1 point)
2. heard (1)
3. don't (1)
4. family (1)
5. guess (1)
6. field (1)
7. buy (1)
8. cousin (1)

Letter Math Add and subtract letters from the words below to make Spelling Words. Write the new words.

9. carrot + nn − rr =
10. having − ing + en't =
11. sour − s + y =
12. want + ' − w + c =
13. guild − g + b =
14. they're + you − they =
15. hadn't + di −ha =

9. cannot (1)
10. haven't (1)
11. your (1)
12. can't (1)
13. build (1)
14. you're (1)
15. didn't (1)

Spelling Words
1. heard
2. your
3. you're
4. field
5. buy
6. friend
7. guess
8. cousin
9. build
10. family
11. can't
12. cannot
13. didn't
14. haven't
15. don't

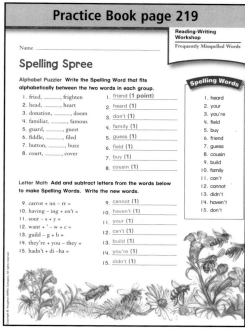

Practice Book page 220

Reading-Writing Workshop
Frequently Misspelled Words

Name _____

Proofreading and Writing

Proofreading Circle the five misspelled Spelling Words in this wanted poster. Then write each word correctly.

HAVE YOU SEEN THIS CAT?

You may have (herd) about the escape of this mountain lion from the county zoo. We have been searching for the past week, but we (have'nt) been able to track her down. Our best (gess) is that she is keeping to wooded areas, but we can't say for sure. As a result, we are asking that you be extremely careful when outdoors, and that you keep an eye on (youre) children and pets. Above all, if you see the cat, (dont) approach her. Instead, call the police, or call us at the zoo at 555-7372.

1. heard (1 point)
2. haven't (1)
3. guess (1)
4. your (1)
5. don't (1)

Spelling Words
1. heard
2. your
3. you're
4. field
5. buy
6. friend
7. guess
8. cousin
9. build
10. family
11. can't
12. cannot
13. didn't
14. haven't
15. don't

——— **Animal Riddles** On a separate piece of paper, write three riddles about animals. Include a Spelling Word in each riddle. Then trade riddles with a classmate and try to guess each other's answers.
Responses will vary. (5)

Practice Book page 279

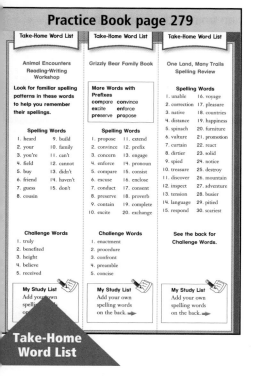

Take-Home Word List

Animal Encounters
Reading-Writing Workshop

Look for familiar spelling patterns in these words to help you remember their spellings.

Spelling Words
1. heard   9. build
2. your   10. family
3. you're   11. can't
4. field   12. cannot
5. buy   13. didn't
6. friend   14. haven't
7. guess   15. don't
8. cousin

Challenge Words
1. truly
2. benefited
3. height
4. believe
5. received

My Study List Add your own spelling words on the back.

Take-Home Word List

Grizzly Bear Family Book

More Words with Prefixes
compare   convince
excite   enforce
preserve   propose

Spelling Words
1. propose   11. extend
2. convince   12. prefix
3. concern   13. engage
4. enforce   14. pronoun
5. compare   15. consist
6. excuse   16. enclose
7. conduct   17. consent
8. preserve   18. proverb
9. contain   19. complete
10. excite   20. exchange

Challenge Words
1. enactment
2. procedure
3. confront
4. preamble
5. concise

My Study List Add your own spelling words on the back.

Take-Home Word List

One Land, Many Trails
Spelling Review

Spelling Words
1. unable   16. voyage
2. correction   17. pleasure
3. native   18. countries
4. distance   19. happiness
5. spinach   20. furniture
6. vulture   21. promotion
7. curtain   22. react
8. dirtier   23. solid
9. spied   24. notice
10. treasure   25. destroy
11. discover   26. mountain
12. inspect   27. adventure
13. tension   28. busier
14. language   29. pitied
15. respond   30. scariest

See the back for Challenge Words.

My Study List Add your own spelling words on the back.

Take-Home Word List

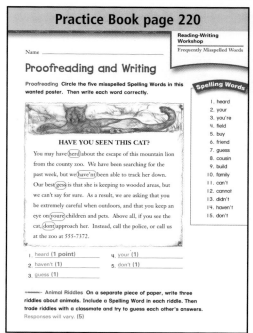

Publishing

Have students publish their persuasive essays.

- Ask them to look back at the publishing ideas they noted when they chose a topic. Discuss the Ideas for Sharing box below.

- Then ask students to decide how they want to publish their writing.

- Tell them to make a neat final copy of their persuasive essay. Remind them to use good penmanship and to be sure that they have fixed all mistakes.

📁 **Portfolio Opportunity**

Save students' final copy of their persuasive essay as an example of the development of their writing skills.

Join Karate

Ideas for Sharing

Write It
- Send your essay as a letter to a newspaper.

Say It
- Present it as a speech.

Show It
- Display your essay on a poster, and illustrate each reason.

- Make slides that illustrate your reasons. Read your essay as you show your slides.

Tips for Creating a Persuasive Poster

- Choose a poster title that states your goal.

- Find photos or make drawings to illustrate each of your reasons clearly.

- Attach your essay to the center of the poster.

- Run string from each reason to its illustration.

- Display your poster where it will be seen by your audience.

Monitoring Student Progress

Student Self-Assessment

- Was your persuasive essay convincing? Why or why not?

- What was most difficult about writing a persuasive essay? What was easiest?

- What advice would you give someone who was writing a persuasive essay for the first time?

- How does this paper compare with other papers you have written?

Evaluating

Have students write responses to the questions in the Student Self-Assessment box.

Evaluate students' writing, using the Writing Traits Scoring Rubric. This rubric is based on the criteria in this workshop and reflects the criteria students used in Revising Your Persuasive Essay on **Practice Book** page 216.

Persuasive Essay

Writing Traits Scoring Rubric

4

IDEAS	The essay focuses on a goal. The goal is supported by at least three important reasons. Each reason is supported by facts and details. The writer answers possible objections.
ORGANIZATION	The introduction states the goal clearly. Each paragraph states a reason and includes supporting facts and details. The conclusion sums up the reasons and restates the goal.
VOICE	The writer's voice confidently expresses his or her feelings about the goal.
WORD CHOICE	The words chosen are persuasive.
SENTENCE FLUENCY	The writing flows well. Sentence length and structure vary.
CONVENTIONS	There are almost no errors in grammar, capitalization, spelling, or usage.
PRESENTATION	The final copy is neat and legible.

3

IDEAS	The essay focuses on a goal. More facts and details would make each reason more convincing. The writer may not answer objections.
ORGANIZATION	The introduction or conclusion may be weak. A few facts or details may be in the wrong paragraphs.
VOICE	The writer's voice is not strong. It may not sound positive.
WORD CHOICE	The writer could have used more persuasive words.
SENTENCE FLUENCY	The essay would benefit from greater sentence variety.
CONVENTIONS	There are a few mistakes, but they do not affect understanding.
PRESENTATION	The final copy is messy in a few places but still legible.

2

IDEAS	The essay does not stay focused on a goal. The writer gives too few reasons, or the reasons are weak. Reasons are not supported by facts and details. Objections are not addressed.
ORGANIZATION	The goal may not be clearly stated. The organization is inconsistent. The conclusion may be missing.
VOICE	The writer may sound angry or unconfident.
WORD CHOICE	Word choice is unpersuasive.
SENTENCE FLUENCY	The essay lacks sentence variety.
CONVENTIONS	Mistakes sometimes make the essay hard to understand.
PRESENTATION	The final copy is messy. It may be illegible in a few places.

1

IDEAS	The goal is not clear. There are no convincing reasons. The supporting facts and details are weak or confusing.
ORGANIZATION	The introduction and the conclusion are missing. Ideas may be presented just as a list.
VOICE	The voice may not show that the writer cares about the goal.
WORD CHOICE	Word choice is vague or uninteresting. It may be confusing.
SENTENCE FLUENCY	Sentences are short, unclear, or repetitive.
CONVENTIONS	Many mistakes make the paper hard to understand.
PRESENTATION	The final copy is messy. It may be illegible in many places.

Lesson Overview

Literature

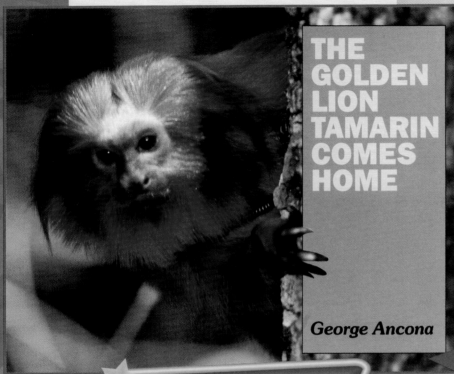

THE GOLDEN LION TAMARIN COMES HOME

George Ancona

Selection Summary

Several captive-born golden lion tamarins travel from the National Zoo in Washington, D.C. to Brazil for reintroduction into the rainforest.

1 Background and Vocabulary

2 Main Selection

The Golden Lion Tamarin Comes Home
Genre: Nonfiction

3 Technology Link

Instructional Support

Planning and Practice

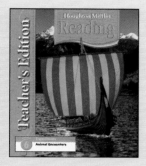

- Planning and classroom management
- Reading instruction
- Skill lessons
- Materials for reaching all learners

- Independent practice for skills

- Newsletters
- Selection Summaries
- Assignment Cards
- Observation Checklists
- Selection Tests

- Transparencies
- Strategy Posters
- Blackline Masters

Reaching All Learners

Coordinated lessons, activities, and projects for additional reading instruction

For
- Classroom Teacher
- Extended Day
- Pull Out
- Resource Teacher

Technology

Audio Selection
The Golden Lion Tamarin Comes Home

Get Set for Reading CD-ROM
- Background building
- Vocabulary support
- Selection Summary in English and Spanish

Accelerated Reader
- Practice quizzes for the selection

www.eduplace.com
Log on to Education Place for more activities related to the selection.

e • Glossary
e • WordGame

Leveled Books for Reaching All Learners

Leveled Readers and Leveled Practice

- Independent reading for building fluency
- Topic, comprehension strategy, and vocabulary linked to main selection
- Lessons in Teacher's Edition, pages 647O–647R
- Leveled practice for every book

Technology

Leveled Readers
Audio available

Book Adventure
- Practice quizzes for the Leveled Theme Paperbacks

www.eduplace.com
Log on to Education Place® for activities related to the Leveled Theme Paperbacks.

● BELOW LEVEL

SAVING SEA TURTLES
by Amy Edgar illustrated by Tom Leonard

▲ ON LEVEL

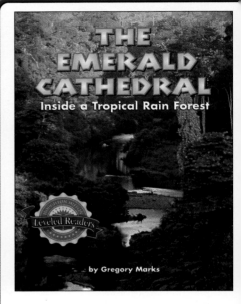

THE EMERALD CATHEDRAL
Inside a Tropical Rain Forest
by Gregory Marks

● Below Level Practice

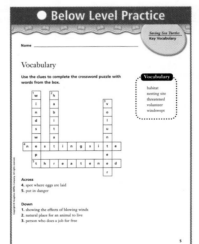

Saving Sea Turtles
Key Vocabulary

Name _____

Vocabulary

Use the clues to complete the crossword puzzle with words from the box.

Vocabulary
habitat
nesting site
threatened
volunteer
windswept

Across
4. spot where eggs are laid
5. put in danger

Down
1. showing the effects of blowing winds
2. natural place for an animal to live
3. person who does a job for free

▲ On Level Practice

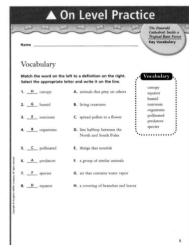

The Emerald Cathedral: Inside a Tropical Rain Forest
Key Vocabulary

Name _____

Vocabulary

Match the word on the left to a definition on the right. Select the appropriate letter and write it on the line.

Vocabulary
canopy
equator
humid
nutrients
organisms
pollinated
predators
species

1. __H__ canopy   A. animals that prey on others
2. __G__ humid   B. living creatures
3. __E__ nutrients   C. spread pollen to a flower
4. __B__ organisms   D. line halfway between the North and South Poles
5. __C__ pollinated   E. things that nourish
6. __A__ predators   F. a group of similar animals
7. __F__ species   G. air that contains water vapor
8. __D__ equator   H. a covering of branches and leaves

● Below Level Practice

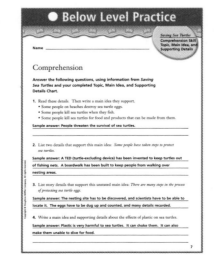

Saving Sea Turtles
Comprehension Skill
Topic, Main Idea, and
Supporting Details

Name _____

Comprehension

Answer the following questions, using information from *Saving Sea Turtles* and your completed Topic, Main Idea, and Supporting Details Chart.

1. Read these details. Then write a main idea they support.
- Some people on beaches destroy sea turtle eggs.
- Some people kill sea turtles when they fish.
- Some people kill sea turtles for food and products that can be made from them.

Sample answer: People threaten the survival of sea turtles.

2. List two details that support this main idea: *Some people have taken steps to protect sea turtles.*

Sample answer: A TED (turtle-excluding device) has been invented to keep turtles out of fishing nets. A boardwalk has been built to keep people from walking over nesting areas.

3. List story details that support this unstated main idea: *There are many steps in the process of protecting sea turtle eggs.*

Sample answer: The nesting site has to be discovered, and scientists have to be able to locate it. The eggs have to be dug up and counted, and many details recorded.

4. Write a main idea and supporting details about the effects of plastic on sea turtles.

Sample answer: Plastic is very harmful to sea turtles. It can choke them. It can also make them unable to dive for food.

▲ On Level Practice

The Emerald Cathedral: Inside a Tropical Rain Forest
Comprehension Skill
Topic, Main Idea, and
Supporting Details

Name _____

Comprehension

Answer the following questions, using information from *The Emerald Cathedral: Inside a Tropical Rain Forest* and your completed Topic, Main Idea, and Details Chart.

1. Define the terms below.
topic: what the selection is about
main idea: the most important points the author makes about the topic
details: support or explain the main idea

2. Reread the section called "The Layered Forest." Write the main idea and two supporting details.

Main idea: The organisms throughout the layers need each other for survival. Details: Each layer looks different. Organisms on the floor eat things from the layers above.

3. Reread the section called "Floor Animals and Hunters." Write the main idea and two supporting details.

Main idea: Some floor animals depend on each other to survive; others just visit. Details: Birds and larger mammals eat insects on the floor; frogs and toads also eat insects.

4. Here are two details. Write the main idea.

Detail #1: The wealth of canopy plants supports most of the rain forest animals.
Detail #2: Plants depend on canopy animals to carry seeds a distance from the parent tree.

Plants and animals in the canopy depend on each other to survive.

Leveled Theme Paperbacks

- Extended independent reading in theme-related trade books
- Lessons in Teacher's Edition, pages R2–R7

■ ABOVE LEVEL

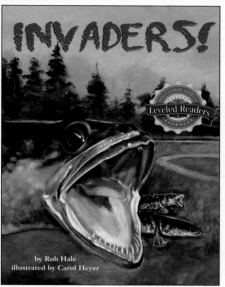

INVADERS!
by Rob Hale
illustrated by Carol Heyer

◆ LANGUAGE SUPPORT

PROTECTING SEA TURTLES
by Amy Edgar   illustrated by Tom Leonard

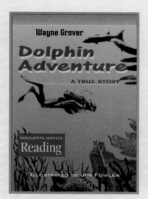

Wayne Grover
Dolphin Adventure
A TRUE STORY
HOUGHTON MIFFLIN Reading
ILLUSTRATED BY JIM FOWLER

Below Level

The TARANTULA in My Purse
and 172 Other Wild Pets
HOUGHTON MIFFLIN Reading
written and illustrated by Jean Craighead George

On Level

■ Above Level Practice

Invaders!
Key Vocabulary

Name _____

Vocabulary

Using the words in the box, complete this letter to the editor of a newspaper, explaining why invading organisms are so dangerous.

Vocabulary
alien
complex
consequences
ecosystem
eradicate
extinction
habitat
predators
vulnerable

To the Editor:

After reading the article on feral pigs in Hawaii in last week's paper, I felt that it was important to write to explain my point of view. __Sample answer: Alien__ invaders such as the feral pig present a __complex__ problem. The __consequences__ are severe and are a threat to the natural __ecosystem.__

Without taking steps to __eradicate__ the invaders, native creatures are left __vulnerable__ to __extinction.__ Some invaders have succeeded in their new __habitat.__ Without __predators,__ these creatures can be dangerous.

Sincerely,
A Faithful Reader

5

◆ Language Support Practice

Protecting Sea Turtles
Build Background

Name _____

Build Background

Read the activities below. Then decide whether each activity might hurt a sea turtle or help to protect it. Write a check mark in the correct column.

Activity	Hurts Sea Turtles	Helps Sea Turtles
hunting sea turtles for their skin, shells, and meat	✔	
helping scientists to learn more about what turtles need to be healthy		✔
throwing trash on the beach or in the water where turtles live	✔	
helping to clean up areas where turtles live		✔
being careful not to step on turtle nests and eggs		✔
stepping on or breaking turtle eggs before they hatch	✔	

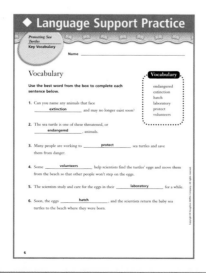

5

■ Above Level Practice

Invaders!
Comprehension Skill Topic, Main Idea, and Supporting Details

Name _____

Comprehension

Answer the following questions, using information from the story *Invaders!* and your completed Topic, Main Idea, and Details Chart.

1. Define the terms *topic, main idea,* and *details.*
The topic is the subject that the paragraphs tell about.
The main idea is an important point about the topic. Details support the main idea.

2. Identify the main idea of the section called "Stowaways and Invited Guests." Then list two supporting details.
Main idea: Alien animals or plants can arrive by accident or deliberately.
Details: Mosquitoes, The Nile perch.

3. What is the main idea of the section called "Guarding the Gates"? List two supporting details.
Main idea: Keeping invaders from a new environment will slow their spread.
Details: Mosquitoes prevented by flushing water barrels. Packers checking for beetles.

4. Here are three details. Write the main idea.
Detail #1: The invading brown snake has exterminated nearly all the native forest birds on the island of Guam.
Detail #2: The crazy ant, an alien from Africa, has taken over at least 8 areas of rain forest on Christmas Island.
Detail #3: When dogs were brought into the island of Hawaii, they destroyed about 20 species of native flightless birds.
Islands are very vulnerable to invaders.

5. How does identifying the topic, main ideas, and details help you to be a more efficient reader?
Sample answer: Understanding the topic, main ideas, and details helps me because I can organize the information to make it easier to read.

7

◆ Language Support Practice

Protecting Sea Turtles
Key Vocabulary

Name _____

Vocabulary

Use the best word from the box to complete each sentence below.

Vocabulary
endangered
extinction
hatch
laboratory
protect
volunteers

1. Can you name any animals that face __extinction__ and may no longer exist soon?

2. The sea turtle is one of these threatened, or __endangered__, animals.

3. Many people are working to __protect__ sea turtles and save them from danger.

4. Some __volunteers__ help scientists find the turtles' eggs and move them from the beach so that other people won't step on the eggs.

5. The scientists study and care for the eggs in their __laboratory__ for a while.

6. Soon, the eggs __hatch__, and the scientists return the baby sea turtles to the beach where they were born.

6

JIM BRANDENBURG
To the Top of the World
➥ ADVENTURES WITH ARCTIC WOLVES
HOUGHTON MIFFLIN Reading

Challenge

Daily Lesson Plans

Technology

Lesson Planner CD-ROM allows you to customize the chart below to develop your own lesson plans.

T Skill tested on Theme Skills Test and/or Integrated Theme Test

DAILY LESSON PLANS

50–60 minutes

Reading
Comprehension

Leveled Readers
- Fluency Practice
- Independent Reading

DAY 1

Teacher Read Aloud, 625S–625T
Nunavut

Building Background, 626

Key Vocabulary, 627

canopy	genes	observation
captive	habitat	predators
dilemma	humid	reintroduction
extinction		

Reading the Selection, 628–641

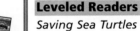 **Comprehension Skill,** 628
Topic, Main Idea, and Supporting Details **T**

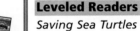 **Comprehension Strategy,** 628
Monitor/Clarify **T**

Leveled Readers
Saving Sea Turtles
The Emerald Cathedral
Invaders!
Protecting Sea Turtles

Lessons and Leveled Practice, 647O–647R

DAY 2

Reading the Selection,
628–641

Comprehension Check, 641

Responding, 642
Think About the Selection

 Comprehension Skill Preview, 631
Topic, Main Idea, and Supporting Details **T**

Leveled Readers
Saving Sea Turtles
The Emerald Cathedral
Invaders!
Protecting Sea Turtles

Lessons and Leveled Practice, 647O–647R

20–30 minutes

Word Work

Phonics/Decoding
Vocabulary
Spelling

Phonics/Decoding, 629
Phonics/Decoding Strategy

Vocabulary, 628–641
Selection Vocabulary

Spelling, 647E
Three-Syllable Words **T**

 Structural Analysis, 647C
Three-Syllable Words **T**

Vocabulary, 628–641
Selection Vocabulary

Spelling, 647E
Three-Syllable Words Review and Practice **T**

20–30 minutes

Writing and Oral Language

Writing
Grammar
Listening/Speaking/Viewing

Writing, 647K
Prewriting a Compare/Contrast Essay

Grammar, 647I
Prepositions **T**

Daily Language Practice
1. The kayakers paddled skillfully through dangurus hamilton gorge. (dangerous; Hamilton Gorge.)
2. Your father and I will sells the proporty as soon as possible. (sell; property)

Listening/Speaking/Viewing,
625S–625T, 635
Teacher Read Aloud, Stop and Think

Writing, 647K
Drafting a Compare/Contrast Essay

Grammar, 647I
Prepositions Practice **T**

Daily Language Practice
3. Dr Provine explained that my skin is very sensitiv to heat and sun. (Dr.; sensitive)
4. Our reguler coach, Joe rockwell, is sick today. (regular; Rockwell)

Listening/Speaking/Viewing, 641, 642
Wrapping Up, Responding

Target Skills of the Week

Comprehension	Monitor/Clarify; Topic, Main Idea, and Supporting Details
Vocabulary	Pronunciations in a Dictionary
Phonics/Decoding	Three-Syllable Words
Fluency	Leveled Readers

DAY 3

Rereading the Selection, 628–641

Comprehension Skill, 647A–647B
Topic, Main Idea, and Supporting Details **T**

Leveled Readers
Saving Sea Turtles
The Emerald Cathedral
Invaders!
Protecting Sea Turtles

Lessons and Leveled Practice, 647O–647R

Phonics Review, 647D
Consonant Alternations

Vocabulary, 647G
Pronunciations in a Dictionary **T**

Spelling, 647F
Vocabulary: Clipped Words; Three-Syllable Words **T**

Writing, 647L
Revising a Compare/Contrast Essay
Combining Sentences with Prepositional Phrases **T**

Grammar, 647J
Prepositional Phrases **T**

Daily Language Practice
5. Last year our family plan a vacashun to the coast of Maine. (planned; vacation)
6. Vegetables weren't my favarite food when i was younger. (favorite; I)

DAY 4

Reading the Technology Link, 644–647
"Tuning in on Animals"

Skill: How to Read a Technology Article

Comprehension Skill Review, 633
Compare and Contrast

Leveled Readers
Saving Sea Turtles
The Emerald Cathedral
Invaders!
Protecting Sea Turtles

Lessons and Leveled Practice, 647O–647R

Phonics/Decoding, 644–647
Apply Phonics/Decoding Strategy to Link

Vocabulary, 647M
Language Center: Building Vocabulary

Spelling, 647F
Three-Syllable Words Game, Proofreading **T**

Writing, 647L
Proofreading a Compare/Contrast Essay

Grammar, 647J
Prepositional Phrases Practice **T**

Daily Language Practice
7. We have tried to edjukate my dog skippy, but he still chases cars. (educate; Skippy)
8. My collection of boston Red Sox baseball caps isn't in very good condision. (Boston; condition)

Listening/Speaking/Viewing, 647
Discuss the Link

DAY 5

Rereading for Fluency, 637

Responding Activities, 642–643
Write a Fax Message
Cross-Curricular Activities

Information and Study Skills, 647H
Evaluating the Effects of Media

Comprehension Skill Review, 639
Making Generalizations

Leveled Readers
Saving Sea Turtles
The Emerald Cathedral
Invaders!
Protecting Sea Turtles

Lessons and Leveled Practice, 647O–647R

Structural Analysis, 647M
Language Center: Three-Syllable Words

Vocabulary, 647M
Language Center: Vocabulary Game

Spelling, 647F
Test: Three-Syllable Words **T**

Writing, 647L
Publishing a Compare/Contrast Essay

Grammar, 647J, 647N
Expanding Sentences
Language Center: Prepositional Phrases

Daily Language Practice
9. Mr. and Mrs Chen called our attenshun to the Chinese scrolls in the museum. (Mrs.; attention)
10. Last night Scott asks me what homework we had for hiztory class. (asked; history)

Listening/Speaking/Viewing, 647N
Language Center: Giving Directions

Managing Flexible Groups

	DAY 1	**DAY 2**
WHOLE CLASS	• Teacher Read Aloud (TE pp. 625S–625T) • Building Background, Introducing Vocabulary (TE pp. 626–627) • Comprehension Strategy: Introduce (TE p. 628) • Comprehension Skill: Introduce (TE p. 628) • Purpose Setting (TE p. 629) **After reading first half of** *The Golden Lion Tamarin* • Stop and Think (TE p. 635)	**After reading** *The Golden Lion Tamarin Comes Home* • Wrapping Up (TE p. 641) • Comprehension Check (Practice Book p. 223) • Responding: Think About the Selection (TE p. 642) • Comprehension Skill: Preview (TE p. 631)
SMALL GROUPS		
Extra Support	**TEACHER-LED** • Preview *The Golden Lion Tamarin Comes Home* to Stop and Think (TE pp. 628–635). • Support reading with Extra Support/ Intervention notes (TE pp. 629, 632, 634, 637, 640).	**Partner or Individual Work** • Reread first half of *The Golden Lion Tamarin Comes Home* (TE pp. 628–635). • Preview, read second half (TE pp. 636–641). • Comprehension Check (Practice Book p. 223)
Challenge	**Individual Work** • Begin "Animal Rescue" (Challenge Handbook p. 50). • Extend reading with Challenge Notes (TE pp. 634, 640).	**Individual Work** • Continue work on activity (Challenge Handbook p. 50).
English Language Learners	**TEACHER-LED** • Preview vocabulary and *The Golden Lion Tamarin Comes Home* to Stop and Think (TE pp. 627–635). • Support reading with English Language Learners notes (TE pp. 626, 631, 639).	**TEACHER-LED** • Review first half of *The Golden Lion Tamarin Comes Home* (TE pp. 628–635). ✔ • Preview, read second half (TE pp. 636–641). • Begin Comprehension Check together (Practice Book p. 223).

FLEXIBLE GROUPS

Leveled Instruction and Leveled Practice

Independent Activities

• Get Set for Reading CD-Rom
• Journals: selection notes, questions
• Complete, review Practice Book (pp. 221–225) and Leveled Readers Practice Blackline Masters (TE pp. 647O–647R).
• Assignment Cards (Teacher's Resource Blackline Masters pp. 91–93)
• Leveled Readers (TE pp. 647O–647R), Leveled Theme Paperbacks (TE pp. R2–R7), or book from Leveled Bibliography (TE pp. 594E–594F)

✔ Opportunity to informally assess oral reading rate

- Rereading (TE pp. 628–641)

- Comprehension Skill: Main lesson
(TE pp. 647A–647B)

- Reading the Technology Link
(TE pp. 644–647): Skill lesson (TE p. 644)

- Rereading the Link (TE pp. 628–641)

- Comprehension Skill: First Comprehension
Review lesson (TE p. 633)

- Responding: Select from Activities
(TE pp. 642–643)

- Information and Study Skills (TE p. 647H)

- Comprehension Skill: Second
Comprehension Review lesson (TE p. 639)

TEACHER-LED

- Reread, review Comprehension check
(Practice Book p. 223).

- Preview Leveled Reader: Below Level
(TE p. 647O), or read book from Leveled
Bibliography (TE pp. 594E-594F). ✔

Partner or Individual Work

- Reread Technology Link (TE pp. 644–647).

- Complete Leveled Reader: Below Level
(TE p. 647O), or read book from Leveled
Bibliography (TE pp. 594E-594F).

TEACHER-LED

- Comprehension Skill: Reteaching lesson
(TE p. R10)

- Reread Leveled Theme Paperback: Below
Level (TE pp. R2–R3), or read book from
Leveled Bibliography (TE pp. 594E-594F). ✔

TEACHER-LED

- Teacher check-in: Assess progress (Challenge
Handbook p. 50).

- Preview Leveled Reader: Above Level
(TE p. 647Q), or read book from Leveled
Bibliography (TE pp. 594E-594F). ✔

Individual Work

- Complete activity (Challenge Handbook
p. 50).

- Complete Leveled Reader: Above Level
(TE p. 647Q), or read book from Leveled
Bibliography (TE pp. 594E-594F).

TEACHER-LED

- Evaluate activity and plan format for sharing
(Challenge Handbook p. 50).

- Reread Leveled Theme Paperback: Above
Level (TE pp. R6–R7), or read book from
Leveled Bibliography (TE pp. 594E-594F). ✔

Partner or Individual Work

- Complete Comprehension Check (Practice
Book p. 223).

- Begin Leveled Reader: Language Support
(TE p. 647R), or read book from Leveled
Bibliography (TE pp. 594E-594F).

TEACHER-LED

- Reread the Technology Link (TE pp. 644–647)
✔ and review Link Skill (TE p. 644).

- Complete Leveled Reader: Language Support
(TE p. 647R), or read book from Leveled
Bibliography (TE pp. 594E-594F). ✔

Partner or Individual Work

- Reread book from Leveled Bibliography
(TE pp. 594E-594F).

- Responding activities (TE pp. 642–643)
- Language Center activities (TE pp. 647M–647N)
- **Fluency Practice:** Reread *The Golden Lion Tamarin Comes Home;*
The Grizzly Bear Family Book. ✔
- Activities relating to *The Golden Lion Tamarin Comes Home* at
Education Place www.eduplace.com

**Turn the page for more
independent activities.**

Classroom Management

CLASSROOM MANAGEMENT

Assign these activities while you work with small groups.

Differentiated Instruction for Small Groups

- **Handbook for English Language Learners**, pp. 218–227

- **Extra Support Handbook**, pp. 214–223

Independent Activities

- Language Center, pp. 647M–647N

- Challenge/Extension Activities, Resources, pp. R11, R17

- **Classroom Management Handbook**, Activity Masters CM6-5–CM6-8

- **Challenge Handbook**, Challenge Masters CH6-3–CH6-4

Look for more activities in the Classroom Management Kit.

Social Studies

Brazil

Groups	⏱ 45 minutes
Objective	Make an informational poster about Brazil.
Materials	Encyclopedia, atlas, art materials, poster board

Work with a group to create a poster about Brazil, home to the golden lion tamarin.

- Use an encyclopedia to research key facts about Brazil, such as land features, natural resources, population, and languages.

- Take notes on information to include on your poster.

- Find a map of Brazil, and copy it onto poster board. Illustrate your poster with symbols for Brazil's major cities, rivers, and rain forests.

- Add key facts about Brazil.

- Add a scale and key to explain the distances and symbols on your map.

Career

Wildlife Workers

👤 Singles	⏱ 30 minutes
Objective	Research a wildlife career.
Materials	Reference sources, anthology

Would you like to work with wild animals? Research a wildlife career.

- Scan the Anthology and other books on wildlife for mention of wildlife careers, such as *biologist, zoo program coordinator,* or *veterinarian.* Choose one career to research.

- Use a reference source such as an encyclopedia or the Internet to learn about that career.

- Write a "Wildlife Career Fact Sheet" that includes descriptions of

  – typical responsibilities and activities

  – necessary training or experience

  – helpful personality traits to have

  – what is fun or interesting about this career

Consider copying and laminating these activities for use in centers.

Science

Layered Living

Pairs	⏱ 40 minutes
Objective	Create a rain forest diagram.
Materials	Encyclopedia, science textbook, art materials, poster board

Did you know that a rain forest contains four distinct layers that depend upon each other for survival? Work with a partner to create a diagram about this unique ecosystem.

- Use a reference source such as an encyclopedia or science textbook to find out about the four layers of the rain forest. Take notes on the kinds of plants and animals that live in each layer.

- Draw a diagram of the four layers on poster board. Illustrate or write notes about the plants and animals in each layer.

- Include a title for your diagram.

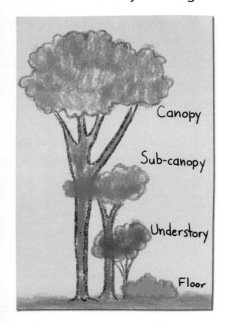

Technology

Global Positioning System

Pairs	⏱ 40 minutes
Objective	Report on the Global Positioning System.
Materials	Reference sources

One type of technology featured in "Tuning in on Animals" is the Global Positioning System (GPS). Work with a partner to write a report on this technology.

- Use reference sources such as the Anthology, an encyclopedia, and the Internet to learn about GPS technology. Take notes on key facts to include in your report.

- Write a one- to two-page report that describes GPS, how and when it was developed, how it works, and what it is used for.

- Illustrate your report with photographs or drawings. Include a title and captions.

Writing

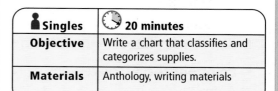

Categorize and Classify

Singles	⏱ 20 minutes
Objective	Write a chart that classifies and categorizes supplies.
Materials	Anthology, writing materials

Observers who track golden lion tamarins must carefully choose the supplies they bring on their trips. Write a chart like the one below to categorize and classify these supplies.

- Read page 638 of the Anthology to find a list of supplies that an observer must carry.

- Scan the rest of the selection to find ideas for other helpful supplies. Add them to the list.

- Write a chart to organize the supplies into categories that would help an observer remember what to pack.

Listening Comprehension

Building Background

Tell students that you will read aloud a non-fiction article about Arctic working dogs.

- Point out the Arctic regions of North America on a map or globe. Nunavut (NOO-nuh-voōt) is a territory of Canada.

Fluency Modeling

Explain that as you read aloud, you will be modeling fluent oral reading. Ask students to listen carefully to your phrasing and your expression, or tone of voice and emphasis.

COMPREHENSION SKILL

Topic, Main Idea, and Details

Explain the following:

- The topic is the subject that a selection is mainly about.
- The main ideas are the most important points the author makes about the topic.
- Details support or explain the main idea.

Purpose Setting Read the selection aloud, asking students to pay attention to the topic, main ideas, and supporting details. Then use the Guiding Comprehension questions to assess understanding. Reread for clarification as needed.

Teacher Read Aloud

Nunavut

❶ Some people who own dogs may chuckle at the thought of their pet going out to work each day. But for the people of Nunavut, Canada, the idea is not unusual. The Inuit use dogs for work and for play. In a place where winter can last nine months and temperatures average -22°F, cars are not the best means of transportation. If you lived along the coast of Cambridge Bay and had a friend in Grise Fjord in the north, you might make the visit by dog sled.

❷ The two most popular breeds of dog in the coldest place in Canada are the Canadian dog and the Siberian husky. The Inuit name for the Canadian dog is *qimmiq*. Long ago, Canadian dogs assisted explorers. Today, they are used for pulling heavy supply sleds and for hunting seals, musk oxen, and polar bears. These powerful dogs have a mixed heritage of Labrador and Greenland dogs. They are also related to the malamute, the Samoyed, and the Siberian husky.

❸ Canadian dogs are medium sized, weighing sixty to one hundred pounds. They are incredibly strong and rugged for their size. They are bred in a variety of color combinations mixing black, white, tan, and gray. Their heads are wedge shaped. Their paws are huge, with fat, thick pads. They have upward-curved tails and magnificent coats. Their thick, dense fur consists of long, coarse outer hairs called guard hairs and a fleecy undercoat called wool. This special fur holds in body heat, allowing these hardy dogs to sleep outdoors comfortably when it is -50°F. The tail is bushy and has a purpose. When a dog curls up to sleep, the tail lies across its delicate nose, eyes, and muzzle, keeping these sensitive areas warm.

Dog teams carrying a heavy sled over rough ice and snow average 25 miles per day. Locals say these intelligent, sturdy dogs are so clever they can catch a two-foot-long fish and eat it in two bites. Their special coats, strength, instinct for survival, and outstanding intelligence permit these dogs to work in one of the harshest climates on the planet.

Most Inuit Siberian huskies are used strictly as sport dogs. The Siberian husky is smaller, more stream-lined, and faster than the Canadian dog. It, too, has a double-layered coat, but the fur is smoother and neater in appearance than that of the Canadian dog. The Siberian husky is gray, black, or tan with lots of markings around the head. The head is round and the legs longer than the Canadian dog's. The friendly husky can have pale blue eyes or even one blue eye and one brown eye. This dog is built for speed rather than endurance. Teams of Siberian huskies have pulled some of the fastest sled speeds ever recorded.

Over time, snowmobiles and all-terrain vehicles have replaced many dog-driven sleds, but some Inuit still prefer to travel by dog sleds.

CRITICAL THINKING

Guiding Comprehension

❶ **TOPIC, MAIN IDEA, AND DETAILS**
What is the topic of the selection?
(types of dogs used by the Inuit)

❷ **TOPIC, MAIN IDEA, AND DETAILS**
What is a main idea from the selection?
(Sample answer: The two most popular dogs in Nunavut are the Canadian dog and the Siberian husky.)

❸ **TOPIC, MAIN IDEA, AND DETAILS**
What details support the idea that Canadian dogs are good sled dogs?
(They are strong and rugged. Their paws have thick pads. They have thick fur that has two layers. They have bushy tails that protect their faces when they sleep.)

Discussion Options

Personal Response Have students discuss what new information about dogs they learned from the selection.

⭐ **Connecting/Comparing** Ask students to compare how dogs in the Arctic have adapted to the cold with how bears described in *The Grizzly Bear Family Book* have adapted.

English Language Learners

Supporting Comprehension

Ask students to identify words that describe dogs (*pet, breeds, Canadian dog, Siberian husky, qimmiq, Labradors, Greenland dogs, malamute, Samoyed, sports dogs, husky*) and terms that tell about ways to travel. (*cars, dog sled, snowmobiles, all-terrain vehicles*) Have students suggest additional terms they know and build word webs for each group of terms.

Building Background

Key Concept: Saving the Golden Lion Tamarin

Remind students that this selection also focuses on connections between people and animals. It tells about efforts to save the golden lion tamarin from extinction. Use "Rescue in the Rain Forest" on Anthology pages 626–627 to build background and introduce Key Vocabulary.

- Have a student read aloud "Rescue in the Rain Forest."

- Have students study the photographs and map. Ask them to discuss reasons why the golden lion tamarin is threatened with extinction.

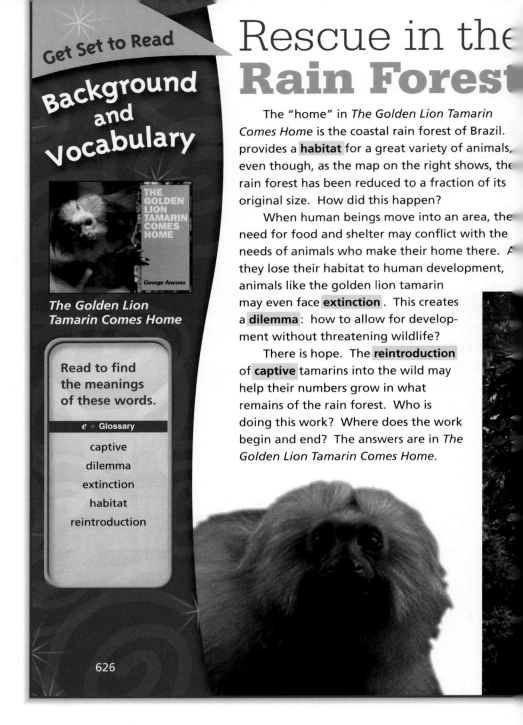

Get Set to Read

Background and Vocabulary

The Golden Lion Tamarin Comes Home

Read to find the meanings of these words.

e • Glossary

captive
dilemma
extinction
habitat
reintroduction

Rescue in the Rain Forest

The "home" in *The Golden Lion Tamarin Comes Home* is the coastal rain forest of Brazil. [ ] provides a **habitat** for a great variety of animals, even though, as the map on the right shows, the rain forest has been reduced to a fraction of its original size. How did this happen?

When human beings move into an area, the need for food and shelter may conflict with the needs of animals who make their home there. A[ ] they lose their habitat to human development, animals like the golden lion tamarin may even face **extinction**. This creates a **dilemma**: how to allow for development without threatening wildlife?

There is hope. The **reintroduction** of **captive** tamarins into the wild may help their numbers grow in what remains of the rain forest. Who is doing this work? Where does the work begin and end? The answers are in *The Golden Lion Tamarin Comes Home*.

626

English Language Learners

Supporting Comprehension

Beginning/Preproduction Have students listen to the article. Then ask students to look at the photographs and to point out the golden lion tamarin's natural habitat.

Early Production and Speech Emergence Use the photographs and map to explain the meaning of *canopy, habitat,* and *extinction.* Have students work in small groups to discuss why it's important to save the golden lion tamarin from extinction.

Intermediate and Advanced Fluency Have students work in small groups to read and then restate in their own words why golden lion tamarins face extinction.

South America
Brazil

Coastal Rain Forest of Brazil
■ Before Europeans arrived
■ Today

627

Introducing Vocabulary

Key Vocabulary

These words support the Key Concept and appear in the selection.

canopy the high, sheltering branches of rain forest trees

captive held against one's will

dilemma a situation in which one is given difficult choices to make

extinction having died out

genes tiny pieces of matter in cells that carry the blueprints for characteristics

habitat a natural environment for native creatures

humid containing a large amount of water vapor

observation the act of paying close attention

predators animals that prey on others

reintroduction the process of returning animals to their native habitats

e • Glossary
e • WordGame

See Vocabulary notes on pages 630, 632, 634, 636, and 638 for additional words to preview.

Display Transparency 6–10.

- Model how to figure out the meaning of *reintroduction* from context clues.

- Ask students to use context clues to figure out the Key Vocabulary words in each remaining sentence.

- Have students look for these words as they read and use them in discussions.

Practice/Homework Assign **Practice Book** page 221.

Introducing Vocabulary 627

Transparency 6–10

Words About Observing

Observation Log

Date: May 14, 1999
Place: Poço das Antas Biological Reserve, Brazil
Goal: To monitor the <u>reintroduction</u> process for a family of golden lion tamarins released into the wild three weeks ago.

Our <u>dilemma</u> has been how to blend six tamarins from two different zoos into one family without intruding in the animals' lives. If we are successful in bringing the tamarins together, it will strengthen the animals' <u>genes</u> and help prevent their <u>extinction</u>.

Notes:

8:10 A.M.: Morning air already hot and <u>humid</u>. So far, no sign of any of the <u>captive</u> tamarins released into the area three weeks ago.

8:25 A.M.: Saw one ocelot. Tamarins still hidden; they may be trying to avoid this <u>predator</u>.

9:40 A.M.: Spotted two tamarins above me in the forest <u>canopy</u>.

11:00 A.M.: Observed three tamarins using vines to travel among treetops. This is a sign that they are adjusting to the rain forest <u>habitat</u>. However, still no sign of the other monkeys.

1:15 P.M.: Spotted three juveniles foraging for natural food. Another sign that they are adjusting to the wild. Even better — the three adults joined them, and the juveniles helped the older monkeys forage for food. They seem to be working together as one family!

Practice Book page 221

The Golden Lion Tamarin Comes Home
Key Vocabulary

Name _____

Saving a Species

Complete each statement with a word from the word box.

Vocabulary
dilemma
extinction
predator
observation
canopy
reintroduction
habitat
captive
humid
genes

1. If you are in the highest branches of the tallest trees in the rain forest, you are in the <u>canopy</u> (1 point)

2. If the air has a lot of moisture in it, the weather is <u>humid</u> (1) _____.

3. If you release animals into a wild area in which their ancestors once lived, you are helping with the <u>reintroduction</u> (1) _____ of a species.

4. If you study the region in which a wild creature lives, you study its <u>habitat</u> (1) _____.

5. If you are faced with a problem that seems to have no good solution, you are faced with a <u>dilemma</u> (1) _____.

6. If you study the material that determines the characteristics of a plant or animal, you study its <u>genes</u> (1) _____.

7. If no members of a species remain alive, that species has suffered <u>extinction</u> (1) _____.

8. If you are being held prisoner, you are a <u>captive</u> (1) _____.

9. If an animal is being watched, it is under <u>observation</u> (1) _____.

10. If an animal hunts other animals for food, it is a <u>predator</u> (1) _____.

COMPREHENSION STRATEGY
Monitor/Clarify

Teacher Modeling Ask a student to read aloud the Strategy Focus. Then have students read the first paragraph on page 630. Model the strategy.

Think Aloud *I wonder what Andreia is looking for in the canopy. I'll read ahead to see if I can find out. In the third paragraph she points out the micos in the trees. They must be what she was looking for, but I don't know what golden lion tamarins are. I'll read ahead to find an answer.*

✓ **Test Prep** When a main idea is not stated directly in a test passage, students can follow these steps:

- Think about the title and other headings.
- Look at illustrations, photographs, and charts. Read the captions.
- Reread the first or last paragraph.
- Read the first and last sentences of paragraphs.

COMPREHENSION SKILL
Topic, Main Idea, and Details

Introduce the Graphic Organizer. Tell students that a Topic, Main Idea, and Details Chart can help them identify important ideas in the selection. Explain that as they read, students will fill out the chart found on **Practice Book** page 222.

- Display **Transparency 6–11.** Have students read Anthology page 630.
- Model how to fill in the main idea and supporting details for this page. Monitor students' work as needed.

Meet the Author/Photographer
George Ancona

Future Traveler: As a boy, Ancona visited the East River docks in New York City with his father. Watching freighters from around the world sparked an interest in other countries.

Study Abroad: While in art school, Ancona traveled to southern Mexico, where he met his parents' families for the first time.

Early Work: Before Ancona became a photographer, he worked for a carpenter, a mechanic, and at an amusement park.

In His Own Words: "I think people are fascinating and I love to find myself in strange places, meeting people, getting to know them and learning about them. This helps me to learn about myself."

Other Titles: Ancona's books reflect his love of travel and other cultures. *Turtle Watch* and *Carnaval* also take place in Brazil, and *Pablo Remembers* was photographed in Mexico.

To find out more about George Ancona, log on to Education Place. **www.eduplace.com/kids**

628

Transparency 6–11

Get the Idea?
Entries will vary. Samples are shown.

Topic: The conservation of golden lion tamarins

(Page 630) Main Idea: The native habitat of the tamarins is a diverse, colorful environment.

Details: Birds sing, insects buzz, cicadas chirp; tangled vines and leaves; orange-gold flash; speckles of sunlight.

(Pages 632–633) Main Idea: Captive-born tamarins need special training before being reintroduced into the wild.

Details:

(Pages 634–637) Main Idea: The observers prepare thoroughly before bringing the tamarins into the wild.

Details:

(Page 638) Main Idea: The observers carefully follow certain steps when releasing the tamarins.

Details:

(Pages 640–641) Main Idea: The observers gradually give less assistance as the tamarins adapt to their environment.

Details:

TRANSPARENCY 6–11
TEACHER'S EDITION PAGES 628 AND 647A

ANIMAL ENCOUNTERS The Golden Lion Tamarin
Graphic Organizer Topic, Main Idea, and Details Chart

ANNOTATED VERSION

Practice Book page 222

The Golden Lion Tamarin Comes Home

Graphic Organizer Topic, Main Idea, and Details Chart

Name _____

Get the Idea?

What are the main ideas of this selection? As you read, find the main ideas on the pages listed below. Then fill in the chart with the main idea and the details that support each main idea. Entries will vary. Samples are shown.

Topic: The conservation of golden lion tamarins

(Page 630) Main Idea: The native habitat of the tamarins is a diverse, colorful environment. **(1)**

Details: Birds sing, insects buzz, cicadas chirp; tangled vines and leaves; orange-gold flash; speckles of sunlight. **(1)**

(Pages 632–633) Main Idea: Captive-born tamarins need special training before being reintroduced into the wild. **(1)**

Details: (1)

(Pages 634–637) Main Idea: The observers prepare thoroughly before bringing the tamarins into the wild. **(1)**

Details: (1)

(Page 638) Main Idea: The observers carefully follow certain steps when releasing the tamarins. **(1)**

Details: (1)

(Pages 640–641) Main Idea: The observers gradually give less assistance as the tamarins adapt to their environment. **(1)**

Details: (1)

Selection 2

THE GOLDEN LION TAMARIN COMES HOME

George Ancona

Strategy Focus

As you read, **monitor** your understanding of how people are trying to help the golden lion tamarin. If necessary, reread or read ahead to **clarify**.

629

Extra Support/Intervention

Selection Preview

pages 629–631 All but two percent of the golden lion tamarin's natural habitat has been destroyed. What effects do you think this has had on the animals?

pages 632–633 Look at the photograph on page 633. How do these surroundings compare to the way most zoos keep animals?

pages 634–636 The tamarins are taken from the zoo and released into cages in the rain forest. What do you think they might do and learn while in these cages?

pages 637–641 Tamarins need the most help from humans during the early stages of their reintroduction into the rain forest. What do you think happens once the tamarins learn to be more independent?

Purpose Setting

- Have students predict what they might learn about golden lion tamarins.

- Have students preview the selection by looking at the photographs. Ask them to predict what they might learn about efforts to save golden lion tamarins from extinction.

- Ask students to monitor and clarify their understanding as they read. Remind students to clarify by rereading or reading ahead.

- Ask students to pay attention to the selection's main ideas and supporting details.

- You may want to preview the Responding questions on Anthology page 642.

Journal ▶ Students can use their journal to record their predictions and any questions they have about tamarins.

STRATEGY REVIEW

Phonics/Decoding

Remind students to use the Phonics/ Decoding Strategy as they read.

Modeling Write this sentence from the selection on the board: *…Dr. A. Coimbra-Filho, a Brazilian biologist, warned of its <u>imminent</u> extinction.* Point to *imminent*.

Think Aloud *I see a vowel followed by two consonants, so it probably has the short vowel sound. The last part, nent, looks like the ending of another word I know, permanent. It might have the same sound, nuhnt. I'll try blending all the sounds together: IHM-uh-nuhnt. That might be right, but I don't know what* imminent *means, so I'll look it up in the dictionary. That word means "about to happen." That makes sense in the sentence.*

CRITICAL THINKING
Guiding Comprehension

❶ MAKING INFERENCES Why do you think the author begins the selection without explaining what Andreia, Carolina, and Renato are looking for? (to put readers in the position of "searching" for tamarins)

❷ CAUSE AND EFFECT What effect did the destruction of Brazil's coastal rain forest have on tamarins? (They became endangered.)

❸ NOTING DETAILS What details does the author include to show why the rain forest is an ideal home for tamarins? (It provides water, food, protection, and routes for traveling.)

❹ DRAWING CONCLUSIONS Why do you think the author calls humans the most dangerous of all the tamarins' predators? (Human poachers are probably the most effective at capturing wild tamarins.)

Vocabulary

canopy the high, sheltering, overlapping branches of rain forest trees

humid containing a large amount of water vapor

teeming full of things

habitat a natural environment where native creatures live

extinction having died out

predators animals that prey on others

diversity variety

poachers people who catch fish or hunt game illegally

❶ Whistling softly as she scans the upper canopy of leaves, Andreia Martins leads her sister Carolina and brother Renato through the rain forest. It is hot and humid. The small group is surrounded by the teeming life of the tropical forest.

Birds sing, insects buzz, cicadas chirp. Nearby they hear a tractor engine, cattle lowing, a rooster, and men at work on a *fazenda*, or "farm." They pick their way carefully along the narrow path to avoid the sharp spines of leaves and the tangle of vines underfoot.

Andreia raises her hand, and the group stops. Above them the leaves rustle and branches sway as streaks of orange-gold flash in the speckles of sunlight. "*Micos*," she whispers to the children, and points to the cluster of golden lion tamarins staring down at them from the branches of the trees. Their high-pitched whistles and squeaks pierce the air.

"Mico" is short for *mico leão dourado*, the Portuguese name for the golden lion tamarin of Brazil. About the size of a squirrel, the monkey is named for its color and lionlike mane.

630

ASSIGNMENT CARD 7

Exploring the Forest

Sensory Imagery

Sensory images are details an author uses to appeal to a reader's senses. Such imagery helps readers to visualize what they read. On the opening page of this selection, the author uses sensory imagery to give readers a strong impression of what the Brazilian rain forest looks, sounds, and feels like. Identify these details and tell what sense each one appeals to. Use a chart like the one below to record your answers.

Sound	Feeling	Sight

Theme 6: Animal Encounters

Teacher's Resource BLM page 92

The golden lion tamarin is found only in the coastal rain forest of southeastern Brazil. Flanked by a mountain range on the west and the Atlantic Ocean on the east, the forest once stretched for 1,500 miles.

When the first Europeans arrived, they cut down the trees to build their homes and towns. They burned the rest of the forest to clear the land for settlements, for coffee and sugar plantations, and for pastures on which to graze livestock. The city of Rio de Janeiro grew and spread. Today only 2 percent of the original rain forest remains, scattered like small islands in a sea of farms and towns.

❷ As its native habitat disappeared, so did the golden lion tamarin. By 1960 there were so few left that Dr. A. Coimbra-Filho, a Brazilian biologist, warned of its imminent extinction. He urged the Brazilian government to set aside the remaining forest as a wildlife refuge. The Poço das Antas Biological Reserve, a protected habitat, was established in 1973.

❸ The tall trees in the tropical rain forest offer the tamarins food, protection from predators, and a network of routes through their territories. The cupped centers of bromeliads, plants that live in host trees, hold water and insects for the monkeys to drink and eat. Tamarins are omnivorous. They eat not only fruits, seeds, and nuts but also bird eggs, insects, frogs, and snakes, which provide additional protein.

The rain forest is alive both day and night with a diversity of wildlife. Among the trees can be seen sloths and other species of monkeys.

❹ Tamarins must always be on guard for predators. Above them fly owls, while on the ground prowl ocelots, feral dogs, and — the most dangerous of all — humans. Poachers trap the tamarins and sell them in illegal animal markets for high prices. If discovered, these pets are confiscated and returned to the reserve.

631

English Language Learners

Language Development

Point out that in the rain forest there are many different sounds. Have students locate words that refer to sounds on page 630. *(sing, buzz, chirp, lowing, rustle, whistles, squeaks)* Encourage volunteers to demonstrate these sounds. Then tell students to look for other sound words as they read the selection.

Comprehension Preview

Topic, Main Idea, and Details

Teach

- Explain that the topic is the subject of a selection or paragraph.
- The main idea is the most important point about the topic. It can be stated or unstated.
- Details support or explain the main idea.

Practice

- Point out that the topic of this selection is the conservation of golden lion tamarins.
- Have students identify the topic of the second paragraph on page 631. (the destruction of the Brazilian rain forest)
- Ask students if there is a sentence that expresses the main idea. If so, which sentence? (yes; the last one)
- Have students identify details that support or explain this statement.

Apply

- Have students work in pairs to identify and list the topic, main idea, and supporting details of the third and fourth paragraphs on page 631.

Target Skill Trace	
Preview; Teach	p. 625S; p.628; p. 631; p. 647A
Reteach	p. R10
Review	pp. M32–M33; p. 611

CRITICAL THINKING
Guiding Comprehension

⑤ CAUSE AND EFFECT Why have captive tamarins lost the ability to survive in the wild? (They don't need survival skills in most zoo habitats.)

⑥ MAKING INFERENCES Why do you think a number is tattooed onto each tamarin at the National Zoo? (so staff members can track each animal)

COMPREHENSION STRATEGY
Monitor/Clarify

Teacher/Student Modeling Model using the Monitor/Clarify strategy.

- How could you clarify understanding about which skills captive-bred tamarins need for reintroduction into the wild? (read ahead)

- How could you get a better idea of where the tamarins live in the National Zoo? (look at the photo on page 633)

Have students read and monitor their comprehension of page 633.

Vocabulary

captive held against one's will

forage to search for food

reintroduction the process of returning animals to their native habitats

territorial protective of one's territory

simulate imitate

dilemma a situation in which one is given difficult choices to make

---

⑤ Today golden lion tamarins are bred in many zoos around the world. These animals do not have the skills to survive in the wild on their own. A captive tamarin lives in a confined space, climbs sturdy poles that don't move, and is served its food in a bowl at regular hours by a familiar keeper. It has never leaped from a vine to a delicate tree branch that sways under its weight. It doesn't know how to forage for its food. It hasn't experienced weather changes — cold, rain, thunder, and lightning. It would be killed by predators or get lost and starve. It needs the help of humans and that of native-born tamarins to learn to survive independently in its original habitat.

Since 1983, Dr. Benjamin Beck and his staff at the National Zoological Park in Washington, D.C., have been trying to find ways to prepare captive-born tamarins for their return to the rain forest. Dr. Beck coordinates the reintroduction of the tamarins into their natural habitat for the Golden Lion Tamarin Conservation Program.

⑥ The tamarins being reintroduced often come from other zoos and are examined carefully when they arrive at the National Zoo. A different number is tattooed onto each animal's leg and entered into a record of all the tamarins born in captivity.

632

Extra Support/Intervention

Strategy Modeling: Monitor/Clarify

If students need help with the strategy, use this example to model it.

On page 632, I read that the golden lion tamarins in zoos don't have the skills to survive in the wild. At first I didn't understand why people would risk returning them to the rain forest. I read ahead and learn that there are people who train the tamarins to live successfully in the wild.

As an experiment, tamarins are being permitted to live free in a wooded section of the zoo. Because they are territorial, they stay close to their nesting boxes, which are wired vertically high in the trees. The nesting box is a modified picnic cooler with two chambers inside, one above the other. In the top chamber is a hole through which the tamarins enter and leave. Should a predator attack, the tamarins huddle in the lower chamber, where a groping paw cannot reach them.

A tamarin claims its territory by rubbing a scent from its body onto tree limbs. The ones that will someday be reintroduced into the wild wear radio collars that transmit a constant beep, enabling the keepers to locate them in the woods. The tamarins are fed by food trays raised to the height of their nesting boxes.

Ropes are hung to simulate vines and to provide a network of treetop highways for the monkeys. The ropes and the nesting boxes are often changed while the tamarins are asleep to help prepare them for the unexpected.

The dilemma for the zoo is how to protect the animals and still expose them to the experiences and dangers they will meet in the wild.

633

Comprehension Review

Compare and Contrast

Review

- Remind students that to compare is to find similarities. To contrast is to find differences.

- Explain that identifying similarities and differences in nonfiction will help them better understand what they read.

Practice/Apply

- Have students reread pages 631–633.

- Draw a Venn diagram like the one shown below.

- Ask: What is the tamarins' rain forest habitat like? What is their zoo habitat like? What do these both have in common?

- Have students complete their own Venn diagrams. Then have students share their responses with the group.

Rain Forest Habitat
many predators, branches and vines form networks, forage for food

Both
homes high in trees, networks for travel

Zoo Habitat
no predators, ropes form networks, zoo workers provide food

Review Skill Trace	
Teach	Theme 4, p. 413A
Reteach	Theme 4, p. R12
▶ Review	p. 633; Theme 4, p. 403; Theme 5, p. 479

ASSIGNMENT CARD 8

Problem and Solution

Create a Chart

Scientists face several problems as they release tamarins into a wooded section of the National Zoo. They must come up with a solution for each one. Reread page 633. Make a chart like the one below, and use it to list each problem the scientists face and the solutions they have devised to overcome each of the problems listed. Compare your chart with those of your classmates when you are finished.

Problem	Solution
protect tamarins from predators	

Theme 6: Animal Encounters

CRITICAL THINKING

Guiding Comprehension

7 MAKING INFERENCES Why is it so important for observers to keep track of tamarins that are reintroduced into the wild? (It helps scientists learn how well the reintroduction process works.)

8 NOTING DETAILS What steps in the process of preparing the tamarins for reintroduction does the author describe? (releasing them into the simulated forest environment, moving them to Brazil, taking steps to strengthen their gene pool, observing them carefully throughout the whole process)

9 MAKING INFERENCES Why do you think the author calls the transported tamarins *immigrants*? (because they have left their home in the zoo to move to a new environment, the rain forest)

7   Observers watch and record everything the monkeys do. To tell the tamarins apart, they mark the tails with hair dye. Each member of the tamarin family has its own distinctive tail marking.

8   When the time is right, the monkeys are shipped by air from Washington, D.C., to Rio de Janeiro.

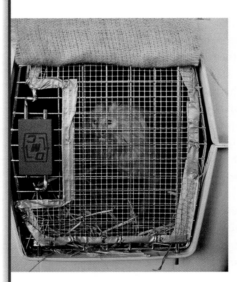

Andreia Martins is one of the many people in Brazil and abroad working to save the golden lion tamarin. She coordinates a team of observers who roam the rain forest, tracking tamarins and observing their behavior. The team's notes are sent to the National Zoo, where scientists in the conservation program use them to help prepare captive-born tamarins for their reintroduction into the rain forest.

In Rio de Janeiro, Andreia and Dionizio Moraes Pessamilio, director of the reserve, carry bags of fruit when they meet a shipment of seven tamarins that arrives from Washington, D.C.

634

Vocabulary

abroad out of one's own country; in foreign places

genes tiny pieces of matter in cells that carry the blueprints for a living thing's characteristics

observation watching or paying attention

REACHING ALL LEARNERS

Extra Support/ Intervention	On Level	Challenge

Review (pages 629–635)

Before students who need extra support join the whole class for Stop and Think on page 635, have them

- take turns modeling Monitor/Clarify and other strategies they used

- help you add to **Transparency 6–11**

- check and revise their Topic, Main Idea, and Details Chart on **Practice Book** page 222, and use it to summarize

Strategy Modeling: Monitor/Clarify

Use this example to model the strategy.

On page 635, I read that the tamarins were transported inside cages. Then the last sentence says that the tamarins are released into the cages where they will get used to the new surroundings. I am confused until I reread the last paragraph and learn that these are different cages. Now I understand.

After the overnight flight, the squealing monkeys are hungry, and they gobble up the pieces of fruit that Andreia and Dionizio squeeze into the cages. Then the noisy cages are loaded into a van for the two-hour trip to the reserve.

Golden lion tamarins tend to be monogamous, which means a male and female will live together and mate only with each other. This shipment includes a family of four from one zoo: the mother, the father, and a pair of one-year-old twins, one male and one female. The other three tamarins come from three different zoos and will be used to create new families.

Because there are so few tamarins left in the wild, they keep reproducing among themselves. Introducing animals that are born in distant zoos helps to strengthen the gene pool of the native tamarins. Genes carry the characteristics of a species from one generation to the next.

The van and the observation team meet on a narrow road in the forest. The tamarins are unloaded and carried into the woods, where large cages await the immigrants. They are released into the cages, where they will grow accustomed to their new surroundings.

635

ASSIGNMENT CARD 6

Literature Discussion

Discuss your own questions and the following questions with a group of your classmates:

- Have you ever seen a wild animal in its natural habitat? If so, describe the experience. If not, name an animal you would like to see in the wild, and tell why you want to.

- How do you think the needs of humans for wood, space, and other resources should be balanced with the needs of wild animals?

- Why do you think scientists keep careful records of all tamarins that are reintroduced to the wild?

- Why do you think some people buy wild animals illegally?

Theme 6: Animal Encounters

Teacher's Resource BLM page 91

Stop and Think

Critical Thinking Questions

1. **MAKING INFERENCES** How do you think scientists in Washington, D.C. use the notes from the observers? (The scientists use the notes about what the monkeys can and can't do in the wild to better prepare other tamarins.)

2. **DRAWING CONCLUSIONS** Why do you think the tamarins are first placed in cages at the Brazilian preserve? (They need time to adjust to the rain forest before they are released.)

Strategies in Action

Have students take turns modeling Monitor/Clarify and other strategies they used.

Discussion Options

You may wish to bring the entire class together to do one or more of the activities below.

- **Review Predictions/Purpose** Review students' predictions and what they have learned. Discuss students' questions, and review main ideas and details about tamarins.

- **Share Group Discussions** Have students share their literature discussions.

- **Summarize** Help students use their Topic, Main Idea, and Details Chart to summarize the story so far.

Monitoring Student Progress

If . . .	Then . . .
students have successfully completed the Extra Support activities on page 634,	have them read the rest of the selection cooperatively or independently.

Reading the Selection 635

CRITICAL THINKING

Guiding Comprehension

10 **TOPIC, MAIN IDEA, AND DETAILS** What is the topic of the last paragraph on page 636 and the first two paragraphs on page 637? (how Andreia's team cares for the tamarins)

11 **CAUSE AND EFFECT** How might learning to dig food out of holes in plastic tubes help the tamarins after their release? (It teaches them to probe for food in trees and logs, as they must in the wild.)

Everything is different: the heat, the tall trees, the noises. The tamarins will get to know their potential prey, such as the insects and small reptiles and mammals that scoot in and out of their cages. Beyond the cages stalk their predators, which they must learn to avoid.

10 The reserve is located a few kilometers from the town of Silva Jardim, where Andreia lives with her mother and ten brothers and sisters. Every morning Andreia and her sister Arleia, who is also an observer, cut up fruit and canned marmoset food. The canned food, which provides needed protein, is exactly what the tamarins ate in the zoo.

636

Vocabulary

potential future capability

marmoset any of various small Central and South American monkeys having thick fur and long tails

extract to pull out

camouflage material designed to look like part of the natural surroundings

The pieces of food are then stuffed into feeders made of plastic tubes wired together to make a square, with holes drilled along the tubes. Andreia crams bits of food into the holes. This encourages the tamarins to use their long fingers and nails to extract the food, just as they will probe in trees and rotted logs once they are released.

Meanwhile, Arleia fills canteens with water. By 7:30 A.M. the van is loaded with feeders and canteens. The sisters tuck their camouflage pants into their socks to keep out insects and jump into the van.

The Golden Lion Tamarin Conservation Program has provided many jobs for people in Silva Jardim. A small town, it is located near the main highway to Rio. The *praça*, or "plaza," with its tall shade trees, band-stand, and playground, sits in the center of town.

Andreia stops at the plaza to pick up more of the observation team. While waiting for them to arrive, she works out the assignment for each one. Every day, an observer is assigned to a different group of tamarins.

11

637

Fluency Practice

Rereading for Fluency Have students choose a favorite part of the story to reread to a partner, or suggest that they read page 637. Encourage students to read expressively.

Extra Support/Intervention

Strategy Modeling: Phonics/Decoding

Model the strategy using the word *predators*.

The first three letters of this word might be the prefix pre-, *but* pree-DAY-tuhrz *doesn't sound right. Maybe the first syllable includes the consonant* d, *which would make the* e *in that syllable short.* PREHD-uh-tuhrz *is a word I know, and it makes sense in the sentence.*

CRITICAL THINKING
Guiding Comprehension

12 **MAKING INFERENCES** Why do you think the author mentions that local farmers have come to accept the reintroduced tamarins? (to show that challenges to the conservation program can be overcome)

13 **DRAWING CONCLUSIONS** What clues does the author give that observing the tamarins is a challenging and even dangerous job? (Observers carry rain gear and snakebite kits; Observers must climb high in the trees to place the nesting boxes.)

COMPREHENSION STRATEGY
Monitor/Clarify

Student Modeling Have students model the strategy by pointing out any places on pages 636–639 where they needed to reread or read ahead to clarify information about how tamarins are reintroduced to the rainforest.

Vocabulary

hesitant reluctant

machete a large, heavy knife with a broad blade

fork a separation into two or more branches

tentative uncertain; hesitant

juvenile a young person or animal

socialize to take part in social activities with others

The observation team is split into two groups. One group goes to the reserve, while the other goes to the fazendas where tamarins have been reintroduced. Originally the *fazenderos*, or "farmers," were hesitant **12** about accepting the monkeys on their forest-land. But now they speak of them as "my micos."

Andreia drives through the forest, stopping every so often to drop off an observer. **13** Each carries a canteen and a machete on a belt, as well as a backpack with food, rain gear, a snakebite kit, and mosquito repellent. Everyone carries a compass, a digital watch, a notebook, and an antenna and radio receiver for tracking the tamarins. A full tamarin feeder, carried on the shoulder, completes the equipment each observer takes into the woods.

Today the newly arrived tamarin family of four will be released. They have spent enough time in the large cage to become accustomed to the climate of the rain forest. In addition to its own tail marking, each monkey has another mark on its body that identifies the family to which it belongs. One tamarin in the group wears a new radio collar.

Andreia and Paulo Caesar, another observer, carry the nesting box into the woods. They have selected a tree in an area that the tamarin family can claim as its own. Paulo Caesar nimbly climbs the tree with a rope and wire on his shoulder. When he reaches a fork about twenty feet above the ground, he drops one end of the rope to Andreia. She ties the end to the nesting box, and Paulo Caesar hoists it up and wires it in place. With the rope draped over a branch, he drops both ends to Andreia so she can raise a feeder up to the box. Finally, Paulo Caesar uncovers the opening of the nesting box and slides down to the ground. Then they both sit down to see what will happen.

638

ASSIGNMENT CARD 9
What Happens First?
Summarize Events Graphically

Reread page 638. Pay attention to the steps the observers take to prepare for the release of the tamarins into the wild. Summarize those steps in a flow chart or other graphic organizer that shows the order in which they occurred. Follow these steps:

- Read each paragraph carefully.
- On a piece of paper, jot down each step the observers take.
- Create an organizer, and list the steps in order in your chart.
- When you are finished, share your graphic organizer with your classmates.

Theme 6: Animal Encounters

Teacher's Resource BLM page 93

A young tamarin pokes its head out of the box, looks around, and squeals. Then the other golden heads appear to take a look. After some tentative moves, the juvenile darts out to the feeder, pokes into it, and stuffs food into its mouth.

Below, Andreia glances at her watch and writes in her notebook. For the first hour, she describes what the entire group is doing — the way they eat, socialize, and rest, and the sounds they make. Then she notes what each member of the family does.

In order not to give the tamarins human characteristics, the observers do not give them names. Instead they identify the monkeys by letters that represent the zoo they came from and numbers that symbolize their position in the group. For example, KO1 is the adult female from the zoo in Cologne, Germany, KO2 is the adult male, and KO3 and KO4 are their offspring.

639

Making Generalizations

Review

- Remind students that generalizations are broad statements that are based on facts and are true most of the time.

- Point out that words such as *most, many, all, always, generally, often,* and *never* often signal generalizations.

Practice/Apply

- Have students identify two generalizations in the first paragraph on page 638. (the third and fourth sentences)

- Ask students if these statements are likely to be true of all *fazenderos*. (probably not)

- Ask students what signal word could be added to make the generalization more valid, or true. (Sample answer: Originally many *fazenderos* were hesitant about accepting the monkeys on their forestland.)

- Have students find and read aloud other generalizations in the selection.

Review Skill Trace	
Teach	p. 623A
Reteach	p. R8
Review	p. 639; Theme 3, p. 277

English Language Learners

Supporting Comprehension

After reading page 639, pause and have students summarize Andreia's activities. Have students begin their summaries by looking back at page 634 and reviewing the photographs. Provide the following prompts: Where does Andreia bring new tamarins? Why does she use special feeders? What does Andreia write in her notebook?

Guiding Comprehension

14 **NOTING DETAILS** What details does the author include to show how difficult it is for the tamarins to adjust to the rain forest? (They may get lost, starve, or be injured or eaten. They don't know how to peel fruit.)

15 **MAKING INFERENCES** Why do you think the observers eventually place the feeders farther from the nest and also place fruit on saplings? (to force the tamarins to venture farther from the nest and to learn how to find food in the wild)

16 **DRAWING CONCLUSIONS** What clues on page 641 tell you that the author feels optimistic about the tamarins' chances for success in the wild? (He describes how infants of reintroduced tamarins do well in the wild.)

At first the newcomers stay close to their nesting box. Away from their new home, they may become disoriented and get lost. Alone, a newly reintroduced tamarin can die of starvation, become injured, or fall prey to a predator. **14**

This is when the tamarins need the most help. They are given plenty of food and water. Oranges and bananas are hung on branches for them. Because the tamarins have always eaten chopped fruit, they don't know how to peel whole fruit. The bananas are partially opened for them, and the oranges have "windows" cut into them.

As the months go by, the feeder is placed farther from the nesting box. Fruits are placed on saplings that will sway when the tamarins leap onto them. **15**

640

Extra Support/ Intervention	On Level	Challenge
Selection Review	**Literature Discussion**	

Selection Review

Before students join in Wrapping Up on page 641, have them

- take turns modeling the reading strategies they used

- help you complete **Transparency 6–11**

- complete their Topic, Main Idea, and Details Charts and summarize the whole selection

Literature Discussion

In mixed-ability small groups, have students discuss their predictions and their questions. Then have students discuss the Responding questions on page 642 of the Anthology.

When the tamarins begin to forage and eat natural foods, the observers reduce their visits to three times a week, then to once a week, and finally to once a month. When the tamarins become independent, all feeding is stopped.

Bit by bit, the family becomes familiar with the rain forest, the younger ones adapting faster than the parents. But only about 30 percent of all reintroduced tamarins survive more than two years. Some die by eating poisonous fruits or snakes. Some are killed by Africanized, or "killer," bees, which sometimes take over a nesting box to make a hive. The infants that are born in the wild fare much better than the reintroduced tamarins. They are more acrobatic and confident as they leap from limb to limb. They are able to deal with surprises, and they don't have to unlearn behaviors that were adequate for zoo life but are useless in the forest.

16

The goal of the Golden Lion Tamarin Conservation Program is to have two thousand tamarins living in the wild by the year 2025. For this to happen, the people who live in and around the rain forest have to help protect the tamarins and their environment. That way, human beings and tamarins will be able to share the Brazilian landscape for years to come.

641

Wrapping Up

Critical Thinking Questions

1. **MAKING JUDGMENTS** What qualities do you think an observer should have? Why? (patience, to watch the tamarin for a long time; knowledge of the rain forest, since tamarins live there)

2. **PREDICTING OUTCOMES** What do you think the Golden Lion Tamarin Conservation Program will have to do to reach its goal of placing 2,000 tamarins in the wild by 2025? (continue the tamarin training program; protect the tamarins' habitat)

Strategies in Action

Have students tell how and where they used the Monitor/Clarify strategy.

Discussion Options

Bring the entire class together to do one or more of the activities below.

Review Predictions/Purpose Discuss students' predictions and any revisions they made.

Share Group Discussions Have students share their literature discussions.

Summarize Ask students to use their Topic, Main Idea, and Details Charts to summarize the selection.

Comprehension Check

Use **Practice Book** page 223 to assess students' comprehension of the selection.

Monitoring Student Progress

If . . .	Then . . .
students score 8 or below on **Practice Book** page 223,	have them form small groups and reread relevant pages in the selection.

Practice Book page 223

The Golden Lion Tamarin
Comes Home
Comprehension Check

Name _____

The Lion Speaks

Fill in the blanks below with information from the story.

1. "I am a golden lion tamarin _____. My native home is in the rain forest of Brazil _____." (2 points)

2. "Unfortunately, humans have cut _____ down many trees and burned _____ much of the forest for their own use. Today I am in danger of extinction _____." (2)

3. "That is why biologists have established a protected habitat _____ for us in the rain forest. Because many of us are bred in zoos _____, however, we must learn new skills _____ before we go into the wild." (2)

4. "We are trained at the National _____ Zoo in Washington, D.C. _____. Then we are shipped to our native country, Brazil _____. There a team of observers _____ first releases us into cages _____ within the rain forest." (2)

5. "When we are ready, they let us out. They watch _____ us carefully and take detailed notes _____ describing our behavior. They also give us food _____ and water _____ until we learn to find these things on our own." (2)

6. "The juveniles _____ among us adapt the fastest. Today only about 30 _____ percent of us survive more than two years _____ in the wild. The Golden Lion Tamarin _____ Conservation Program hopes to have 2,000 _____ of us living in the wild by the year 2025 _____." (2)

Think About the Selection

Have students discuss or write their answers. Sample answers are provided; accept reasonable responses.

1. **MAKING JUDGMENTS** yes, because they needed wood for homes and land for towns, farms, and pastures; no, because the forest animals and plants also needed land

2. **DRAWING CONCLUSIONS** Tamarins born in captivity have to unlearn old habits and develop new skills. Animals born in the wild learn survival skills early on.

3. **NOTING DETAILS** From page 640: *Away from their new home, they may become disoriented and get lost. Alone, a newly introduced tamarin can die of starvation, become injured, or fall prey to a predator.*

4. **EXPRESSING PERSONAL OPINIONS** Answers will vary.

5. **EXPRESSING PERSONAL OPINIONS** Answers will vary.

6. **MAKING JUDGMENTS** Yes, it is a sign of success that any captive-born tamarins survive in the wild. Also, their native-born young will enjoy a better survival rate; No, the animals might not escape extinction if their survival rate does not improve.

7.  **Connecting/Comparing** Sample answers: grizzlies, because they have a larger population; tamarins, because many people are working to save them

---

Think About the Selection

1. Do you think the settlers' reasons for cutting down the rain forest were good ones? Why or why not?

2. Why do you think tamarins born in the wild do better than tamarins who return to the rain forest after living in captivity?

3. Find evidence in the text to support this idea: Tamarins need the most help just after they return to the rain forest.

4. Do you agree with the observers' decision on page 639 not to name the tamarins? Why or why not?

5. Would you want to be part of a conservation program? If so, what would you like to do? If not, why not?

6. Do you think the efforts to return tamarins to the forest are worthwhile, even though only 30% of them survive? Explain.

7. **Connecting/Comparing** Which animal's survival do you feel more hopeful about — the grizzly's or the golden lion tamarin's? Why

 **Informing**

Write a Fax Message

A conservation team leader might send a fax to tamarin observers. Write a fax that tells what jobs they will do, what equipment they will need, and where and when they will be picked up.

Tips
- Keep your message brief and clear.
- Include a cover page giving your name and the name of the person you're faxing.

642

English Language Learners

Supporting Comprehension

Beginning/Preproduction Have students mime a step in the reintroduction and care of the tamarins. Ask them questions about the process that can be answered by *yes* or *no*.

Early Production and Speech Emergence Have students look at the pictures in the selection and describe the tamarin's natural habitat.

Intermediate and Advanced Fluency Have students summarize the process of returning captive-born tamarins to the rain forest.

Science

Make a Fact Chart

Use the information in the selection to make a chart of facts about the golden lion tamarin. Create rows with category headings such as *Size, Color, Habitat, Food, Predators,* and *Family.* Then fill in the rows to show what you have learned.

Bonus Make a similar fact chart for another kind of monkey, and then compare the two animals.

Golden Lion Tamarin

Size	
Food	
Color	

Listening and Speaking

Give a Talk

Are you concerned about the golden lion tamarin? Do you agree that it should be returned to the rain forest? Use the selection to prepare a talk about the Golden Lion Tamarin Conservation Program and present it to your class.

Tips

- Use note cards instead of writing out your whole talk. Practice using your notes.
- Speak at an even pace. Be sure that everyone in your audience can hear you.

Internet

E-Mail a Friend

What did you learn from reading *The Golden Lion Tamarin Comes Home?* What did you think about what you read? Send an e-mail message to a friend, telling about the selection.

643

Additional Responses

Personal Response Invite students to share their personal responses to *The Golden Lion Tamarin Comes Home.*

Journal ▶ Ask students to write in their journals about what it would be like to work with the tamarins.

Selection Connections Remind students to add to **Practice Book** pages 199 and 200.

Practice Book page 199

Launching the Theme
Selection Connections

Name _____

Animal Encounters

The selections in this theme explore some special relationships between people and wild creatures. After reading each selection, fill in this chart to show what you learned.

	What kind of writing is the selection an example of?	What creature or creatures does the selection describe?
Grizzly Bear Family Book	first-person narrative nonfiction **(2.5 points)**	grizzly bears **(2.5)**
The Golden Lion Tamarin Comes Home	expository nonfiction **(2.5)**	golden lion tamarins **(2.5)**
My Side of the Mountain	fiction **(2.5)**	many small creatures of the forest, such as raccoons and a falcon **(2.5)**

Practice Book page 200

Launching the Theme
Selection Connections

Name _____

Animal Encounters continued

	What is the purpose of the encounter between humans and animals?	What are the results of the encounter?
Grizzly Bear Family Book	Michio Hoshino wants to learn as much as he can about grizzly bears. He wants to photograph them. **(2.5)**	People learn more about grizzly bears and how they live. **(2.5)**
The Golden Lion Tamarin Comes Home	The people of the Golden Lion Tamarin Conservation Program want to return golden lion tamarins to the forests where they naturally live. **(2.5)**	The golden lion tamarin population increases in the rain forest of Brazil. The monkeys are protected in the preserve. **(2.5)**
My Side of the Mountain	Sam wants to experience the wilderness and be self-sufficient in it. He sees the animals as companions and even friends. **(2.5)**	Sam learns more about himself and about the creatures with whom he shares his woodland home. **(2.5)**

What are some ways in which people can help wild animals? **(2)**
People can help wild animals in zoos learn to live in the wild again. People can
protect wild animals' natural habitats. People can teach others about wild animals
to try to get them to care about the animals and understand their needs.

Monitoring Student Progress

End-of-Selection Assessment

Selection Test Use the test on page 151 in the **Teacher's Resource Blackline Masters** to assess selection comprehension and vocabulary.

Student Self-Assessment Have students assess their reading with additional questions such as

- Which parts of this selection were difficult? Why?
- What strategies helped me understand the story?
- Would I recommend this story to my friends? Why?

Responding 643

Technology Link

Skill: How to Read a Technology Article

- **Introduce** "Tuning in on Animals," a technology article about tracking animals.

- **Discuss** the Skill Lesson on Anthology page 644.

- **Model** reading the first two paragraphs to identify the topic of the article. (tracking animals) Then model how to read the diagram on page 647.

- **Explain** that using a K-W-L Chart will help students get the information they want from the article. Draw a K-W-L Chart like the one below on the board.

- **Set a purpose** for reading. First, have students help fill in the top K and W boxes. Then, have the students copy the chart, fill in more K and W boxes, and read to find answers for the L column.

K	W	L
What I Know	What I Want to Learn	What I Learned
Animal tracking means locating and monitoring wild animals.	What methods have scientists come up with to track animals today?	

Vocabulary

receiver the unit of a communications system, such as a radio or television, that receives an incoming signal and converts it into sound or light

transmitter a device used in a communications system that generates a signal and sends it forth by means of an antenna

Technology Link

Skill: How to Read a Technology Article

Before you read . . .

- Identify the **topic** of the article.

- Look through the article for **diagrams** or **illustrations** that help explain the technology.

As you read . . .

- If you come to an unfamiliar **term**, try rereading or reading ahead to find its definition.

- If you come to an unfamiliar **abbreviation**, scan back to the first time it appears. The full name is usually given there.

644

Tuning in on Animals

Golden lion tamarins are not the only species scientists are listening to. New technologies have changed the way we keep in touch with animals, and have taught us surprising things about their behavior.

In the fall of 1994, a Florida manatee, an endangered sea mammal, was spotted off the coast of Maryland. Scientists know that manatees migrate north over the summer, but they were puzzled that this one had not returned south yet. Clearly there was a lot more they needed to know about manatees. They caught the animal, but before bringing it back to Florida waters, they fitted it with a special radio collar around the base of its tail. From this collar, the scientists could track the manatee's movements and location and learn more about manatee migration.

Animal tracking means following the location of an animal as it walks, runs, swims, or flies. By tracking many single animals over time, scientists can learn how a whole species migrates with the seasons. They also learn details about animal behavior that may help them in protecting endangered species.

Tags and Telemetry

The simplest way to track an animal is to follow one and keep it in view. But physically tracking an animal is not always possible. (Think of how quickly a bird can fly out of sight.) So, almost two hundred years ago, researchers began catching individual animals, fitting them with tags, and letting them go. This method was better, but still flawed: if scientists wanted to learn about the animal, they would have to catch it again later.

The next development was *telemetry* — using radio signals to track animals.

Here's an example of how it works. A single animal, such as a lynx, is fitted with a small device that transmits a radio signal. Using a receiver, scientists pick up the signals from a distance on land or from an airplane. Over days or weeks, they chart where the lynx goes. This method is still used today, but it has limitations. The receiver must be within a few hundred yards of the transmitter. And telemetry won't work everywhere. Radio signals cannot penetrate heavy jungle vegetation or below the surface of the ocean.

Once this lynx is fitted with a radio transmitter (left), it can be tracked using a portable radio antenna and receiver (above).

645

REACHING ALL LEARNERS

Extra Support/Intervention

Keeping Track of Tracking Methods

Suggest that as students read they keep a list about the methods scientists have developed to track animals. They can also note the problems or drawbacks of each method.

Satellite Signals

Perhaps the most accurate and powerful type of animal tracking today is the Global Positioning System (GPS). This system uses 26 satellites orbiting 11,000 miles above the earth to follow the animals being tracked.

Instead of carrying a transmitter, a waved albatross, for example, would be fitted with a receiver. At regular intervals, the receiver automatically selects the four GPS satellites that are closest to the albatross. The receiver picks up the signals from these satellites and passes them on to a computer. The computer then calculates the position of the albatross by processing the information collected from the four satellites. The location that the GPS system calculates is accurate, on average, to within 30 meters (33 yards).

Satellite tracking has revealed fascinating and important information about many kinds of animals. Scientists have learned that albatross parents fly thousands of miles to find food for a single chick.

They have discovered that leatherback turtles swim more than a thousand miles in the open sea, along routes that they return to again and again. And studies have shown that great white sharks hunt around the clock, not just in the daytime as researchers had previously believed.

Scientists are constantly working on improvements in animal tracking. One group of researchers fits sharks with special tags that relay information to receivers on buoys floating in the water. Radio transmitters as light as seven-tenths of an ounce can be attached to even very small birds, and scientists are working to make them still lighter.

Perhaps the most exciting aspect of present-day animal tracking is that, using the Internet, anyone can find out the most up-to-date information that scientists are gathering. By logging onto the Web sites of animal trackers, you can learn where an animal goes each month or week, or even every day. And maybe the next time a manatee surfaces in an unusual place, you'll be one of the first to know.

To feed their young, albatrosses scan the ocean for fish. Trackers scan for albatrosses.

646

Vocabulary

calculates finds an answer or a result by using mathematics

buoys floats

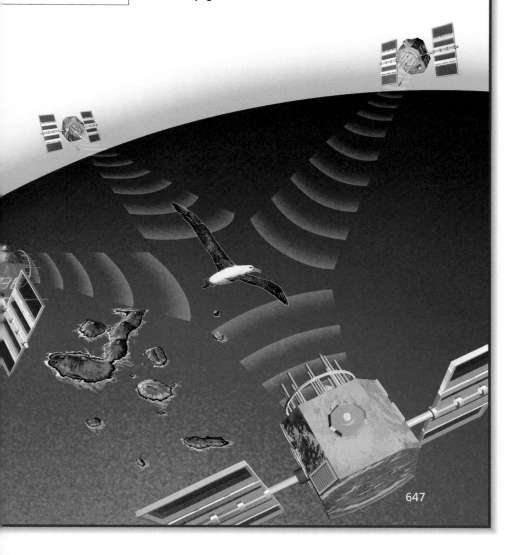

In GPS tracking, 26 satellites with transmitters orbit the Earth (left). At regular intervals, the four satellites closest to a waved albatross (below) send signals to the bird's receiver, which records its location.

Using this data, biologists with the Albatross Project are able to track the flights of waved albatrosses with great accuracy from the birds' breeding site on tiny Española, one of the Galapagos Islands off the coast of Ecuador.

647

Challenge

Research

Have students visit Education Place at **www.eduplace.com/kids** and locate links that provide up-to-date information about animal tracking. Ask them to work individually or in pairs, and to visit the links on at least three different days. Then ask students to write a summary of what they learned there. They can share their summaries with the class.

Wrapping Up

Critical Thinking Questions

Ask students to use the article to answer these questions.

1. **MAKING INFERENCES** Why might it be helpful for scientists to know that leatherback turtles migrate along special routes in the open sea? (It helps them make rules for protecting turtles in that area.)

2. **MAKING INFERENCES** Why do you think humans put time, energy, and resources into protecting animals? (Sample answer: Many people love animals; Animals are an important part of life on earth.)

3. **COMPARE AND CONTRAST** How does the tracking technology used to monitor tamarins in the wild compare to the GPS technology? (The tamarins wear radio transmitters on their collars, while animals tracked with the GPS technology wear receivers and are located by satellite.)

OBJECTIVES

- Identify the topic, main ideas, and details in a selection.
- Identify the main idea and key details in a paragraph or passage.
- Learn academic language: *topic, main idea, details.*

Target Skill Trace

Preview; Teach	pp. 624S; 628; 631; p. 647A
Reteach	p. R10
Review	pp. M32–M33; p. 611
See	*Extra Support Handbook,* pp. 216–217; pp. 222–223

Transparency 6–11

Get the Idea?

Entries will vary. Samples are shown.

Topic: The conservation of golden lion tamarins

(Page 630) Main Idea: The native habitat of the tamarins is a diverse, colorful environment.

Details: Birds sing, insects buzz, cicadas chirp; tangled vines and leaves; orange-gold flash; speckles of sunlight.

(Pages 632–633) Main Idea: Captive-born tamarins need special training before being reintroduced into the wild.

Details:

(Pages 634–637) Main Idea: The observers prepare thoroughly before bringing the tamarins into the wild.

Details:

(Page 638) Main Idea: The observers carefully follow certain steps when releasing the tamarins.

Details:

(Pages 640–641) Main Idea: The observers gradually give less assistance as the tamarins adapt to their environment.

Details:

TRANSPARENCY 6–11
TEACHER'S EDITION PAGES 628 AND 647A

ANIMAL ENCOUNTERS The Golden Lion Tamarin
Graphic Organizer Topic, Main Idea, and Details Chart
ANNOTATED VERSION

Practice Book page 222

Name _____

The Golden Lion Tamarin Comes Home

Graphic Organizer Topic, Main Idea, and Details Chart

Get the Idea?

What are the main ideas of this selection? As you read, find the main ideas on the pages listed below. Then fill in the chart with the main idea and the details that support each main idea. Entries will vary. Samples are shown.

Topic: The conservation of golden lion tamarins.

(Page 630) Main Idea: The native habitat of the tamarins is a diverse, colorful environment. (1)

Details: Birds sing, insects buzz, cicadas chirp; tangled vines and leaves; orange-gold flash; speckles of sunlight. (1)

(Pages 632–633) Main Idea: Captive-born tamarins need special training before being reintroduced into the wild. (1)

Details: (1)

(Pages 634–637) Main Idea: The observers prepare thoroughly before bringing the tamarins into the wild. (1)

Details: (1)

(Page 638) Main Idea: The observers carefully follow certain steps when releasing the tamarins. (1)

Details: (1)

(Pages 640–641) Main Idea: The observers gradually give less assistance as the tamarins adapt to their environment. (1)

Details: (1)

COMPREHENSION: Topic, Main Idea, and Supporting Details

TARGET SKILL

❶ Teach

Review topic, main idea, and supporting details. Remind students that they will read with better understanding if they focus on the relationship among topic, main idea, and details.

- The topic is the subject of a selection or paragraph.
- A main idea is the most important idea or point about the topic.
- Key details support or explain the main idea.
- Sometimes a main idea is stated directly in a sentence. Other times it must be inferred from details.

Review topic, main idea, and supporting details in *The Golden Lion Tamarin Comes Home*. Display **Transparency 6–11.** (Sample answers are shown.) Discuss the topic of the selection and the main ideas and supporting details on each page. Students may refer to **Practice Book** page 222.

Model inferring a main idea from details. Use the third paragraph on page 633 as an example of an unstated main idea.

Think Aloud *The first sentence describes how scientists use ropes to simulate vines, and the second tells how they try to prepare the tamarins for the unexpected. The main idea isn't stated—only these details. But after thinking about what these details have in common, I can infer the main idea: "Scientists use different methods to prepare the tamarins for life in the wild."*

❷ Guided Practice

Have students identify main ideas and details. Have students read the first paragraph on page 632 and identify the main idea. Then have partners complete a chart like the one below.

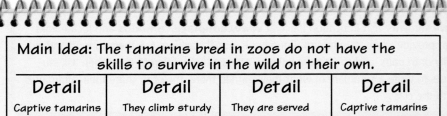

Main Idea: The tamarins bred in zoos do not have the skills to survive in the wild on their own.			
Detail	**Detail**	**Detail**	**Detail**
Captive tamarins live in confined spaces; they have never experienced weather changes.	They climb sturdy poles; they have never leaped from a vine to a tree branch.	They are served food in a bowl by a keeper, and do not know how to forage for food.	Captive tamarins need the help of humans. Otherwise, they could be killed, get lost, or starve.

❸ Apply

Assign Practice Book pages 224–225. Also have students apply this skill as they read their **Leveled Readers** for this week. You may also select books from the Leveled Bibliography for this theme, pages 594E–594F.

✔️ **Test Prep** Tell students that when there is a nonfiction passage on a test, there will usually be questions about topic, main idea, and supporting details. Suggest that as soon as they realize that they are reading a nonfiction passage, they should start looking for these elements.

Leveled Readers and Leveled Practice

Students at all levels apply the comprehension skill as they read their Leveled Readers. See lessons on pages 647O–647R.

● **BELOW LEVEL** ▲ **ON LEVEL** ■ **ABOVE LEVEL** ◆ **LANGUAGE SUPPORT**

Reading Traits

As students develop the ability to identify topic, main idea, and details, they are learning to "read the lines" of a selection. This comprehension skill supports the reading trait **Establishing Comprehension**.

Practice Book page 224

Name _____

The Golden Lion Tamarin Comes Home

Comprehension Skill Topic, Main Ideas, and Details

Mind the Main Idea

Read the passage. Then complete the activity on page 225.

The Decline of the Tiger

Once, many different types of tigers roamed throughout Asia. These were the Indian, Indochinese, Chinese, Siberian, Sumatran, Caspian, Javan, and Balinese tigers. Today, three of these eight types are extinct and several of the others are rare. Wild tigers can still be found only in some parts of Southeast Asia and Siberia.

Two main factors have caused the decline of tiger populations. One factor is the destruction of tigers' habitats. In central Asia, for example, farmers burned wooded areas along waterways to clear the land for farming. Thousands of acres of forest were also set on fire. As a result, much of the tigers' natural prey disappeared. Without enough food to support their roughly four-hundred-pound bodies, the tigers have disappeared as well.

Hunting is the second factor that has caused the decline of tiger populations. With the loss of their habitats and natural prey, tigers began to hunt closer to people. Farmers shot them to protect their livestock. Others hunted them for sport or for their fur.

Today, efforts are being made in many regions to protect wild tigers. India and Nepal have set aside reserves for them. Many countries have outlawed the import or sale of tiger skins. Successful captive breeding programs in zoos are also helping to ensure that the survival of these great cats continues.

Practice Book page 225

Name _____

The Golden Lion Tamarin Comes Home

Comprehension Skill Topic, Main Ideas, and Details

Mind the Main Idea *continued*

Answer the questions below. Use information from the passage on page 224. Sample answers are shown.

1. What is the topic of the passage? tigers **(3 points)**
2. Write the main idea or supporting details of the following paragraphs below.

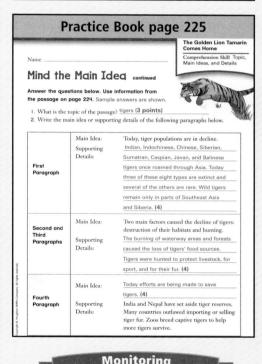

First Paragraph	Main Idea:	Today, tiger populations are in decline.
	Supporting Details:	Indian, Indochinese, Chinese, Siberian, Sumatran, Caspian, Javan, and Balinese tigers once roamed through Asia. Today three of these eight types are extinct and several of the others are rare. Wild tigers remain only in parts of Southeast Asia and Siberia. **(4)**
Second and Third Paragraphs	Main Idea:	Two main factors caused the decline of tigers: destruction of their habitats and hunting.
	Supporting Details:	The burning of waterway areas and forests caused the loss of tigers' food sources. Tigers were hunted to protect livestock, for sport, and for their fur. **(4)**
Fourth Paragraph	Main Idea:	Today efforts are being made to save tigers. **(4)**
	Supporting Details:	India and Nepal have set aside tiger reserves. Many countries outlawed importing or selling tiger fur. Zoos breed captive tigers to help more tigers survive.

Monitoring Student Progress

If . . .	Then . . .
students score 11 or below on **Practice Book** page 225,	use the Reteaching lesson on Teacher's Edition page R10.
students have successfully met the lesson objectives,	have them do the Challenge/Extension activities on Teacher's Edition page R11.

OBJECTIVES

- Read words with three syllables.
- Use the Phonics/Decoding Strategy to decode longer words.

Target Skill Trace

Teach	p. 647C
Reteach	p. R16
Review	pp. M34–M35
See	Handbook for English Language Learners, p. 219; Extra Support Handbook, pp. 214–215; pp. 218–219

TARGET SKILL

STRUCTURAL ANALYSIS/ VOCABULARY: Three-Syllable Words

❶ Teach

Introduce three-syllable words. Remind students that they have learned many tools to help them decode three-syllable words.

- Tools include looking for base words and using various syllabication patterns.
- Using the most obvious syllabication will not always help to decode the word.

Explain the three-syllable word *plantation*. Write *They burned the forest for sugar* <u>plantations</u>.

- Readers might recognize the base word *plant* in *plantations*, and divide and pronounce the word as *plant-AY-shuhnz*.
- Because this word has the VCCV pattern, it is divided in a different way: *plan-TAY-shuhnz*.

Model the Phonics/Decoding Strategy. Write *Each member of the tamarin family has its own* <u>distinctive</u> *tail marking*. Model decoding *distinctive*.

Think Aloud *I recognize the base word* distinct. *I'll try saying the whole word, dih-STIHNGKT-ihv. That doesn't sound quite right. The base word is not always divided the same way in a longer word, so I'll try saying dih-STIHNGK-tihv. That sounds right, and it makes sense in the sentence.*

❷ Guided Practice

Have students decode three-syllable words. Display the phrases below. Call on volunteers to try different strategies for decoding the underlined three-syllable words and figuring out their meanings.

<u>permitted</u> to live free

<u>assignment</u> for each one

<u>potential</u> prey

after some <u>tentative</u> moves

❸ Apply

Assign Practice Book page 226.

Practice Book page 226

Name _____

The Golden Lion Tamarin Comes Home

Structural Analysis Three-Syllable Words

Syllable Sensations

Read the sentences. Then circle the correct way to divide the syllables of the underlined word. Check the syllable pattern that applies to the word.

	VCV	VCCV
1. In zoos, ropes are hung to <u>simulate</u> vines for the tamarins. si/mul/ate (sim/u/late) (1 point)	✔ (1)	
2. Nesting boxes are made for the tamarins from <u>modified</u> picnic coolers. (mod/i/fied) mod/if/ied (1)	✔ (1)	
3. After returning to the rain forest, the tamarins grow <u>accustomed</u> to their new surroundings. (ac/cus/tomed) (1) acc/ust/omed		✔ (1)
4. As <u>immigrants</u>, the newly arrived tamarins have a great deal to learn. imm/ig/rants (im/mi/grants) (1)		✔ (1)
5. Human <u>observers</u> watch and record everything the tamarins do. (ob/ser/vers) (1) obs/erv/ers		✔ (1)
6. Bit by bit, the tamarins become <u>familiar</u> with the rain forest. (fa/mil/iar) (1) fam/i/liar	✔ (1)	
7. Older tamarins must unlearn behaviors that were <u>adequate</u> for zoo life but are useless in the forest. a/deq/uate (ad/e/quate) (1)	✔ (1)	

Monitoring Student Progress

If . . .	Then . . .
students score 10 or below on **Practice Book** page 226,	use the Reteaching lesson on Teacher's Edition page R16.

PHONICS REVIEW:
Consonant Alternations

OBJECTIVES

- Read pairs of words with consonant alterations.
- Use the Phonics/Decoding Strategy to decode longer words.

❶ Teach

Review consonant alternations. Tell students that the same consonant in related words can be pronounced differently.

- Silent consonants can become sounded, as in *sign* and *signal*.
- The letter *c* can change between the /s/ and the /k/ sound, as in *practice* and *practical*.
- The letter *t* can change to the /ch/ or /sh/ sound, as in *fact* and *factual*.

Model the Phonics/Decoding Strategy. Write *Tamarins have long nails for the* <u>extraction</u> *of food.* Model decoding *extraction*.

Think Aloud *In the base word, I recognize the prefix* ex- *and I can sound out* trakt. *When I sound out the whole word the way it looks, I get* ihk-STRAKT-eeuhn. *That doesn't sound right. Sometimes the letter* t *changes sounds, so I'll try* ihk-STRAK-shuhn. *That sounds familiar, and it makes sense.*

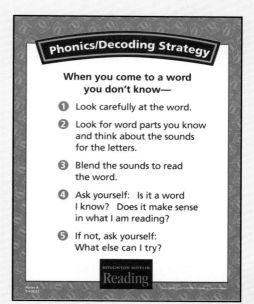

Phonics/Decoding Strategy

When you come to a word you don't know—

❶ Look carefully at the word.

❷ Look for word parts you know and think about the sounds for the letters.

❸ Blend the sounds to read the word.

❹ Ask yourself: Is it a word I know? Does it make sense in what I am reading?

❺ If not, ask yourself: What else can I try?

HOUGHTON MIFFLIN
Reading

❷ Guided Practice

Help students decode words with consonant alternations. Write these sentences. Have students circle the letter that changes sound in the underlined words. Have volunteers pronounce the words and check to see if the words make sense in the sentences.

1. Biologists warned of its imminent <u>extinction</u>. She didn't want them to become <u>extinct</u>.
2. The tamarins are being <u>reintroduced</u> in their native habitat. She is part of the <u>reintroduction</u> program.
3. Vines are used to <u>simulate</u> a forest. The <u>simulation</u> is very convincing.
4. The <u>creation</u> of new families is a goal of the zoos. They hope to <u>create</u> a viable population in the wild.

❸ Apply

Have students use words with consonant alternations. Have students decode these word pairs and use each word in a sentence.

protected/protection	critic/criticize
depart/departure	edit/edition
bomb/bombard	contaminate/contamination
locate/location	part/partial

SPELLING: Three-Syllable Words

OBJECTIVES

- Write Spelling Words that have three syllables.

SPELLING WORDS

Basic

dangerous*	potato
history	natural*
vacation	sensitive
popular	energy
favorite	emotion
memory	period
personal	property
educate	condition
regular*	imagine
continue	attention

Review	**Challenge**
together*	juvenile*
beautiful	astonish
library	ovation
hospital	amateur
another*	obvious

Forms of these words appear in the literature.

Extra Support/ Intervention

Basic Word List You may want to use only the left column of Basic Words with students who need extra support.

Challenge

Challenge Word Practice Ask students to use the Challenge Words to write a short review of a live performance they have seen.

DAY 1 INSTRUCTION

Three-Syllable Words

Pretest Use the Day 5 Test sentences.

Teach Tell students that to spell three-syllable words, they can divide the words into syllables, paying attention to syllables with less stress.

- Write *vacation* and *educate* on the board. Have students repeat them.
- Draw lines to syllabicate the words, and underline the stressed syllables. (va|<u>ca</u>|tion, <u>ed</u>|u|cate)
- Point out that in each word, one syllable is stressed and two have less stress. Mention that three-syllable words are usually stressed on the first or second syllable.
- Erase the board; write these column heads: *Stressed First Syllable; Stressed Second Syllable*. Have students say each Basic Word and identify the stressed syllable. Write the word below the correct head.

Practice/Homework Assign **Practice Book** page 281.

Practice Book page 281

Take-Home Word List	Take-Home Word List	Take-Home Word List
Animal Encounters Spelling Review	My Side of the Mountain	The Golden Lion Tamarin Comes Home
	Words with -ent, -ant; -able, -ible	Three-Syllable Words
	/ent/ → student, merchant	va|ca|tion /va kā' shən/
	/ə bəl/ → suitable, possible	ed|u|cate /ěj' ə kāt/
Spelling Words		dan|ger|ous /dăn' jər əs/
1. excite 16. preserve	**Spelling Words**	e|mo|tion /ĭ mō' shən/
2. concern 17. dangerous	1. fashionable 11. absent	
3. imagine 18. vacation	2. comfortable 12. vacant	**Spelling Words**
4. continue 19. terrible	3. different 13. servant	1. dangerous 11. potato
5. enforce 20. accident	4. suitable 14. valuable	2. history 12. natural
6. propose 21. complete	5. merchant 15. accident	3. vacation 13. sensitive
7. condition 22. regular	6. profitable 16. horrible	4. popular 14. energy
8. resident 23. potato	7. student 17. honorable	5. favorite 15. emotion
9. possible 24. laughable	8. possible 18. reasonable	6. memory 16. period
10. fashionable 25. remarkable	9. resident 19. remarkable	7. personal 17. property
11. consist 26. proverb	10. terrible 20. laughable	8. educate 18. condition
12. prefix 27. natural		9. regular 19. imagine
13. sensitive 28. emotion		10. continue 20. attention
14. suitable 29. merchant	**Challenge Words**	**Challenge Words**
15. vacant 30. enclose	1. excellent 4. durable	1. juvenile 4. amateur
	2. prominent 5. reversible	2. astonish 5. obvious
	3. extravagant	3. ovation
See the back for Challenge Words.		
My Study List Add your own spelling words on the back.	**My Study List** Add your own spelling words on the back.	**My Study List** Add your own spelling words on the...

Take-Home Word List

DAY 2 REVIEW & PRACTICE

Reviewing the Principle

Go over the principle of three-syllable words with students.

Practice/Homework Assign **Practice Book** page 227.

Practice Book page 227

The Golden Lion Tamarin Comes Home

Spelling Three-Syllable Words

Name _____

Three-Syllable Words

A three-syllable word has one stressed syllable and two syllables with less stress. To help you spell the word, divide it into its syllables. Note the spelling of the syllables that have less stress.

va | ca | tion /vă kā' shən/
ed | u | cate /ěj' ə kāt/

Write each Spelling Word under the heading that names its stressed syllable. Order of answers for each category may vary.

Stressed First Syllable

dangerous (1 point)	regular (1)
history (1)	natural (1)
popular (1)	sensitive (1)
favorite (1)	energy (1)
memory (1)	period (1)
personal (1)	property (1)
educate (1)	

Stressed Second Syllable

vacation (1)	condition (1)
continue (1)	imagine (1)
potato (1)	attention (1)
emotion (1)	

Spelling Words

1. dangerous
2. history
3. vacation
4. popular
5. favorite
6. memory
7. personal
8. educate
9. regular
10. continue
11. potato
12. natural
13. sensitive
14. energy
15. emotion
16. period
17. property
18. condition
19. imagine
20. attention

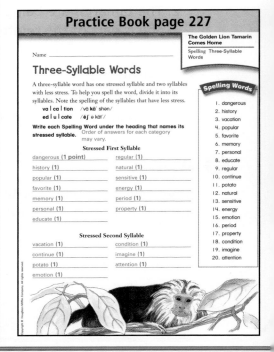

DAY 3 VOCABULARY

Clipped Words

Write *popular* on the board.

- Ask students to suggest a shorter word made from *popular* that makes sense in this sentence: They are famous _____ singers. (*pop*)

- Explain that *pop* in this context is a clipped word, a shortened form of a longer word.

- Ask students to supply the clipped form of each of these words: *graduate, dormitory, limousine, newspaper, influenza.* (*grad, dorm, limo, paper, flu*)

- List the Basic Words on the board. Have students use each word orally in a sentence. (Sentences will vary.)

Practice/Homework For spelling practice, assign **Practice Book** page 228.

Practice Book page 228

Name _____

The Golden Lion Tamarin Comes Home
Spelling Three-Syllable Words

Spelling Spree

Syllable Scramble Rearrange the syllables to write a Spelling Word. One syllable in each item is extra.

1. ue con gel tin   1. continue (1 point)
2. gy ro en er   2. energy (1)
3. po to tion ta   3. potato (1)
4. at tion men ten   4. attention (1)
5. let vor fa ite   5. favorite (1)
6. sen ring tive si 6. sensitive (1)
7. u ed gan cate   7. educate (1)

Word Maze Begin at the arrow and follow the Word Maze to find eight Spelling Words. Write the words in order.

8. regular (1)   12. personal (1)
9. imagine (1)   13. popular (1)
10. emotion (1)   14. memory (1)
11. dangerous (1) 15. vacation (1)

Spelling Words
1. dangerous
2. history
3. vacation
4. popular
5. favorite
6. memory
7. personal
8. educate
9. regular
10. continue
11. potato
12. natural
13. sensitive
14. energy
15. emotion
16. period
17. property
18. condition
19. imagine
20. attention

DAY 4 PROOFREADING

Game: What's My Word?

Have students work in even-numbered groups. Ask the groups to make cards for the Basic Words, leaving space on each card to write a sentence or two. Then ask each group to split into 2 teams, and tell each team to randomly choose 10 cards. Team members add a riddle or meaning clue to each card.

- To play, a member of Team 1 picks a card and reads the clue aloud to Team 2, who try to guess the word and spell it correctly.

- Teams alternate giving each other clues.

- Each correctly guessed and spelled word earns a point, and the higher-scoring team wins.

Practice/Homework For proofreading and writing practice, assign **Practice Book** page 229.

Practice Book page 229

Name _____

The Golden Lion Tamarin Comes Home
Spelling Three-Syllable Words

Proofreading and Writing

Proofreading Circle the five misspelled Spelling Words in this brochure. Then write each word correctly.

The golden lion tamarin has a sad (histrey). Over a (perriod) of years, much of Brazil's rain forest was cut down. The tamarin, therefore, was driven out of its (naturel) habitat. Most of the forest was turned into private (propety.) Brazil's government has now set aside some of the remaining forest as a wildlife refuge. Since then, the tamarins' (condishun) has improved. There is still much to be done, however. Won't you help us continue our work?

1. history (1 point)   4. property (1)
2. period (1)   5. condition (1)
3. natural (1)

Spelling Words
1. dangerous
2. history
3. vacation
4. popular
5. favorite
6. memory
7. personal
8. educate
9. regular
10. continue
11. potato
12. natural
13. sensitive
14. energy
15. emotion
16. period
17. property
18. condition
19. imagine
20. attention

Write an Opinion Only three out of every ten reintroduced tamarins survive for more than two years in the wild. Do you think the time and money spent in this effort is worth it? Why or why not?

On a separate piece of paper, write your opinion of the Golden Lion Tamarin Conservation Program. Use Spelling Words from the list. Responses will vary. (5)

DAY 5 ASSESSMENT

Spelling Test

Say each underlined word, read the sentence, and then repeat the word. Have students write only the underlined word.

Basic Words

1. Swimming alone is **dangerous**.
2. I'm studying the **history** of popular music.
3. She took a **vacation** to China.
4. Everyone reads that **popular** magazine.
5. Dan tore his **favorite** shirt.
6. An actor needs a good **memory**.
7. Don't ask me any **personal** questions.
8. A teacher's job is to **educate** students.
9. Lunch today will be at the **regular** time.
10. The game will **continue** later today.
11. Sue ordered a baked **potato** for lunch.
12. Eating **natural** foods helps me stay healthy.
13. My skin is **sensitive** to the sun.
14. Exercise increases my **energy**.
15. The actor showed no **emotion**.
16. Should I use a **period** or a question mark?
17. This seaside **property** belongs to me.
18. My bike is in good **condition**.
19. I can't **imagine** a better movie.
20. Mrs. Dasho tried to get our **attention**.

Challenge Words

21. Children's books are in the **juvenile** section.
22. This trick will **astonish** you.
23. The singer received an **ovation**.
24. She acts with an **amateur** theater group.
25. The mistake is **obvious**.

OBJECTIVES

- Use a dictionary to find out that some words have more than one acceptable pronunciation.

Target Skill Trace

Teach	p. 647G
Extend	p. R17
Review	pp. M36–M37
See	*Handbook for English Language Learners*, p. 223

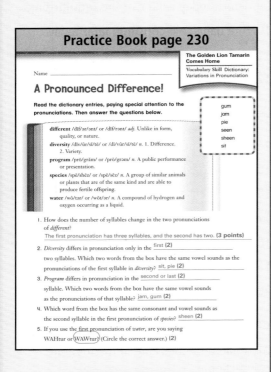

Practice Book page 230

Name _____

The Golden Lion Tamarin Comes Home

Vocabulary Skill Dictionary: Variations in Pronunciation

A Pronounced Difference!

Read the dictionary entries, paying special attention to the pronunciations. Then answer the questions below.

gum
jam
pie
seen
sheen
sit

different /dĭf/ər/ənt/ or /dĭf/rənt/ *adj.* Unlike in form, quality, or nature.
diversity /dĭv/ûr/sĭ/tē/ or /dī/vûr/sĭ/tē/ *n.* 1. Difference. 2. Variety.
program /prō/grăm/ or /prō/grəm/ *n.* A public performance or presentation.
species /spē/shēz/ or /spē/sēz/ *n.* A group of similar animals or plants that are of the same kind and are able to produce fertile offspring.
water /wô/tər/ or /wŏt/ər/ *n.* A compound of hydrogen and oxygen occurring as a liquid.

1. How does the number of syllables change in the two pronunciations of *different*?
The first pronunciation has three syllables, and the second has two. **(3 points)**

2. *Diversity* differs in pronunciation only in the first **(2)** two syllables. Which two words from the box have the same vowel sounds as the pronunciations of the first syllable in *diversity*? sit, pie **(2)**

3. *Program* differs in pronunciation in the second or last **(2)** syllable. Which two words from the box have the same vowel sounds as the pronunciations of that syllable? jam, gum **(2)**

4. Which word from the box has the same consonant and vowel sounds as the second syllable in the first pronunciation of *species*? sheen **(2)**

5. If you use the first pronunciation of *water*, are you saying WAHtur or (WAWtur) (Circle the correct answer.) **(2)**

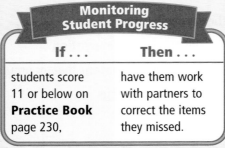

Monitoring Student Progress

If . . .	Then . . .
students score 11 or below on **Practice Book** page 230,	have them work with partners to correct the items they missed.

VOCABULARY: Pronunciations in a Dictionary

❶ Teach

Explain variations in pronunciation. Some words have more than one acceptable pronunciation. Dictionaries generally list all acceptable pronunciations of a word. The most common pronunciation is listed first.

Model variations in pronunciation. Write this sentence and sample dictionary entry. Use them to model how you figure out the pronunciation of *route*.

> The tall trees function as a network of <u>routes</u> through their territories.

> **route** (*rōōt, rout*) *n.* A way for travel.

Think Aloud *This word looks as if it should be pronounced* rowt, *but I haven't heard that word before. The dictionary shows that the word can be pronounced two ways:* root *and* rowt. *The first pronunciation is the one I'm familiar with. It means "a pathway or road." Now I know I can pronounce it two different ways.*

❷ Guided Practice

Give students practice using variations in pronunciation. Write these sentences on the board and have students copy the underlined words. Have partners look up each word in a dictionary to find the acceptable pronunciations. Suggest that partners read the sentence aloud twice, using each pronunciation of the word.

1. <u>Cicadas</u> chirp.
2. It doesn't know how to <u>forage</u> for its food.
3. <u>Sloths</u> can be seen among the trees.
4. Everyone carries a <u>compass</u>.
5. The juvenile darts out to the <u>feeder</u>.

❸ Apply

Assign Practice Book page 230.

STUDY SKILL: Evaluating the Effects of Media

OBJECTIVES
- Identify the media's messages.
- Evaluate the media's part in shaping people's values, attitudes, and wants.

❶ Teach

Introduce the effects of media.

- Define *media* as systems that deliver information and entertainment.

- The media affect people's daily lives. The contents of programs, publications, and movies often shape people's opinions.

- Through commercials, advertisers promote goods and services in all types of media.

Model evaluating the effects of media on daily life.

- Point out that people around the world have learned about endangered species such as the golden lion tamarin through many media sources. As a result, many people took action to protect their habitats.

- Discuss television shows or movies that have contributed ideas, phrases, styles, fashions, or music to daily life. Invite students to offer examples.

- Discuss familiar advertisements. Ask: How have advertisements shaped your opinions or influenced your decisions?

❷ Practice/Apply

Give students practice in evaluating the effects of media on daily life.

- Have students discuss the impact of the media on people's lives by writing and sharing answers to the following questions.

  – How does the media influence the choices you make in fashion and recreation, and in your opinions about people, places, and events?

  – How has your opinion about endangered species been affected by something you have seen on TV or read, including advertisements or commercials?

- Have pairs of students prepare an oral presentation about a TV program, magazine article, advertisement, or website. Ask students to speculate on the effects its creators wanted it to have on the audience.

INFORMATION & STUDY SKILLS

The Golden Lion Tamarin Comes Home

GRAMMAR: Prepositions

OBJECTIVES

- Identify prepositions and their objects.
- Identify and write prepositional phrases.
- Proofread and correct sentences with grammar and spelling errors.
- Add prepositional phrases to expand sentences and improve writing.
- Learn academic language: *preposition, prepositional phrase.*

DAY 1 — INSTRUCTION

Prepositions

Teach Go over these definitions:

- A preposition relates the noun or the pronoun that follows it to another word in the sentence.
- The object of the preposition is the noun or the pronoun that follows the preposition.

- Display the example sentences at the top of **Transparency 6–13.**
- Point out that the underlined word in each sentence relates the noun *tree* to the verb in the sentence. Explain that the underlined words are prepositions. Ask students what the object of each preposition is. (*tree*)
- Have volunteers underline each preposition and circle the object of each preposition in Sentences 1–6.

Daily Language Practice
Have students correct Sentences 1 and 2 on **Transparency 6–12.**

DAY 2 — PRACTICE

Independent Work

Practice/Homework Assign **Practice Book** page 231.

Daily Language Practice
Have students correct Sentences 3 and 4 on **Transparency 6–12.**

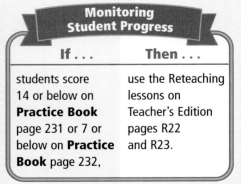

Transparency 6–12

Daily Language Practice

Correct two sentences each day.

1. The kayakers paddled skillfully through dangurus hamilton gorge.
   The kayakers paddled skillfully through dangerous Hamilton Gorge.
2. Your father and I will sells the proporty as soon as possible.
   Your father and I will sell the property as soon as possible.
3. Dr Provine explained that my skin is very sensitiv to heat and sun.
   Dr. Provine explained that my skin is very sensitive to heat and sun.
4. Our reguler coach, Joe rockwell, is sick today.
   Our regular coach, Joe Rockwell, is sick today.
5. Last year our family plan a vacashun to the coast of Maine.
   Last year our family planned a vacation to the coast of Maine.
6. Vegetables weren't my favarite food when i was younger.
   Vegetables weren't my favorite food when I was younger.
7. We have tried to edjukate my dog skippy, but he still chases cars.
   We have tried to educate my dog Skippy, but he still chases cars.
8. My collection of boston Red Sox baseball caps isn't in very good condision.
   My collection of Boston Red Sox baseball caps isn't in very good condition.
9. Mr. and Mrs Chen called our attenshun to the Chinese scrolls in the museum.
   Mr. and Mrs. Chen called our attention to the Chinese scrolls in the museum.
10. Last night Scott asks me what homework we had for hiztory class.
    Last night Scott asked me what homework we had for history class.

Monitoring Student Progress

If . . .	Then . . .
students score 14 or below on **Practice Book** page 231 or 7 or below on **Practice Book** page 232,	use the Reteaching lessons on Teacher's Edition pages R22 and R23.

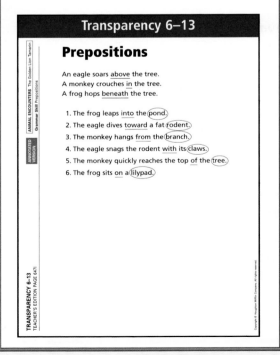

Transparency 6–13

Prepositions

An eagle soars <u>above</u> the tree.
A monkey crouches <u>in</u> the tree.
A frog hops <u>beneath</u> the tree.

1. The frog leaps into the pond.
2. The eagle dives toward a fat rodent.
3. The monkey hangs from the branch.
4. The eagle snags the rodent with its claws.
5. The monkey quickly reaches the top of the tree.
6. The frog sits on a lilypad.

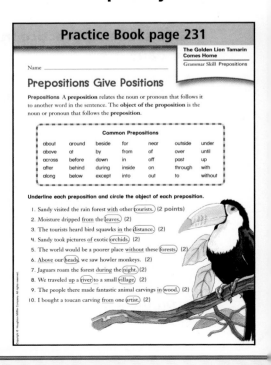

Practice Book page 231

The Golden Lion Tamarin Comes Home
Grammar Skill Prepositions

Name _____

Prepositions Give Positions

Prepositions A **preposition** relates the noun or pronoun that follows it to another word in the sentence. The **object of the preposition** is the noun or pronoun that follows the **preposition.**

Common Prepositions

about	around	beside	for	near	outside	under
above	at	by	from	of	over	until
across	before	down	in	off	past	up
after	behind	during	inside	on	through	with
along	below	except	into	out	to	without

Underline each preposition and circle the object of each preposition.

1. Sandy visited the rain forest with other tourists. (2 points)
2. Moisture dripped from the leaves. (2)
3. The tourists heard bird squawks in the distance. (2)
4. Sandy took pictures of exotic orchids. (2)
5. The world would be a poorer place without these forests. (2)
6. Above our heads, we saw howler monkeys. (2)
7. Jaguars roam the forest during the night. (2)
8. We traveled up a river to a small village. (2)
9. The people there made fantastic animal carvings in wood. (2)
10. I bought a toucan carving from one artist. (2)

6471 THEME 6: Animal Encounters

Prepositional Phrases

Teach Go over this definition:

- A prepositional phrase is made up of a preposition, the object of the preposition, and all the words in between.

- Display the sentences at the top of **Transparency 6–14.** Ask students what kind of word appears at the beginning of each underlined phrase. (a preposition) Ask what appears at the end of each phrase. (the object of that preposition)

- Point out that a prepositional phrase can come at the beginning, middle, or end of a sentence.

- Ask volunteers to complete each numbered sentence by writing a prepositional phrase on the line. Have them underline each preposition and circle its object.

Daily Language Practice
Have students correct Sentences 5 and 6 on **Transparency 6–12.**

Transparency 6–14

Prepositional Phrases

In the early morning the deer are thirsty.
The heat of the noonday sun drives some creatures underground.
The deer find shade in a narrow canyon.

1. The naturalist took a photograph _____.
2. Then she saw a golden lion tamarin _____.
3. _____ she spotted another one.
4. Sometimes she uses a camera _____.
5. At dusk she waited patiently _____.
6. A tamarin _____ is not easy to photograph.

Responses will vary, but prepositions should be underlined and objects of prepositions circled.

Independent Work

Practice/Homework Assign **Practice Book** page 232.

Daily Language Practice
Have students correct Sentences 7 and 8 on **Transparency 6–12.**

Practice Book page 232

The Golden Lion Tamarin Comes Home

Grammar Skill Prepositional Phrases

Name _____

Prepositional Phrases Don't Faze Us

Prepositional Phrases A prepositional phrase is made up of a preposition, the object of the preposition, and all the words in between.
Write each prepositional phrase on the line.

1. My friend Molly watches birds in her backyard.
   in her backyard **(1 point)**
2. Molly's family lives far from town.
   from town **(1)**
3. In the field wildflowers grow.
   in the field **(1)**
4. Animals leave tracks by the pond.
   by the pond **(1)**
5. The hoots of an owl fill the air.
   of an owl **(1)**
6. Sometimes we camp out in the yard.
   in the yard **(1)**
7. At night stars twinkle in the sky.
   At night, in the sky **(1)**
8. We make out constellations above our heads.
   above our heads **(1)**
9. We tell ghost stories inside the tent.
   inside the tent **(1)**
10. We can hardly sleep during the night.
    during the night **(1)**

Expanding Sentences

Teach Inform students that a good writer may add prepositional phrases to sentences to make them say more.

- Model adding a prepositional phrase to a sentence to improve a description:
  - We noticed fresh hoof prints beside the river.
  - *Expanded:* We noticed fresh hoof prints <u>in the soft mud</u> beside the river.

- Have students look for a sentence in their writing that could be improved by adding a prepositional phrase. Ask them to share their revised sentences with the class.

Practice/Homework Assign **Practice Book** page 233.

Daily Language Practice
Have students correct Sentences 9 and 10 on **Transparency 6–12.**

Practice Book page 233

The Golden Lion Tamarin Comes Home

Grammar Skill Prepositional Phrases

Name _____

Expanding Isn't Demanding

Expanding Sentences with Prepositional Phrases A good writer can make sentences say more by adding prepositional phrases.
I took a walk.
Expanded: I took a walk along the path through the woods.

Read Charlie's paragraph. Add details to his description by adding prepositional phrases in the blanks. Ask yourself, Where? When? How? What? Use your imagination!
Answers will vary. Sample answers shown.

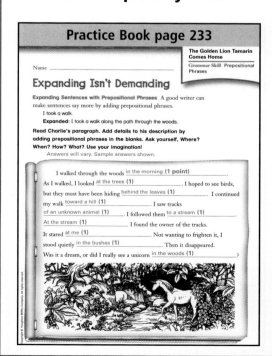

I walked through the woods in the morning **(1 point)** _____.
As I walked, I looked at the trees **(1)** _____. I hoped to see birds, but they must have been hiding behind the leaves **(1)** _____. I continued my walk toward a hill **(1)** _____. I saw tracks of an unknown animal **(1)** _____. I followed them to a stream **(1)** _____.
At the stream **(1)** _____ I found the owner of the tracks.
It stared at me **(1)** _____. Not wanting to frighten it, I stood quietly in the bushes **(1)** _____. Then it disappeared.
Was it a dream, or did I really see a unicorn in the woods **(1)** _____?

WRITING: Compare/Contrast Essay

WRITING

OBJECTIVES

- Identify characteristics of a good compare/contrast essay.
- Write a compare/contrast essay.
- Improve writing by combining sentences with prepositional phrases.

Writing Traits

Conventions As you teach the lesson on Day 3, emphasize the importance of conventions. Discuss these points.

- When combining sentences, be sure to use the correct punctuation in order to make it easier for others to read what you have written.
- Paying attention to capitalization, spelling, and usage is part of making your ideas clear.

DAY 1 PREWRITING

Introducing the Format

Define a compare/contrast essay.

- A compare/contrast essay explains the similarities and differences between two or more items.
- To compare is to show likenesses.
- To contrast is to show differences.

Start students thinking about compare/contrast essays.

- Have students discuss the similarities and differences between grizzly bears and golden lion tamarins.
- Have partners discuss possible elements to be compared between the two animals, for example: physical characteristics, diets, habits, habitat, or endangerment status.
- Have students save their notes.

DAY 2 DRAFTING

Discussing the Model

Display Transparency 6–15. Ask:

- What is being compared and contrasted? (the tamarins' life in their native habitat with life in the zoo)
- Where is the topic stated? (in the first paragraph)
- Which parts compare or show likenesses between the things being discussed? (the last paragraph)
- Which parts contrast or show differences? (the second and third paragraphs)
- How does the writer conclude the essay? (with a conclusion statement)

Display Transparency 6–16, and discuss the guidelines.

Have students draft a compare/contrast essay.

- Have students choose two animals to compare and contrast.
- Have them use their notes from Day 1.
- Assign **Practice Book** page 234 to help students organize their writing.
- Provide support as needed.

Transparency 6–15

A Compare / Contrast Essay

Introduction (topic statement and compare/contrast overview) — Tamarins are an endangered species. Zoos around the world are cooperating to reintroduce tamarins raised in captivity back into their natural habitat in Brazil. However, life for golden lion tamarins in a zoo is very different from life in their natural habitat.

Contrast: details about zoo environment — First of all, in a zoo, food and shelter are provided, and the tamarins do not have to learn wilderness survival behaviors. A familiar human delivers chopped fruit in a bowl to the tamarins in a safe, enclosed living area. The tamarins climb up fixed poles that do not sway under their weight. No predators enter their safe environment, so they do not have to learn to avoid any other animals. They are sheltered from severe weather.

Contrast: details about natural environment — On the other hand, tamarins in the wild must forage for their own food, avoid predators including human hunters and poachers, avoid poisonous foods and snakes, find shelter from storms, live out in the open, and move among tree limbs and vines that sway and bend when they jump onto them.

Comparison details — Whether the tamarins live in the zoos or in the wild in Brazil, they are all endangered. All are counted and observed very carefully. The fur of individuals and families is marked with dyes, and the tamarins, especially those being introduced to the wild, wear radio collars to help observers locate, track, and study them. Scientists hope that gradually more and more golden lion tamarins will survive and raise families in their natural rain forest habitat.

Concluding statement

Transparency 6–16

Guidelines for Writing a Compare/Contrast Essay

Follow these guidelines when you write a compare/contrast essay.

- Choose two subjects that have likenesses and differences that you can compare.
- Make a Venn diagram to list likenesses and differences.
- In the opening paragraph, clearly state the things to be compared and contrasted.
- Group details that compare and details that contrast in the paragraphs that follow.
- Use clue words to help the reader identify likenesses and differences.
- End with a concluding statement.

Practice Book page 234

The Golden Lion Tamarin Comes Home
Writing Skill Compare/Contrast Essay

Name _____

Writing a Compare/Contrast Essay

In *The Golden Lion Tamarin Comes Home*, you read about similarities and differences between captive-born golden lion tamarins and those born in the wild. Both eat fruit, for example, but golden lion tamarins born in zoos do not know how to hunt or forage for food. One way to explain similarities and differences is by writing a **compare/contrast essay.** Comparing shows how things are alike, and contrasting shows how they are different.

Using the Venn diagram, gather and organize details that compare and contrast grizzly bears with golden lion tamarins. Jot down facts about the two species, including their habitats, their diets, and threats to their survival.

Grizzly Bears (2 points) — Both (2) — Golden Lion Tamarins (2)

Write a compare/contrast essay about grizzly bears and golden lion tamarins on a separate sheet of paper. In the opening paragraph, clearly state the subject being compared and contrasted. In the following paragraphs, present details from your Venn diagram. Group details that compare and details that contrast in a clear manner. Use clue words such as *both* or *same* to help readers identify likenesses and *in contrast* or *although* to help them identify differences. (4)

647K THEME 6: Animal Encounters

DAY 3 REVISING

Improving Writing: Combining Sentences

Explain combining sentences with prepositional phrases.

- Review prepositional phrases.
- Sentences that have a repeated subject but differing prepositional phrases can be combined to streamline writing.

Display Transparency 6–17.

- Have students identify the prepositional phrases in Passage A.
- Identify how Passage B removes the repeated words by combining sentences.
- Repeat the procedure for Passage C. Ask students to suggest ways to streamline Passage C by combining prepositions.
- Show students passage D.

Assign Practice Book page 235.

Have students revise their drafts.

- Display **Transparency 6–16** again.
- Have partners hold a writing conference.
- See Writing Traits on page 647K.
- Ask students to revise any parts of their essays that still need work.

Transparency 6–17

Combining Sentences with Prepositional Phrases

Passage A
The observation team meets the van on a narrow road. The narrow road is in the tropical rain forest. The forest is within the Poço das Antas Biological Reserve. The Biological Preserve is near Rio de Janeiro, Brazil.

Passage B
The observation team meets the van on a narrow road in the tropical rain forest within the Poço das Antas Biological Reserve near Rio de Janeiro, Brazil.

Passage C
The tamarins are inside their cages. They are in the rain forest. The tamarins eat a diet of insects and small animals that scoot into those enclosures.

Passage D
Inside their cages in the rain forest, the tamarins eat a diet of insects and small animals that scoot into those enclosures.

TRANSPARENCY 6–17
TEACHER'S EDITION PAGE 647L

ANIMAL ENCOUNTERS The Golden Lion Tamarin
Writing Skill Improving Your Writing
ANNOTATED VERSION

DAY 4 PROOFREADING

Checking for Errors

Have students proofread for errors in grammar, spelling, punctuation, or usage.

- Students can use the proofreading checklist on **Practice Book** page 287 to help them proofread their compare/contrast essays.
- Students can also use the proofreading marks on **Practice Book** page 288.

Practice Book page 235

Name _____

The Golden Lion Tamarin Comes Home
Writing Skill Improving Your Writing

Combining Sentences

Good writers are always looking for ways to improve their writing. One method to streamline your writing is to combine short sentences that have a repeated subject but differing prepositional phrases into a single sentence with consecutive prepositional phrases.

> The biologist was **in a tropical rain forest**. He stood **beneath some tall trees**. He peered **into the green vines**. He spotted a few golden lion tamarins **above him**.

> Standing **beneath some tall trees in a tropical rain forest**, the biologist peered **into the green vines above him** and spotted a few golden lion tamarins.

Revise these field notes. Combine short sentences that have a repeated subject but differing prepositional phrases into a single sentence. Write the revised notes on the lines. (12 points)

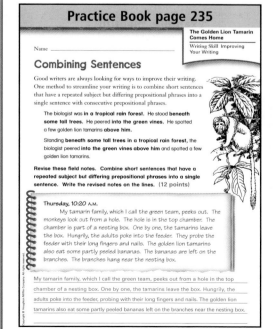

Thursday, 10:20 A.M.
My tamarin family, which I call the green team, peeks out. The monkeys look out from a hole. The hole is in the top chamber. The chamber is part of a nesting box. One by one, the tamarins leave the box. Hungrily, the adults poke into the feeder. They probe the feeder with their long fingers and nails. The golden lion tamarins also eat some partly peeled bananas. The bananas are left on the branches. The branches hang near the nesting box.

My tamarin family, which I call the green team, peeks out from a hole in the top chamber of a nesting box. One by one, the tamarins leave the box. Hungrily, the adults poke into the feeder, probing with their long fingers and nails. The golden lion tamarins also eat some partly peeled bananas left on the branches near the nesting box.

DAY 5 PUBLISHING

Sharing Compare/Contrast Essays

Consider these publishing options.

- Ask students to read their compare/contrast essays or some other piece of writing from the Author's Chair.
- Encourage students to illustrate their compare/contrast essays and bring them home to share.

Portfolio Opportunity

Save students' compare/contrast essays as samples of their writing development.

Monitoring Student Progress

If . . .	Then . . .
students' writing does not follow the guidelines on **Transparency 6–16,**	work with students to improve specific parts of their writing.

Independent Activities

Language Center

VOCABULARY

Building Vocabulary

👥 Pairs	🕐 20 minutes
Objective	Explore place names and proper adjectives.
Materials	Dictionary, writing materials

The Golden Lion Tamarin Comes Home takes place in Brazil. When speaking of someone or something from Brazil you use the word *Brazilian*. This proper adjective combines the proper noun *Brazil* with the adjective ending *-ian*.

• With a partner, make a list of country names and their proper adjectives. HINT: Not all proper adjectives are formed in the same way. If you need help use a dictionary.

Country Name	Proper Adjective
Peru	Peruvian
Germany	German
Chile	
Italy	
Norway	
Ireland	
Pakistan	
Vietnam	

STRUCTURAL ANALYSIS

Three-Syllable Words

👥 Pairs	🕐 20 minutes
Objective	Divide three-syllable words.
Materials	Anthology, writing materials

With a partner, use what you know about syllabication patterns, prefixes, and suffixes to divide a list of words into syllables.

• Review the stories in this theme for three-syllable words. Make a list of twenty words.

• Study the example below. Then divide each word on your list into three parts.

> **Example: plentiful = plen/ti/ful**
>
> I see the VCCV pattern, and the suffix *-ful*. I will divide the base word between the two consonants, then separate the suffix.

VOCABULARY

Vocabulary Game

👥 Groups	🕐 45 minutes
Objective	Play a "Go Fish" card game.
Materials	Activity Master 6–3, index cards, scissors

Play a "Go Fish" word game.

• Complete Activity Master 6–3.

• Write each word from Activity Master 6–3 on an index card.

• Shuffle the deck and deal five cards to each player. Stack the remaining cards face down.

• To begin, players check their cards for synonym matches, placing pairs face up on the table.

• Next, Player 1 asks another player for a card that matches one in his or her hand. If that player has a match, he or she must hand it over. If not, he or she says "Go Fish." Player 1 then draws a new card from the deck, and Player 2 takes a turn.

• Play continues until one player's hand is empty. The player with the most matched pairs wins.

Consider copying and laminating these activities for use in centers.

LISTENING/SPEAKING

Giving Directions

👥 Pairs	🕐 40 minutes
Objective	Prepare a set of oral directions.

As part of their job, the observers who work with the golden lion tamarins must listen to, follow, and give directions. Throughout your daily life, you will often be called upon to give and follow directions.

- With a partner, plan and practice giving a set of directions out loud. Pick your own topic, or select one of these:

  – how to prepare a golden lion tamarin nesting box or feeder

  – how to make a paper airplane

  – what to do during a fire drill

  – how to clean your desk

- As you plan, make cue cards or notes. Follow the guidelines below.

Tips for Giving Directions

Think through each step before explaining the directions.

Design your directions to fit your audience.

Use sequence words to present the steps in order. Include every step.

Speak slowly and clearly in a polite, helpful tone.

GRAMMAR

Prepositional Phrases

👤 Singles	🕐 25 minutes
Objective	Add prepositional phrases to a piece of your writing.
Materials	Writing samples

When you write, you can improve your sentences by adding prepositional phrases.

- Prepositional phrases begin with a preposition, such as *of, in, on, above, under, over, beneath,* or *between*.

- Note how the underlined prepositional phrases make sentences more specific:

  – <u>At the stroke of dawn</u>, the birds began to chirp.

  – The sound <u>of their melodic voices</u> makes the rain forest come alive.

  – Some tropical birds nest high up <u>in the canopy</u>.

- Review a piece of your writing. Make your sentences say more by adding prepositional phrases to five sentences.

LEVELED READERS

Saving Sea Turtles

Summary *Many scientists think that sea turtles have been swimming the oceans since the days of the dinosaurs, but Saving Sea Turtles focuses on how sea turtles are nearing extinction at an alarming rate. While all sea turtles are endangered, the book concentrates on the small Kemp's Ridley sea turtle, which is dangerously close to extinction.*

Vocabulary

Introduce the Key Vocabulary and ask students to complete the BLM.

habitat* a natural environment for native creatures, *p. 3*

windswept having winds blow across, *p. 8*

threatened put in danger, *p. 10*

volunteer someone doing a job for free, *p. 14*

nesting site spot where eggs are laid, *p. 15*

*Forms of these words are Anthology Key Vocabulary words.

Building Background and Vocabulary

Have students share what they know about sea turtles, including kinds of turtles, how turtles swim and breathe, and how they lay their eggs. Preview the story with students, using the story vocabulary when possible.

⌾ Comprehension Skill: Topic, Main Idea, and Supporting Details

Have students read the Strategy Focus on the book flap. Remind students to use the strategy and to think about the topic, main idea, and supporting details as they read the book. (See the Leveled Readers Teacher's Guide for **Vocabulary and Comprehension Practice Masters.**)

Responding

Have partners discuss how to answer the questions on the inside back cover.

Think About the Selection Sample answers:

1. the Kemp's Ridley sea turtle
2. Humans have harmed the turtles and the turtle's natural habitat.
3. Even though sea turtles like the Kemp's Ridley are in danger, there are things that we can do to help them survive.
4. Scientists are helping sea turtles by hatching their eggs in laboratories, and protecting the baby turtles from predators when they are released.

Making Connections Responses will vary.

⌾ Building Fluency

Model Read aloud the captions on page 3. Point out that the captions help explain the pictures above them.

Practice Have partners find other examples of captions in the book and take turns reading them aloud to each other as they look at the pictures.

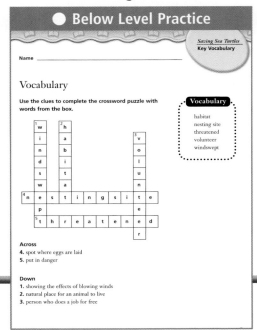

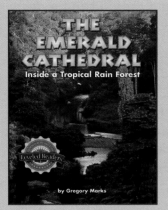

The Emerald Cathedral: Inside a Tropical Rain Forest

by Gregory Marks

The Emerald Cathedral: Inside a Tropical Rain Forest

Summary The Emerald Cathedral: Inside a Tropical Rain Forest *provides history and statistics on the Amazon tropical rain forest.*

Vocabulary

Introduce the Key Vocabulary and ask students to complete the BLM.

equator imaginary line that circles the middle of the earth, *p. 4*

humid* containing a large amount of water vapor, damp, *p. 4*

canopy* the high, sheltering branches of rain forest trees, *p. 5*

nutrients substances that provide nourishment, *p. 6*

organisms living things, *p. 7*

predators* animals that prey on others, *p. 9*

pollinated transferred pollen to a flower, *p. 16*

species a class of similar animals or plants, *p. 21*

*Forms of these words are Anthology Key Vocabulary words.

▲ ON LEVEL

Building Background and Vocabulary

Have students share what they know about tropical rain forests. Preview the story with students, using the story vocabulary when possible.

Comprehension Skill: Topic, Main Idea, and Supporting Details

Have students read the Strategy Focus on the book flap. Remind students to use the strategy and to think about the topic, main idea, and supporting details as they read the book. (See the Leveled Readers Teacher's Guide for **Vocabulary and Comprehension Practice Masters**.)

Responding

Have partners discuss how to answer the questions on the inside back cover.

Think About the Selection Sample answers:

1. It is hot and wet, and temperatures don't change much.
2. Possible response: Some floor animals eat fruit, then scatter the seeds away from the parent tree. Other animals plant seeds by digging. All this spreads growth.
3. Possible response: Only a little light slips through the growth. Few plants grow in the darkest shadows. It seems hushed and still.
4. Responses will vary.

Making Connections Responses will vary.

Building Fluency

Model Read aloud the first paragraph on page 4. Point out the dash and explain that readers should pause when they reach a dash in a sentence. Also point out that the text after the dash often explains the text before it.

Practice Have volunteers find and read appropriately other sentences with dashes from the book.

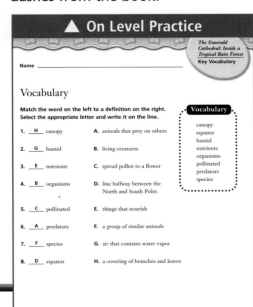

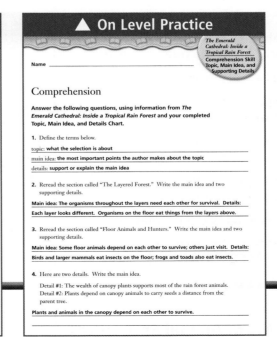

LEVELED READERS

Invaders!

Summary *The selection explores how invasions of nonnative plants and animals, and attempts to eradicate them, can cause catastrophic results.*

Vocabulary

Introduce the Key Vocabulary and ask students to complete the BLM.

extinction* the condition of having died out, *p. 4*

alien introduced to a new region, *p. 4*

ecosystem community of organisms and their environment, *p. 4*

habitat* a natural environment for native creatures, *p. 8*

vulnerable open to attack, *p. 11*

predators* animals that prey on others, *p. 12*

complex complicated, involved, *p. 15*

eradicate remove or destroy completely, *p. 15*

consequences outcomes, *p. 23*

*Forms of these words are Anthology Key Vocabulary words.

■ ABOVE LEVEL

Building Background and Vocabulary

Explain that plants and animals that aren't native to a region can be destructive. Preview the story with students, using the story vocabulary.

Comprehension Skill: Topic, Main Idea, and Supporting Details

Have students read the Strategy Focus on the book flap. Remind students to use the strategy and to think about the topic, main idea, and supporting details as they read the book. (See the Leveled Readers Teacher's Guide for **Vocabulary and Comprehension Practice Masters.**)

Responding

Have partners discuss how to answer the questions on the inside back cover.

Think About the Selection Sample answers:

1. It carried a disease that caused the extinction of ten species of birds.

2. Yes, because they haven't built up defenses against new predators and have no escape.

3. They can occur by accident, as with the arrival of the Asian Longhorned Beetle. They can occur by people bringing them deliberately, as with the Nile perch.

4. Students might say he should have thought about the consequences.

Making Connections Responses will vary.

Building Fluency

Model Read aloud the third paragraph on page 4. Explain that the reader must pause at the colon. Also explain that the part of the sentence that comes before the colon introduces the part that follows the colon.

Practice Have small groups work together to find another sentence with a colon, each member of the group reading the sentence appropriately.

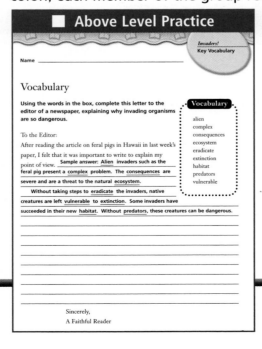

Protecting Sea Turtles

Summary *Sea turtles, which have existed since the days of the dinosaurs, are now endangered. After explaining the dangers these turtles face from humans, the author describes the efforts scientists and volunteers are making to save these sea creatures.*

Vocabulary

Introduce the Key Vocabulary and ask students to complete the BLM.

endangered in danger, threatened, *p. 3*

extinction* the condition of having died out, *p. 3*

protect keep safe from harm or attack; guard, *p. 8*

hatch to come out of an egg, *p. 9*

volunteers people who do a job without pay, *p. 14*

laboratory a place for doing scientific research and experiments, *p. 14*

*Forms of these words are Anthology Key Vocabulary words.

◆ LANGUAGE SUPPORT

Building Background and Vocabulary

Show students the picture of the sea turtle on the cover. Explain that this animal is endangered. Distribute the **Build Background Practice Master** and read aloud the direction and activities. Have children decide whether each activity hurts or helps the turtles.

Comprehension Skill: Topic, Main Idea, and Supporting Details

Have students read the Strategy Focus on the book flap. Remind students to use the strategy and to notice main ideas and details as they read the book. (See the Leveled Readers Teacher's Guide for **Build Background, Vocabulary, and Graphic Organizer Masters.**)

Responding

Have partners discuss how to answer the questions on the inside back cover.

Think About the Selection Sample answers:

1. Kemp's Ridley sea turtles are in the greatest danger.
2. They can swim and get to the ocean when they are born.
3. Protecting the eggs helps more baby turtles hatch, and gives them a better chance of getting to the ocean.
4. Responses will vary.

Making Connections Responses will vary.

Building Fluency

Model Have students follow along in their books as they listen to pages 3–4 of the recording on audio CD.

Practice Have students read along with the recording until they can read the text on their own accurately and with expression.

◆ Language Support Practice

Protecting Sea Turtles
Build Background

Name _____

Build Background

Read the activities below. Then decide whether each activity might hurt a sea turtle or help to protect it. Write a check mark in the correct column.

Activity	Hurts Sea Turtles	Helps Sea Turtles
hunting sea turtles for their skin, shells, and meat	✔	
helping scientists to learn more about what turtles need to be healthy		✔
throwing trash on the beach or in the water where turtles live	✔	
helping to clean up areas where turtles live		✔
being careful not to step on turtle nests and eggs		✔
stepping on and breaking turtle eggs before they hatch	✔	

◆ Language Support Practice

Protecting Sea Turtles
Key Vocabulary

Name _____

Vocabulary

Use the best word from the box to complete each sentence below.

Vocabulary
endangered
extinction
hatch
laboratory
protect
volunteers

1. Can you name any animals that face _____ **extinction** _____ and may no longer exist soon?

2. The sea turtle is one of these threatened, or _____ **endangered** _____ , animals.

3. Many people are working to _____ **protect** _____ sea turtles and save them from danger.

4. Some _____ **volunteers** _____ help scientists find the turtles' eggs and move them from the beach so that other people won't step on the eggs.

5. The scientists study and care for the eggs in their _____ **laboratory** _____ for a while.

6. Soon, the eggs _____ **hatch** _____ , and the scientists return the baby sea turtles to the beach where they were born.

Lesson Overview

Literature

MY SIDE OF
THE MOUNTAIN
Jean Craighead George

Selection Summary

Sam Gribley learns to live off of the land after he sets up house in a hollow tree in the Catskill Mountains.

1 Background and Vocabulary

2 Main Selection

My Side of the Mountain
Genre: Realistic Fiction

3 Career Link

Robin Hughes: Wildlife Doctor

Dr. Robin Hughes could give Sam Gribley advice. She formerly worked as wildlife veterinarian at the Virginia Living Museum in Newport News, Virginia.

by Susan Yoder Ackerman

Instructional Support

Planning and Practice

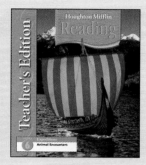

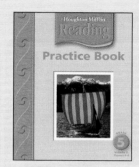

- Planning and classroom management
- Reading instruction
- Skill lessons
- Materials for reaching all learners

- Independent practice for skills

- Newsletters
- Selection Summaries
- Assignment Cards
- Observation Checklists
- Selection Tests

- Transparencies
- Strategy Posters
- Blackline Masters

Reaching All Learners

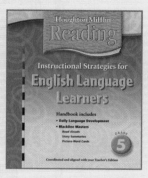

Coordinated lessons, activities, and projects for additional reading instruction

For
- Classroom Teacher
- Extended Day
- Pull Out
- Resource Teacher

Technology

Audio Selection

My Side of the Mountain

Get Set for Reading CD-ROM
- Background building
- Vocabulary support
- Selection Summary in English and Spanish

Accelerated Reader
- Practice quizzes for the selection

www.eduplace.com

Log on to Education Place for more activities related to the selection.

e • **Glossary**
e • **WordGame**

Leveled Books for Reaching All Learners

Leveled Readers and Leveled Practice

- Independent reading for building fluency
- Topic, comprehension strategy, and vocabulary linked to main selection
- Lessons in Teacher's Edition, pages 671O–671R
- Leveled practice for every book

Technology

Leveled Readers
Audio available

Book Adventure

- Practice quizzes for the Leveled Theme Paperbacks

www.eduplace.com

Log on to Education Place® for activities related to the Leveled Theme Paperbacks.

● **BELOW LEVEL**

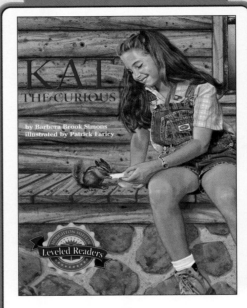

▲ **ON LEVEL**

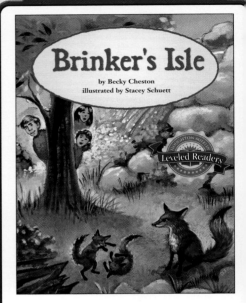

Brinker's Isle
by Becky Cheston
illustrated by Stacey Schuett

● Below Level Practice

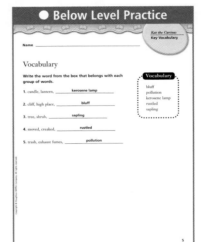

▲ On Level Practice

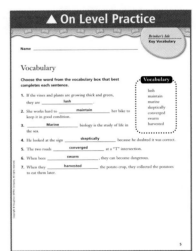

● Below Level Practice

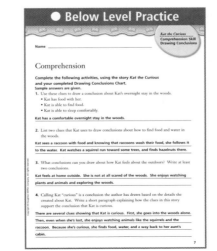

▲ On Level Practice

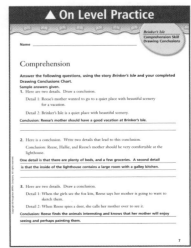

Leveled Theme Paperbacks

- Extended independent reading in theme-related trade books
- Lessons in Teacher's Edition, pages R2–R7

Wayne Grover
Dolphin Adventure
A TRUE STORY

HOUGHTON MIFFLIN
Reading

ILLUSTRATED BY JIM FOWLER

Below Level

■ ABOVE LEVEL

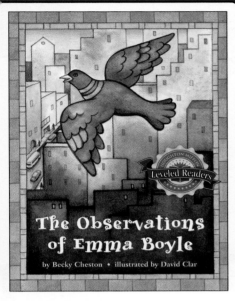

HOUGHTON MIFFLIN
Leveled Readers

The Observations of Emma Boyle

by Becky Cheston • illustrated by David Clar

◆ LANGUAGE SUPPORT

CURIOUS
KAT

by Barbara Brook Simons
illustrated by Patrick Faricy

HOUGHTON MIFFLIN
Leveled Readers

The **TARANTULA in My Purse** and 172 Other Wild Pets

HOUGHTON MIFFLIN
Reading

written and illustrated by
Jean Craighead George

On Level

■ Above Level Practice

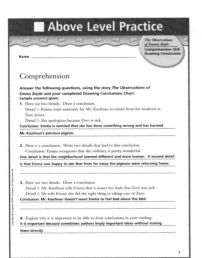

The Observations of Emma Boyle
Key Vocabulary

Name _____

Vocabulary

Write the word from the box that best completes the sentence.

Vocabulary
harsh
constructive
inscription
trough
contagious
occupation
strategy
survive

1. Chicken pox is a ___contagious___ disease.

2. Paula apologized for speaking ___harsh___ words to her friend.

3. Sara thought of a good ___strategy___ for accomplishing her long list of chores.

4. Mr. Kaufman was jailed during the ___occupation___ of Czechoslovakia.

5. "Do you think the plants will ___survive___ in this heat?" asked Rosa.

6. Mike couldn't remember the last time he filled the hamster's ___trough___.

7. Watching television is not a ___constructive___ way to use your time.

8. Ben couldn't wait to read the ___inscription___ on his trophy.

◆ Language Support Practice

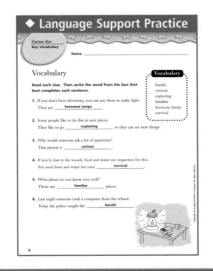

Curious Kat
Build Background

Name _____

Build Background

Read the list of suggestions of what to do if you are lost. Think about which ones you should do if you get lost in the city and which ones you should do if you get lost in the woods. Some suggestions may be good for both the city and the woods. Put a check mark in the correct column of the chart. Then write your own suggestion and put a check mark to show where you would use it.

What to Do If You Are Lost	In the City	In the Woods	Both Places
Ask a policeman for help.	✔		
Look for a road that might lead to people.		✔	
Make sure you have enough to eat.			✔
Call someone who can help you.	✔		
Find a safe place to wait.			✔
Stay out of the rain and cold.			✔
Be careful with wild animals.		✔	
Make light at night with a flashlight.			✔
Ask for help in a store.	✔		
Answers will vary.			

JIM BRANDENBURG
To the Top of the World
ADVENTURES WITH ARCTIC WOLVES

HOUGHTON MIFFLIN
Reading

Challenge

■ Above Level Practice

The Observations of Emma Boyle
Comprehension Skill
Drawing Conclusions

Name _____

Comprehension

Answer the following questions, using the story *The Observations of Emma Boyle* and your completed Drawing Conclusions Chart. Sample answers given.

1. Here are two details. Draw a conclusion.
   Detail 1: Emma waits anxiously for Mr. Kaufman to return from his weekend in New Jersey.
   Detail 2: She apologizes because Zero is sick.
   Conclusion: Emma is worried that she has done something wrong and has harmed Mr. Kaufman's precious pigeon.

2. Here is a conclusion. Write two details that lead to this conclusion.
   Conclusion: Emma recognizes that the ordinary is pretty wonderful.
   One detail is that the neighborhood seemed different and more human. A second detail is that Emma was happy to see that from far away the pigeons were returning home.

3. Here are two details. Draw a conclusion.
   Detail 1: Mr. Kaufman tells Emma that it wasn't her fault that Zero was sick.
   Detail 2: He tells Emma she did the right thing in taking care of Zero.
   Conclusion: Mr. Kaufman doesn't want Emma to feel bad about the bird.

4. Explain why it is important to be able to draw conclusions in your reading.
   It is important because sometimes authors imply important ideas without stating them directly.

◆ Language Support Practice

Curious Kat
Key Vocabulary

Name _____

Vocabulary

Read each clue. Then write the word from the box that best completes each sentence.

Vocabulary
bandit
curious
exploring
familiar
kerosene lamps
survival

1. If you don't have electricity, you can use these to make light.
   They are ___kerosene lamps___.

2. Some people like to do this in new places.
   They like to go ___exploring___ so they can see new things.

3. Why would someone ask a lot of questions?
   That person is ___curious___.

4. If you're lost in the woods, food and water are important for this.
   You need food and water for your ___survival___.

5. What places do you know very well?
   Those are ___familiar___ places.

6. Last night someone took a computer from the school.
   Today the police caught the ___bandit___.

Daily Lesson Plans

T Skill tested on Theme Skills Test and/or Integrated Theme Test

DAILY LESSON PLANS

Reading
Comprehension

50–60 minutes

Leveled Readers
- Fluency Practice
- Independent Reading

Word Work

20–30 minutes

Phonics/Decoding
Vocabulary
Spelling

Writing and Oral Language

20–30 minutes

Writing
Grammar
Listening/Speaking/Viewing

DAY 1

Teacher Read Aloud, 647CC–647DD
Giving Wildlife a Second Chance

Building Background, 648

Key Vocabulary, 649
cache	harvesting	storehouse
fashion	migration	survival
harsh		

Reading the Selection, 650–665
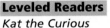 **Comprehension Skill,** 650
Drawing Conclusions **T**
 **Comprehension Strategy,** 650
Summarize

Leveled Readers
Kat the Curious
Brinker's Isle
The Observations of Emma Boyle
Curious Kat

Lessons and Leveled Practice, 671O–671R

Phonics/Decoding, 651
Phonics/Decoding Strategy
Vocabulary, 650–665
Selection Vocabulary
Spelling, 671E
-ent, -ant; -able, -ible **T**

 Writing, 671K
Prewriting an Answer to an Essay Question

Grammar, 671I
Object Pronouns in Prepositional Phrases **T**

Daily Language Practice
1. The only rezident of the cave was a large, furry hibernating bear. (resident; furry,)
2. "When did the accidant occur?" the police officers asks the witness. (accident; ask)

Listening/Speaking/Viewing, 647CC–647DD, 659
Teacher Read Aloud, Stop and Think

DAY 2

Reading the Selection, 650–665

Comprehension Check, 665

Responding, 666
Think About the Selection

 Comprehension Skill Preview, 657
Drawing Conclusions **T**

Leveled Readers
Kat the Curious
Brinker's Isle
The Observations of Emma Boyle
Curious Kat

Lessons and Leveled Practice, 671O–671R

 Structural Analysis, 671C
Suffixes -ent, -ant, -able, -ible **T**
Vocabulary, 650–665
Selection Vocabulary
Spelling, 671E
-ent, -ant; -able, -ible Review and Practice **T**

Writing, 671K
Drafting an Answer to an Essay Question

Grammar, 671I
Object Pronouns in Prepositional Phrases Practice **T**

Daily Language Practice
3. This is the more comfortable chair in our whole house. (most; comfortable)
4. Dan thinks most science-fiction movies is terribel. (are; terrible.)

Listening/Speaking/Viewing, 665, 666
Wrapping Up, Responding

Target Skills of the Week

Comprehension	Summarize; Drawing Conclusions
Vocabulary	Run-on Dictionary Entries
Phonics/Decoding	Suffixes -ent, -ant; -able, -ible
Fluency	Leveled Readers

DAY 3

Rereading the Selection, 650–665

Comprehension Skill, 671A–671B
Drawing Conclusions T

Leveled Readers
Kat the Curious
Brinker's Isle
The Observations of
  Emma Boyle
Curious Kat

Lessons and Leveled Practice, 671O–671R

Phonics Review, 671D
Vowel Alternations

Vocabulary, 671G
Run-on Dictionary Entries T

Spelling, 671F
Vocabulary: Idioms; -ent, -ant; -able, -ible
Practice T

Writing, 671L
Revising an Answer to an Essay Question

Grammar, 671J
Pronouns As Compound Objects of
Prepositions T

Daily Language Practice
5. This old dictionary is most valuble than that
biography of George Washington. (more; valuable)
6. Angela's sweater is warm colorful, and fashionabel.
(warm,; fashionable.)

DAY 4

Robin Hughes:
Wildlife Doctor

Reading the Career Link,
668–671
"Robin Hughes: Wildlife
Doctor"

Skill: How to Categorize
Information

Comprehension Skill Review, 661
Making Judgments

Leveled Readers
Kat the Curious
Brinker's Isle
The Observations of
  Emma Boyle
Curious Kat

Lessons and Leveled Practice, 671O–671R

Phonics/Decoding, 668–671
Apply Phonics/Decoding Strategy to Link

Vocabulary, 671M
Language Center: Building Vocabulary

Spelling, 671F
Ending Suffixes Game, Proofreading T

Writing, 671L
Proofreading an Answer to an Essay Question
Placing Prepositional Phrases Correctly

Grammar, 671J
Pronouns As Compound Objects of
Prepositions Practice T

Daily Language Practice
7. Rock climbing has been a remarkable experience
for Juan and I. (remarkable; me.)
8. I watch as the servent pour ice water for each of
the guests. (servant; pours)

Listening/Speaking/Viewing, 671
Discuss the Link

DAY 5

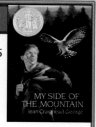

Rereading for Fluency, 655

Responding Activities, 666–667
Write Directions
Cross-Curricular Activities

Information and Study Skills, 671H
Completing Applications and Forms T

Comprehension Skill Review, 663
Following Directions

Leveled Readers
Kat the Curious
Brinker's Isle
The Observations of
  Emma Boyle
Curious Kat

Lessons and Leveled Practice, 671O–671R

Structural Analysis, 671M
Language Center: Suffixes -ent, -ant, -able, -ible

Vocabulary, 671M
Language Center: Vocabulary Game

Spelling, 671F
Test: -ent, -ant; -able, -ible T

Writing, 671L
Publishing an Answer to an Essay Question

Grammar, 671J, 671N
The Correct Pronoun
Language Center: Object Pronouns

Daily Language Practice
9. To Dorla and I, the confusion about our names is
laffable. (me,; laughable.)
10. We can be abcent from school if we are sick,
have a doctor's appointment or take part in a field
trip. (absent; appointment,)

Listening/Speaking/Viewing, 671N
Language Center: Viewing for Information
and Details

Managing Flexible Groups

FLEXIBLE GROUPS

Leveled Instruction and Leveled Practice

	DAY 1	**DAY 2**
WHOLE CLASS	• Teacher Read Aloud (TE pp. 647CC–647DD) • Building Background, Introducing Vocabulary (TE pp. 648–649) • Comprehension Strategy: Introduce (TE p. 650) • Comprehension Skill: Introduce (TE p. 650) • Purpose Setting (TE p. 651) **After reading first half of *My Side of the Mountain*** • Stop and Think (TE p. 659)	**After reading *My Side of the Mountain*** • Wrapping Up (TE p. 665) • Comprehension Check (Practice Book p. 238) • Responding: Think About the Selection (TE p. 666) • Comprehension Skill: Preview (TE p. 657)
SMALL GROUPS **Extra Support**	**TEACHER-LED** • Preview *My Side of the Mountain* to Stop and Think (TE pp. 650–659). • Support reading with Extra Support/Intervention notes (TE pp. 651, 654, 658, 662, 663, 664).	**Partner or Individual Work** • Reread first half of *My Side of the Mountain* (TE pp. 650–659). • Preview, read second half (TE pp. 660–665). • Comprehension Check (Practice Book p. 238)
Challenge	**Individual Work** • Begin "Wild Animal Park" (Challenge Handbook p. 52). • Extend reading with Challenge Notes (TE p. 664).	**Individual Work** • Continue work on activity (Challenge Handbook p. 52).
English Language Learners	**TEACHER-LED** • Preview vocabulary and *My Side of the Mountain* to Stop and Think (TE pp. 649–659). • Support reading with English Language Learners notes (TE pp. 648, 652, 656, 658).	**TEACHER-LED** • Review first half of *My Side of the Mountain* (TE pp. 650–659). ✔ • Preview, read second half (TE pp. 660–665). • Begin Comprehension Check together (Practice Book p. 238).

Independent Activities

- Get Set for Reading CD-Rom
- Journals: selection notes, questions
- Complete, review Practice Book (pp. 236–240) and Leveled Readers Practice Blackline Masters (TE pp. 671O–671R).
- Assignment Cards (Teacher's Resource Blackline Masters pp. 94–95)
- Leveled Readers (TE pp. 671O–671R), Leveled Theme Paperbacks (TE pp. R2–R7), or book from Leveled Bibliography (TE pp. 594E–594F)

✔ **Opportunity to informally assess oral reading rate**

DAY 3

- Rereading (TE pp. 650–665)
- Comprehension Skill: Main lesson (TE pp. 671A–671B)

DAY 4

- Reading the Career Link (TE pp. 668–671): Skill lesson (TE p. 668)
- Rereading the Link (TE pp. 668–671)
- Comprehension Skill: First Comprehension Review lesson (TE p. 661)

DAY 5

- Responding: Select from Activities (TE pp. 666–667)
- Information and Study Skills (TE p. 671H)
- Comprehension Skill: Second Comprehension Review lesson (TE p. 663)

TEACHER-LED

- Reread, review Comprehension check (Practice Book p. 238).
- Preview Leveled Reader: Below Level (TE p. 671O), or read book from Leveled Bibliography (TE pp. 594E–594F). ✔

Partner or Individual Work

- Reread Career Link (TE pp. 668–671).
- Complete Leveled Reader: Below Level (TE p. 671O), or read book from Leveled Bibliography (TE pp. 594E–594F).

TEACHER-LED

- Comprehension Skill: Reteaching lesson (TE p. R12)
- Reread Leveled Theme Paperback: Below Level (TE pp. R2–R3), or read book from Leveled Bibliography (TE pp. 594E–594F). ✔

TEACHER-LED

- Teacher check-in: Assess progress (Challenge Handbook p. 52).
- Preview Leveled Reader: Above Level (TE p. 671Q), or read book from Leveled Bibliography (TE pp. 594E–594F). ✔

Individual Work

- Complete activity (Challenge Handbook p. 52).
- Complete Leveled Reader: Above Level (TE p. 671Q), or read book from Leveled Bibliography (TE pp. 594E–594F).

TEACHER-LED

- Evaluate activity and plan format for sharing (Challenge Handbook p. 52).
- Reread Leveled Theme Paperback: Above Level (TE pp. R6–R7), or read book from Leveled Bibliography (TE pp. 594E–594F). ✔

Partner or Individual Work

- Complete Comprehension Check (Practice Book p. 238).
- Begin Leveled Reader: Language Support (TE p. 671R), or read book from Leveled Bibliography (TE pp. 594E–594F).

TEACHER-LED

- Reread the Career Link (TE pp. 668–671) ✔ and review Link Skill (TE p. 668).
- Complete Leveled Reader: Language Support (TE p. 671R), or read book from Leveled Bibliography (TE pp. 594E–594F). ✔

Partner or Individual Work

- Reread book from Leveled Bibliography (TE pp. 594E–594F).

- Responding activities (TE pp. 666–667)
- Language Center activities (TE pp. 671M–671N)
- **Fluency Practice:** Reread *My Side of the Mountain; The Golden Lion Tamarin Comes Home; The Grizzly Bear Family Book.* ✔
- Activities relating to *My Side of the Mountain* at Education Place www.eduplace.com

Turn the page for more independent activities.

Classroom Management

Independent Activities

Assign these activities while you work with small groups.

Differentiated Instruction for Small Groups

- **Handbook for English Language Learners**, pp. 228–237

- **Extra Support Handbook**, pp. 224–233

Independent Activities

- Language Center, pp. 671M–671N

- Challenge/Extension Activities, Resources, pp. R13, R19

- **Classroom Management Handbook**, Activity Masters CM6-9–CM6-12

- **Challenge Handbook**, Challenge Masters CH6-5–CH6-6

Look for more activities in the Classroom Management Kit.

Health

Plant Hazards

👥 Pairs	🕐 45 minutes
Objective	Create a brochure of poisonous plants.
Materials	Reference sources, art materials, stapler

Do you know which plants to avoid? Work with a partner to write a brochure of toxic plants.

- Use reference sources such as an encyclopedia, the Internet, or a plant guide to research poisonous plants. Choose four to report on.

- Take notes on important characteristics of the plants.

- Fold two sheets of paper in half lengthwise and staple these together at the fold to create your brochure. Write a title and short introduction on the first page.

- Write and illustrate your brochure. For each plant, include key information to help someone to identify it.

Media

Q&A

👤 Singles	🕐 30 minutes
Objective	Write an interview.
Materials	Anthology, sample magazine interview

Write questions and sample answers for an interview with Dr. Robin Hughes, as if you were a magazine writer.

- Reread "Robin Hughes: Wildlife Doctor" in the Anthology. As you read, think about questions that you would want to ask Dr. Hughes in an interview.

- Take notes on what Dr. Hughes might answer, based on information given in the selection.

- Write the interview, following the question and answer (Q&A) format used in many magazines. Place a *Q:* before each question and an *A:* before each answer.

- Sample:
  Q: What is the most challenging aspect of your job?
  A: Figuring out the best way to treat so many different wild animals.

Consider copying and laminating these activities for use in centers.

Science

Kinds of Eaters

👥 Pairs	🕐 40 minutes
Objective	Create an Animal Eaters chart.
Materials	Reference sources, Anthology

Did you know that animals may be classified according to what they eat? Work with a partner to create a "Kinds of Eaters" chart.

- Copy the chart shown below onto a sheet of paper.
- Scan *My Side of the Mountain* and "Robin Hughes: Wildlife Doctor" to identify different animals that are mentioned.
- Use reference sources such as an encyclopedia or the Internet to find out what type of food each animal eats.
- List each animal under the appropriate heading in your chart.

Herbivore (eats plants)	Carnivore (eats meat)
Insectivore (eats insects)	Omnivore (eats everything)

Writing

Only in Fiction

👤 Singles	🕐 20 minutes
Objective	Create fictional characters.
Materials	Anthology, writing materials

In some fantasies and fairy tales, people are changed into forest creatures. What if the opposite thing happened and the animals changed into people?

- List the names of four animals from *My Side of the Mountain*. Next to each name, write a short description of the animal's personality traits.
- What type of human character might have the same personality traits? Write a short description for each human character you invent.

Science

Falcon Feats

👥 Pairs	🕐 30 minutes
Objective	Write a report on falconry.
Materials	Reference sources, art materials

In *My Side of the Mountain,* one of Sam's companions is Frightful, the falcon. Work with a partner to write a report about falconry, the practice of taming falcons.

- Use an encyclopedia, the Internet, or another reference source to find some basic facts about falcons and falconry.
- Take notes on the bird's physical characteristics, habitat, and behavior. Include information about the type of training and equipment that is used in falconry.
- Write and illustrate your report.

Listening Comprehension

OBJECTIVES

- Listen to draw conclusions about ideas not directly stated in the text.

Building Background

Tell students that you will read aloud a non-fiction article about a place where people take care of wild animals that need help.

- Ask students to discuss what such a place might do to return injured animals to the wild.

Fluency Modeling

Explain that as you read aloud, you will be modeling fluent oral reading. Ask students to listen carefully to your phrasing and your expression, or tone of voice and emphasis.

COMPREHENSION SKILL

Drawing Conclusions

Explain that readers can draw conclusions

- by thinking about statements the author makes
- by adding up facts and details to come to an understanding of their own

Purpose Setting Read the selection aloud, asking students to think about conclusions they can draw from selection details as they listen. Then use the Guiding Comprehension questions to assess students' understanding. Reread the selection for clarification as needed.

Teacher Read Aloud

Giving Wildlife a Second Chance
by Connie Goldsmith

Ten thousand furred and scaly feet come through its doors each year. Raptors peer down from their high perches, screeching out greetings to each new arrival. The mouse dairy farm provides a ready supply of milk for injured infant rodents. Chirping barrels of live, crunchy crickets line the walls. Platters of tasty worms await their destiny as dinner. The library has rabbits and rats that can be checked out for a week.

What kind of place is this, anyway?

This is the Lindsay Wildlife Museum, located near a park at the foot of Mount Diablo in Walnut Creek, California. Surrounded by spring green hills, Lindsay Museum has fostered connections between people and nature for forty-four years. It is one of the largest and most active wildlife rehabilitation hospitals in the United States, treating thousands of injured or orphaned wild animals each year. The museum also has many educational programs for both children and adults in the community.

The first thing I notice when I tour this small museum is a row of large glass cages winding across the exhibit hall. Giant birds sit on wooden platforms on top of the cages. My guide, the museum's rehabilitation director, tells me these birds cannot return to the wild because they could no longer survive there. They have been too badly injured—some have been poisoned and need ❶ special diets, and others are no longer afraid of humans. Instead, they split their time between being on display and having a vacation in a volunteer's home—three months on and three months off.

Below, in the large glass cages, are the rescued mammals. These animals also will not be released but will spend their lives on display. The gray fox and the bobcat are too tame for the wild, and the raccoon is too injured. They join the birds who sit above them as living reminders of the sad clash between people and nature—a conflict that nature seldom wins. In fact, nearly all of the animals at the museum are there because of harmful encounters with humans. There is also a reptile and amphibian section, and even a large tank holding native freshwater fish.

We next tour the museum's hospital wing, where there's a holding area for new arrivals, a treatment room, a laboratory, a baby bird section, and an isolation ward for sick creatures. There is also a modern, bright white kitchen with a refrigerator but no stove. "After all," my guide says, "animals do not eat cooked food in the wild."

We leave the hospital area to see the "school animals." These birds and small mammals are permanent residents of the museum and regularly visit schools. They are not to be handled or touched because they are not meant to be pets. By treating these animals as wild creatures, students begin to understand how complex and different the natural world is from their own.

But what about wildlife that can be rehabilitated and released? If an animal is not too used to humans and it looks as if it may recover, it will go home with a volunteer rehabilitation specialist, who prepares the animals for release into the wild.

❷ The animals most often brought to the museum are squirrels, mice, raccoons, opossums, and rabbits. Other patients include deer and even bobcats or coyotes. Many kinds of birds come in, too—owls, hawks, eagles, seabirds, songbirds, ravens, and crows. Once an oil-tanker crew member brought an injured albatross into the museum.

❸ When asked why the museum tries to help animals as common as rabbits or raccoons, the director says, "It is not up to us to decide which animals are important enough to save. We don't really know what animal may become rare in the future. Working with any wild animal gives people a link with nature—a chance to appreciate and value all animals." This amazing museum offers a second chance to wildlife, an opportunity to recover and return to the woods, hills, and fields where they belong.

CRITICAL THINKING
Guiding Comprehension

❶ **DRAWING CONCLUSIONS** Why do you think animals can't be returned to the wild if they lose their fear of humans? (They might be too trusting of people who want to hurt them or rely too much on people for food.)

❷ **DRAWING CONCLUSIONS** Why do you think squirrels, mice, raccoons, opossums, and rabbits are common at the museum? (Their habitats often bring them into contact with humans, increasing their chances of becoming injured or dependent on people for food.)

❸ **DRAWING CONCLUSIONS** What conclusion has the museum director reached about all animals, even common ones? (Sample answer: They are all valuable links with nature.)

Discussion Options

Personal Response Ask students what they find most interesting about the Lindsay Wildlife Museum.

⭐ **Connecting/Comparing** Have students compare how people at the Lindsay Wildlife Museum and people in *The Golden Lion Tamarin Comes Home* help animals.

English Language Learners

Supporting Comprehension

Write *rehabilitation* on the board, and explain that the word means "the act of restoring, or returning, to health or useful life." Tell students that words that end with *-ion* are usually nouns. Ask volunteers to suggest other words that end with *-ion.* (*cooperation, investigation, donation*) Have partners use the words in sentences.

Building Background

Key Concept: Wilderness Survival

Point out that this selection is about a fictional character who has close encounters with wild animals. Discuss what a person could learn from wild animals about surviving in the woods. Then use "Living on the Land" on Anthology pages 648–649 to build background and introduce Key Vocabulary.

- Ask a student to read aloud "Living on the Land."

- Have students use the illustration to discuss the challenges of survival in the wilderness without store-bought food and modern equipment, using only the resources one might find there.

- Encourage students to share their responses to the questions on page 648.

Background and Vocabulary

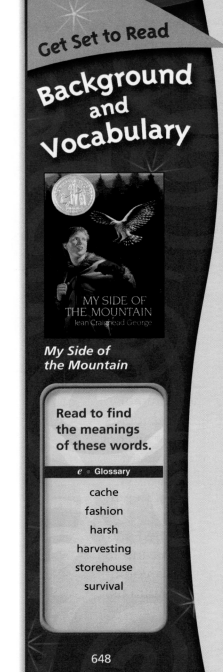

My Side of the Mountain

Read to find the meanings of these words.

e ● Glossary

cache
fashion
harsh
harvesting
storehouse
survival

648

Living on the Land

In *My Side of the Mountain*, a boy chooses to "live on the land" in a forest. His **survival** depends on being able to use what he finds in nature to meet his needs.

Think about what those needs would be. A person living on the land would need to give a lot of attention to food, clothing, and shelter. How would someone go about **harvesting** food from edible plants in the area? How much work would it be to build up a **cache** of food that would last through the winter? Or to create a **storehouse** where food would not spoil or be eaten by wild animals?

Naturally, a forest dweller would also need a place to live. What kind of shelter would that person **fashion** out of materials found in the woods? What qualities in a shelter would help keep out a **harsh** winter? What would make the warmest clothing?

There is one more need to think about. Even if food, shelter, and clothing were taken care of, a person would need to keep from being lonely. What kind of friendship might someone find in the forest?

 English Language Learners

Supporting Comprehension

Beginning/Preproduction Have students listen to the article. Then have students point to items in the illustration that could be harvested. Ask them to draw other foods that could be harvested outdoors.

Early Production and Speech Emergence Mime *harvesting*, *migration*, and the verb *fashion*. Explain the meanings of *cache*, *storehouse*, and *survival*. Ask students to use these words as they discuss what it might be like to live in the wilderness.

Intermediate and Advanced Fluency Have students work in small groups to read and then summarize in their own words the challenges of wilderness survival.

649

Introducing Vocabulary

Key Vocabulary

These words support the Key Concept and appear in the selection.

cache hidden store of goods

fashion to make into a particular form

harsh cruel and severe

harvesting gathering plant parts to be eaten later

migration mass movement of an animal group to a different habitat, usually in search of food

storehouse place where supplies are stored for future use

survival the preservation of one's life; the continuing of life

e • **Glossary**
e • **WordGame**

See Vocabulary notes on pages 652, 654, 656, 658, 660, 662, and 664 for additional words to preview.

Transparency 6–18

Words About Survival

Friday, October 12

Today is my first day at the mountain lake. I came up here on Tuesday with my parents, who stayed a few days to watch the fall bird migration. Now most of the birds have headed south to their winter homes, and my parents have said good-bye.

By myself at last, I am anxious to try out the survival skills I learned this past summer at camp. First thing tomorrow, I'm going to set up a storehouse, where I can keep the food I'll need this winter. I think I'll fashion the storage area out of rocks, and seal the cracks with mud. I'll also need to find a cave or hollow log nearby to use as a cache for extra food, just in case my main supply gets raided by animals.

Once those two areas are ready, I can begin harvesting roots and berries. I'll also need to catch and smoke some fish. With luck I'll be able to put together enough supplies to last through the harsh winter months, when food is much harder to find.

With so much to do before the first snow, I won't have much time for sightseeing. But for right now I need to get some rest. Goodnight.

Practice Book page 236

Name _____

Late Autumn in the Woods

Complete the paragraph below with words from the word box.

Vocabulary

storehouse
harsh
survival
cache
harvesting
fashion
migration

The leaves have turned colors and fallen from the trees. Most birds have made their migration **(1 point)** south to warmer lands. Farmers have finished harvesting **(1)** the last of the wheat and rye, and they have filled crates with apples and have placed them in a cool storehouse **(1)** . Each squirrel is busy adding a few more nuts to its cache **(1)** of food for winter. Bears gorge themselves on one last meal of berries, for they need to have a thick layer of fat to ensure survival **(1)** through the long winter. The few settlers who have come to the wild lands late in the season hurry to fashion **(1)** shelter that will protect them from the harsh **(1)** weather soon to arrive.

Write three more sentences using words from the box to continue the paragraph.

(3) _____

_____

_____

_____

Display Transparency 6–18.

- Model how to figure out the meaning of *migration* from context clues.

- Ask students to figure out the meaning of each remaining Key Vocabulary word using context clues. Have students explain how they figured out the meaning of each word.

- Have students look for these words as they read and use them to discuss what they learn about survival in the woods.

Practice/Homework Assign **Practice Book** page 236.

Introducing Vocabulary **649**

COMPREHENSION STRATEGY
Summarize

Teacher Modeling Ask a student to read aloud the Strategy Focus. Explain that when readers summarize a story, they include only the most important events. Have students read pages 652–653. Then model the strategy.

Think Aloud *To summarize what I've read so far, I'll identify the most important events. Sam watches mice, squirrels, and chipmunks gathering food. He sees birds move to the south. He begins to gather food for himself.*

Test Prep Students can quickly summarize a test passage before they answer a question, thinking in particular about the order of facts or events. Creating this kind of mental "outline" will help them decide where to look to find the answer.

COMPREHENSION SKILL
Drawing Conclusions

Introduce the Graphic Organizer. Explain that a Conclusions Chart can help students add up story clues and details to draw conclusions about the story. As they read, students will fill out the Conclusions Chart on **Practice Book** page 237.

- Display **Transparency 6–19.** Have students read Anthology pages 654–655.
- Model how to fill in the second row. Monitor students' work as needed.

MEET THE AUTHOR
Jean Craighead George

Jean Craighead George's family lived in Washington, D.C., and her father often took her and her brothers into the surrounding countryside to teach them about plants and animals. She also learned some of the survival skills that Sam Gribley uses, including building a lean-to, and making a fishhook and line out of wood and wood fiber. Of her writing, George says, "I write for children. Children are still in love with the wonders of nature, and I am too."

Among over seventy other books dealing with nature, George has extended the story of *My Side of the Mountain* in two sequels: *On the Far Side of the Mountain* and *Frightful's Mountain*.

MEET THE ILLUSTRATOR
Gary Aagaard

Gary Aagaard grew up in Seattle, Washington. He remembers being energetic as a child and full of curiosity. To illustrate *My Side of the Mountain*, Aagaard traveled to upstate New York, where the story takes place. There he took pictures of the outdoors, using a friend's son as a model for Sam. Aagaard currently lives in New York City.

Learn more about Jean Craighead George and Gary Aagaard at Education Place. **www.eduplace.com/kids**

650

Transparency 6–19
Use the Clues

Story Clues			Conclusions
pages 652–653 Mice, squirrels, and chipmunks collected seeds and nuts.	+	Sam gathers various roots and smokes fish and rabbit.	= On the wooded mountain where Sam is living, food is scarce in the winter.
pages 654–655 The animals are growing thick coats of fur and making warm shelters for winter.	+	Sam realizes he needs to build a small fireplace to warm his shelter.	= Sam's clothing and his current shelter aren't enough to protect him from the cold of winter.
pages 656–658 Sam playfully chases the Baron Weasel up the mountain.	+	Sam runs after Frightful because he is warned the falcon has left him.	= Sam relies on the animals to keep him from feeling too lonely.
pages 660–665 The Baron comes to get food from Sam, but doesn't let him get too close.	+	The raccoons make a mess of Sam's food supply.	= Even though Sam enjoys the animals' company, he must remain alert around these wild creatures.

TRANSPARENCY 6–19
TEACHER'S EDITION PAGES 650 AND 671A

Practice Book page 237

My Side of the Mountain
Graphic Organizer
Conclusions Chart

Name _____

Use the Clues

Read the story clues and conclusions provided in the boxes below. Fill in the missing information with text from the selection.

Story Clues			Conclusions
pages 652–653 Mice, squirrels, and chipmunks collected seeds and nuts.	+	Sam gathers various roots and smokes fish and rabbit.	= On the wooded mountain where Sam is living, food is scarce in the winter.
pages 654–655 The animals are growing thick coats of fur and making warm shelters for winter. **(2 points)**	+	Sam realizes he needs to build a small fireplace to warm his shelter. **(2)**	= Sam's clothing and his current shelter aren't enough to protect him from the cold of winter.
pages 656–658 Sam playfully chases the Baron Weasel up the mountain.	+	Sam runs after Frightful because he is warned the falcon has left him.	= Sam relies on the animals to keep him from feeling too lonely. **(2)**
pages 660–665 The Baron comes to get food from Sam, but doesn't let him get too close. **(2)**	+	The raccoons make a mess of Sam's food supply. **(2)**	= Even though Sam enjoys the animals' company, he must remain alert around these wild creatures.

Selection 3

MY SIDE OF THE MOUNTAIN
Jean Craighead George

Strategy Focus

Sam Gribley is living alone in a mountain forest. As you read, **summarize** how Sam solves his problems and interacts with animals.

651

Extra Support/Intervention

Selection Preview

pages 651–655 Sam notices animals growing new coats and preparing their homes for winter. What preparations do you think Sam will have to make to survive winter in the wilderness?

pages 656–658 Sam's pet falcon, Frightful, flies off and Sam worries that she might not return. Do you think the falcon will return?

pages 659–661 Sam's entry on page 659 is called IN WHICH *We All Learn About Halloween*. Who is *we*, and what do you think they will learn about Halloween?

pages 662–665 Look at the illustration on page 664. How do you think Sam feels at this moment?

Purpose Setting

- Remind students that this selection tells about Sam Gribley, who lives in the wilderness.

- Have students preview the selection and predict what encounters Sam will have with wild animals.

- Have students stop from time to time as they read to summarize the main events and information that they have read.

- Ask students to use selection details to draw conclusions about story events and characters.

- You may wish to preview with students the Responding questions on Anthology page 666.

Journal ▸ Students can use their journals to record their predictions and summaries.

STRATEGY REVIEW

Phonics/Decoding

Remind students to use the Phonics/Decoding Strategy as they read.

Modeling Write this sentence from *My Side of the Mountain* on the board: *As I got used to the* <u>indignity</u> *and the smell, I saw the raccoons cavort around my fireplace and dodge past me.* Point to *indignity*.

Think Aloud *I recognize the prefix* in- *and the suffix* -ity. *The part that's left looks like the word* sign, *but with a* d *instead of an* s. *That would make the word* ihn-DYN-ih-tee. *That doesn't sound like a word I've heard. It might be* ihn-DIHG-nih-tee. *I've heard of* dignity, *so* indignity *must mean that the boy is in a situation where he has no dignity.*

READ & COMPREHEND

My Side of the Mountain

Reading the Selection 651

CRITICAL THINKING

Guiding Comprehension

1 **MAKING INFERENCES** Why do you think Sam refers to September as *she*? (He feels a personal relationship to autumn.)

2 **DRAWING CONCLUSIONS** What does Sam's description of his feelings on page 653 tell you about him? (He enjoys being out in nature.)

3 **NOTING DETAILS** What does the episode with the crickets show about Sam? (He has a sense of humor.)

4 **DRAWING CONCLUSIONS** What do you think the author means by *the goodness of the earth*? (the rich supply of food that comes from the ground)

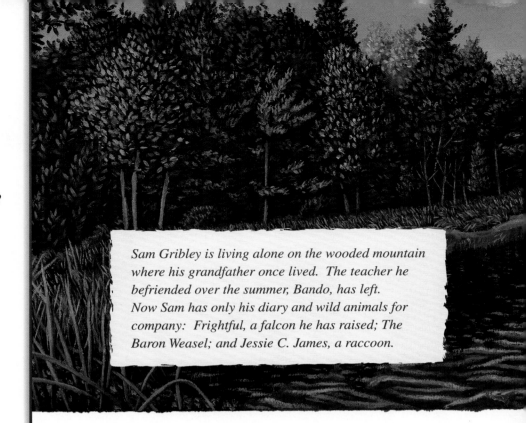

Sam Gribley is living alone on the wooded mountain where his grandfather once lived. The teacher he befriended over the summer, Bando, has left. Now Sam has only his diary and wild animals for company: Frightful, a falcon he has raised; The Baron Weasel; and Jessie C. James, a raccoon.

IN WHICH

The Autumn Provides Food and Loneliness

1 September blazed a trail into the mountains. First she burned the grasses. The grasses seeded and were harvested by the mice and the winds.

Then she sent the squirrels and chipmunks running boldly through the forest, collecting and hiding nuts.

Then she frosted the aspen leaves and left them sunshine yellow.

Then she gathered the birds together in flocks, and the mountaintop was full of songs and twitterings and flashing wings. The birds were ready to move to the south.

652

Vocabulary

blazed marked or cut, as when making a trail

aspen a western tree whose leaves flutter readily in the wind

bulbs underground stems or roots

tubers swollen stems, usually underground, such as potatoes

sedges plants resembling grasses, with solid rather than hollow stems

talons the claws of a bird of prey

English Language Learners

Language Development

Read aloud the phrases *she burned the grasses, she sent the squirrels, she frosted the aspen leaves,* and *she gathered the birds* on page 652.

- Ask students who *she* is. (September)

- Point out that the author *personifies* (verb), or gives human characteristics to, a nonliving thing, the month of September. This process is called *personification* (noun).

And I, Sam Gribley, felt just wonderful, just wonderful.

I pushed the raft down the stream and gathered arrowleaf bulbs, cattail tubers, bulrush roots, and the nutlike tubers of the sedges.

And then the crop of crickets appeared and Frightful hopped all over the meadow snagging them in her great talons and eating them. I tried them, because I had heard they are good. I think it was another species of cricket that was meant. I think the field cricket would taste excellent if you were starving. I was not starving, so I preferred to listen to them. I abandoned the crickets and went back to the goodness of the earth.

I smoked fish and rabbit, dug wild onions by the pouchful, and raced September for her crop.

2

3

4

653

CRITICAL THINKING
Guiding Comprehension

5 **CAUSE AND EFFECT** Why is Sam fearful? What causes his fear? (He is afraid of a harsh winter. He sees the animals preparing for winter.)

6 **MAKING INFERENCES** Why do you think thoughts of scarecrows and Halloween make Sam feel lonely? (because Halloween can be fun to spend with friends, but he will be alone)

COMPREHENSION STRATEGY
Summarize

Teacher/Student Modeling Model how to summarize pages 652–654.

- What important events are described here? (Fall arrives in the mountains. Sam sees animals preparing for winter.)

- Should I include the detail about digging wild onions? Why? (no, because it is not the most important information)

Have students summarize pages 655–659. (Sam builds the fireplace and continues to prepare for winter.)

Vocabulary

mantle a covering; a cloak

harsh cruel and severe

burrows holes or tunnels dug by small animals for homes or shelter

fashion to make into a particular form

warblers small birds, many of which have yellowish feathers and markings

---

"October 15

"Today The Baron Weasel looked moldy. I couldn't get near enough to see what was the matter with him, but it occurs to me that he might be changing his summer fur for his white winter mantle. If he is, it is an itchy process. He scratches a lot."

5 Seeing The Baron changing his mantle for winter awoke the first fears in me. I wrote that note on a little birch bark, curled up on my bed, and shivered.

The snow and the cold and the long lifeless months are ahead, I thought. The wind was blowing hard and cool across the mountain. I lit my candle, took out the rabbit and squirrel hides I had been saving, and began rubbing and kneading them to softness.

The Baron was getting a new suit for winter. I must have one too. Some fur underwear, some mittens, fur-lined socks.

Frightful, who was sitting on the foot post of the bed, yawned, fluffed, and thrust her head into the slate-gray feathers of her back. She slept. I worked for several hours.

I must say here that I was beginning to wonder if I should not go home for the winter and come back again in the spring. Everything in the forest was getting prepared for the harsh months. Jessie Coon James was as fat as a barrel. He came down the tree slowly, his fat falling in a roll over his shoulders. The squirrels were working and storing food. They were building leaf nests. The skunks had burrows and plugged themselves in at dawn with bunches of leaves. No drafts could reach them.

As I thought of the skunks and all the animals preparing themselves against the winter, I realized suddenly that my tree would be as cold as the air if I did not somehow find a way to heat it.

"notes:

"Today I rafted out into the deep pools of the creek to fish. It was a lazy sort of autumn day, the sky clear, the leaves beginning to brighten, the air warm. I stretched out on my back because the fish weren't biting, and hummed.

"My line jerked and I sat up to pull, but was too late. However, I was not too late to notice that I had drifted into the bank — the very bank where Bando had dug the clay for the jam pots.

654

Extra Support/Intervention

Strategy Modeling: Summarize

Model the strategy with the "notes" section on pages 654–655.

I could sum up the "notes" section this way: While fishing, Sam gets an idea to build a clay fireplace for the winter. I would not include the detail about the brightening leaves. It's a nice image, but it isn't the most important information.

"At that moment I knew what I was going to do. I was going to build a fireplace of clay, even fashion a little chimney of clay. It would be small, but enough to warm the tree during the long winter.

"Next day

"I dragged the clay up the mountain to my tree in my second best pair of city pants. I tied the bottoms of the legs, stuffed them full, and as I looked down on my strange cargo, I thought of scarecrows and Halloween. Suddenly I was terribly lonely. The air smelled of leaves and the cool wind from the stream hugged me. The warblers in the trees above me seemed gay and glad about their trip south. I stopped halfway up the mountain and dropped my head. I was lonely and on the verge of tears. Suddenly there was a flash, a pricking sensation on my leg, and I looked down in time to see The Baron leap from my pants to the cover of fern.

655

 **Fluency Practice**

Rereading for Fluency Have students choose a favorite part of the story to reread to a partner, or suggest that they read page 655. Encourage students to read expressively.

Guiding Comprehension

7 MAKING INFERENCES What does Sam mean by *He scared the loneliness right out of me*? (The Baron startles Sam and makes him forget about being alone.)

8 DRAWING CONCLUSIONS Why does it take three days for Sam to finish the fireplace? (He has trouble figuring out how to seal it so that smoke won't pour into his tree.)

9 NOTING DETAILS What details does the author include on page 657 to show how much Sam cares for Frightful? (Sam tries hard to lure her back. He also says *my heart was sore* after she flew away.)

7 "He scared the loneliness right out of me. I ran after him and chased him up the mountain, losing him from time to time in the ferns and crowfeet. We stormed into camp an awful sight, The Baron bouncing and screaming ahead of me, and me dragging that half scarecrow of clay.

"Frightful took one look and flew to the end of her leash. She doesn't like The Baron, and watches him — well, like a hawk. I don't like to leave her alone. End notes. Must make fireplace."

8 It took three days to get the fireplace worked out so that it didn't smoke me out of the tree like a bee. It was an enormous problem. In the first place, the chimney sagged because the clay was too heavy to hold itself up, so I had to get some dry grasses to work into it so it could hold its own weight.

I whittled out one of the old knotholes to let the smoke out, and built the chimney down from this. Of course when the clay dried, it pulled away from the tree, and all the smoke poured back in on me.

So I tried sealing the leak with pine pitch, and that worked all right, but then the funnel over the fire bed cracked, and I had to put wooden props under that.

The wooden props burned, and I could see that this wasn't going to work either; so I went down the mountain to the site of the old Gribley farmhouse and looked around for some iron spikes or some sort of metal.

656

Vocabulary

funnel a shaft, flue, or stack for the passage of smoke

props devices used to support something

lure a bunch of feathers attached to a long cord, used in falconry to bring a hawk back

migration a mass movement of an animal group to a different habitat, usually in search of food or to bear young

English Language Learners

Supporting Comprehension

Encourage students to discuss how Sam's feelings have changed so far. Offer these prompts.

- How does Sam feel on pages 652–653? (*just wonderful*)
- How do his feelings change on pages 654–657? (He is worried about winter and feels lonely.)
- How do you think you would feel if you lived alone on a mountain? (Answers will vary.)

READ & COMPREHEND

I took the wooden shovel that I had carved from the board and dug around what I thought must have been the back door or possibly the woodhouse.

I found a hinge, old hand-made nails that would come in handy, and finally, treasure of treasures, the axle of an old wagon. It was much too big. I had no hacksaw to cut it into smaller pieces, and I was not strong enough to heat it and hammer it apart. Besides, I didn't have anything but a small wooden mallet I had made.

I carried my trophies home and sat down before my tree to fix dinner and feed Frightful. The evening was cooling down for a frost. I looked at Frightful's warm feathers. I didn't even have a deer hide for a blanket. I had used the two I had for a door and a pair of pants. I wished that I might grow feathers.

I tossed Frightful off my fist and she flashed through the trees and out over the meadow. She went with a determination strange to her. "She is going to leave," I cried. "I have never seen her fly so wildly." I pushed the smoked fish aside and ran to the meadow. I whistled and whistled and whistled until my mouth was dry and no more whistle came.

I ran onto the big boulder. I could not see her. Wildly I waved the lure. I licked my lips and whistled again. The sun was a cold steely color as it dipped below the mountain. The air was now brisk, and Frightful was gone. I was sure that she had suddenly taken off on the migration; my heart was sore and ⑨

657

Comprehension Preview

Drawing Conclusions

Teach

- Explain that readers can use selection details to draw conclusions about something that is not stated in the text.

Practice

- Read aloud paragraph three on page 656 through paragraph four on page 657.

- Ask students to draw conclusions about the type of person Sam is based on story details. Record responses in a chart like the one below. (Sample answers shown.)

Apply

- Have students draw conclusions about Sam's feelings for each of the wild animals.

- Tell students to create their own charts to record their conclusions.

Story Clue +	Story Clue =	Conclusion
Sam uses dry grass to keep the clay chimney from sagging.	Sam has made a wooden shovel and mallet.	Sam is very resourceful.

Target Skill Trace	
Preview; Teach	p. 647CC; p. 650; p. 657; p. 671A
Reteach	p. R12
Review	Theme 5, p. 509

ASSIGNMENT CARD 12

Will It Work?

Problem Solving

Sam says it takes him three days to figure out how to get his fireplace to work properly. Look back on pages 656 and 657 to identify the problems with the chimney and the solutions Sam uses. Figure out which problem he still must solve. Then work with a partner to make a list of solutions to that problem. Keep your list in mind as you read on to find out what Sam does finally to get the fireplace to work. Compare his solution to the ones you devised.

Theme 6: Animal Encounters

Teacher's Resource BLM page 95

CRITICAL THINKING

Guiding Comprehension

10 NOTING DETAILS Why do you think the author calls the sun *cold* and *steely*? (to remind readers that the cold, harsh winter is approaching)

11 DRAWING CONCLUSIONS In what ways does Frightful help Sam on pages 658–659? (She leads him to the flat stone and she helps him realize that he needs to let more air into the room.)

pounding. I had enough food, I was sure. Frightful was not absolutely necessary for my survival; but I was now so fond of her. She was more than a bird. I knew I must have her back to talk to and play with if I was going to make it through the winter.

I whistled. Then I heard a cry in the grasses up near the white birches.

In the gathering darkness I saw movement. I think I flew to the spot. And there she was; she had caught herself a bird. I rolled into the grass beside her and clutched her jesses. She didn't intend to leave, but I was going to make sure that she didn't. I grabbed so swiftly that my hand hit a rock and I bruised my knuckles.

The rock was flat and narrow and long; it was the answer to my fireplace.

 I picked up Frightful in one hand and the stone in the other; and I laughed at the cold steely sun as it slipped out of sight, because I knew I was going to be warm. This flat stone was what I needed to hold up the funnel and finish my fireplace.

And that's what I did with it. I broke it into two pieces, set one on each side under the funnel, lit the fire, closed the flap of the door and listened to the wind bring the first frost to the mountain. I was warm.

658

Vocabulary

survival preservation of life; continuing of life

jesses short straps fastened around the legs of a hawk to which a leash may be attached

ventilate to let fresh air into a place

harvesting gathering plant parts to be eaten later

tethered bound with a rope or chain to limit how far one can move

REACHING ALL LEARNERS

Extra Support/ Intervention

Review (pages 652–659)

Before students who need extra support join the whole class for Stop and Think on page 659, have them

- check predictions
- take turns modeling Monitor/Clarify and other strategies they used
- help you add to **Transparency 6–19**
- check and revise their Conclusions Chart on **Practice Book** page 237, and use it to summarize

English Language Learners

Language Development

Have students locate the words *hit* and *set* on page 658. Ask them to identify the part of speech (verbs) and the tense. (past) Point out that the spelling of some verbs does not change in the past tense. Have students write *cut, let,* and *put.* Encourage them to write short sentences using these verbs.

Then I noticed something dreadful. Frightful was sitting on the bedpost, her head under her wings. She was toppling. She jerked her head out of her feathers. Her eyes looked glassy. She is sick, I said. I picked her up and stroked her, and we both might have died there if I had not opened the tent flap to get her some water. The cold night air revived her. "Air," I said. "The fireplace used up all the oxygen. I've got to ventilate this place."

We sat out in the cold for a long time because I was more than a little afraid of what our end might have been.

I put out the fire, took the door down and wrapped up in it. Frightful and I slept with the good frost nipping our faces.

"notes:
"I cut out several more knotholes to let air in and out of the tree room. I tried it today. I have Frightful on my fist watching her. It's been about two hours and she hasn't fainted and I haven't gone numb. I can still write and see clearly.
"Test: Frightful's healthy face."

11

IN WHICH
We All Learn About Halloween

"October 28
"I have been up and down the mountain every day for a week, watching to see if walnuts and hickory nuts are ripe. Today I found the squirrels all over the trees, harvesting them furiously, and so I have decided that ripe or not, I must gather them. It's me or the squirrels.

"I tethered Frightful in the hickory tree while I went to the walnut tree and filled pouches. Frightful protected the hickory nuts. She keeps the squirrels so busy scolding her that they don't have time to take the nuts. They are quite terrified by her. It is a good scheme. I shout and bang the tree and keep them away while I gather.

659

Stop and Think

Critical Thinking Questions

1. **MAKING JUDGMENTS** Do you think Sam would make a good friend? Why or why not? (Sample answer: yes, because he is resourceful and has a sense of humor)

2. **DRAWING CONCLUSIONS** Is Sam prepared for the winter? Explain. (Yes. He has collected food and built a fireplace to keep warm.)

Strategies in Action

Have students take turns modeling Summarize and other strategies they used.

Discussion Options

You may wish to bring the entire class together to do one or more of the activities below.

• **Review Predictions/Purpose** Review students' predictions. Discuss students' questions, what they have learned, and any conclusions they have drawn about Sam.

• **Share Group Discussions** Have students share their literature discussions.

• **Summarize** Have students use their Conclusions Charts to summarize the story so far.

Monitoring Student Progress

If . . .	Then . . .
students have successfully completed the Extra Support activities on page 658,	have them read the rest of the selection cooperatively or independently.

Reading the Selection 659

CRITICAL THINKING
Guiding Comprehension

12 **SEQUENCE OF EVENTS** What happens just before Sam takes out his calendar stick? What happens after? (Baron weasel enters, eats some soup, and leaves. Then Sam decides to have a Halloween party.)

13 **COMPARE AND CONTRAST** How does Sam feel about the forest animals before he remembers that it is Halloween? How do his feelings change after he remembers Halloween? (Before, he thinks of them as his rivals for food. After, he wants to share his food with them as *treats*.)

"I have never seen so many squirrels. They hang from the slender branches, they bounce through the limbs, they seem to come from the whole forest. They must pass messages along to each other — messages that tell what kind of nuts and where the trees are."

A few days later, my storehouse rolling with nuts, I began the race for apples. Entering this race were squirrels, raccoons, and a fat old skunk who looked as if he could eat not another bite. He was ready to sleep his autumn meal off, and I resented him because he did not need my apples. However, I did not toy with him.

I gathered what apples I could, cut some in slices, and dried them on the boulder in the sun. Some I put in the storeroom tree to eat right away. They were a little wormy, but it was wonderful to eat an apple again.

Then one night this was all done, the crop was gathered. I sat down to make a few notes when The Baron came sprinting into sight.

12 He actually bounced up and licked the edges of my turtle-shell bowl, stormed Frightful, and came to my feet.

"Baron Weasel," I said. "It is nearing Halloween. Are you playing tricks or treats?" I handed him the remains of my turtle soup dinner, and, fascinated, watched him devour it.

"note:

"The Baron chews with his back molars, and chews with a ferocity I have not seen in him before. His eyes gleam, the lips curl back from his white pointed teeth, and he frowns like an angry man. If I move toward him, a rumble starts in his chest that keeps me back. He flashes glances at me. It is indeed strange to be looked in the eye by this fearless wild animal. There is something human about his beady glance. Perhaps because that glance tells me something. It tells me he knows who I am and that he does not want me to come any closer."

The Baron Weasel departed after his feast. Frightful, who was drawn up as skinny as a stick, relaxed and fluffed her feathers, and then I said to her,

660

Vocabulary

storehouse a place where supplies are stored for future use

ferocity the condition of being extremely savage or fierce

beady small, round, and shiny

propped kept from falling; supported

---

660 **THEME 6: Animal Encounters**

"See, he got his treats. No tricks." Then something occurred to me. I reached inside the door and pulled out my calendar stick. I counted 28, 29, 30, 31.

"Frightful, that old weasel knows. It is Halloween. Let's have a Halloween party."

Swiftly I made piles of cracked nuts, smoked rabbit, and crayfish. I even added two of my apples. This food was an invitation to the squirrels, foxes, raccoons, opossums, even the birds that lived around me to come have a party.

When Frightful is tethered to her stump, some of the animals and birds will only come close enough to scream at her. So bird and I went inside the tree, propped open the flap, and waited.

Not much happened that night. I learned that it takes a little time for the woodland messages to get around. But they do. Before the party I had been very careful about leaving food out because I needed every mouthful. I took the precaution of rolling a stone in front of my store tree. The harvest moon rose. Frightful and I went to sleep.

At dawn, we abandoned the party. I left the treats out, however. Since it was a snappy gold-colored day, we went off to get some more rabbit skins to finish my winter underwear.

13

661

Making Judgments

Review

- Remind students that judgments are opinions based on consideration of personal values and facts. Point out that there is no one correct judgment.

- Tell them that good readers use story details and personal values to make judgments about whether something is true or false and right or wrong.

Practice/Apply

- Have a volunteer read aloud the second paragraph on page 659, below the heading IN WHICH *We All Learn About Halloween*.

- Ask students whether or not they think it is right for Sam to keep Frightful tethered, and why. Ask students to write a list of reasons that support their judgments. (Answers will vary.)

- Then have students work in pairs to make judgments about whether or not Sam should feed the wild animals, and why. (Answers will vary.)

- Invite students to share their judgments and supporting reasons.

Review Skill Trace	
Teach	Theme 5, p. 547A
Reteach	Theme 5, p. R12
▶ Review	p. 661; Theme 5, p. 635

ASSIGNMENT CARD 13

Survival Techniques

Comparing Details

Look back through the story and make a list of all the things the animals do in preparation for the harsh winter months. Then work with a group of your classmates to create another list of ways in which people prepare for winter weather. Think about:

- the way people dress

- the things people do to their cars or other vehicles

- how people prepare their homes

When you have finished, compare animals' preparations with those of humans. How are they alike? How are they different?

Theme 6: Animal Encounters

Teacher's Resource BLM page 95

CRITICAL THINKING
Guiding Comprehension

14 **WRITER'S CRAFT** How does the author create suspense? (by having Frightful seem nervous and having Sam wonder why)

15 **NOTING DETAILS** How does Sam react when he discovers that raccoons have entered his house on page 663? (At first, he is startled. Then he is dismayed to find the mess they are making.)

COMPREHENSION STRATEGY
Summarize

Student Modeling Have students model the strategy by summarizing pages 659–663.

Vocabulary

ox bow a U-shaped bend in a river or stream

hemlock a type of evergreen tree with short, flat needles and small cones

lingering delaying departure

cache a hidden store of goods

We had lunch along the creek — stewed mussels and wild potatoes. We didn't get back until dusk because I discovered some wild rice in an ox bow of the stream. There was no more than a handful.

Home that night, everything seemed peaceful enough. A few nuts were gone, to the squirrels, I thought. I baked a fish in leaves, and ate a small, precious amount of wild rice. It was marvelous! As I settled down to scrape the rabbit skins of the day, my neighbor the skunk marched right into the campground and set to work on the smoked rabbit. I made some Halloween notes:

"The moon is coming up behind the aspens. It is as big as a pumpkin and as orange. The winds are cool, the stars are like electric light bulbs. I am just inside the doorway, with my turtle-shell lamp burning so that I can see to write this.

"Something is moving beyond the second hemlock. Frightful is very alert, as if there are things all around us. Halloween was over at midnight last night, but for us it is just beginning. That's how I feel, anyhow, but it just may be my imagination.

14 "I wish Frightful would stop pulling her feathers in and drawing herself up like a spring. I keep thinking that she feels things.

662

"Here comes Jessie C. James. He will want the venison.

"He didn't get the venison. There was a snarl, and a big raccoon I've never seen walked past him, growling and looking ferocious. Jessie C. stood motionless — I might say, scared stiff. He held his head at an angle and let the big fellow eat. If Jessie so much as rolled his eyes that old coon would sputter at him."

It grew dark, and I couldn't see much. An eerie yelp behind the boulder announced that the red fox of the meadow was nearing. He gave me goose bumps. He stayed just beyond my store tree, weaving back and forth on silent feet. Every now and then he would cry — a wavery owl-like cry. I wrote some more.

"The light from my turtle lamp casts leaping shadows. To the beechnuts has come a small gray animal. I can't make out what — now, I see it. It's a flying squirrel. That surprises me, I've never seen a flying squirrel around here, but of course I haven't been up much after sunset."

When it grew too dark to see, I lit a fire, hoping it would not end the party. It did not, and the more I watched, the more I realized that all these animals were familiar with my camp. A white-footed mouse walked over my woodpile as if it were his.

I put out my candle and fell asleep when the fire turned to coals. Much later I was awakened by screaming. I lifted my head and looked into the moonlit forest. A few guests, still lingering at the party, saw me move, and dashed bashfully into the ground cover. One was big and slender. I thought perhaps a mink. As I slowly came awake, I realized that screaming was coming from behind me. Something was in my house. I jumped up and shouted, and two raccoons skittered under my feet. I reached for my candle, slipped on hundreds of nuts, and fell. When I finally got a light and looked about me, I was dismayed to see what a mess my guests had made of my tree house. They had found the cache of acorns and beechnuts and had tossed them all over my bed and floor. The party was getting rough.

663

Extra Support/Intervention

Strategy Modeling: Phonics/Decoding

Model the strategy using *awakened* from page 663.

I see -ed *and the suffix* -en *at the end of this word. The first part looks like* uh-WAHK, *but that doesn't sound right. Maybe the final* e *was dropped when the suffix was added. Then the first part would be* uh-WAYK *and the whole word would be* uh-WAY-kuhnd. *That word makes sense in the sentence.*

Following Directions

Review

- Review with students these steps for following directions.
  - Read all the directions carefully. Use numbers or order words to figure out the correct sequence of steps.
  - Gather any necessary materials.
  - Follow each step in order, and finish each step before going on to the next.
  - Reread or ask questions if you don't understand.

Practice/Apply

- Remind students that Sam built a fireplace inside his tree house.
- Ask students to reread pages 655–659 to figure out the steps involved in the process.
- Have students work in pairs to write a set of directions for making a tree house fireplace. (Sample answers shown.)

1. Gather supplies, such as clay, dry grasses, a funnel, and long, flat stones.
2. Mix the clay and grasses, and build the chimney in the tree house.
3. Support the funnel under the chimney by propping it up with stones.
4. Make air holes in the tree house.

Review Skill Trace	
Teach	Theme 3, p. 333A
Reteach	Theme 3, p. R12
Review	p. 663; Theme 4, p. 383

READ & COMPREHEND

My Side of the Mountain

CRITICAL THINKING

Guiding Comprehension

16 **DRAWING CONCLUSIONS** What does Sam mean when he writes *Smelling to the sky…*? (that the skunk's spray left him with a strong, terrible smell)

17 **DRAWING CONCLUSIONS** What does Sam mean by *to animals, might is right*? (that the strongest animal gets to decide what should happen)

18 **NOTING DETAILS** How does Sam get rid of the visitors? Why does he choose this method? (He makes the fire bigger, shouts, snarls, and growls; He realizes that he is the biggest animal there.)

664

Vocabulary

winged flew

laced drew closed with a cord

Extra Support/ Intervention	On Level	Challenge

Selection Review

Before students join in Wrapping Up on page 665, have them

- review and discuss their predictions
- take turns modeling the reading strategies they used
- help you complete **Transparency 6–19**
- complete their Conclusions Charts and use them to summarize the story

Literature Discussion

Have students work in mixed-ability small groups to discuss their predictions and questions. Then have students discuss the Responding questions on Anthology page 666.

I chased the raccoons into the night and stumbled over a third animal and was struck by a wet stinging spray. It was skunk! I was drenched. As I got used to the indignity and the smell, I saw the raccoons cavort around my fireplace and dodge past me. They were back in my tree before I could stop them.

A bat winged in from the darkness and circled the tallow candle. It was Halloween and the goblins were at work.

Having invited all these neighbors, I was now faced with the problem of getting rid of them. The raccoons were feeling so much at home that they snatched up beechnuts, bits of dried fish and venison and tossed them playfully into the air. They were too full to eat any more, but were having a marvelous time making toys out of my hard-won winter food supply.

I herded the raccoons out of the tree and laced the door. I was breathing "relief" when I turned my head to the left, for I sensed someone watching me. There in the moonlight, his big ears erect on his head, sat the red fox. He was smiling — I know he was. I shouted, "Stop laughing!" and he vanished like a magician's handkerchief.

All this had awakened Frightful, who was flopping in the dark in the tree. I reached in around the deer flap to stroke her back to calmness. She grabbed me so hard I yelled — and the visitors moved to the edge of my camp at my cry.

Smelling to the sky, bleeding in the hand, and robbed of part of my hard-won food, I threw wood on the fire and sent an enormous shaft of light into the night. Then I shouted. The skunk moved farther away. The raccoons galloped off a few feet and galloped back. I snarled at them. They went to the edge of the darkness and stared at me. I had learned something that night from that very raccoon bossing Jessie C. James — to animals, might is right. I was biggest and I was oldest, and I was going to tell them so. I growled and snarled and hissed and snorted. It worked. They understood and moved away. Some looked back and their eyes glowed. The red eyes chilled me. Never had there been a more real Halloween night. The last bat of the season darted in the moonlight. I dove on my bed, and tied the door. There are no more notes about Halloween.

16

17

18

665

Wrapping Up

Critical Thinking Questions

1. **MAKING JUDGMENTS** Which animal do you think Sam learns from the most? Explain. (Sample answer: On page 665, Sam learns from the bossy raccoon that he must show the other animals that he is in charge.)

2. **MAKING INFERENCES** How do you think Sam feels at the end of the story? Explain. (He is upset about the mischief of the Halloween party, tired, and relieved to go to bed.)

Strategies in Action

Have students tell how and where they used the Summarize strategy.

Discussion Options

Bring the entire class together to do one or more of the activities below.

Review Predictions/Purpose Discuss students' predictions of what Sam would do as winter approached.

Share Group Discussions Have students share their literature discussions.

Summarize Ask students to summarize the selection using their Conclusions Charts.

Comprehension Check

Use **Practice Book** page 238 to assess students' comprehension of the selection.

Practice Book page 238

My Side of the Mountain
Comprehension Check

Name _____

Autumn Adventures

The adventures Sam has that are recounted in this story begin in September and end just after Halloween. Use the sequence chart below to write the most important events in the order in which they occurred.

September

Sam watches the coming of autumn. He gathers roots and tubers and smokes fish and rabbit. **(2 points)**

October 15

The weasel's winter coat, the raccoon's rolls of fat, and the other animals' winter preparations make Sam realize that he must figure out a way to stay warm in the winter. **(2)**

The next three days

Sam brings clay back to his tree and fashions a chimney. He then tries several different ways to keep the smoke from going into his home. **(2)**

October 31

After the Baron visits, Sam realizes that it is Halloween. He decides to put out food so the animals will come to a Halloween party. **(2)**

November 1

The animals finally show up and there is a wild party in which Sam learns that he must always show the animals that he is the strongest. **(2)**

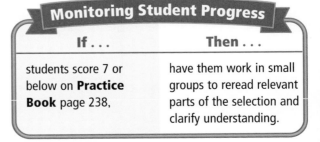

Monitoring Student Progress	
If . . .	**Then . . .**
students score 7 or below on **Practice Book** page 238,	have them work in small groups to reread relevant parts of the selection and clarify understanding.

Responding

Think About the Selection

Have students discuss or write their answers. Sample answers are provided; accept reasonable responses.

1. **DRAWING CONCLUSIONS** He is a resourceful problem solver.

2. **CONNECTING TO PERSONAL EXPERIENCES** Cold, wet winter weather can make you feel gloomy; Warm spring weather can make you feel happy.

3. **MAKING INFERENCES** The night was scary and exciting, as Halloween can be.

4. **DRAWING CONCLUSIONS** Based on how friendly and careful Sam is towards the wild animals, I think he likes and respects them.

5. **EXPRESSING PERSONAL OPINIONS** Answers will vary.

6. **EXPRESSING PERSONAL OPINIONS** Answers will vary.

7. **Connecting/Comparing** Alike—All three respect wild creatures and feel comfortable in the wilderness. Different—Hoshino and Martin each focus on one kind of animal, but Sam gets to know many creatures.

READ & COMPREHEND

Think About the Selection

1. What does Sam's solution for staying warm through the winter tell you about him?

2. Think about Sam's loneliness on page 655. What are some ways a time of year can affect a person's feelings?

3. On page 665, Sam says that he has never experienced a "more real" Halloween night. What do you think he means?

4. How do you think Sam feels about the wild woodland creatures that live around him? Use details from the story to support your answer.

5. If it were up to you, would you have tried to persuade Sam to leave the wilderness? Why or why not?

6. Do you think you would enjoy a wilderness experience similar to Sam's? Why or why not?

7. **Connecting/Comparing** Compare Sam's fictional woodland adventure with the real-life wilderness experiences of Michio Hoshino and Andrei Martins in this theme. How are they different? How are they alike?

Explaining

Write Directions

A person who relies on food from the forest would need to know what food to eat and how to prepare it. Use information in the selection to write directions for making a wilderness meal. Include choices for a main course, side dish, and dessert.

Tips

- List the ingredients needed for each course of the meal.
- Use a sequence of steps to explain how to gather and prepare the food.

666

English Language Learners

Supporting Comprehension

Beginning/Preproduction Invite students to mime their favorite event from the story.

Early Production and Speech Emergence Remind students that Sam lives with animals in the forest. Have students list and describe wild animals that are characters in the selection.

Intermediate and Advanced Fluency Ask students to describe ways in which people in their parents' home country may appreciate nature.

Social Studies

Make a Picture Map

With a partner, take notes about Sam's camp and the trees, animals, and land he describes. Then make a picture map, using small pictures to show the camp and its surroundings. Include a key that explains the pictures you have used.

Bonus Give a presentation in which you compare a picture map to another kind of map, such as a road map or a contour map. Tell in what situation each map would be useful.

Viewing

Update an Illustration

Choose an illustration from the selection. Study it carefully. Then show in a drawing or describe in a paragraph how the scene in that illustration might look hours later, one month later, or one year later.

Tips

- Ask yourself how the illustration would look in a different season.
- If the illustration shows the day, consider how it might look at night — or vice versa.

Internet

Complete a Web Word Find

You've learned a lot of vocabulary words related to Sam's experience living on the land. Try finding those words in a puzzle that can be printed from Education Place. **www.eduplace.com/kids**

667

Additional Responses

Personal Response Invite students to share their personal responses to *My Side of the Mountain*.

Journal ▶ Ask students to write about what it would be like to live with animals as their only companions.

Selection Connections Remind students to add to **Practice Book** pages 199–200.

Practice Book page 199

Name _____

Launching the Theme
Selection Connections

Animal Encounters

The selections in this theme explore some special relationships between people and wild creatures. After reading each selection, fill in this chart to show what you learned.

	What kind of writing is the selection an example of?	What creature or creatures does the selection describe?
Grizzly Bear Family Book	first-person narrative nonfiction (2.5 points)	grizzly bears (2.5)
The Golden Lion Tamarin Comes Home	expository nonfiction (2.5)	golden lion tamarins (2.5)
My Side of the Mountain	fiction (2.5)	many small creatures of the forest, such as raccoons and a falcon (2.5)

Practice Book page 200

Name _____

Launching the Theme
Selection Connections

Animal Encounters continued

	What is the purpose of the encounter between humans and animals?	What are the results of the encounter?
Grizzly Bear Family Book	Michio Hoshino wants to learn as much as he can about grizzly bears. He wants to photograph them. (2.5)	People learn more about grizzly bears and how they live. (2.5)
The Golden Lion Tamarin Comes Home	The people of the Golden Lion Tamarin Conservation Program want to return golden lion tamarins to the forests where they naturally live. (2.5)	The golden lion tamarin population increases in the rain forest of Brazil. The monkeys are protected in the preserve. (2.5)
My Side of the Mountain	Sam wants to experience the wilderness and be self-sufficient in it. He sees the animals as companions and even friends. (2.5)	Sam learns more about himself and about the creatures with whom he shares his woodland home. (2.5)

What are some ways in which people can help wild animals?(2)
People can help wild animals in zoos learn to live in the wild again. People can
protect wild animals' natural habitats. People can teach others about wild animals
to try to get them to care about the animals and understand their needs.

Monitoring Student Progress

End-of-Selection Assessment

Selection Test Use the test on page 153 in the **Teacher's Resource Blackline Masters** to assess selection comprehension and vocabulary.

Student Self-Assessment Have students assess their reading with additional questions such as

- Which parts of this selection were difficult for me? Why?
- What strategies helped me understand the story?
- Would I recommend this story to my friends? Why?

Responding 667

Career Link

Skill: How to Categorize Information

- **Introduce** "Robin Hughes: Wildlife Doctor," a nonfiction article about the work a veterinarian does.

- **Discuss** the Skill Lesson on Anthology page 668. Explain that categorizing helps readers remember details and make comparisons.

- **Model** how to divide broad categories into narrower categories. Read aloud the first paragraph of the "Career File" on page 671, and break the broad category of *animals* into narrower categories. (House Pets, Wild Animals, Farm Animals, Zoo Animals)

- **Explain** that the article describes the many animals Robin treats. This information can be classified into categories. Tell students that some animals may fit more than one category.

- **Set a purpose** for reading. Have students read the article. Then have them create categories and classify the animals into these categories. Suggest that they use Summarize and other strategies to help them determine what different animals have in common.

Vocabulary

ibises large wading birds related to the stork, with long downward-curving bills

Gila monster a poisonous lizard having black and orange or yellow markings

dosage amount of medicine given at one time

ferrets North American mammals similar to the weasel

anatomy the structure of an animal

Career Link

Skill: How to Categorize Information

Categorizing helps you to organize ideas by **classifying** items that have something in common.

As you read . . .

- If you come to a group of items or ideas, identify what **category** they have in common. Use **headings** for each category, such as Animal Injuries, or Medical Instruments.

- Divide a broad category into two or more **narrower categories**. For example, the category Animals could be divided into Endangered Animals and Pets.

668

Robin Hughes: Wildlife Doctor

Dr. Robin Hughes could give Sam Gribley advice. She formerly worked as wildlife veterinarian at the Virginia Living Museum in Newport News, Virginia.

by Susan Yoder Ackerman

As I walked into her office, Robin was on the phone. "Yes," she was saying, "hummingbirds need more than sugar water. They need protein. Fruit flies are perfect for them!"

Robin's understanding of small wild birds is no wonder, growing up as she did with the name Robin. While her friends were selling Kool-Aid on hot days, little Robin set up a veterinary stand. She stocked it with her stethoscope, long sticks for splints, and lots of gauze. The neighborhood pets showed up with their sore paws and torn ears.

Sometimes Dr. Hughes's work takes her out of the office and into the woods. After tranquilizing this deer to work on its overgrown hoof, Dr. Hughes (center) administers medicine to wake him up.

As she got older, Robin decided to go to veterinary school to learn all she could about dogs and cats and horses. But she didn't stop there. Pursuing her interest in wild animals, she cared for gazelles at the Kansas City Zoo. She learned to follow the white ibises who feed on fiddler crabs on Pumpkin Seed Island in South Carolina. She worried over the growth on a Gila monster's tongue in California's Living Desert.

So, when Robin finally became Dr. Robin Hughes, she wasn't content in private practice treating mostly cats and dogs. She came to the Virginia Living Museum, where she has the care of live-animal exhibits that reflect Virginia's wildlife in its native habitat. And though she uses all the training she's had, sometimes she feels as if she's writing her own medical book. How do you

medicate a sick beaver? Just figure out the dosage for a very large guinea pig! What about an otter? Try what's good for ferrets. A skunk with heart disease? Perhaps the treatment for a small dog would be most appropriate. Robin studies diet, behavior, tooth structure, and anatomy to figure out the best way to treat her patients. Has she ever treated a wild animal she couldn't match to a domestic one?

"A possum!" she said with a laugh. "Possums are clearly in a class of their own! *The Care and Treatment of Possums* is a book nobody has written yet."

669

Extra Support/Intervention

Categorizing

Help students to categorize the information in the article. Have a volunteer read aloud the first four paragraphs. Ask: What types of animals does Robin Hughes care for? Have students use their responses to create categories.

Besides nursing raccoons and giving advice on the diet of hummingbirds, what does Robin do in the course of a day? Happily for her, every day is different. As curator of animals and a veterinarian, she may find herself out on a trawler in the York River, using a seine net to find new fish for the aquarium display. She might be rescuing injured waterfowl to bring to the outdoor wetlands aviary. She might travel to a distant wooded lake and release half-grown beavers into the wild. Other days she adjusts the diets for all the animals on the museum grounds.

And then there are the days when Robin really shows her stuff. Such as the day she needed to operate on an eastern diamondback rattlesnake to remove a mass growing under its eye. A fungal infection was causing inflammatory tissue to form into a granuloma. Robin said that snakes in the wild often get abscesses and tumors, but she didn't want any snake under her care to crawl off into a corner to die. So she scrubbed up and got started.

Robin vented anesthetic gas through a small hose in the lid of a sealed aquarium until the snake was asleep. (Since a sleeping snake doesn't look a whole lot different from a snake that's awake, this was the tricky part.) Then, taking the snake out of the aquarium, she put a tube down its windpipe to control the amount of anesthesia until the procedure was over.

Cutting into the skin so near the venomous fangs was also risky. Just to be safe, Robin placed corks over the fangs during surgery. And, to save herself a lot of trouble, she closed the incision with sutures that would dissolve all by themselves. A rattlesnake might not want to hold still to get its stitches taken out.

Sometimes Robin finds herself running a maternity ward. A couple of newborn baby otters stole the show at the museum for months, and black-crowned night herons hatched their young in the outdoor aviary. One year Robin and everyone else tiptoed around the bald eagle enclosure for thirty-eight days, hoping that the eggs the pair was guarding would hatch. They never did, but Robin hopes that the adult birds, injured by hunters in the wild, will someday produce perfect little bald eagles that can fly wherever they wish.

Vocabulary

curator a person who manages a zoo, museum, or library

inflammatory characterized by redness, heat, swelling, and pain

tissue a group of animal or plant cells that are similar in form and function

anesthesia something that causes one not to feel pain

venomous poisonous

maternity associated with being a mother

vaccinated given a substance to prevent getting a particular disease

REACHING ALL LEARNERS
English Language Learners

Language Development

Explain that a *veterinarian* is a doctor for animals. As students read, encourage them to notice what the doctor does to care for animals. Point out the following words: *diet* (page 669), *operate*, and *maternity* (page 670). Guide students to use sentence context to figure out what the words mean.

Then there are the exciting outdoor dramas that take place when the larger animals get vaccinated. The deer, foxes, and otter don't like injections any more than people do, so Robin has to come prepared. Sometimes she uses a dart gun to carry the vaccine; sometimes she'll throw a net around the animal to hold it still. Even so, there can be surprises, such as the time the thirty-pound bobcat leaped onto Robin's back when she turned to get the vaccine ready! She wasn't injured, but the incident made her aware that he was still a wild animal, even though he'd been hand-raised as an orphan. She never turns her back to him now if she has to enter his enclosure.

Bobcat, rattlesnake, hummingbird, raccoon — Dr. Robin is there for them. She also cares about the half million people who visit the Virginia Living Museum each year. Robin wants visitors to walk away with a greater appreciation and concern for Virginia's wildlife.

Career File

Veterinarian

Do you like taking care of animals? If so, consider becoming a veterinarian. As a vet, you'll have a chance to help house pets, wild animals, farm or zoo animals by . . .

- caring for them when they're sick or injured
- making sure they eat healthy diets
- giving them the medicine or vitamins they need
- studying diseases that could affect them

After college, you'll need a degree from a four-year veterinary school. You'll also need to pass a state exam in the state where you want to work. In the meantime, you can learn more about what a veterinarian does by volunteering at a local animal hospital, humane society, zoo, or farm.

671

Wrapping Up

Critical Thinking Questions

Have students use their categories and the selection to answer these questions.

1. **DRAWING CONCLUSIONS** How can you tell that Robin's veterinary training did not include specific information on how to treat beavers, otters, skunks, or possums? (because she said she sometimes feels as if she's writing her own medical books)

2. **MAKING INFERENCES** How does Robin use her knowledge of some types of animals to help her treat other types? (She compares their diets, behavior, and anatomy, and treats similar animals in a similar way.)

3. **NOTING DETAILS** How can you tell that Robin likes the various challenges of working at the Virginia Living Museum? (The article says she is happy that every day is different.)

4. **COMPARE AND CONTRAST** How does Robin's experience with the bobcat compare with Sam's experience at the Halloween party? How are their experiences different? (Alike—Both learn that they must be on guard around wild animals. Different—Sam treats the animals as friends, while Robin takes care of sick animals.)

REACHING ALL LEARNERS

Challenge

Science

Have students use reference sources such as electronic or print encyclopedias to find out about the wildlife native to their state. Encourage them to contact a local zoo or a wildlife protection agency to gather more information. Ask students to create a chart that classifies the different animals into categories such as *Mammals*, *Birds*, *Fish*, and *Reptiles*.

OBJECTIVES

- Use facts and details from the selection to come to an understanding of something not directly stated in the text.

Target Skill Trace

Preview; Teach	p. 647CC, p. 650, p. 657; p. 671A
Reteach	R12
Review	pp. M32–M33; Theme 4, p. 349; Theme 5, p. 509
See	*Extra Support Handbook,* pp. 226–227; pp. 232–233

Transparency 6–19

Use the Clues

ANIMAL ENCOUNTERS: My Side of the Mountain
Graphic Organizer Conclusions Chart
ANNOTATED VERSION

Story Clues		Conclusions
pages 652–653 Mice, squirrels, and chipmunks collected seeds and nuts.	+ Sam gathers various roots and smokes fish and rabbit.	= On the wooded mountain where Sam is living, food is scarce in the winter.
pages 654–655 The animals are growing thick coats of fur and making warm shelters for winter.	+ Sam realizes he needs to build a small fireplace to warm his shelter.	= Sam's clothing and his current shelter aren't enough to protect him from the cold of winter.
pages 656–658 Sam playfully chases the Baron Weasel up the mountain.	+ Sam runs after Frightful because he is warned the falcon has left him.	= Sam relies on the animals to keep him from feeling too lonely.
pages 660–665 The Baron comes to get food from Sam, but doesn't let him get too close.	+ The raccoons make a mess of Sam's food supply.	= Even though Sam enjoys the animals' company, he must remain alert around these wild creatures.

TRANSPARENCY 6–19
TEACHER'S EDITION PAGES 650 AND 671A

Practice Book page 237

My Side of the Mountain
Graphic Organizer Conclusions Chart

Name _____

Use the Clues

Read the story clues and conclusions provided in the boxes below. Fill in the missing information with text from the selection.

Story Clues		Conclusions
pages 652–653 Mice, squirrels, and chipmunks collected seeds and nuts.	+ Sam gathers various roots and smokes fish and rabbit.	On the wooded mountain where Sam is living, food is scarce in the winter.
pages 654–655 The animals are growing thick coats of fur and making warm shelters for winter. (2 points)	+ Sam realizes he needs to build a small fireplace to warm his shelter. (2)	= Sam's clothing and his current shelter aren't enough to protect him from the cold of winter.
pages 656–658 Sam playfully chases the Baron Weasel up the mountain.	+ Sam runs after Frightful because he is warned the falcon has left him.	= Sam relies on the animals to keep him from feeling too lonely. (2)
pages 660–665 The Baron comes to get food from Sam, but doesn't let him get too close. (2)	+ The raccoons make a mess of Sam's food supply. (2)	= Even though Sam enjoys the animals' company, he must remain alert around these wild creatures.

TARGET SKILL COMPREHENSION: Drawing Conclusions

❶ Teach

Review drawing conclusions in *My Side of the Mountain*. Remind students that authors do not always state everything directly. Sometimes readers must add up facts and details to draw their own conclusions. Display **Transparency 6–19.**

- Review how details from pages 652 and 653 help them draw the conclusion that food on the mountain is scarce in the winter. (Animals collect seeds and nuts; Sam smokes fish and rabbit.)
- Have students use **Practice Book** page 237 to discuss other conclusions they drew about Sam.

Model drawing conclusions. Have students turn to page 653. Model using story details to draw another conclusion.

Think Aloud *The author doesn't say directly that Sam Gribley has chosen to live in the wilderness, but by adding up story details, I can draw that conclusion. On page 653, Sam says he "felt just wonderful." A person stranded in the wilderness probably wouldn't feel this way. On page 654, Sam wonders whether he should return home for the winter. That tells me he can if he wants to. Both these details help me conclude that Sam is in the wilderness by choice.*

❷ Guided Practice

Have students draw conclusions. Have partners answer the following questions by recording story details in a chart, as below.

- Why does Sam throw a Halloween party for the animals? (because he is lonely and has been thinking about Halloween)
- Does Sam consider the Halloween party a success? (yes, because it was a real Halloween)

Detail	Detail	Detail	Conclusion
Sam thinks of Halloween and feels lonely. (page 655)	+ Sam asks Baron Weasel if he is playing tricks or treats. (page 660)	+ Sam tells Frightful that Baron Weasel knows it's Halloween. (page 661)	= Sam throws a Halloween party because he is lonely and has been thinking about Halloween.

❸ Apply

Assign Practice Book pages 239–240. Also have students apply this skill as they read their **Leveled Readers** for this week. You may also select books from the Leveled Bibliography for this theme (pages 594E–594F).

 **Test Prep** Emphasize that many questions on reading tests ask students to draw conclusions. Explain that for these questions students will have to find details in the passage that they can use to form and support their conclusions.

Leveled Readers and Leveled Practice

Students at all levels apply the comprehension skill as they read their Leveled Readers. See lessons on pages 671O–671R.

● BELOW LEVEL ▲ ON LEVEL ■ ABOVE LEVEL ◆ LANGUAGE SUPPORT

Reading Traits

Teaching students how to draw conclusions is one way of encouraging them to "read between the lines" of a selection. This comprehension skill supports the reading trait **Developing Interpretations.**

Practice Book page 239

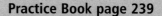

My Side of the Mountain
Comprehension Skill
Drawing Conclusions

Name _____

Gather the Clues

Read the passage. Then answer the questions on page 240.

Taking Stock

It was nearing dusk when I got back to camp. The crickets were just launching into their evening serenade. I set my backpack down on the slab of granite I used as my table and began to unpack the treasures of the day.

I pulled out the sack of miner's lettuce that I'd gathered near the waterfall. Next, I lifted out a pouch of wild blackberries packed in a soft cushion of moss. From the bottom of the pack I drew handfuls of walnuts. The berries I'd expected to find, but the walnuts were an unexpected luxury, from a walnut tree I'd discovered in a grove of tan oaks. I carefully laid the food out on the stone. I had smoked two small trout the day before; these I had wrapped in paper and stored in a tree, away from hungry bears. The trout, nuts, and lettuce, with the berries as dessert, would make a feast indeed.

I then turned my attention to building a fire. The day had been a hot one, but I knew how fast the temperature would drop when the sun went down. After I had the campfire crackling cheerfully, I sat down to take stock.

Some things had gone better than I'd expected. Staying warm and dry had been easy. Even the rainstorm on the second night didn't soak any of my belongings. Other things, like finding enough to eat, had proved harder than I'd expected. An hour of picking lettuce resulted in a very small pile of greens. Overall, though, I couldn't complain. I thought about my two-way radio inside the tent. I hadn't had to use it yet. With luck, I wouldn't need to unpack it at all.

Practice Book page 240

My Side of the Mountain
Comprehension Skill
Drawing Conclusions

Name _____

Gather the Clues continued

Answer these questions about the passage on page 239.

1. Where is the narrator? How do you know?
She is in a wilderness area where there are mountains. I can tell because she gathers food in the wilderness and camps near a waterfall. **(3 points)**

2. Is the narrator stranded or did she choose to be there? How can you tell?
She chose to be there. She seems confident and well-prepared. She talks about her expectations, so she thought about the trip beforehand. **(3)**

3. What time of year do you think it is? Why?
It is summer or close to summer. There are crickets at night, the days are hot, and there are fresh berries, nuts, and lettuce. **(3)**

4. What do you think the two-way radio might be used for? Why do you think this?
I think it might be used to call for help in an emergency. The narrator says she hasn't had to use it yet and hopes that she won't have to. **(3)**

5. Do you think the narrator has had other experiences in the wilderness? Why or why not?
Yes. She knows how to gather food in the wilderness, catch and smoke fish, build a fire, and protect her food from bears. **(3)**

Monitoring Student Progress

If . . .	Then . . .
students score 11 or below on **Practice Book** page 240,	use the Reteaching lesson on Teacher's Edition page R12.
students have successfully met the lesson objectives,	have them do the Challenge/Extension activities on Teacher's Edition page R13.

OBJECTIVES

- Read words that have the suffixes *-ent*, *-ant*, *-able*, and *-ible*.
- Use the Phonics/Decoding Strategy to decode longer words.

Target Skill Trace

Teach	p. 671C
Reteach	p. R18
Review	pp. M34–M35
See	*Handbook for English Language Learners*, p. 228; *Extra Support Handbook*, pp. 224–225; pp. 228–229

STRUCTURAL ANALYSIS

Practice Book page 241

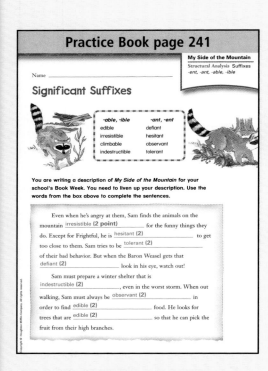

Monitoring Student Progress

If . . .	Then . . .
students score 12 or below on **Practice Book** page 241,	use the Reteaching lesson on Teacher's Edition page R18.

STRUCTURAL ANALYSIS/ VOCABULARY: More Suffixes

❶ Teach

Introduce suffixes. Explain that a suffix is a word part that comes after a base word or root and changes its meaning.

Discuss the suffixes -ent and -ant. Write *I think field crickets would taste excellent if you were starving.* Circle the suffix *-ent* in *excellent*. Underline the base word *excel*.

- Explain that the suffixes *-ent* and *-ant* turn many base words into adjectives.
- The base word *excel* means "to be the best."
- The whole word *excellent* means "of the best quality."

Discuss the suffixes -able and -ible. Write *The apples were perishable.* Circle the suffix *-able* in *perishable*. Underline *perish*.

- Explain that the suffixes *-able* and *-ible* can mean "capable of."
- Cover the suffix to reveal the base word *perish* and explain that in this sentence it means "to spoil."
- Define the whole word as "capable of spoiling."

Model the Phonics/Decoding Strategy. Write *Sam was persist-ent in trying to build a chimney.* Model decoding *persistent*.

Think Aloud *I see* persist, *which means "to keep doing," and the suffix* -ent. *The whole word must be* per-SIS-tuhnt, *which probably means "keeping at it." That makes sense in the sentence.*

❷ Guided Practice

Have students use suffixes to decode. Display the phrases below and have students copy each underlined word. Have partners circle the suffix, decode the word, and give its meaning, using a dictionary if necessary.

the sunset was <u>incredible</u>

the moon's light was <u>radiant</u>

<u>different</u> animals lurked in the darkness

a <u>pleasant</u> meal

❸ Apply

Assign Practice Book page 241.

PHONICS REVIEW:
Vowel Alternations

❶ Teach

Review vowel alternations. Tell students that words that are related in meaning are often related in spelling, even though the same vowel may have a different sound in each word. Point out:

- The vowel representing the long vowel sound can change to the short vowel sound, as in *unite* and *unity*.

- The vowel representing the schwa sound can change to the long vowel sound, as in *equal* and *equation*.

- The vowel representing the schwa sound can change to the short vowel sound, as in *mortal* and *mortality*.

Model the Phonics/Decoding Strategy. Write *This food was an invitation to the squirrels.* Then model how to decode *invitation*.

Think Aloud *The beginning of this word looks like the word* invite. *But* ihn-VYT-ay-shuhn *sounds wrong. In related words, the vowel's sound can change. I'll try* ihn-vih-TAY-shuhn. *That makes sense in the sentence.*

❷ Guided Practice

Help students decode words with vowel alternations. Write these sentence pairs and have students copy the underlined words:

   1. <u>Nature</u> can be unpredictable. The <u>natural</u> world is beautiful.

   2. Animals <u>compete</u> for food. The forest is full of <u>competition</u>.

   3. He chews with <u>ferocity</u>. He lets out a <u>ferocious</u> growl.

Tell partners to circle the vowel that changes sound in each pair of underlined words. Have them then pronounce the two words and check to see if they make sense in the sentences.

❸ Apply

Have students decode words with vowel alternations. Write the following words and page numbers. Have partners find a related word on the page indicated. (species, preferred, wildly, realized) Ask students to tell how the vowel sound changes.

special	p. 653	wilderness	p. 657
preference	p. 653	realization	p. 663

OBJECTIVES

- Read words that are related in spelling but have different vowel sounds.
- Use the Phonics/Decoding Strategy to decode longer words.

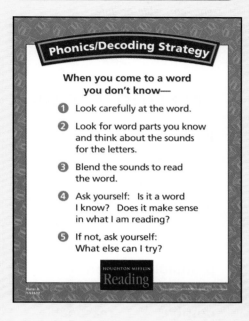

Phonics/Decoding Strategy

When you come to a word you don't know—

❶ Look carefully at the word.

❷ Look for word parts you know and think about the sounds for the letters.

❸ Blend the sounds to read the word.

❹ Ask yourself: Is it a word I know? Does it make sense in what I am reading?

❺ If not, ask yourself: What else can I try?

HOUGHTON MIFFLIN
Reading

SPELLING: -ent, -ant; -able, -ible

SPELLING

- Write Spelling Words that end with *-ent, -ant, -able,* or *-ible.*

SPELLING WORDS

Basic

fashionable*	absent
comfortable	vacant
different	servant
suitable*	valuable
merchant	accident
profitable	horrible
student	honorable
possible	reasonable
resident	remarkable
terrible*	laughable*

Review
current
important
moment*
silent*
parent

Challenge
excellent*
prominent
extravagant
durable
reversible

Forms of these words appear in the literature.

Extra Support/ Intervention

Basic Word List You may want to use only the left column of Basic Words with students who need extra support.

Challenge

Challenge Word Practice Have students use the Challenge Words to write silly or serious recommendations for handy wilderness products. Ask students to share their recommendations with the class.

DAY 1 INSTRUCTION

-ent, -ant; -able, -ible

Pretest Use the Day 5 Test sentences.

Teach Display the following:

/ənt/	/əbəl/
student	suitable
merchant	possible

- Say *student* and *merchant* and have students repeat them. Explain that because the suffixes *-ent* and *-ant* have the same pronunciation, students should remember the spellings of words ending with /ənt/.

- Present *-able* and *-ible* in the same way, using *suitable* and *possible* as examples of words ending with /əbəl/.

- Add *reside* to the board, erase the final e, and add *-ent.* Explain that when *-ent, -ant, -able,* or *-ible* is added to a base word that ends with e, the e is dropped.

- List the remaining Basic Words, asking students to say each word.

Practice/Homework Assign **Practice Book** page 281.

Practice Book page 281

Take-Home Word List	Take-Home Word List	Take-Home Word List
Animal Encounters Spelling Review	**My Side of the Mountain**	**The Golden Lion Tamarin Comes Home**

Take-Home Word List

DAY 2 REVIEW & PRACTICE

Reviewing the Principle

Go over the spelling principles of words that end with *-ent, -ant, -able,* or *-ible.*

Practice/Homework Assign **Practice Book** page 242.

Practice Book page 242

My Side of the Mountain
Spelling Words with *-ent, -ant; -able, -ible*

Name _____

Words with *-ent, -ant; -able, -ible*

The suffixes *-ent* and *-ant* and the suffixes *-able* and *-ible* sound alike but are spelled differently. You have to remember the spellings of these suffixes because they begin with a schwa sound.

/ənt/	student, merchant
/əbəl/	suitable, possible

Write each Spelling Word under its suffix.
Order of answers for each category may vary.

-ent
different (1 point)
student (1)
resident (1)
absent (1)
accident (1)

-ant
merchant (1)
vacant (1)
servant (1)

-able
fashionable (1)
comfortable (1)
suitable (1)
profitable (1)
valuable (1)
honorable (1)
reasonable (1)
remarkable (1)
laughable (1)

-ible
possible (1)
terrible (1)
horrible (1)

Spelling Words
1. fashionable
2. comfortable
3. different
4. suitable
5. merchant
6. profitable
7. student
8. possible
9. resident
10. terrible
11. absent
12. vacant
13. servant
14. valuable
15. accident
16. horrible
17. honorable
18. reasonable
19. remarkable
20. laughable

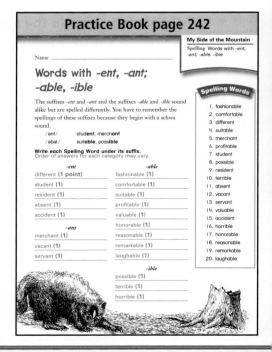

Idioms

Tell students that an idiom is an expression whose meaning is different from the meanings of its separate words.

- Write this example on the board: *a horse of a different color.* Explain that this expression is not literally referring to an oddly colored horse; rather, it means "another matter altogether."

- Have small groups brainstorm other idioms they have heard, and then share their idioms with the class. (Responses will vary.)

- List the Basic Words on the board. Have students use each word orally in a sentence. (Sentences will vary.)

Practice/Homework For spelling practice, assign **Practice Book** page 243.

Game: Spelling Go Fish!

Have pairs of students create a word card for each Basic and Review Word. Tell players to shuffle the cards, deal 7 cards to each player, and stack the remaining cards face-down. Explain that the object is to obtain pairs of word cards with the same suffix.

- Player 1 asks Player 2 for a card, saying, for example, "Do you have a word card that ends with i-b-l-e?"

- If Player 2 has such a card, he or she reads the word aloud. Player 1 must then spell the word correctly to obtain the card.

- If Player 2 doesn't have the card or if Player 1 misspells the word, Player 2 says "Go fish!" and Player 1 draws a card from the stack.

- Players can lay pairs from their hands face-up on the table at any time. Play ends when a player has laid down all his or her cards.

Practice/Homework For proofreading and writing practice, assign **Practice Book** page 244.

Spelling Test

Say each underlined word, read the sentence, and then repeat the word. Have students write only the underlined word.

Basic Words

1. My old coat is still **fashionable**.
2. The soft chair is **comfortable**.
3. Mexico and Spain are **different** countries.
4. Wear clothes **suitable** for a picnic.
5. The **merchant** sold me a hat.
6. Selling our house was **profitable**.
7. The **student** worked hard in class.
8. Is it **possible** to land on Mars?
9. Are you our new town **resident**?
10. The flood was **terrible**.
11. I was **absent** from school yesterday.
12. Is that old house **vacant**?
13. A police officer is a public **servant**.
14. Her diamond pin is **valuable**.
15. I met Jack by **accident**.
16. That plant has a **horrible** skunk smell.
17. Leah behaved in an **honorable** way.
18. Two dollars for markers is **reasonable**.
19. You did a **remarkable** job.
20. That excuse is **laughable**.

Challenge Words

21. You should be proud of your **excellent** grades.
22. The **prominent** judge lives in a huge house.
23. I am **extravagant** with my money.
24. This heavy cloth should be **durable**.
25. My winter coat is **reversible**.

Practice Book page 243

My Side of the Mountain
Spelling Words with -ent, -ant; -able, -ible

Name _____

Spelling Spree

Finding Words Each word below is hidden in a Spelling Word. Write the Spelling Word.

1. chant merchant **(1 point)**
2. sent absent **(1)**
3. fit profitable **(1)**
4. side resident **(1)**
5. rent different **(1)**
6. suit suitable **(1)**
7. fort comfortable **(1)**

Crack the Code Some Spelling Words have been written in the code below. Use the code to figure out each word. Then write the words correctly.

8. DHAKHIAP — 8. valuable **(1)**
9. URLLSIAP — 9. horrible **(1)**
10. BHMUSRFHIAP — 10. fashionable **(1)**
11. WPLLSIAP — 11. terrible **(1)**
12. MWKOPFW — 12. student **(1)**
13. MPLDHFW — 13. servant **(1)**
14. URFRLHIAP — 14. honorable **(1)**
15. YRMMSIAP — 15. possible **(1)**

CODE: H I X O P B N U S A C F R Y L M W K D
LETTER: a b c d e f g h i l m n o p r s t u v

Spelling Words
1. fashionable
2. comfortable
3. different
4. suitable
5. merchant
6. profitable
7. student
8. possible
9. resident
10. terrible
11. absent
12. vacant
13. servant
14. valuable
15. accident
16. horrible
17. honorable
18. reasonable
19. remarkable
20. laughable

Practice Book page 244

My Side of the Mountain
Spelling Words with -ent, -ant; -able, -ible

Name _____

Proofreading and Writing

Proofreading Circle the five misspelled Spelling Words in this news report. Then write each word correctly.

Finally tonight, remarkabel stories continue to filter in. We have learned of a wild boy living on a nearby mountain. Most of the sightings have been near a vacant farm lot. Town leaders are dismissing the claims as laughible. Still, as one resident put it, "I don't think it's an accidant that these sightings keep coming in. If that many people say they've seen him, there's a reasonabel chance he's out there."

1. remarkable **(1 point)**
2. vacant **(1)**
3. laughable **(1)**
4. accident **(1)**
5. reasonable **(1)**

Spelling Words
1. fashionable
2. comfortable
3. different
4. suitable
5. merchant
6. profitable
7. student
8. possible
9. resident
10. terrible
11. absent
12. vacant
13. servant
14. valuable
15. accident
16. horrible
17. honorable
18. reasonable
19. remarkable
20. laughable

Write a Character Sketch Sam Gribley finds food and shelter in the wilderness. He also makes friends with wild animals. What do you think this says about him?

On a separate piece of paper, write a brief character sketch of Sam. Use Spelling Words from the list. Responses will vary. (5)

OBJECTIVES

- Learn that idioms are phrases with special meanings that can be located under key words in the dictionary.
- Learn that run-on entries are forms of a base word.
- Use a dictionary to find both idioms and run-on entries.
- Learn academic language: *idiom.*

Target Skill Trace

Teach	p. 671G
Extend	p. R19
Review	pp. M36–M37
See	*Handbook for English Language Learners,* p. 233

Transparency 6–20

ANIMAL ENCOUNTERS *My Side of the Mountain*
Vocabulary Skill
Run-On Dictionary Entries
ANNOTATED VERSION

Run-On Dictionary Entries

time *n.* A continuous succession in which events occur from the past through the present to the future. —**idioms. for the time being.** Temporarily. **from time to time.** Once in a while.

lonely *adj.* Without companions; alone. —**loneliness** *n.*

home *n.* A place where one lives; residence. —**idioms. at home.** Comfortable and relaxed. **home free.** Free of tension and stress.

He <u>bent over backward</u> to make Halloween a fun night.

<u>Suddenly</u> I was terribly lonely.

In the gathering <u>darkness</u> I saw movement.

The raccoon gave the others a <u>dirty look.</u>

A few guests dashed <u>bashfully</u> into the ground cover.

I reached in around the deer flap to stroke her back to <u>calmness.</u>

"I'll <u>take you at your word,</u>" I said happily.

TRANSPARENCY 6–20
TEACHER'S EDITION PAGE 671G

Monitoring Student Progress

If . . .	Then . . .
students score 8 or below on **Practice Book** page 245,	have them work with partners to correct the items they missed.

VOCABULARY: Run-on Dictionary Entries

❶ Teach

Introduce idioms and run-on entries. Explain that after the last definition of a dictionary entry word, an **idiom** or a **run-on entry** often shows a different use or form of the word.

Display Transparency 6–20. Cover the lower part.

- Point to the entry word *time.* Have a volunteer read aloud the meaning of the idiom *from time to time.* (once in a while)

- Explain that an idiom is a phrase with a special meaning that is different from the meanings of the words that make it up.

- Point to the run-on entry *loneliness.* Explain that a run-on entry is a word made by adding a suffix to an entry word. The *n.* after the word shows that *loneliness* is the noun form of *lonely.*

Model how to find the meaning of idioms. Write *The raccoons were feeling so much <u>at home</u> that they snatched up beechnuts and tossed them into the air.* Use **Transparency 6–20** and the Think Aloud to model defining *at home.*

Think Aloud *If I don't understand* at home, *I'll look under the entry word* home *in a dictionary. After the definition, I see* idioms *followed by* at home *meaning "comfortable and relaxed." That describes the raccoons.*

❷ Guided Practice

Give students practice in using idioms and run-on entries. Have partners complete **Transparency 6–20,** using a dictionary to find the definitions of the underlined words or phrases.

- Remind students to identify the base words for run-on entries as well as the key words for idioms. (bend; word)

- Have students discuss the meanings as a class.

❸ Apply

Assign Practice Book page 245.

Practice Book page 245

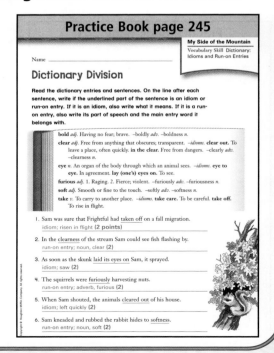

My Side of the Mountain
Vocabulary Skill Dictionary: Idioms and Run-on Entries

Name _____

Dictionary Division

Read the dictionary entries and sentences. On the line after each sentence, write if the underlined part of the sentence is an idiom or run-on entry. If it is an idiom, also write what it means. If it is a run-on entry, also write its part of speech and the main entry word it belongs with.

bold *adj.* Having no fear; brave. —**boldly** *adv.* —**boldness** *n.*
clear *adj.* Free from anything that obscures; transparent. —*idioms.* **clear out.** To leave a place, often quickly. **in the clear.** Free from dangers. —**clearly** *adv.* —**clearness** *n.*
eye *n.* An organ of the body through which an animal sees. —*idioms.* **eye to eye.** In agreement. **lay (one's) eyes on.** To see.
furious *adj.* 1. Raging. 2. Fierce; violent. —**furiously** *adv.* —**furiousness** *n.*
soft *adj.* Smooth or fine to the touch. —**softly** *adv.* —**softness** *n.*
take *v.* To carry to another place. —*idioms.* **take care.** To be careful. **take off.** To rise in flight.

1. Sam was sure that Frightful had <u>taken off</u> on a fall migration.
   idiom; risen in flight (2 points)

2. In the <u>clearness</u> of the stream Sam could see fish flashing by.
   run-on entry; noun, clear (2)

3. As soon as the skunk <u>laid its eyes on</u> Sam, it sprayed.
   idiom; saw (2)

4. The squirrels were <u>furiously</u> harvesting nuts.
   run-on entry; adverb, furious (2)

5. When Sam shouted, the animals <u>cleared out</u> of his house.
   idiom; left quickly (2)

6. Sam kneaded and rubbed the rabbit hides to <u>softness.</u>
   run-on entry; noun, soft (2)

STUDY SKILL: Completing Applications and Forms

❶ Teach

Introduce applications and forms.

- Forms and applications are required for such needs as library cards, memberships, jobs, driver's licenses, and passports.

- Knowing how to complete these forms correctly can save time and help people get what they need.

Review completing applications and forms.

- Skim the entire form and read all the directions before writing.

- Complete the form, following the directions for each step. Print clearly or type, according to directions.

- Check to make sure everything has been filled in correctly.

- If you find a mistake, erase thoroughly, cross out neatly, or cover with correction fluid. Rewrite clearly.

Model looking over an application.

- Display **Transparency 6–21.**

- Demonstrate how you would look over the first part of the application form.

- Point out the deadline, the directions to type or print, and the order in which to write the name.

❷ Practice/Apply

Give practice in completing applications and forms.

- Duplicate **Transparency 6–21** and give each student a copy. Have them complete Part 1.

- Ask the following questions:

  - If you put the application in the mailbox on May 1, will it meet the deadline? Explain. (yes, if it reaches the post office that day)

  - When do you write a different address under Mailing Address from the one under Street Address? (when you receive mail at a different address from your home)

  - What could you do if you didn't know the full name of a recreation organization you belonged to? (Look the organization up in a telephone directory.)

- Have students skim over Part 2, ask questions, and complete it, using made-up information.

Transparency 6–21

An Application Form

APPLICATION FOR PINE MOUNTAIN WILDERNESS CAMP

Print or type only. Application must be postmarked no later than May 1.

Part 1

Name _____

| Last | First | Middle |

Date of birth: ☐☐ ☐☐ ☐☐ ☐ Male ☐ Female

Mo. Day Yr.

Street Address _____

City _____ State _____ ZIP _____

Mailing Address (if different from above)

City _____ State _____ ZIP _____

Home Phone Number (include area code) _____

Name of school _____ Grade _____

Scout groups or other organizations that you belong to:

Part 2

Have you attended Wilderness Camp before? _____

If yes, when? _____

Session that you would like to attend. (Write 1 for your first choice, 2 for your second choice, and 3 for your third choice.)

☐ July 10–15 ☐ July 17–22 ☐ July 24–29

☐ July 31–Aug 5 ☐ Aug 7–12 ☐ Aug 14–19

In 100 words or less, tell why you would like to attend Pine Mountain Wilderness Camp. Please type or write your answer neatly and attach it to this form.

Signature _____ Date _____

Signature of Parent or Guardian

ANIMAL ENCOUNTERS *My Side of the Mountain*
Information and Study Skills
An Application Form

ANNOTATED VERSION

TRANSPARENCY 6–21
TEACHER'S EDITION PAGE 671H

GRAMMAR: Object Pronouns

OBJECTIVES

- Identify and use object pronouns as objects in prepositional phrases.
- Use pronouns as part of the compound object of a prepositional phrase.
- Proofread and correct sentences with grammar and spelling errors.
- Use pronouns correctly in compound objects of prepositions to improve writing.
- Learn academic language: *object pronoun, compound.*

DAY 1 PRACTICE

Prepositional Phrases

Teach Go over the following:

- The object pronouns are *me, you, him, her, it, us,* and *them.*
- Use object pronouns as objects in prepositional phrases.

- Display the example sentences at the top of **Transparency 6–23.** Ask students which sentence is correct. (the second) Have them explain why. (*To* is a preposition. The object of the preposition must be an object pronoun—*him.*)

- Ask volunteers to underline the correct pronoun in parentheses in Sentences 1–8.

DAY 2 PRACTICE

Independent Work

Practice/Homework Assign **Practice Book** page 246.

Transparency 6–22

Daily Language Practice

Correct two sentences each day.

1. The only rezident of the cave was a large, furry hibernating bear.
   The only resident of the cave was a large, furry, hibernating bear.
2. "When did the accidant occur?" the police officers asks the witness.
   "When did the accident occur?" the police officers ask the witness.
3. This is the more comfitable chair in our whole house.
   This is the most comfortable chair in our whole house.
4. Dan thinks most science-fiction movies is terribel.
   Dan thinks most science-fiction movies are terrible.
5. This old dictionary is most valuble than that biography of George Washington.
   This rare dictionary is more valuable than that biography of George Washington.
6. Angela's sweater is warm colorful, and fashionabel.
   Angela's sweater is warm, colorful, and fashionable.
7. Rock climbing has been a remarkable experience for Juan and I.
   Rock climbing has been a remarkable experience for Juan and me.
8. I watch as the servent pour ice water for each of the guests.
   I watch as the servant pours ice water for each of the guests.
9. To Dorla and I, the confusion about our names is laffable.
   To Dorla and me, the confusion about our names is laughable.
10. We can be abcent from school if we are sick, have a doctor's appointment or take part in a field trip.
    We can be absent from school if we are sick, have a doctor's appointment, or take part in a field trip.

Monitoring Student Progress

If . . .	Then . . .
students score 7 or below on **Practice Book** page 246 or 247,	use the Reteaching lessons on Teacher's Edition pages R24 and R25.

Daily Language Practice
Have students correct Sentences 1 and 20 on **Transparency 6–22.**

Transparency 6–23

Object Pronouns in Prepositional Phrases

Several of Sam's animal friends were helpful to he.
Several of Sam's animal friends were helpful to him.

1. My friends Rich and Zoila went on a survival hike with (I, me).
2. Zoila brought a compass with (she, her).
3. (She, Her) also brought water bottles.
4. Because Rich forgot his water bottle, she lent one to (he, him).
5. The two of (they, them) hiked swiftly.
6. I rested at the two-mile mark, but (they, them) kept going.
7. My mother reserved a campsite for (us, we).
8. The dinner we prepared tasted good to (me, I).

Daily Language Practice
Have students correct Sentences 3 and 4 on **Transparency 6–22.**

Practice Book page 246

My Side of the Mountain
Grammar Skill Object Pronouns in Prepositional Phrases

Name _____

I Don't Object to Objects

Object Pronouns in Prepositional Phrases Use **object pronouns** as objects in prepositional phrases.

Object Pronouns	
Singular	**Plural**
me	us
you	you
him, her, it	them

Underline the pronoun in parentheses that correctly completes each sentence. (1 point each)

1. Randy and his dog Maggie came with (I/me) on my walk up Mt. Hunter.
2. It seemed to (he/him) that we had found an old farmhouse.
3. We imagined the people who once lived here and told stories about (they/them).
4. For (we/us), the old farm was a window into the past.
5. Maggie barked, and we walked toward (she/her).
6. A squirrel in a tree chittered, and Maggie barked at (him/he).
7. More squirrels chittered, and we looked up at (them/they).
8. I guess to (they/them), we were enemies.
9. To (I/me), however, the squirrels were a surprise.
10. We went home. The day had been a success for (we/us).

Compound Objects

Teach Remind students that a compound object is made up of two or more simple objects and one or more may be an object pronoun.

- Go over these points:
  - Use object pronouns in compound objects of a preposition.
  - If you can't decide which pronoun to use in a compound, say the sentence aloud without the other part of the compound.
- Display the example sentences at the top of **Transparency 6–24.** Ask students which is correct. (first) Cover up the words *Neil and,* showing how students can check whether the pronoun in a compound object is correct.

  Ask volunteers to underline the correct pronouns in parentheses in Sentences 1–6.

Daily Language Practice
Have students correct Sentences 5 and 6 on **Transparency 6–22.**

Independent Work

Practice/Homework Assign **Practice Book** page 247.

Daily Language Practice
Have students correct Sentences 7 and 8 on **Transparency 6–22.**

The Correct Pronoun

Teach Inform students that a good writer is careful to use subject pronouns in compound subjects and to use object pronouns in compound objects of a preposition.

- Model correcting an incorrect pronoun in a compound structure.
  - To Rich and I, spring is the best time of year. Sandra thinks summer is the best time for her brothers and she.
  - *Corrected:* To Rich and me, spring is the best time of year. Sandra thinks summer is the best time for her brothers and her.
- Have students proofread a piece of their writing for correct use of pronouns in compound structures.

Practice/Homework Assign **Practice Book** page 248.

Daily Language Practice
Have students correct Sentences 9 and 10 on **Transparency 6–22.**

Transparency 6–24

ANIMAL ENCOUNTERS My Side of the Mountain
Grammar Skill Pronouns in Prepositional Phrases with Compound Objects

Pronouns in Prepositional Phrases with Compound Objects

My cousin built a tree house for Neil and me.
My cousin built a tree house for Neil and I.

1. Neil shares his field glasses with my cousin and (I, me).
2. Neil and (I, me) are experienced bird watchers.
3. The tree house is the perfect spot for my cousin and (we, us).
4. She watches birds with Neil and (I, me).
5. She even lent her guidebook to (he and I, him and me).
6. Neil took pictures of (she and I, her and me) in the tree house.

TRANSPARENCY 6–24
TEACHER'S EDITION PAGE 671J

Practice Book page 247

My Side of the Mountain
Grammar Skill Pronouns in Prepositional Phrases with Compound Objects

Name

Pronoun Pronouncements

Pronouns in Prepositional Phrases with Compound Objects Use an object pronoun in a compound object of a preposition. To see whether a pronoun is correct, say the sentence aloud without the other part of the compound.

Underline the pronoun in parentheses that correctly completes each sentence. (1 point each)

1. Lois gave a book about bats to Marjorie and (I/me).
2. We called for Todd and then looked for (he/him) and Adam.
3. Todd stood behind Adam and (I/me) as we looked for bats under the eaves.
4. Lois gave a flashlight to Adam and (we/us).
5. Suddenly, a bat flew in the direction of Adam and (she/her)!
6. Would it fly near Todd and (we/us) too?
7. Marjorie wasn't afraid since she had read the book Lois gave to (she/her) and me.
8. I knew that the bat did not care about Todd or (we/us).
9. Lois did not know that the bat would not fly at the boys or (she/her).
10. The bat flew away, and I gave the book to Todd and (she/her).

Practice Book page 248

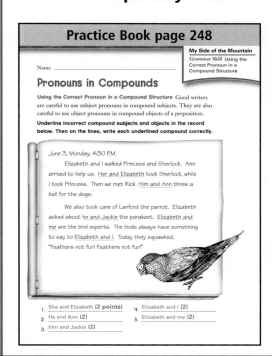

My Side of the Mountain
Grammar Skill Using the Correct Pronoun in a Compound Structure

Name

Pronouns in Compounds

Using the Correct Pronoun in a Compound Structure Good writers are careful to use subject pronouns in compound subjects. They are also careful to use object pronouns in compound objects of a preposition.

Underline incorrect compound subjects and objects in the record below. Then on the lines, write each underlined compound correctly.

June 3, Monday, 4:30 P.M.

Elizabeth and I walked Princess and Sherlock. Ann arrived to help us. Her and Elizabeth took Sherlock, while I took Princess. Then we met Rick. Him and Ann threw a ball for the dogs.

We also took care of Lanford the parrot. Elizabeth asked about he and Jackie the parakeet. Elizabeth and me are the bird experts. The birds always have something to say to Elizabeth and I. Today they squawked, "Feathers not fur! Feathers not fur!"

1. She and Elizabeth **(2 points)**
2. He and Ann **(2)**
3. him and Jackie **(2)**
4. Elizabeth and I **(2)**
5. Elizabeth and me **(2)**

WRITING: Answer to an Essay Question

OBJECTIVES

- Identify the characteristics of a good answer to an essay question.
- Write an answer to an essay question.
- Place prepositional phrases correctly to improve writing.

Writing Traits

Word Choice As students are revising their drafts on **Day 3,** remind them to choose strong nouns and verbs.

- Exact words help details come alive.
- Energetic verbs help to convey the steps in a process.
- Avoiding clichés and tired language makes an essay more persuasive.

DAY 1 PREWRITING

Introducing the Format

Explain an answer to an essay question.

- An essay question is a test question that asks for a written answer of one or more paragraphs.
- There are many types of essay questions, including ones that ask to
  – write about an experience
  – give a personal opinion and back it up with reasons and examples
  – explain a process
  – persuade someone

Start students thinking about an answer to an essay question.

- Ask students to use their experience or selection details to make notes about one of the following:
  – three of their outdoor experiences
  – the process Sam Gribley went through to create his fireplace
  – the process of bringing golden lion tamarins from zoo to rainforest
- Have students save their notes.

DAY 2 DRAFTING

Discussing the Model

Display Transparency 6–25.

- Ask students to restate what the essay question calls for. (a summary of a year in the life of a grizzly bear)
- Ask what type of writing is required. (presenting events in time order)
- Have students read the response, and discuss how it answers the question. (It describes the sequence of events in the bears' lives.)

Display Transparency 6–26, and discuss the guidelines.

Have students draft an answer to an essay question.

- Assign **Practice Book** page 249 to help students choose a topic and organize their writing.
- Have them use their notes from Day 1.
- Provide support as needed.

Transparency 6–25

Answering an Essay Question

Essay Question:
Beginning with the midwinter season, summarize a year in the life of a grizzly bear in Alaska.

Essay Response:
In midwinter, grizzly bears are sound asleep in dens underground. Cubs are born at this time. In the spring, bears come out of their dens, with their cubs following behind. Adult bears are at their thinnest in the spring because they have not eaten all winter. They may feed at first on the bodies of animals that died during the cold season; when the snow melts they will begin to eat green plants and roots. Often they catch ground squirrels that supplement their diet. In the summer, when the salmon migrate upstream, the bears gather at the rivers and streams and enjoy an abundant feast of salmon. This is the only time when many bears are found close together in the same region. Usually bears are solitary creatures who avoid one another. Although the adult grizzlies do not socialize, their cubs do. In fact, if a cub becomes an orphan, another mother bear may adopt it. The young bears learn to fish, hunt, and gather food by watching and imitating their mothers. In late summer, when the salmon stop running, the bears head for the mountains, where berries are ripening. Throughout the fall, the bears eat huge amounts of berries, which helps them store fat before they go back into hibernation for the winter months.

Transparency 6–26

Guidelines for Writing an Answer to an Essay Question

- Carefully read the essay question. Identify key words that tell what kind of answer is needed. Think about the meaning of the key words.
- Decide what type of writing and organization you need. Are you explaining? Telling a story? Persuading? Presenting steps in a process?
- Plan your answer. Jot down main ideas and details.
- Arrange your ideas in order.
- Begin your answer by restating the question.
- Check your answer. Does your response answer the question? Edit your response to make sure it does.

Practice Book page 249

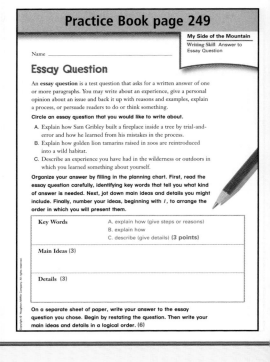

My Side of the Mountain
Writing Skill Answer to an Essay Question

Name _____

Essay Question

An **essay question** is a test question that asks for a written answer of one or more paragraphs. You may write about an experience, give a personal opinion about an issue and back it up with reasons and examples, explain a process, or persuade readers to do or think something.

Circle an essay question that you would like to write about.

A. Explain how Sam Gribley built a fireplace inside a tree by trial-and-error and how he learned from his mistakes in the process.
B. Explain how golden lion tamarins raised in zoos are reintroduced into a wild habitat.
C. Describe an experience you have had in the wilderness or outdoors in which you learned something about yourself.

Organize your answer by filling in the planning chart. First, read the essay question carefully, identifying key words that tell you what kind of answer is needed. Next, jot down main ideas and details you might include. Finally, number your ideas, beginning with 1, to arrange the order in which you will present them.

Key Words	A. explain how (give steps or reasons) B. explain how C. describe (give details) (3 points)
Main Ideas (3)	
Details (3)	

On a separate sheet of paper, write your answer to the essay question you chose. Begin by restating the question. Then write your main ideas and details in a logical order. (6)

Evaluating to Revise

Display Transparency 6–26.

Ask students to use the guidelines to decide how to make their writing better. Encourage students to turn each point into a question: Did I…?

- Students may work with a partner in a writing conference.

- Ask students to revise any parts of their writing that still need work.

See Writing Traits on page 671K.

Improving Writing: Placing Prepositional Phrases Correctly

Explain placing prepositional phrases.

- A prepositional phrase can confuse the reader if it is positioned wrong.

- Most prepositional phrases should be next to words or phrases they modify.

Display Transparency 6–27.

- Have a volunteer identify the prepositional phrases in Example A.

- Ask which prepositional phrase is confusing and why. (*Inside the tree;* Was the speaker or just the fireplace inside the tree?)

- Have students change the order. Compare their suggestion to Example B.

- Repeat the exercise with Examples C and D.

Assign Practice Book page 250.

- Students can use the checklist on **Practice Book** page 287 and the chart of proofreading marks on **Practice Book** page 288 to help them proofread their answers.

- Have students review their answers, checking for correct placement of prepositional phrases and for other errors.

Sharing Answers to an Essay Question

Consider these publishing options.

- Ask students to read their answers or some other piece of writing from the Author's Chair.

- Have volunteers gather all essays into a class book, divided into three sections by essay question. Make it available in the classroom library.

Portfolio Opportunity

Save students' answers as samples of their writing development.

Transparency 6–27

Placing Prepositional Phrases Correctly

Example A:
Inside the tree I planned to build the fireplace <u>at the base of the trunk.</u>

Suggested changes to clarify meaning:

Example B:
I planned to build the fireplace inside the tree at the base of the trunk.

Example C:
Through a chimney the smoke was let <u>out of the tree</u> leading <u>up to a knothole.</u>

Suggested changes to clarify meaning:

Example D:
The smoke was let out of the tree through a chimney leading up to a knothole.

Practice Book page 250

My Side of the Mountain
Writing Skill Improving Your Writing

Name _____

Placing Prepositional Phrases Correctly

Careful writers check the placement of prepositional phrases in their writing. If prepositional phrases appear in the wrong places in a sentence, they can make a sentence unclear. To avoid confusion, place prepositional phrases as close as possible to the words or phrases that they describe.

On a boulder Sam Gribley dried apple slices **in the sun.**
Sam Gribley dried apple slices **on a boulder in the sun.**

Revise the sentences from notes that Sam Gribley might have written. Make the meaning of each sentence clearer by moving one prepositional phrase as close as possible to the word that it describes. Circle the misplaced prepositional phrase, and then draw an arrow to show where it should go. (2 points each)

1. I steered my raft down the creek with a long stick to deep pools.
2. In the icy water I drifted with my line for an hour.
3. Suddenly the line jerked from my hand behind the raft. Dinner!
4. I pulled a fish onto the dry logs from the blue water of my raft.
5. Then I pushed near my home the raft to the muddy banks.
6. I sprinkled dried herbs on the fresh fish from a leather pouch.
7. Over a fire I grilled the fish outside my tree for a delicious meal.

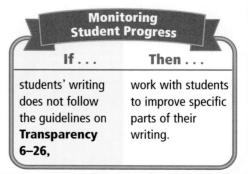

Monitoring Student Progress

If . . .	Then . . .
students' writing does not follow the guidelines on **Transparency 6–26,**	work with students to improve specific parts of their writing.

Independent Activities

Language Center

	VOCABULARY	STRUCTURAL ANALYSIS	VOCABULARY

VOCABULARY

Building Vocabulary

👥 Pairs	🕐 30 minutes
Objective	Explore botanical words.
Materials	Encyclopedia, dictionary, writing materials

My Side of the Mountain takes place in the wilderness and contains many references to plant life. Create a botanical word web of plant words in the story.

- With a partner, make a word web similar to the one shown below.

- Then go through the story and find seven names of plants. Write them in the circles.

- In each circle, include a descriptive word or phrase. Look up any unfamiliar names in an encyclopedia or dictionary.

STRUCTURAL ANALYSIS

Suffixes -ent, -ant, -able, -ible

👥 Pairs	🕐 35 minutes
Objective	Play a suffixes card game.
Materials	Index cards, writing materials

The suffixes *-ent* and *-ant* mean "having the quality of." The suffixes *-able* and *-ible* mean "capable of; inclined to." Explore words with these suffixes.

- Write each suffix on a separate index card.

- Write the following words and word roots on index cards: *abs-, comfort, horr-, poss-, profit, reason, reside, serve, stud-, terr-, vac-, valu-*.

- Work with a partner to practice forming words with the cards.

- Use a dictionary to check your answers.

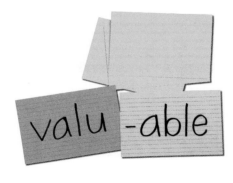

VOCABULARY

Vocabulary Game

👥 Pairs	🕐 45 minutes
Objective	Create a crossword puzzle.
Materials	Activity Master 6–4, graph paper, pencil and eraser

Use the Key Vocabulary to make a crossword puzzle. Have your partner solve it.

- Copy these Key Vocabulary words: *cache, fashion* (verb), *harsh, harvesting, migration, storehouse, survival*.

- Plan your puzzle on a piece of graph paper. Add one word at a time, intersecting the words at matching letters.

- Write a clue for each word.

- Number the first box of each word and match it with the number of the clue. Include both a *Down* and an *Across* section of clues.

- Copy your finished puzzle onto Activity Master 6–4. Leave out the words themselves. Put the clues on the back.

- Trade puzzles with your partner, and work to solve each other's puzzle.

Consider copying and laminating these activities for use in centers.

VIEWING

Viewing for Information and Details

👥 Pairs	🕐 20 minutes
Objective	Use visuals to answer questions.
Materials	Anthology, writing materials

A nonfiction article like "Tuning in on Animals" on Anthology pages 644–647 uses visuals to present information.

- Read over the guidelines for getting information from visual forms. Then write answers to the following questions by viewing Anthology pages 644–647.

  – What does a radio transmitter look like?

  – How does GPS work?

  – How are transmitters or receivers attached to animals?

  – What kinds of animals do scientists track?

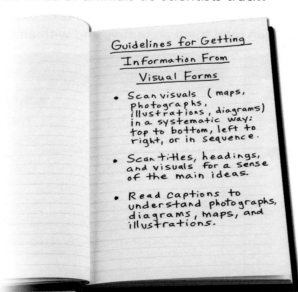

Guidelines for Getting Information From Visual Forms

- Scan visuals (maps, photographs, illustrations, diagrams) in a systematic way: top to bottom, left to right, or in sequence.
- Scan titles, headings, and visuals for a sense of the main ideas.
- Read captions to understand photographs, diagrams, maps, and illustrations.

GRAMMAR

Object Pronouns

🧍 Singles	🕐 30 minutes
Objective	Write a story using object pronouns.
Materials	Anthology, writing materials

Write a short story about Sam, from *My Side of the Mountain,* meeting up with another animal. Use at least five object pronouns in your story.

- The object pronouns are *me, you, him, her, it, us,* and *them.*
- Object pronouns are used after prepositions, such as *above, to,* and *of.*

LEVELED READERS

Kat the Curious

Summary *Kat the Curious is realistic fiction about a girl's adventure in the wild. Kat's parents drop her off for a visit at her aunt's cabin. Although a note from Aunt Helen says that she will return shortly, Kat decides not to wait. Curious and restless, Kat leaves a note and wanders off, sure that she knows the way. She gets lost but isn't frightened to spend the night in the woods. By observing animals, she discovers food and water. The next morning, she follows a raccoon she names Bandit back to her aunt's cabin.*

Vocabulary

Introduce the Key Vocabulary and ask students to complete the BLM.

kerosene lamps lamps fueled by burning oil, *p. 5*

pollution something that can be harmful to living things, *p. 7*

rustled moved with a fluttering sound, *p. 7*

bluff a high, steep cliff, *p. 10*

saplings slender young trees, *p. 16*

Building Background and Vocabulary

Ask students what a person would need to stay in the woods overnight. Preview the story with students, using the story vocabulary when possible.

◉ Comprehension Skill: Drawing Conclusions

Have students read the Strategy Focus on the book flap. Remind students to use the strategy and to draw conclusions as they read the book. (See the Leveled Readers Teacher's Guide for **Vocabulary and Comprehension Practice Masters.**)

Responding

Have partners discuss how to answer the questions on the inside back cover.

Think About the Selection   Sample answers:

1. Kat gets lost because she goes off alone, thinking she knows the way through the woods near her aunt's house.

2. She takes care of herself by eating what she sees animals eating, finding shelter, drinking water, and building a small fire.

3. that Bandit was the raccoon in Aunt Helen's garbage can the day before

4. He eats out of Helen's garbage can, so he is familiar with humans and has learned not to fear them.

Making Connections   Responses will vary.

◉ Building Fluency

Model   Read aloud page 3. Explain that italic text shows emphasis and that the italicized word should be stressed.

Practice   Have students work in pairs to find other examples of italics in the book. Once they find other sentences with italic text, they can take turns reading the sentences until they can read them accurately and with emphasis.

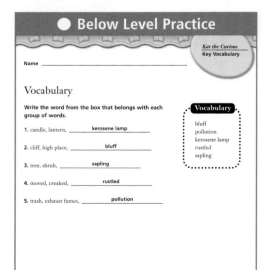

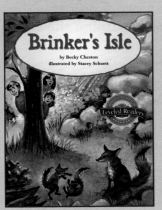

Brinker's Isle
by Becky Cheston
illustrated by Stacey Schuett

Brinker's Isle

Summary *Reese thinks that staying on Brinker's Isle will be boring. She and her friend, Hallie, will stay at an old lighthouse so her mother can paint. When the girls meet Sam, a college student, he shows them around the island.*

Vocabulary

Introduce the Key Vocabulary and ask students to complete the BLM.

lush growing thick and very green, *p. 6*

maintain to keep in proper condition, *p. 7*

marine having to do with the sea, *p. 8*

skeptically doubtfully, *p. 8*

converged merged, came together, *p. 11*

swarm gather in large numbers, *p. 12*

harvested* gathered to be eaten later, *p. 16*

*Forms of these words are Anthology Key Vocabulary words.

▲ ON LEVEL

Building Background and Vocabulary

Ask students what they think living in an isolated area, such as an island, might be like. Invite them to speculate what they might do to amuse themselves for two weeks with no television, computer, or phone. Preview the story with students, using the story vocabulary when possible.

Comprehension Skill: Drawing Conclusions

Have students read the Strategy Focus on the book flap. Remind students to use the strategy and to draw conclusions as they read the book. (See the Leveled Readers Teacher's Guide for **Vocabulary and Comprehension Practice Masters.**)

Responding

Have partners discuss how to answer the questions on the inside back cover.

Think About the Selection Sample answers:

1. being in the city, going to the mall, surfing the Internet
2. He's nice to them, he shows Hallie and Reese the secret places on the island.
3. She realizes there is a lot to do and see; there are animals that don't live in the city, such as birds, fox, and deer; Reese and Hallie go swimming and have a secret cave.
4. Responses will vary.

Making Connections Responses will vary.

Building Fluency

Model Read aloud page 5. Explain that phrases following dialogue, like *said Reese hopefully*, can tell how something is said.

Practice Have students work in pairs to find other examples of phrases that tell how a character speaks. Have them read the dialogue to their partners in the manner indicated by the words.

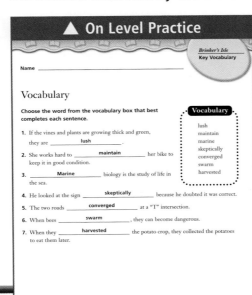

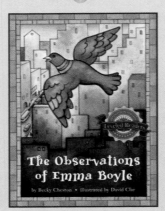

The Observations of Emma Boyle

Summary *When Emma needs to observe a bird for a science project, her mother suggests Mr. Kaufman's pigeons. However, when Mr. Kaufman tells her the history of pigeons, she agrees to take over part of their care.*

Vocabulary

Introduce the Key Vocabulary and ask students to complete the BLM.

harsh* severe, *p. 3*

constructive practical, useful, *p. 5*

inscription engraving, *p. 9*

trough long, narrow container for holding animal feed, *p. 9*

occupation possession or control of a territory, *p. 12*

contagious carrying disease, *p. 12*

strategy plan of action, *p. 14*

survive to manage to live through, *p. 15*

*Forms of these words are Anthology Key Vocabulary words.

■ ABOVE LEVEL

Building Background and Vocabulary

Have students share what they know about homing pigeons and how they are trained and cared for. Preview the story with students, using the story vocabulary when possible.

⊙ Comprehension Skill: Drawing Conclusions

Have students read the Strategy Focus on the book flap. Remind students to use the strategy and to draw conclusions as they read the book. (See the Leveled Readers Teacher's Guide for **Vocabulary and Comprehension Practice Masters.**)

Responding

Have partners discuss how to answer the questions on the inside back cover.

Think About the Selection Sample answers:

1. Possible response: She didn't know Mr. Kaufman very well, she was too busy, she thought pigeons were nasty, she didn't want to do what her mother said.

2. Possible response: She came to see the city in a new way because of him.

3. She thought of her classmate who was sick.

4. Possible response: Mr. Kaufman had been in prison under a harsh government, and his birds symbolize freedom.

Making Connections Responses will vary.

⊙ Building Fluency

Model Read aloud pages 3 and 13, modeling changing your rate of reading. Read the passage on page 3 more slowly than the one on page 13 because on page 13 Emma is hurrying around, trying to save a sick pigeon. Explain that a reader chooses to read faster or slower based on the action in the story.

Practice Have volunteers read aloud the two passages at the appropriate speed.

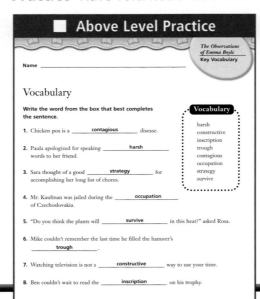

Leveled Readers

Curious Kat

Summary *Kat goes for a hike near her Aunt Helen's cabin and gets lost while in search of her favorite spot in the woods. She uses her intelligence, survival skills, and curiosity to get through a night in the woods.*

Vocabulary

Introduce the Key Vocabulary and ask students to complete the BLM.

curious eager to find out about something, *p. 3*

kerosene lamps lamps that burn an oil called kerosene, *p. 5*

rustling a soft fluttering sound, *p. 9*

exploring going to an unknown or unfamiliar place to look around, *p. 9*

familiar well known from experience, *p. 12*

survival* the preservation of one's life; the continuing of life, *p. 13*

bandit a robber, someone who steals, *p. 15*

*Forms of these words are Anthology Key Vocabulary words.

◆ LANGUAGE SUPPORT

Building Background and Vocabulary

Explain that in this story, a girl gets lost in the woods. Ask students what they might do if they got lost in the woods. Then distribute the **Build Background Practice Master.** Read aloud the directions and each item in the first column. Have students decide where they would do each item.

Comprehension Skill: Drawing Conclusions

Have students read the Strategy Focus on the book flap. Remind students to use the strategy and to draw conclusions as they read the book. (See the Leveled Readers Teacher's Guide for **Build Background, Vocabulary, and Graphic Organizer Masters.**)

Responding

Have partners discuss how to answer the questions on the inside back cover.

Think About the Selection Sample answers:

1. She wants to see her favorite place again.
2. She brings food and water with her, and she finds more food and water in the woods.
3. She knows what to do to stay safe in the woods at night.
4. Answers will vary.

Making Connections Answers will vary.

Building Fluency

Model Read aloud page 16 as students follow along in their books.

Practice Have partners read the pages out loud together several times, until they can read the text accurately and with expression.

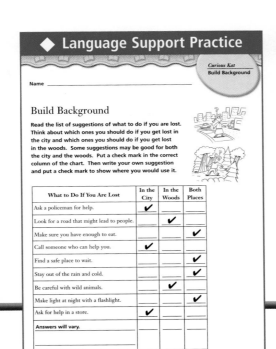

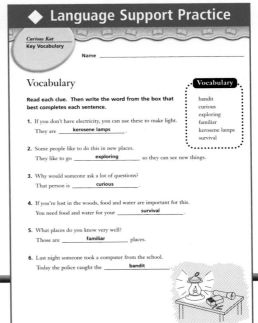

Connecting and Comparing Literature

Check Your Progress

Use these Paired Selections to help students make connections with other theme literature and to wrap up the theme.

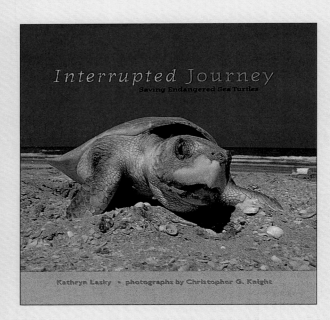

Interrupted Journey: Saving Endangered Sea Turtles
Genre: Nonfiction

Max is a volunteer who helps save sea turtles on the beaches of Cape Cod. When he discovers a sick sea turtle, he knows exactly what to do.

The Rabbit's Judgment
Genre: Fiction (Folktale)

A man creates an unusual problem for himself when he rescues a tiger. His future is uncertain until a rabbit comes along with a clever solution.

Preparing for Tests

Taking Tests: Strategies

Use this material to prepare for tests, to teach strategies, and to practice test formats.

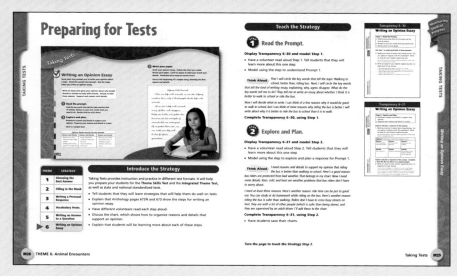

Skill Review

Use these lessons and supporting activities to review tested skills in this theme.

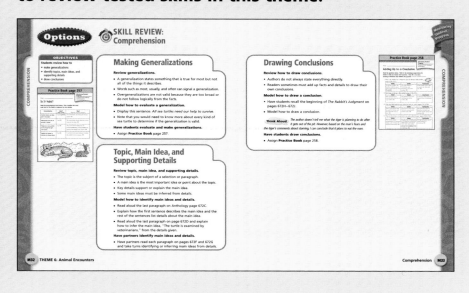

- Independent practice for skills

- Transparencies
- Strategy Posters
- Blackline Masters

Technology

Audio Selections
Interrupted Journey: Saving Endangered Sea Turtles

The Rabbit's Judgment

www.eduplace.com
Log on to Education Place for vocabulary support—
e•Glossary
e•WordGame

Theme Connections

Anthology Literature

Activities to help students think critically

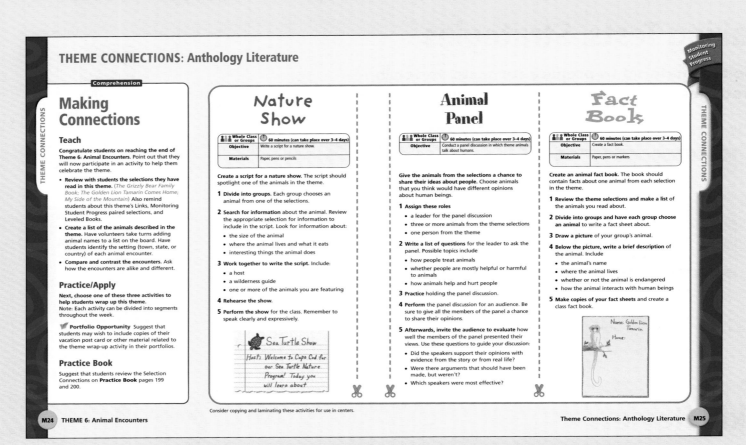

THEME CONNECTIONS: Anthology Literature

Comprehension

Making Connections

Teach

Congratulate students on reaching the end of Theme 6: Animal Encounters. Point out that they will now participate in an activity to help them celebrate the theme.

- **Review** with students the selections they have read in this theme. (*The Grizzly Bear Family Book; The Golden Lion Tamarin Comes Home; My Side of the Mountain*) Also remind students about this theme's Links, Monitoring Student Progress paired selections, and Leveled Books.
- **Create a list** of the animals described in the theme. Have volunteers take turns adding animal names to a list on the board. Have students identify the setting (town, state, or country) of each animal encounter.
- **Compare and contrast** the encounters. Ask how the encounters are alike and different.

Practice/Apply

Next, choose one of these three activities to help students wrap up this theme.
Note: Each activity can be divided into segments throughout the week.

Portfolio Opportunity Suggest that students may wish to include copies of their vacation post card or other material related to the theme wrap-up activity in their portfolios.

Practice Book

Suggest that students review the Selection Connections on **Practice Book** pages 199 and 200.

Nature Show

Whole Class or Groups	**60 minutes (can take place over 3–4 days)**
Objective	Write a script for a nature show.
Materials	Paper, pens or pencils

Create a script for a nature show. The script should spotlight one of the animals in the theme.

1 Divide into groups. Each group chooses an animal from one of the selections.

2 Search for information about the animal. Review the appropriate selection for information to include in the script. Look for information about:
- the size of the animal
- where the animal lives and what it eats
- interesting things the animal does

3 Work together to write the script. Include:
- a host
- a wilderness guide
- one or more of the animals you are featuring

4 Rehearse the show.

5 Perform the show for the class. Remember to speak clearly and expressively.

Animal Panel

Whole Class or Groups	**60 minutes (can take place over 3–4 days)**
Objective	Conduct a panel discussion in which theme animals talk about humans.

Give the animals from the selections a chance to share their ideas about people. Choose animals that you think would have different opinions about human beings.

1 Assign these roles
- a leader for the panel discussion
- three or more animals from the theme selections
- one person from the theme

2 Write a list of questions for the leader to ask the panel. Possible topics include
- how people treat animals
- whether people are mostly helpful or harmful to animals
- how animals help and hurt people

3 Practice holding the panel discussion.

4 Perform the panel discussion for an audience. Be sure to give all the members of the panel a chance to share their opinions.

5 Afterwards, invite the audience to evaluate how well the members of the panel presented their views. Use these questions to guide your discussion:
- Did the speakers support their opinions with evidence from the story or from real life?
- Were there arguments that should have been made, but weren't?
- Which speakers were most effective?

Fact Book

Whole Class or Groups	**60 minutes (can take place over 3–4 days)**
Objective	Create a fact book.
Materials	Paper, pens or markers

Create an animal fact book. The book should contain facts about one animal from each selection in the theme.

1 Review the theme selections and make a list of the animals you read about.

2 Divide into groups and have each group choose an animal to write a fact sheet about.

3 Draw a picture of your group's animal.

4 Below the picture, write a brief description of the animal. Include
- the animal's name
- where the animal lives
- whether or not the animal is endangered
- how the animal interacts with human beings

5 Make copies of your fact sheets and create a class fact book.

Consider copying and laminating these activities for use in centers.

Three Main Selections

The Grizzly Bear Family Book
Michio Hoshino

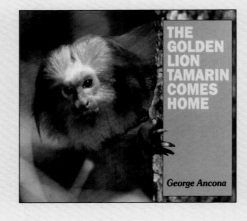

THE GOLDEN LION TAMARIN COMES HOME
George Ancona

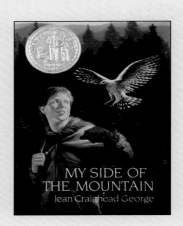

MY SIDE OF THE MOUNTAIN
Jean Craighead George

Leveled Books

Activities to help students connect and compare

Independent Activities

While you work with small groups, students can choose from a wealth of books to complete these activities.

Leveled Readers . . .

for *The Grizzly Bear Family Book*
The Hyrax of Top-Knot Island
The Bald Eagle Is Back
The Return of Wild Whoopers
The Hyrax: An Interesting Puzzle

for *The Golden Lion Tamarin Comes Home*
Saving Sea Turtles
The Emerald Cathedral: Inside a Tropical Rain Forest
Invaders!
Protecting Sea Turtles

for *My Side of the Mountain*
Kat the Curious
Brinker's Isle
The Observations of Emma Boyle
Curious Kat

Leveled Theme Paperbacks
Dolphin Adventure
The Tarantula in My Purse: and 172 Other Wild Pets
To the Top of the World: Adventures with Arctic Wolves

Leveled Bibliography
pp. 594E–594F

THEME CONNECTIONS:
Leveled Books

Monitoring Student Progress

Animal Postcards

👥 Pairs	⏱ 30 minutes
Objective	Write a postcard describing an animal encounter.

Select an animal encounter you read about in one of the books for this theme. Imagine that you had that encounter. Create a postcard to a friend back home that describes the experience. On the front, draw a picture of your animal encounter. On the back, write your message.

You might include details about
- the animal you encountered
- where your encounter took place
- what happened during the encounter

Trade your postcard with a partner. Compare your encounter with the encounter your partner wrote about.

Use these questions to guide your discussion:
- How did the characters feel about the encounters?
- How might the animals have felt during the encounters?
- What did the characters learn from their encounters?

Visitor's Guide

🧍 Singles	⏱ 45 minutes
Objective	Create a visitor's guide for people who observe animals.
Materials	Colored pens or pencils, markers

Choose an animal from one of the books you have read for this theme. Then create a visitor's guide for people who want to observe the animal in its natural environment.

Include visitor information about
- where to look for the animal
- how not to disturb the animal

Also include a list of clothing and other supplies that visitors should bring with them. You might also include a list of what *not* to bring to the animal's home.

Create illustrations to accompany the guide. Then display it so other animal observers can know what to expect on their visit.

Fact File

👥 Groups	⏱ 45 minutes
Objective	Design an educational fact file.
Materials	Reference sources, index cards

Make an index card fact file for animals you read about in the books for this theme.

List the animals you read about. Gather facts about each animal using the books and reference sources such as an encyclopedia. Include facts such as
- where each animal lives
- what each animal eats
- how the animal behaves
- whether the animal is endangered and what people are doing to help it

Use index cards to organize your facts. Write information about the animal on one side of a card. Then draw or paste a picture of the animal on the other side.

Organize your cards in alphabetical order. Then present your fact file to the class or to a small group.

✂ ✂ ✂

Consider copying and laminating these activities for use in centers.

Twelve Leveled Readers

Three Leveled Theme Paperbacks

Daily Lesson Plans

 **Technology**

Lesson Planner CD-ROM allows you to customize the chart below to develop your own lesson plans.

T Skill tested on Theme Skills Test and/or Integrated Theme Test

 50–60 minutes

DAILY LESSON PLANS

Connecting and Comparing Literature

CHECK YOUR PROGRESS

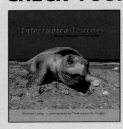 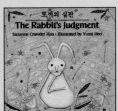

Leveled Readers
- Fluency Practice
- Independent Reading

 40–60 minutes

Preparing for Tests

TAKING TESTS: Strategies

SKILL REVIEW OPTIONS
Comprehension
Structural Analysis
Vocabulary
Spelling
Grammar
Prompts for Writing

DAY 1

Introducing Paired Selections

Key Vocabulary, M9

endangered	analyzing
veterinarian	feisty
fatal	

Reading the Selection, M10–M15
Interrupted Journey

Comprehension Strategy, M10
Monitor/Clarify **T**

Classroom Management Activities, M6–M7

Leveled Readers
The Hyrax of Top-Knot Island
The Bald Eagle Is Back
The Return of Wild Whoopers
The Hyrax: An Interesting Puzzle

Introduce the Strategy, M28
Writing an Opinion Essay

Comprehension, M32–M33
Skill Review Options **T**
Structural Analysis, M34–M35
Skill Review Options **T**
Vocabulary, M36–M37
Skill Review Options **T**

Spelling, M38
More Prefixes **T**

Grammar, M40
Negatives **T**

Prompts for Writing, M42
Opinion Paragraph/Avoiding Double Negatives **T**

DAY 2

Reading the Selection,
Interrupted Journey

Connecting and Comparing
Making Generalizations, M11
Topic, Main Idea, and Details, M13
Making Judgments, M15

Stop and Think, M16

Classroom Management Activities, M6–M7

Leveled Readers
Saving Sea Turtles
The Emerald Cathedral:
   Inside a Tropical Rain Forest
Invaders!
Protecting Sea Turtles

Step 1: Read the Prompt, M29

Comprehension, M32–M33
Skill Review Options **T**
Structural Analysis, M34–M35
Skill Review Options **T**
Vocabulary, M36–M37
Skill Review Options **T**

Spelling, M40
Three-Syllable Words **T**

Grammar, M42
Prepositions **T**

Prompts for Writing, M44
Compare-Contrast Essay/Combining Sentences **T**

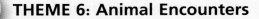

Target Skills of the Week

Comprehension
Vocabulary
Phonics/Decoding
Fluency

Monitoring Student Progress

DAILY LESSON PLANS

DAY 3

Key Vocabulary, M17

doomed	gratefulness
situation	opinion
diligently	judgment

Reading the Selection, M18–M22
The Rabbit's Judgment

Comprehension Strategy, M22
Monitor/Clarify **T**

Classroom Management Activities, M6–M7

Leveled Readers
Kat the Curious
Brinker's Isle
The Observations of Emma Boyle
Curious Kat

Step 2: Explore and Plan, M29

Comprehension, M32–M33
Skill Review Options **T**
Structural Analysis, M34–M35
Skill Review Options **T**
Vocabulary, M36–M37
Skill Review Options **T**

Spelling, M39
-ent, -ant; -able, -ible **T**

Grammar, M41
Prepositions **T**

Prompts for Writing, M43
Answer to an Essay Question/Placing Prepositional Phrases Correctly

DAY 4

Reading the Selection,
Blizzard!

Connecting and Comparing
Making Generalizations, M19
Author's Viewpoint, M21

Think and Compare, M25

Theme Connections: Anthology Literature, M26–M27

Classroom Management Activities, M6–M7

Leveled Readers
Theme Connections: Leveled Books, M26–M27

Step 3: Write Your Paper, M30

Comprehension, M32–M33
Skill Review Options **T**
Structural Analysis, M34–M35
Skill Review Options **T**
Vocabulary, M36–M37
Skill Review Options **T**

Spelling, M39
Final Sounds

Grammar, M41
Object Pronouns **T**

Prompts for Writing, M43
Summary/Paraphrasing

DAY 5

Theme Connections: Anthology Literature, M26–M27

Rereading for Fluency, M13, M22

Classroom Management Activities, M6–M7

Leveled Readers
Theme Connections: Leveled Books, M26–M27

Test Practice: Writing to a Prompt, M31

Comprehension, M32–M33
Skill Review Options **T**
Structural Analysis, M34–M35
Skill Review Options **T**
Vocabulary, M36–M37
Skill Review Options **T**

Spelling Test, M39

Grammar, M41
Object Pronouns **T**

Prompts for Writing, M43
Persuasive Essay **T** /Correcting Run-On Sentences

Classroom Management

Assign these activities while you work with small groups.

Suggest that students include copies of their work in their portfolios.

Folktale

Folktale Collage

👥 Pairs	🕐 40 minutes
Objective	Create a folktale collage.
Materials	Paste, colored paper, cloth, string, magazine pictures

The Rabbit's Judgment is illustrated with striking collages. Artists create collages by pasting cloth, colored paper, string, or pictures onto paper. Working with a partner, create your own collage to illustrate a folktale.

- Choose a folktale that you know to illustrate. (Hint: "Hansel and Gretel," "Goldilocks and the Three Bears," and "Little Red Riding Hood" are all folktales.)
- Pick an important scene from the tale to illustrate.
- Create a collage illustrating the scene.

Math

Water Speedsters

👥 Pairs	🕐 30 minutes
Objective	Make a bar graph comparing animals' speeds.
Materials	Reference sources, graph paper

A sea turtle can swim up to 20 miles per hour. Make a graph that compares this speed to that of other water creatures.

- With a partner, use an encyclopedia, an almanac, or the Internet to find out how fast sharks, dolphins, and whales swim.
- Then draw a bar graph like the one shown below onto graph paper. Plot the animal names on the horizontal axis. On the vertical axis, mark speeds at equal intervals of 20 miles per hour.
- Complete your graph by plotting the speeds from your research.

miles per hour	Speeds of Sea Creatures
80	
60	
40	
20	
0	
	turtle shark dolphin whale

Look for more activities in the Classroom Management Kit.

Consider copying and laminating these activities for use in centers.

CLASSROOM MANAGEMENT

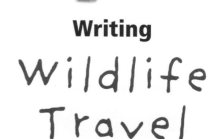

Science

Hibernation

Singles	30 minutes
Objective	Write a paragraph about hibernation.
Materials	Reference sources

In *Interrupted Journey*, the author describes one survival mechanism used by turtles—they slow their heartbeat and cool their body temperature to conserve energy and keep vital organs working. This is a form of *hibernation*.

- Use an encyclopedia, the Internet, or an animal book to research hibernation. Find answers to the questions below.
- Write a paragraph that explains how grizzly bears and other hibernating animals survive the winter.
- Be sure to include a topic sentence and to place your supporting sentences in logical order.

Research Questions

- What is hibernation?
- Which animals hibernate, and when?
- What happens to animals while they hibernate?
- How does this process help animals survive?

Media

TV Animal Encounters

Pairs	40 minutes
Objective	Plan a wildlife news television program.

What's new in the animal kingdom? Work with a partner to plan a one-hour television show reporting on encounters between humans and wildlife.

- Look through the selections for this theme and choose three subjects for news segments. Each segment should focus on an encounter between humans and wildlife.
- Brainstorm what each segment should show and the information that should be told to viewers. Plan for about fifteen minutes per segment.
- Write out the plan for your news report. Give your show a title. Then describe each segment in a short paragraph.

Writing

Wildlife Travel

Singles	30 minutes
Objective	Write a travel advertisement.
Materials	Art materials.

Animal lovers go out of their way to see wildlife while on vacation. Write a magazine ad for a travel company that runs wildlife trips.

- Create a name for the company.
- Tell what the trip will be like.
- Include what types of animals and scenery visitors might see.
- Add an illustration.

Connecting and Comparing Literature

Theme Wrap-Up

Check Your Progress

In this theme you have been reading about how people meet — and often help — wild animals. The next two selections bring you new animal encounters to read about and compare.

Before you begin, return to George Ancona's letter on pages 596–598. Think about how other characters in the theme show the patience and awareness he writes about.

People helping animals is the subject of the following selections. Compare the kinds of help the humans give, and the results of that help. Then give some thought to what all the theme selections tell about how people should act toward wild animals.

672

Read and Compare

A boy finds an endangered sea turtle and brings in others to help save its life.

Try these strategies:
Monitor and Clarify
Summarize

토끼의 심판
The Rabbit's Judgment
Suzanne Crowder Han • Illustrated by Yumi Heo

In this Korean folktale, a man helps an ungrateful tiger and needs to be saved by a clever rabbit.

Try these strategies:
Predict and Infer
Question

Strategies in Action *Remember to put all your reading strategies to work as you read.*

672 A

Use Paired Selections: Check Your Progress

Have students read page 672. Discuss these questions:

- What do the people in this theme have in common? (All of them have unusual experiences with animals.)

Have students read page 672A. Ask these questions:

- How might *Interrupted Journey* be similar to the other selections in the theme? (Sample answer: Like *The Golden Lion Tamarin Comes Home*, *Interrupted Journey* is nonfiction that tells about a real-life animal rescue.)

- How do you think *The Rabbit's Judgment* will be different from other selections? (Sample answer: It is a folktale, not nonfiction.)

Strategies in Action Remind students to use all their reading strategies, including the Monitor/Clarify strategy, as they read the Paired Selections.

Rescue Words

Carmen was walking in the park one Saturday morning when she spotted something strange. A small bird was flapping in the grass. The bird looked feisty, but it was clear to Carmen that it was hurt.

Carmen called the SPCA. A volunteer picked up the bird and took it to an animal hospital. At the hospital, a veterinarian named Sarah carefully examined the bird. She took x-rays of the bird's injured wing. After analyzing the x-rays, Sarah told Carmen the bird's wing was broken. She also said that its injuries shouldn't be fatal, and the bird would survive. Carmen felt relieved.

Sarah then told Carmen some surprising news. The bird was a Kirtland's warbler, a rare and endangered bird. By bringing the bird in, Carmen had done a little bit to keep the Kirtland's warbler from dying out.

ANIMAL ENCOUNTERS *Interrupted Journey*
Monitoring Student Progress
Key Vocabulary

ANNOTATED VERSION

TRANSPARENCY 6–28
TEACHER'S EDITION PAGE M9

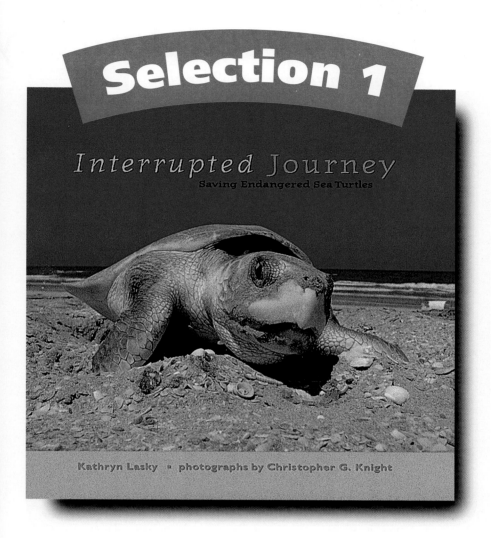

Selection 1

Interrupted Journey
Saving Endangered Sea Turtles

Kathryn Lasky • photographs by Christopher G. Knight

Introducing Vocabulary

Key Vocabulary
These words appear in the selection.

endangered close to dying out

veterinarian a person trained to give medical care to animals

fatal causing death

analyzing carefully examining

feisty lively

 e • Glossary
e • WordGame

See Vocabulary notes on pages M10, M12, and M14 for additional words to preview.

Have students locate Key Vocabulary words in the story.

- Have volunteers read aloud each sentence containing a highlighted Key Vocabulary word in the selection.

Display Transparency 6–28.

- Model how to use context clues to find the meaning of *feisty*.

- For each remaining sentence, ask students to use context clues to understand each Key Vocabulary word.

Practice/Homework Assign **Practice Book** page 251.

Introduce the Graphic Organizer.
Tell students to fill in **Practice Book** page 252 as they read the Paired Selections.

Practice Book page 251

Name _____

Monitoring Student Progress
Key Vocabulary

Animal Care Words

Fill in each blank with the Vocabulary word that best replaces each underlined word or phrase.

Vocabulary
endangered
veterinarian
fatal
analyzing
feisty

1. Marcus is a <u>doctor who treats sick animals.</u>
   veterinarian (2 points)

2. Some animals are calm and obedient during their examinations. Other animals are so <u>active</u> their owners must be called in to hold them still. feisty (2)

3. Most animals are brought into the office for regular checkups. In a few cases, Marcus has treated animals with <u>deadly</u> illnesses.
   fatal (2)

4. When Marcus suspects that an animal has a broken bone, he takes an x-ray. By <u>studying</u> the results, Marcus can tell where the break is and how to fix it. analyzing (2)

5. When Marcus isn't working at the office, he volunteers at a wildlife sanctuary. He believes it is important to help <u>threatened</u> animals. endangered (2)

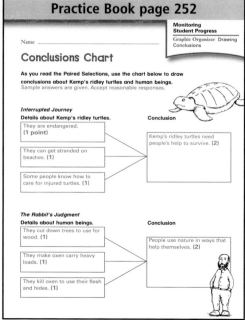

Practice Book page 252

Name _____

Monitoring Student Progress
Graphic Organizer Drawing Conclusions

Conclusions Chart

As you read the Paired Selections, use the chart below to draw conclusions about Kemp's ridley turtles and human beings.
Sample answers are given. Accept reasonable responses.

Interrupted Journey
Details about Kemp's ridley turtles.

They are endangered. (1 point)

They can get stranded on beaches. (1)

Some people know how to care for injured turtles. (1)

Conclusion

Kemp's ridley turtles need people's help to survive. (2)

The Rabbit's Judgment
Details about human beings.

They cut down trees to use for wood. (1)

They make oxen carry heavy loads. (1)

They kill oxen to use their flesh and hides. (1)

Conclusion

People use nature in ways that help themselves. (2)

Reading the Paired Selections M9

Guiding Comprehension

1 MAKING INFERENCES How do you think Max feels when he finds a sick sea turtle? (Sample answer: He feels excited about finding the turtle, but he is also worried about its health.)

2 NOTING DETAILS What symptoms does the sick sea turtle exhibit? (a cold body, floppy flippers, open eyes but no movement)

3 PREDICTING OUTCOMES What do you think will happen next to the sea turtle? (Sample answer: It will be taken to an animal hospital.)

TARGET SKILL

COMPREHENSION STRATEGY

Monitor/Clarify

Teacher Modeling Remind students that if they come to a part of the selection they do not understand, they should reread or read ahead to clarify. Read aloud the first two paragraphs on page 672B. Then model the strategy:

Think Aloud *After reading the first paragraph, I wonder what happens to cold and confused sea turtles. When I read ahead I see that volunteers patrol beaches looking for stranded turtles. Some must wash up on beaches when they become cold and confused.*

Vocabulary

plankton tiny animals that float on the ocean's surface

endangered close to dying out

READ & COMPARE

Interrupted Journey
Saving Endangered Sea Turtles

by Kathryn Lasky
photographs by Christopher G. Knight

The young turtle has been swimming for three months now in the same warm shallow bay, grazing on small crabs and plankton, basking in an endless dream of calm water and plentiful food. But as the days begin to shorten and the light drains out of the sky earlier and earlier, the water grows colder. It drops to fifty degrees Fahrenheit. The turtle is confused. Swimming is harder. Its heartbeat slows — and almost stops.

Ten days before Thanksgiving, on a beach where Pilgrims once walked, Max Nolan, a ten-year-old boy, and his mother begin their patrol. The Nolans are among volunteers who walk Cape Cod's beaches during November and December to search for turtles who are often cold and stunned and seem dead — turtles whose lives they may be able to save.

It is a blustery day on Ellis Landing Beach. At twenty-five knots the bitter northwest wind stings Max's face like sharp needles. It makes his eyes water but he keeps looking — looking above the high-water mark through the clumps of seaweed, looking below the tide line where the sand is hard and sleek and lapped by surf — looking for a dark greenish-brown mound about the size of a pie plate, looking for a Kemp's ridley turtle that is dying and perhaps can be saved.

Max and his mother and the other volunteers work for a vital cause. All sea turtles are threatened or endangered; Kemp's ridleys are the most endangered of all. Right now on our planet there are fewer than eight thousand Kemp's ridley turtles left. They are a vanishing species.

672B

REACHING ALL LEARNERS

Challenge

Additional Reading

Students may be interested in reading other books by Kathryn Lasky. To learn more about the author, visit Education Place at **www.eduplace.com/kids**.

On Ellis Landing Beach, snow squalls begin to whirl down. The waves are building, and as they begin to break, the white froth whips across their steep faces. So far there is no sign of a turtle.

Max is far ahead of his mother when he sees the hump in the sand being washed by the surf. He runs up to it and shouts to his mom, "Got one!" The turtle is cold. Its flippers are floppy. Its eyes are open, but the turtle is not moving at all. It might be dead, but then again, it might not.

Max remembers the instructions given to all rescuers. He picks up the turtle, which weighs about five pounds, and moves it above the high-tide mark to keep it from washing out to sea. Then he runs to find seaweed to protect it from the wind. He finds a stick to mark the spot, and next, he and his mother go to the nearest telephone and call the sea-turtle rescue line of the Massachusetts Audubon Society.

1

2

3

672**C**

Connecting and Comparing

Making Generalizations

- Ask students: How does the information in this theme support the generalization that some animals need help to survive? (Sample answer: Some golden lion tamarins, manatees, and Kemp's ridley turtles need special training or care to survive in the wild.)

- From reading the selections in this theme, what can you tell about the people who work to save endangered animals? (Sample answer: They are kind and compassionate. They work hard.)

Extra Support/Intervention

Selection Preview

pages 672B–672C Max and his mother belong to a volunteer group that patrols the shores of Cape Cod in Massachusetts, looking for sick sea turtles. How do you think the group helps the turtles?

pages 672D–672E What is happening to the turtles in these pictures? Where do you think they are now?

pages 672F–672G How do you think the medical team will care for the turtles?

Reading the Paired Selections **M11**

CRITICAL THINKING
Guiding Comprehension

4 **TEXT ORGANIZATION** How is the information presented to readers in this selection? (by sequence of events)

5 **NOTING DETAILS** What will analyzing the turtle's blood tell the veterinarians? (how well the turtle's organs are working)

6 **MAKING JUDGMENTS** Do you think caring for sick turtles is a difficult job? Why or why not? (Sample answer: Yes. It is hard to tell whether the turtles are alive or dead.)

COMPREHENSION STRATEGY
Monitor/Clarify

Teacher/Student Modeling Ask students to model how they would reread or read ahead if they were unsure of why the turtles were in a *cold, stunned condition* when they were rescued.

Vocabulary

veterinarian a person trained to give medical care to animals

fatal causing death

dehydrated lacking water

analyzing carefully examining

vestigial something that once was important but now no longer serves a purpose

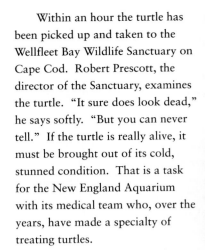

4 Within an hour the turtle has been picked up and taken to the Wellfleet Bay Wildlife Sanctuary on Cape Cod. Robert Prescott, the director of the Sanctuary, examines the turtle. "It sure does look dead," he says softly. "But you can never tell." If the turtle is really alive, it must be brought out of its cold, stunned condition. That is a task for the New England Aquarium with its medical team who, over the years, have made a specialty of treating turtles.

Robert puts the new turtle in a plastic wading pool with another turtle that is quite lively. Max crouches by the edge and watches his turtle. It is as still as a stone. He gently touches a flipper. Nothing moves. Then after about twenty minutes, he thinks he might see a flicker in the turtle's left eyelid. He leans closer. "Hey, it's moving!" It wasn't just the eyelid. He saw the right rear flipper move a fraction of an inch. Over the next five minutes, he sees the turtle make three or four microscopically small motions with its right rear flipper. Soon, the rescue team from the New England Aquarium arrives.

Beth Chittick is a vet at the New England Aquarium. When the turtles arrive she is ready for them. The turtles are taken immediately into the examination room. Beth is joined by head veterinarian, Howard Crum. They insert a thermometer into the cloaca, the opening under the turtle's tail. The temperature of the turtle Max found is fifty degrees Fahrenheit. Normal temperature for a turtle is usually about seventy-five degrees. Howard next tries to find a heartbeat. He listens intently. "I think I can hear a faint sound . . ." He holds the stiff turtle against his ear as one might hold a seashell. "Why, gee whiz, I can hear the ocean," he jokes.

672D

Challenge

Research Kemp's Ridley Turtles

Have groups collect facts about Kemp's ridley turtles, such as their anatomy and life cycle. Then ask them to use the information to create an illustrated fact file for the animal.

Howard is still not convinced that the turtle is dead. "With turtles," Howard says, "death is a relative term." Turtles can operate, can survive, even when their hearts slow down for periods of time. Events that might damage the larger, more complicated brains of other animals will not always prove fatal to turtles.

In fact, a turtle's heartbeat naturally slows down at times to just one or two beats per minute in order to conserve oxygen and keep vital organs like the brain working. So Howard won't give up on this turtle yet. The turtle does not seem dehydrated. The skin on its limbs is not wrinkled — a good sign.

An assistant swabs down an area on the turtle's neck, from which a blood sample will be taken. By analyzing the blood, Howard and Beth will be able to see how the turtle's kidneys and other organs are functioning. **5**

Next the turtle is cleaned. The algae are washed and wiped from its shell. The doctors detect movement in its tail and then see some of the same movements that Max saw in its flippers. They are the motions a turtle makes when it swims. They do not necessarily mean that it is alive, though. It has been speculated that these movements could be what are sometimes called vestigial motions, echoes of long-ago actions, fossil behaviors embedded in the brain of an ancient creature. The turtle could be swimming in death or swimming toward life. **6**

672E

Connecting and Comparing

Topic, Main Idea, and Details

- Ask students: How are the topics of *Interrupted Journey* and *The Golden Lion Tamarin Comes Home* similar? (Both selections focus on ways people help endangered animals survive.)

- Have students identify the types of details that can be found in both selections. (Sample answer: Both explain the medical care given to each animal and describe where the animals live.)

Fluency Practice

Rereading for Fluency Suggest that students reread the first two paragraphs on page 672E. Encourage them to read expressively.

Guiding Comprehension

➐ NOTING DETAILS Why does Howard give the lively turtle only a fifty-percent survival rate? (He thinks there is a good chance it could still get sick.)

➑ COMPARE AND CONTRAST How is Orange's behavior different from Yellow-Blue's? (Orange is feisty and then paddles with its flippers. Yellow-Blue barely moves.)

Summarize Have students use what they wrote on their Drawing Conclusions Graphic Organizers to summarize *Interrupted Journey*.

Nonetheless, the vets hook up the turtle to an intravenous needle through which fluids will be pumped very slowly at a temperature slightly higher than the turtle's body. Beth and Howard have learned much about the condition of this turtle but they are still not sure if it is really alive or dead.

Finally the turtle is tagged with a yellow-blue band. It will be known as Yellow-Blue. It is put in the Intensive Care Unit, a large temperature-controlled stainless steel box with a glass window. Inside, the turtle is placed on a soft pile of towels so its shell is supported and it will not have to rest on its ventrum, or bottom shell.

Then the team turn their attention to another turtle, which is definitely alive. Howard picks up the turtle and talks to it as its flippers thrash madly. "Okay, little man!" This turtle's temperature is sixty-two degrees. When they take its blood, the sample appears much redder than the nearly brown-ish blood of Yellow-Blue, which indicates that there is more oxygen in it.

672**F**

Vocabulary

intravenous inserted into a vein

pneumonia a disease that affects the lungs

feisty lively

 English Language Learners

Language Development

Explain to students that an Intensive Care Unit is an area in a hospital where very sick patients are watched closely by nurses and doctors. Tell students that an x-ray is a picture of the inside of a patient's body. Doctors x-ray patients to determine the health of their bones and organs.

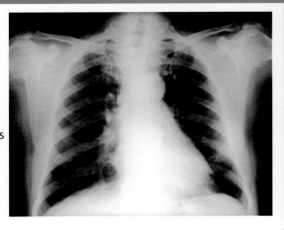

But as lively as this one is, Howard gives it only a fifty-percent survival rate. There is a good chance that pneumonia could still develop. They insert an intravenous tube for rehydration. Then they tag the animal with a plain yellow band. There are other turtles also being treated. One, Orange, needs to have its eyes lubricated and then be weighed and examined. The turtle is feisty and needs to be sedated. This is done without drugs, simply by shielding the top of its head from the ceiling lights. There is a gland inside a turtle's head that is sensitive to light, and it is speculated that when the gland is covered, it helps the turtle settle down into a relaxed, near-sleeping state.

7

8

In this peaceful state, Orange begins to "swim" on the table, its flippers making the paddling motions that have since birth propelled it through thousands of miles of sea. Its heart rate, at thirty-six beats a minute, is good. Its respiration rate is still slow. It takes only one breath every minute. Its temperature is near seventy degrees. Orange is x-rayed for signs of pneumonia. The lungs are clear.

Whatever the outcome for these three turtles, Beth, Howard, Robert, Max, and his mother all know they are doing their part to help return the turtles to health, to help return them to the sea.

672**G**

Connecting and Comparing

Making Judgments

- Ask students: Who has the harder job—the tamarin observers in Brazil or the turtle volunteers in Cape Cod? Why? (Sample answer: the tamarin observers; They feed and care for the animals in their natural habitat and send notes about them to the National Zoo. The volunteers only find the sick turtles and call the rescuers.)

- Ask students: Which animal do you think has a better chance of surviving in its natural habitat—the turtles or the tamarins? Why? (Sample answer: the turtles; They are healthy when they leave the aquarium and they have lived in their natural environment before.)

Stop and Think

Critical Thinking Questions

1. **COMPARE AND CONTRAST** How is Max's animal encounter in *Interrupted Journey* different from Michio's animal encounter in *The Grizzly Bear Family Book?* (Max helps rescue sick sea turtles that wash up on the beach in Massachusetts; Michio observes and photographs grizzly bears in Alaska.)

2. **PREDICTING OUTCOMES** What do you think will happen to the turtles that recover? (Sample answer: They will be returned to the sea near Cape Cod.)

3. **MAKING JUDGMENTS** Which animal that you read about in the theme needs the most help from people? Why? (Answers will vary.)

Strategies in Action Have students model how they used Monitor/Clarify and other strategies to help them understand this selection.

Connecting and Comparing

Compare and Contrast

- Remind students that a topic is the subject of a paragraph or selection, a main idea is the main point it makes about a topic, and a detail supports a topic or main idea.

- Have students skim through *The Grizzly Bear Family Book* and *Interrupted Journey*. Work with them to identify and compare topics and main ideas.

- Have students use **Practice Book** page 253 to identify supporting details in each selection.

Practice Book page 253

Monitoring Student Progress
Connecting and Comparing

Name _____

Details Make a Difference

Read the information in the chart below. Write at least two details that support the selected main ideas.
Sample answers are given. Accept reasonable responses.

Interrupted Journey: Saving Endangered Sea Turtles

Main Idea	Supporting Details
page 672C: Max knows what to do when he finds a sick turtle on the beach.	He picks up the turtle and moves it above the high-tide mark to keep it from washing out to sea. He finds seaweed to protect it from the wind. He finds a stick to mark the spot and calls the sea-turtle rescue line of the Massachusetts Audubon Society. (**2 points:** 1 per detail)
page 672E: Live turtles can seem to be dead.	Things that might damage the brains of larger animals do not kill turtles. Turtles can survive even when their hearts slow down. A turtle's heartbeat naturally slows down at times in order to save oxygen and keep vital organs working. (**2 points:** 1 per detail)

The Grizzly Bear Family Book

Main Idea	Supporting Details
pages 604–605: Mother bears behave similarly to human mothers.	Mother bears play tag with their cubs. They hug their cubs and have fun together. They nurse and care for their cubs the same way a human mother would with her children. (**2 points:** 1 per detail)
pages 608–609: Bears create a dominance order when together in a group.	The stronger, more aggressive bears have the best places. When a bear joins a group, there is a brief struggle. Bears try to avoid fighting, but sometimes bears may fight for the higher position. When two bears who have already fought meet again, the loser will give up its place to the winner. (**2 points:** 1 per detail)

Extra Support/Intervention

Strategy Review: Monitor/Clarify

Have students discuss how they clarified information they did not understand in *Interrupted Journey*. How and where did rereading or reading ahead help them?

Monitoring Student Progress

If . . .	Then . . .
students have difficulty answering Guiding Comprehension questions,	guide them in reading aloud relevant portions of the text and discussing their answers.

Selection 2

토끼의 심판

The Rabbit's Judgment

Suzanne Crowder Han • Illustrated by Yumi Heo

Introducing Vocabulary

Key Vocabulary
These words appear in the selection.

doomed headed for an unhappy end

gratefulness thankfulness

situation position

opinion a belief

diligently in a steady, hard-working way

judgment a decision made after careful thought

e • Glossary
e • WordGame

See Vocabulary notes on pages M18, and M22 for additional words to preview.

Have students locate Key Vocabulary words in the story.

- Have volunteers read aloud each sentence containing a highlighted Key Vocabulary word in the selection.

Display Transparency 6–29.

- Work with students to complete the sentences, using Key Vocabulary words.

Practice/Homework Assign **Practice Book** page 254.

Transparency 6–29

Competition Words

doomed	gratefulness	situation
opinion	diligently	judgment

Chloe had practiced ___diligently___ for months to prepare for the state piano competition. She was determined to win first prize this year. However, just as she was about to perform, all the lights in the concert hall suddenly went out. It was so dark that Chloe could barely see the piano. She felt ___doomed___ to failure. Then one of the judges opened a door to let in some light. Although it was still dark, Chloe could at least see the keys on the piano. Chloe felt sudden ___gratefulness___ to her piano teacher for making her memorize the music. She took a deep breath, and began her performance.

After she finished, Chloe was pleased. In her ___opinion___, she had performed well despite a difficult ___situation___. As she waited to hear the panel's final ___judgment___, Chloe hoped that the judges would agree.

Practice Book page 254

Monitoring Student Progress
Key Vocabulary

Name _____

Decision Words

Write the word from the list that best fits each word or phrase.

		Vocabulary
1. in a serious and steady way	diligently **(1 point)**	doomed
2. state of affairs	situation **(1)**	gratefulness
3. thoughtful decision	judgment **(1)**	situation
4. headed for big trouble	doomed **(1)**	opinion
5. thought or feeling	opinion **(1)**	diligently
6. thankfulness	gratefulness **(1)**	judgment

7. Now write a paragraph about a situation in which you had to make a judgment.
Answers will vary. **(4)**

_____
_____
_____
_____
_____

CRITICAL THINKING

Guiding Comprehension

❶ FANTASY AND REALISM Is this story realistic, or does it use fantasy? How can you tell? (It uses fantasy; It contains talking animals.)

❷ PREDICTING OUTCOMES What do you think will happen to the man? (Sample answers: The tiger will eat him; He will outsmart the tiger and run away.)

Vocabulary

hoarse low and rough in voice

doomed headed for an unhappy end

refuse to turn down or reject

pitiful sad or pathetic

The Rabbit's Judgment

by Suzanne Crowder Han • illustrated by Yumi Heo

❶ $\quad$ Long, long ago, when plants and animals talked, a tiger fell into a deep pit while roaming through the forest in search of food. He tried over and over to get out but the walls were too steep for him to climb and he could not jump high enough to reach the opening. He called for help but none came.

The next morning he called for help until he was hoarse. Hungry and exhausted, he slumped down on the ground, thinking that he was doomed to die in the pit. But then he heard footsteps.

"Help! Help!" he cried desperately.

"Oh! A tiger!" said a man, peering over the side of the pit.

"Please! Please help me out of here!" pleaded the tiger. "If you help me, I won't forget you as long as I live."

The man felt sorry for the tiger but he was afraid of being eaten. "I would like to help you but, I'm sorry, the thought of what might happen makes me refuse. Please forgive me. I must be on my way," said the man and he began walking down the path.

"No! No! Please don't think like that! Please help me!" cried the tiger. "You don't have to worry, I promise. I won't hurt you. Please help me out. Please! I beg you! If you get me out, I'll be forever grateful to you. Please!"

The tiger sounded so pitiful that the man turned around and walked back to the pit. He looked around until he found a big log. "Here, climb up this," he said, lowering the log into the pit.

The tiger climbed up the log and came face to face with the man.
❷ His mouth watered and he began circling him.

672**H**

Extra Support/Intervention

Selection Preview

pages 672H–672I A tiger trapped in a deep pit asks a man for help. The tiger promises not to eat the man. Do you think the tiger will keep his promise?

pages 672J–672K What do you think the ox and the pine tree will tell the tiger to do?

page 672L What do you think the rabbit will say? Why?

672I

Connecting and Comparing

Making Generalizations

- Have students discuss how the man in *The Rabbit's Judgment* is similar to other people in this theme. (He cares about animals.)

- Ask students: What evidence in this theme supports the generalization that some animals can be dangerous? (This man is almost eaten by a tiger, photographer Michio Hoshino is scared by two bears, and Sam Gribley meets destructive animal guests after Halloween.)

Guiding Comprehension

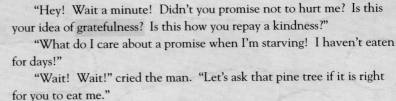

❸ MAKING JUDGMENTS Do you think the tiger treats the man fairly? Why or why not? (Sample answer: No. The tiger promises not to hurt the man, but then decides to eat him.)

❹ COMPARE AND CONTRAST What do the pine tree and the ox have in common? Why? (They both dislike and distrust people because they feel mistreated by them.)

READ & COMPARE

❸
"Hey! Wait a minute! Didn't you promise not to hurt me? Is this your idea of gratefulness? Is this how you repay a kindness?"

"What do I care about a promise when I'm starving! I haven't eaten for days!"

"Wait! Wait!" cried the man. "Let's ask that pine tree if it is right for you to eat me."

"All right," said the tiger. "But I'm awfully hungry."

The tiger and the man explained the situation to the pine tree.

"What do men know about gratefulness?" said the pine tree. "Why, your kind take our leaves and limbs to make fires to heat your homes and cook your food. And it takes us years to grow big but when we finally do, you cut us down and cut us up to make timber and planks for houses and furniture and the like. Moreover, it was a man that dug that pit. Gratefulness, indeed! Don't give it another thought, Tiger. You just go ahead and satisfy your hunger!"

"Now what do you think of that?" asked the tiger, smacking his lips loudly and slinking toward the man.

Just at that moment an ox wandered by. "Wait! Wait!" cried the man. "Let's ask that ox to judge."

The tiger agreed, so they explained everything to the ox and asked his opinion.

"Well, as far as I'm concerned, there's no question about what to do," said the ox, turning to the tiger. "You should eat him up!"

672J

Challenge

Act Out or Retell Folktales

Explain to students that this story is a *folktale*, a story handed down in a culture. Have small groups of students find other folktales to retell or act out for the class. For example, have students use an Anansi story from West Africa or a Coyote tale from Native American folklore.

Vocabulary

gratefulness thankfulness

situation position

opinion a belief

diligently in a steady, hard-working way

"You see, from the time we're born we oxen work diligently for men. We carry heavy loads on our backs and plow up the ground so they can grow food. But what do they do when we're old? They kill us and eat our flesh and use our hides to make all kinds of things. So don't talk to me about being grateful to him. Just eat him!"

"See! Everyone agrees. Now get ready to die," said the tiger, crouching to pounce.

The man thought that it must surely be his time to die. But then a rabbit came hopping by.

"Wait, Tiger! Wait!" shouted the man.

"Now what?" roared the tiger.

"Please give me one last chance," begged the man. "Let's ask that rabbit to judge whether I should be eaten or not."

"Oh, what's the use? You know the answer will be the same."

"Please, please," pleaded the man.

"Oh, all right. But this is the last time. I'm starving!"

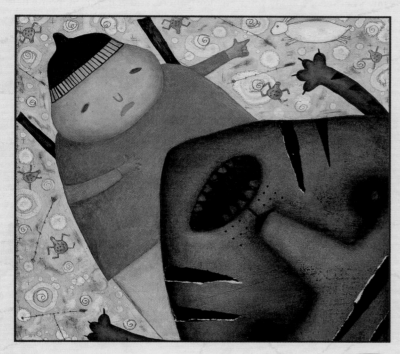

672**K**

Connecting and Comparing

Author's Viewpoint

- Have students reread what the pine tree and ox have to say about people. Then compare their feelings with the author's feelings about trophy hunters on page 615 of *The Grizzly Bear Family Book*. What do both authors seem to think about people? (They think some people have no respect for animals and nature.)

- Ask: Do you agree with this opinion? Why or why not? (Answers will vary.)

English Language Learners

Language Development

Some students may be unfamiliar with the phrase *smacking his lips.* Explain its meaning and have students demonstrate it to show their comprehension.

Reading the Paired Selections **M21**

CRITICAL THINKING

Guiding Comprehension

5 DRAWING CONCLUSIONS Who benefits most from the rabbit's judgment? How? (the man; He is no longer in danger of being eaten.)

6 MAKING JUDGMENTS Do you agree with the rabbit's advice? Why or why not? (Answers will vary.)

TARGET SKILL
COMPREHENSION STRATEGY
Monitor/Clarify

Student Modeling Have students model rereading or reading ahead to clarify any aspect of the rabbit's judgment they don't understand. If necessary, use this prompt: Why does the rabbit tell the tiger to return to his position in the pit?

TARGET SKILL

Fluency Practice

Rereading for Fluency Have students choose a favorite part of the selection to reread to a partner. Remind students to read with expression.

Finish the Graphic Organizer Have students share and discuss their completed Drawing Conclusions Graphic Organizers.

So the tiger and the man told the rabbit their story. The rabbit listened carefully. Then he closed his eyes and stroked one of his long ears. After a few seconds he opened his eyes and spoke slowly and deliberately. "I well understand what the two of you have said. But if I am to make a wise judgment we should go to that pit and you should tell me again what happened. So lead the way."

The tiger and the man led the rabbit the few short steps to the pit.

"Well, it certainly is deep," said the rabbit, looking down into the pit. "Let's see, you say you were down there, and you were standing here like this?" he said to the tiger and then to the man. "Well, if you get in those positions, then I can make a judgment."

Without giving it a second thought, the hungry tiger jumped down into the pit. The man peered over the edge.

5
6 "So, that is how the two of you were," said the rabbit. "Now I can judge. The problem started when this man helped that tiger out of this pit. In other words, if the man had not shown any kindness and had left the tiger in the pit, there wouldn't be a problem. So I think the man should continue his journey and the tiger should remain in the pit.

"Now, a good day to the both of you," said the clever rabbit and he hopped away.

672L

Think and Compare

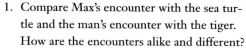

1. Compare Max's encounter with the sea turtle and the man's encounter with the tiger. How are the encounters alike and different?

2. Compare the efforts to save the sea turtle and the efforts to save the tamarins in *The Golden Lion Tamarin Comes Home*. Do you think the efforts will be successful? Why or why not?

3. The ox and the pine tree don't have good things to say about people in *The Rabbit's Judgment*. What do you think the grizzly bear, the tamarin, and Sam Gribley's animal neighbors would say about people?

4. Do you agree with the ox and the pine tree's opinions? How would you respond to them?

5. Think about the different ways people interact with animals in the theme. Which person would you most like to trade places with? Explain why.

Strategies in Action Tell about two or three places in *Interrupted Journey* where you used reading strategies.

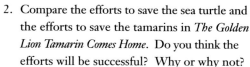

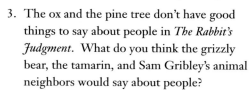

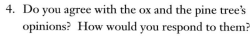

Expressing

Write an Essay

Write a brief essay telling what kind of responsibility people should have toward wild animals. Use examples from the selections.

Tips
- Think of a sentence stating the main point you want to make.
- Think of reasons to back up that main point.
- Think of details that support those reasons.

672**M**

Think and Compare

READ & COMPARE

Discuss or Write Have students discuss or write their answers. Sample answers are provided; accept reasonable responses.

1. Both encounters show people helping animals in need. When Max helps the sea turtle, he is in no danger, but when the man helps the tiger, he is in danger of becoming the tiger's next meal.

2. yes, because in both cases there are many determined people working to save the animals

3. The grizzly bear might say that people are peaceful observers. The tamarin might say that some people are violent and destructive, while others are nurturing and kind. Sam Gribley's animal neighbors might say people are generous hosts.

4. Answers will vary.

5. Answers will vary.

Strategies in Action Have students take turns modeling how and where they used Monitor/Clarify and other reading strategies.

REACHING ALL LEARNERS

Extra Support/Intervention

Strategy Review: Monitor/Clarify

Have students discuss how they clarified information they did not understand in *The Rabbit's Judgment.* How and where did rereading or reading ahead help them?

Monitoring Student Progress

If . . .	Then . . .
students have difficulty answering more than 2 Think and Compare questions,	guide them in reading aloud relevant portions of the text and discussing their answers.

Comprehension

Making Connections

Teach

Congratulate students on reaching the end of Theme 6: Animal Encounters. Point out that they will now participate in an activity to help them celebrate the theme.

- **Review with students the selections they have read in this theme.** (*The Grizzly Bear Family Book; The Golden Lion Tamarin Comes Home; My Side of the Mountain*) Also remind students about this theme's Links, Monitoring Student Progress paired selections, and Leveled Books.

- **Create a list of the animals described in the theme.** Have volunteers take turns adding animal names to a list on the board. Have students identify the setting (town, state, or country) of each animal encounter.

- **Compare and contrast the encounters.** Ask how the encounters are alike and different.

Practice/Apply

Next, choose one of these three activities to help students wrap up this theme.
Note: Each activity can be divided into segments throughout the week.

✍ **Portfolio Opportunity** Suggest that students may wish to include copies of their vacation post card or other material related to the theme wrap-up activity in their portfolios.

Practice Book

Suggest that students review the Selection Connections on **Practice Book** pages 199 and 200.

Nature Show

👥👥 Whole Class or Groups	🕐 60 minutes (can take place over 3–4 days)
Objective	Write a script for a nature show.
Materials	Paper, pens or pencils

Create a script for a nature show. The script should spotlight one of the animals in the theme.

1 Divide into groups. Each group chooses an animal from one of the selections.

2 Search for information about the animal. Review the appropriate selection for information to include in the script. Look for information about:

- the size of the animal
- where the animal lives and what it eats
- interesting things the animal does

3 Work together to write the script. Include:

- a host
- a wilderness guide
- one or more of the animals you are featuring

4 Rehearse the show.

5 Perform the show for the class. Remember to speak clearly and expressively.

Sea Turtle Show

Host: Welcome to Cape Cod for our Sea Turtle Nature Program! Today you will learn about

Consider copying and laminating these activities for use in centers.

Animal Panel

![Whole Class or Groups] Whole Class or Groups	![clock] 60 minutes (can take place over 3–4 days)	
Objective	Conduct a panel discussion in which theme animals talk about humans.

Give the animals from the selections a chance to share their ideas about people. Choose animals that you think would have different opinions about human beings.

1 Assign these roles

- a leader for the panel discussion
- three or more animals from the theme selections
- one person from the theme

2 Write a list of questions for the leader to ask the panel. Possible topics include

- how people treat animals
- whether people are mostly helpful or harmful to animals
- how animals help and hurt people

3 Practice holding the panel discussion.

4 Perform the panel discussion for an audience. Be sure to give all the members of the panel a chance to share their opinions.

5 Afterwards, invite the audience to evaluate how well the members of the panel presented their views. Use these questions to guide your discussion:

- Did the speakers support their opinions with evidence from the story or from real life?
- Were there arguments that should have been made, but weren't?
- Which speakers were most effective?

Fact Book

![Whole Class or Groups] Whole Class or Groups	![clock] 60 minutes (can take place over 3–4 days)	
Objective	Create a fact book.
Materials	Paper, pens or markers

Create an animal fact book. The book should contain facts about one animal from each selection in the theme.

1 Review the theme selections and make a list of the animals you read about.

2 Divide into groups and have each group choose an animal to write a fact sheet about.

3 Draw a picture of your group's animal.

4 Below the picture, write a brief description of the animal. Include

- the animal's name
- where the animal lives
- whether or not the animal is endangered
- how the animal interacts with human beings

5 Make copies of your fact sheets and create a class fact book.

THEME CONNECTIONS: Leveled Books

While you work with small groups, students can choose from a wealth of books to complete these activities.

Leveled Readers . . .

for *The Grizzly Bear Family Book*
The Hyrax of Top-Knot Island
The Bald Eagle Is Back
The Return of Wild Whoopers
The Hyrax: An Interesting Puzzle

for *The Golden Lion Tamarin Comes Home*
Saving Sea Turtles
The Emerald Cathedral: Inside a Tropical Rain Forest
Invaders!
Protecting Sea Turtles

for *My Side of the Mountain*
Kat the Curious
Brinker's Isle
The Observations of Emma Boyle
Curious Kat

Leveled Theme Paperbacks

Dolphin Adventure
The Tarantula in My Purse: and 172 Other Wild Pets
To the Top of the World: Adventures with Arctic Wolves

Leveled Bibliography

pp. 594E–594F

Animal Postcards

👥 **Pairs**	🕐 **30 minutes**
Objective	Write a postcard describing an animal encounter.

Select an animal encounter you read about in one of the books for this theme. Imagine that you had that encounter. Create a postcard to a friend back home that describes the experience. On the front, draw a picture of your animal encounter. On the back, write your message.

You might include details about

- the animal you encountered
- where your encounter took place
- what happened during the encounter

Trade your postcard with a partner. Compare your encounter with the encounter your partner wrote about.

Use these questions to guide your discussion:

- How did the characters feel about the encounters?
- How might the animals have felt during the encounters?
- What did the characters learn from their encounters?

Consider copying and laminating these activities for use in centers.

Visitor's Guide

Singles	45 minutes
Objective	Create a visitor's guide for people who observe animals.
Materials	Colored pens or pencils, markers

Choose an animal from one of the books you have read for this theme. Then create a visitor's guide for people who want to observe the animal in its natural environment.

Include visitor information about

- where to look for the animal
- how not to disturb the animal

Also include a list of clothing and other supplies that visitors should bring with them. You might also include a list of what *not* to bring to the animal's home.

Create illustrations to accompany the guide. Then display it so other animal observers can know what to expect on their visit.

Fact File

Groups	45 minutes
Objective	Design an educational fact file.
Materials	Reference sources, index cards

Make an index card fact file for animals you read about in the books for this theme.

List the animals you read about. Gather facts about each animal using the books and reference sources such as an encyclopedia. Include facts such as

- where each animal lives
- what each animal eats
- how the animal behaves
- whether the animal is endangered and what people are doing to help it

Use index cards to organize your facts. Write information about the animal on one side of a card. Then draw or paste a picture of the animal on the other side.

Organize your cards in alphabetical order. Then present your fact file to the class or to a small group.

Preparing for Tests

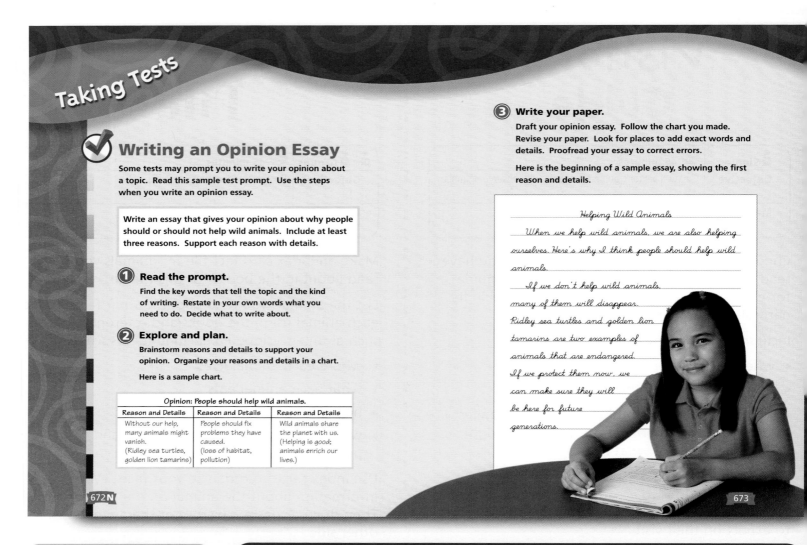

Taking Tests

✓ Writing an Opinion Essay

Some tests may prompt you to write your opinion about a topic. Read this sample test prompt. Use the steps when you write an opinion essay.

> Write an essay that gives your opinion about why people should or should not help wild animals. Include at least three reasons. Support each reason with details.

1 Read the prompt.

Find the key words that tell the topic and the kind of writing. Restate in your own words what you need to do. Decide what to write about.

2 Explore and plan.

Brainstorm reasons and details to support your opinion. Organize your reasons and details in a chart.

Here is a sample chart.

Opinion: People should help wild animals.		
Reason and Details	**Reason and Details**	**Reason and Details**
Without our help, many animals might vanish. (Ridley sea turtles, golden lion tamarins)	People should fix problems they have caused. (loss of habitat, pollution)	Wild animals share the planet with us. (Helping is good; animals enrich our lives.)

3 Write your paper.

Draft your opinion essay. Follow the chart you made. Revise your paper. Look for places to add exact words and details. Proofread your essay to correct errors.

Here is the beginning of a sample essay, showing the first reason and details.

> ### Helping Wild Animals
> When we help wild animals, we are also helping ourselves. Here's why I think people should help wild animals.
> If we don't help wild animals, many of them will disappear. Ridley sea turtles and golden lion tamarins are two examples of animals that are endangered. If we protect them now, we can make sure they will be here for future generations.

672N · 673

THEME	STRATEGY
1	Choosing the Best Answer
2	Filling in the Blank
3	Writing a Personal Response
4	Vocabulary Items
5	Writing an Answer to a Question
▶ **6**	Writing an Opinion Essay

Introduce the Strategy

Taking Tests provides instruction and practice in different test formats. It will help you prepare your students for the **Theme Skills Test** and the **Integrated Theme Test,** as well as state and national standardized tests.

- Tell students that they will learn strategies that will help them do well on tests.
- Explain that Anthology pages 672N and 673 show the steps for writing an opinion essay.
- Have different volunteers read each step aloud.
- Discuss the chart, which shows how to organize reasons and details that support an opinion.
- Explain that students will be learning more about each of these steps.

Teach the Strategy

 Read the Prompt.

Display Transparency 6–30 and model Step 1.

- Have a volunteer read aloud Step 1. Tell students that they will learn more about this one step.
- Model using the step to understand Prompt 1.

Think Aloud *First I will circle the key words that tell the topic:* Walking to school, better than, riding bus. *Next, I will circle the key words that tell the kind of writing:* essay, explaining, why, agree, disagree. *What do the key words tell me to do? They tell me to write an essay about whether I think it is better to walk to school or ride the bus.*

Now I will decide what to write. I can think of a few reasons why it would be good to walk to school, but I can think of more reasons why riding the bus is better. I will write about why it is better to ride the bus to school than it is to walk.

Complete Transparency 6–30, using Step 1.

 Explore and Plan.

Display Transparency 6–31 and model Step 2.

- Have a volunteer read aloud Step 2. Tell students that they will learn more about this one step.
- Model using the step to explore and plan a response for Prompt 1.

Think Aloud *I need reasons and details to support my opinion that riding the bus is better than walking to school. Here's a good reason: bus riders are protected from bad weather. That belongs in my chart. Now I need some details. Rain, cold, and heat are weather problems that bus riders don't have to worry about.*

I need at least three reasons. Here's another reason: ride time can be put to good use. You can study or do homework while riding on the bus. Here's another reason: riding the bus is safer than walking. Riders don't have to cross busy streets on foot, they are with a lot of other people (which is safer than being alone), and they are supervised by an adult driver. I'll add these to the chart.

Complete Transparency 6–31, using Step 2.

- Have students save their charts.

Turn the page to teach the Strategy Step 3.

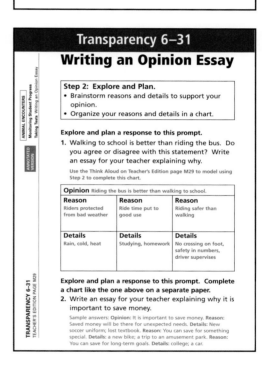

Transparency 6–32

Writing an Opinion Essay

ANNOTATED VERSION | **ANIMAL ENCOUNTERS** Monitoring Student Progress Taking Tests Writing an Opinion Essay

Step 3: Write Your Paper.
• Draft your opinion essay. Follow the chart you made.
• Revise your paper. Add exact words and details.
• Proofread your essay to correct errors.

Discuss a response to this prompt.

1. Walking to school is better than riding the bus. Do you agree or disagree with this statement? Write an essay for your teacher explaining why.

Use the questions on Teacher's Edition page M30 to discuss this model.

The best way to get to school is riding the bus. I am not sure why anyone would prefer to walk.

Riding the bus is better than walking to school because riders are protected from the weather. They do not get wet in the rain. When it is cold outside, they stay warm. When it is hot, they catch a breeze through an open window.

The second reason is that bus riders can put the time between home and school to good use. They can study for exams, jot down notes, or get a head start on homework.

The last reason is that it is safer to ride the bus. Riders do not cross busy streets on foot. Everyone knows there is safety in numbers. On a bus, riders are surrounded by other students. Also, students are supervised by the driver.

Comfort, time management, and safety are all reasons that make riding the bus better than walking.

Write a response to this prompt on a separate paper. Use the chart you made for Step 2.

2. Write an essay for your teacher explaining why it is important to save money.

TRANSPARENCY 6–32 TEACHER'S EDITION PAGE M30

Teach the Strategy continued

STEP 3 — Write Your Paper.

Display Transparency 6–32 and discuss Step 3.

- Have a volunteer read aloud Step 3.
- Tell students that they will learn more about writing an essay by studying a model of a response to Prompt 1.

Discuss the model. Ask these questions.

- Where does the writer state the opinion? (introduction)
- Where does the writer state each reason? (topic sentence of second, third, and fourth paragraphs)
- What details support each reason? (See underscored details in the Annotated Version.)
- What details did the writer add during drafting? (Sample answers: catch a breeze through an open window; free up time for other activities; walkers are often alone)
- What exact words or phrases does the writer use? (Sample answers: *breeze; jot; safety in numbers; comfort; time management*)
- What does the writer do in the conclusion? (restates opinion, reasons)

Complete Transparency 6–32, using Step 3.

- When students have finished, ask them to read their paper aloud to a partner and discuss places where they could add more details.

English Language Learners

REACHING ALL LEARNERS

Teach English language learners how to read a writing prompt before asking them to respond to one.

- Introduce students to the kinds of writing they might find on standardized tests, such as narrative, persuasive essay, or instructions.
- Then share and discuss prompts that ask for each kind of writing. Model restating a prompt in your own words, identifying the kind of writing. Ask students to do the same for several different prompts.
- Have students write a response to a prompt you have already discussed. Later give them practice in responding to prompts you haven't discussed. Encourage them to use words they already know.

Apply the Strategy

Test Practice: Writing to a Prompt

Give students practice with timed writing.

- Many writing assessments are timed.

- If the writing assessment used in your state or district is timed, you might set a time limit for students as they work on their essay.

- This will help students get used to pacing themselves.

Discuss how to revise a response to an opinion prompt.

- Take a short break before revising your paper. Stretch, stare out the window, or close your eyes and relax for a minute.

- Reread your paper. Check to be sure that your opinion fits the prompt and that you stated it clearly in introduction.

- Make sure you wrote at least three reasons. Look for places to add details to support each reason.

- Check to be sure that you wrote a separate paragraph for each reason and the details that support it.

- Look for places to add exact words.

- Check for mistakes. Make sure you used clear handwriting.

Assign Practice Book pages 255 and 256.

- Provide students with practice responding to an additional prompt for an opinion essay.

- Emphasize that students should use all three steps to respond to this prompt.

Practice Book page 255

Test Practice

Use the three steps you've learned to write a response to this prompt. Complete the chart. Then write your essay on the lines below and on page 256. Use the checklist on page 256 to revise.

Write an essay for your teacher explaining why you like going places with a group of friends. Be sure to include reasons and details. Use the Revising Checklist to score each student's essay.

Opinion (Answers will vary.)		
Reason	Reason	Reason
Details	Details	Details

Continue on page 256.

Practice Book page 256

Test Practice continued

Use another piece of paper if you need to.

Revising Checklist

✔ Does my opinion fit the prompt? Did I state it clearly in the introduction? (7 points)
✔ Did I write at least three reasons? (7)
✔ Did I write enough details to support each reason? (6)
✔ Did I write a separate paragraph for each reason? (5)
✔ Did I use exact words? (5)
✔ Did I use clear handwriting and correct any mistakes? (5)

Read your essay aloud to a partner. Then discuss your answers to the questions on the checklist. Make any other changes that you think are necessary.

Additional Resources

Teacher's Assessment Handbook

Suggests more strategies for preparing students for standardized tests

Support for Writing Tests

Provides strategy instruction and practice for open-response questions and writing to prompts at Grades 1–6

TAKING TESTS

Writing an Opinion Essay

**Options**

**SKILL REVIEW: Comprehension**

COMPREHENSION

Practice Book page 257

Name _____

Monitoring Student Progress
Comprehension Making Generalizations

Is It Valid?

Read the generalizations listed below. Then complete the chart.
Look back at *The Rabbit's Judgment* for story details.

Generalization	Valid? (Yes or No)	Why? (Sample answers shown.)
Hunters always use deep pits to trap tigers.	No (1 point)	Not all hunters use deep pits to trap tigers. (1)
Most people take pity on animals in danger.	Yes (1)	My experience shows that this is true most of the time. (1)
People are never grateful for the things they get from nature.	No (1)	The word *never* makes this an overgeneralization. Some people are grateful for things from nature. (1)
Rabbits that appear in folktales are always clever.	No (1)	I've heard and read folktales in which the rabbit is not so clever. (1)

Making Generalizations

Review generalizations.

- A generalization states something that is true for most but not all of the things it describes.
- Words such as *most, usually,* and *often* can signal a generalization.
- Overgeneralizations are not valid because they are too broad or do not follow logically from the facts.

Model how to evaluate a generalization.

- Display this sentence: *All sea turtles need our help to survive.*
- Note that you would need to know more about every kind of sea turtle to determine if the generalization is valid.

Have students evaluate and make generalizations.

- Assign **Practice Book** page 257.

Topic, Main Idea, and Supporting Details

Review topic, main idea, and supporting details.

- The topic is the subject of a selection or paragraph.
- A main idea is the most important idea or point about the topic.
- Key details support or explain the main idea.
- Some main ideas must be inferred from details.

Model how to identify main ideas and details.

- Read aloud the last paragraph on Anthology page 672C.
- Explain how the first sentence describes the main idea and the rest of the sentences list details about the main idea.
- Read aloud the last paragraph on page 672D and explain how to infer the main idea, "The turtle is examined by veterinarians," from the details given.

Have partners identify main ideas and details.

- Have partners read each paragraph on pages 672F and 672G and take turns identifying or inferring main ideas from details.

Drawing Conclusions

Review how to draw conclusions.

- Authors do not always state everything directly.
- Readers sometimes must add up facts and details to draw their own conclusions.

Model how to draw a conclusion.

- Have students recall the beginning of *The Rabbit's Judgment* on pages 672H–672J.
- Model how to draw a conclusion.

Think Aloud *The author doesn't tell me what the tiger is planning to do after it gets out of the pit. However, based on the man's fears and the tiger's comments about starving, I can conclude that it plans to eat the man.*

Have students draw conclusions.

- Assign **Practice Book** page 258.

Practice Book page 258

Monitoring Student Progress

Comprehension Drawing Conclusions

Name _____

Adding Up to a Conclusion

Read the questions below. Refer to the Anthology pages below for details to help you answer each question. Then fill in the chart, drawing a conclusion that answers the question. Sample answers shown.

1. Why is the shallow bay a dangerous place for Kemp's ridley turtles? (pages 672B–672C)

Detail +	Detail =	Conclusion
For three months, the shallow water is warm. Then it gets cold quickly. **(1 point)**	The cold water in November and December stuns the turtles. **(1)**	If the turtles aren't able to warm up, they will die. **(1)**

2. How large are Kemp's ridley turtles? (pages 672B–672C)

Detail +	Detail =	Conclusion
Max searches for a mound about the size of a pie plate. **(1)**	The photos show him holding one of the turtles. **(1)**	A Kemp's ridley turtle is about a foot in diameter. **(1)**

3. Why does Mark mark the spot where he finds the turtle? (pages 672C–672D)

Detail +	Detail =	Conclusion
After marking the spot, he and his mother call the sea-turtle rescue line. **(1)**	Less than an hour later, rescuers come to pick up the turtle. **(1)**	He marks the spot so that the rescuers can find the turtle easily and quickly. **(1)**

4. What are the chances of survival of the turtle called Orange? (pages 672D–672G)

Detail +	Detail =	Conclusion
The normal body temperature of a Kemp's ridley turtle is about 75 degrees Fahrenheit. **(1)**	Orange has a temperature of 70 degrees Fahrenheit, clear lungs, and a good heart rate, and makes swimming motions, even though his breathing rate is still low. **(1)**	Orange probably has a good chance of surviving. **(1)**

SKILL REVIEW:
Structural Analysis/Vocabulary

OBJECTIVES

Students review how to
- decode words with prefixes
- decode three-syllable words
- decode words with suffixes

More Prefixes

Review the prefixes *con-*, *ex-*, *com-*, *en-*, *pre-*, and *pro-*.

- Recognizing prefixes can help readers break words into syllables and locate base words or word roots.

- *Con-*, *com-*, *ex-*, *en-*, *pre-*, and *pro-* are common prefixes.

Model how to decode a word with the prefix *en-*.

- Display this sentence: *All sea turtles are threatened or <u>endangered</u>.* Model how to decode *endangered*.

> **Think Aloud** *I see the prefix* en-, *which can mean "put into." I also see the word* danger *and the ending* -ed. *I'll blend the syllables:* ehn-DAYN-juhrd. *That means "put in danger of extinction." That makes sense.*

Have students decode words.

- Display <u>propelled</u> forward, a <u>stunned</u> condition, almost <u>extinct</u>, a <u>complicated</u> situation, <u>embedded</u> in the sand, the <u>preceding</u> day.

- Have students decode each underlined word and explain its meaning, using a dictionary as needed.

Three-Syllable Words

Review how to decode three-syllable words.

- Look for base words, prefixes, suffixes, and endings.
- Try various syllabication patterns.

Model how to decode a three-syllable word.

- Display this phrase: *heat <u>sensitive</u>.* Model decoding *sensitive*.

> **Think Aloud** *I see a word part that looks like the base word* sense. *I'll try pronouncing the word:* SEHNS-iht-ihv. *That doesn't sound quite right. Maybe the VCCV pattern should be divided between the consonants. Then I get* SEHN-sih-tihv. *That's a word I've heard before, and it makes sense here.*

Have partners decode words.

- Display <u>operate</u> the machine, lungs are <u>functioning</u>, animal <u>behaviors</u>, a <u>blustery</u> day, <u>volunteer</u> work, a <u>specialty</u> practice.

- Have partners decode each underlined word, explaining how they figured it out.

More Suffixes

Review suffixes *-ent, -ant, -able,* and *-ible.*

- A suffix is added to the end of a base word or word root and changes the meaning of the word.

- The suffixes *-ent* and *-ant* turn many base words into adjectives.

- The suffixes *-able* and *-ible* can mean "capable of" or "inclined to."

Model how to decode a word with *-able.*

- Display this sentence: *She made a <u>questionable</u> decision.* Model decoding *questionable.*

Think Aloud *I don't recognize this word, but I see the suffix -able. If I cover it up, I see the base word* question. *If I join the two parts, I get* KWEHS-chuh-nuh-buhl. *That sounds familiar, and means "capable of being questioned, or open to challenge."*

Have students decode words.

- Assign **Practice Book** page 259.

Practice Book page 259

Name _____

Monitoring Student Progress

Structural Analysis More Suffixes

Suffix Sort

Read the sentences. Circle the word in each sentence to which the suffix *-ant, -ent, -able,* or *-ible* has been added. Write the base word and suffix on the line. Then write the word's meaning.

1. Their story was not very (believable).
   believe, -able; "able to be believed" **(2 points)**

2. Is seaweed (digestible) for turtles?
   digest, -ible; "able to be digested" **(2)**

3. Sometimes monkeys can be quite (approachable).
   approach, -able; "able to be approached" **(2)**

4. Wolves are the (dominant) species in this area.
   dominate, -ant; "adjective form of dominate" **(2)**

5. The turtles are (dependent) on people for their survival.
   depend, -ent; "adjective form of depend" **(2)**

6. With the help of volunteers, the forests will be (sustainable).
   sustain, -able; "able to be sustained" **(2)**

OBJECTIVES

Students review how to

- use context to figure out a word's meaning
- use pronunciation variations listed in a dictionary to figure out words
- use idioms and run-on entries in a dictionary

Using Context

Review how to use context.

- The position of a word in a sentence can tell its part of speech.
- Nearby words often give clues about an unfamiliar word's meaning. Check a dictionary to confirm a word's meaning.

Model using context to find the meaning of *diligently*.

- Display *Oxen carry heavy loads, working <u>diligently</u> for farmers.*

Think Aloud *Diligently is an adverb because it comes after the verb working and describes how the work is performed. The words* carrying heavy loads *give clues to its meaning. I think* diligently *means "in a way that is hard-working." I'll check that in a dictionary .*

Have students use context to determine meaning.

- *Display I am filled with <u>gratitude</u> for your help. He spoke slowly and <u>deliberately</u>. Have students use context to figure out the meanings of the underlined words.*

Pronunciations in a Dictionary

Review variations in pronunciation.

- Some words have more than one pronunciation.
- Dictionaries usually list all acceptable pronunciations of a word.
- The most common pronunciation is listed first.

Model using variations in pronunciation.

- Display this dictionary entry: **me•ow** (mē ou′, myou) The high-pitched, whining cry of a cat.
- Pronounce each variation of *meow* and explain that both are correct.

Have students use variations in pronunciation.

- Display these words: *hoof, moustache, sorry, nuisance.*
- Have students look up the acceptable pronunciations of each word.
- Have students use each pronunciation aloud in a sentence.

Run-on Dictionary Entries

Review how to use idioms and run-on entries.

- Idioms or run-on dictionary entries may follow the last definition of an entry word.
- Idioms are expressions with special meanings different from the usual meanings of the words.
- Run-on entries show words formed by adding suffixes to the entry word.

Model finding the meaning of an idiom.

- Display this phrase: *He is not <u>cut out</u> for the job*.
- Model finding the meaning of *cut out*.

Think Aloud *I'm not sure what* cut out *means in this sentence. I'll look under* cut *in the dictionary. After all the definitions I see a list of idioms.* Cut out *means "to be suited." The sentence means "He is not suited for the job." That makes sense.*

Have students use definitions of idioms and run-on entries to determine meaning.

- Assign **Practice Book** page 260.

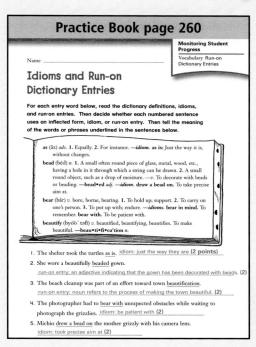

VOCABULARY

Vocabulary **M37**

SKILL REVIEW: Spelling

OBJECTIVES

Students review
- words that have prefixes
- words that have three syllables
- words that end with -ent, -ant, -able, or -ible
- words that have final /n/ or /ən/, /chər/, or /zhər/ sounds

SPELLING WORDS

Basic

excite	preserve
concern	dangerous
imagine	vacation
continue	terrible
enforce	accident
propose	complete
condition	regular
resident	potato
possible	laughable
fashionable	remarkable
consist	proverb
prefix	natural
sensitive	emotion
suitable	merchant
vacant	enclose

Challenge

confront	enactment
preamble	juvenile
astonish	amateur
excellent	extravagant
reversible	durable

DAY 1 — MORE PREFIXES

Pretest Use the Day 5 sentences.

Review words that have prefixes.

- Display the words *engage, prefix, pronoun, conduct, compare,* and *extend.* Read the words aloud.
- Underline the prefix in each word. Explain that the underlined word parts are prefixes—word parts added to the beginning of a word that add meaning.

Have students identify words with prefixes.

- Have students make a six-column chart with these headings: *ex-, con-, com-, en-, pro-, pre-.*
- Display *preserve, excite, propose, concern, prefix, complete, enforce, consist, enclose,* and *proverb.*
- Have students write each word in the correct column in their chart.
- Repeat this process with the Challenge Words *confront, enactment,* and *preamble,* if appropriate.

Practice/Homework Assign **Practice Book** page 281.

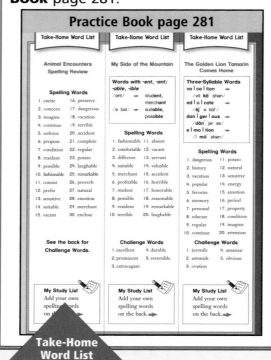

DAY 2 — THREE-SYLLABLE WORDS

Review three-syllable words.

- Display the words *memory* and *period.* Say each word aloud.
- Divide the words into syllables. Underline the stressed syllable in each word. (*mem|o|ry, con|tin|ue*)
- Point out that one syllable is stressed more heavily than the other two. Explain that three-syllable words are usually stressed on the first or second syllable.

Have students identify stressed syllables.

- Have students create a chart with the headings *Stressed First Syllable* and *Stressed Second Syllable.*
- Display these words: *imagine, continue, condition, emotion, sensitive, natural, dangerous, vacation, regular, potato.*
- Have students identify the stressed syllable in each word and write the word in the proper column.

Practice/Homework Assign **Practice Book** page 261.

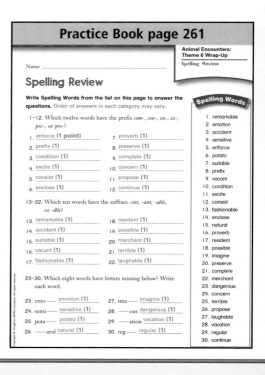

DAY 3 — -ent, -ant; -able, -ible

Review words that end with -ent, -ant, -able, or -ible.

- Display *different* and *servant*. Say each word aloud. Underline *-ent* and *-ant*. Explain that they have the same pronunciation: /ənt/.

- Display *horrible* and *valuable*. Say each word aloud. Underline *-ible* and *-able*. Point out that they have the same pronunciation: /ə//bəl/.

- Point out that words ending in *e* drop the final *e* before adding *-ent, -ant, -ible,* or *-able.*

Have students identify words with -ent, -ant, -able, or -ible.

- Display *vac___, resid___, accid___, merch___.*

- Have students write the words, adding *-ent* or *-ant.*

- Display *fashion_____, suit_____, terr_____, remark_____, laugh_____, poss_____.*

- Have students write the words, adding *-able* or *-ible.*

Practice/Homework Assign **Practice Book** page 262.

Practice Book page 262

Animal Encounters:
Theme 6 Wrap-Up
Spelling Review

Name _____

Spelling Spree

Hint and Hunt Write the Spelling Word that best answers each question.

Spelling Words
1. enforce
2. continue
3. emotion
4. prefix
5. merchant
6. remarkable
7. natural
8. dangerous
9. potato
10. fashionable
11. excite
12. preserve
13. possible
14. terrible
15. proverb

1. What word could describe lions and mountain climbing?
   dangerous (1 point)

2. What word refers to nature? natural (1)

3. What vegetable grows in the ground? potato (1)

4. What is a short saying that states an idea or truth?
   proverb (1)

5. What do you call a person who dresses in the latest styles?
   fashionable (1)

6. What do police officers and principals do with rules?
   enforce (1) them

7. What word means "strong feeling"?
   emotion (1)

8. What is the word for a person who buys and sells things?
   merchant (1)

Contrast Clues Write the Spelling Word that means the opposite of the following words.

9. not *to bore,* but to excite (1)
10. not *to destroy,* but to preserve (1)
11. not a *suffix,* but a prefix (1)
12. not *impossible,* but possible (1)
13. not *ordinary,* but remarkable (1)
14. not *wonderful,* but terrible (1)
15. not *to stop,* but to continue (1)

DAY 4 — FINAL SOUNDS

Review words that have final /n/ or /ən/, /chər/, or /zhər/ sounds.

- Display *mountain, denture,* and *measure.* Read each word aloud.

- Point out the *ain* spelling for the final /ən/ sounds in *mountain.*

- Point out the *ture* spelling for the final /chər/ sounds in *denture.*

- Point out the *sure* spelling for the final /zhər/ sounds in *measure.*

Have students identify words that have final /n/ or /ən/, /chər/, or /zhər/ sounds.

- Have students make a three-column chart with these headings: *Final /n/ or /ən/, Final /chər/, Final /zhər/.*

- Display *mixture, pleasure, captain, moisture, culture, fountain,* and *sculpture.*

- Have students write each word in the correct column.

Practice/Homework Assign **Practice Book** page 263.

Practice Book page 263

Animal Encounters:
Theme 6 Wrap-Up
Spelling Review

Name _____

Proofreading and Writing

Proofreading Circle the six misspelled Spelling Words in this paragraph. Then write each word correctly.

Spelling Words
1. imagine
2. vacation
3. resident
4. vacant
5. sensitive
6. laughable
7. consist
8. complete
9. enclose
10. concern
11. propose
12. regular
13. suitable
14. accident
15. condition

Before we went on (vacashion) I tried to (majine) what animals we might see. First we saw a small bird who was a (residunt) of the rain forest. It lived in a (vakant) hollow tree trunk. We thought it might be (sensative) to noise, so we watched quietly. It was (laffable) how it tried to catch a fly.

1. vacation (1 point)   4. vacant (1)
2. imagine (1)   5. sensitive (1)
3. resident (1)   6. laughable (1)

Half Notes Write Spelling Words to complete these notes.

What does a spider web consist (1) of?

If I write down everything I see, my notes will be complete (1)

Should it concern (1) me that a snake is sleeping in my tent?

I propose (1) that we wake at dawn each day.

At home my regular (1) breakfast is cereal, but here I eat powdered eggs. Yuck!

A cold northern region is a suitable (1) habitat for a polar bear.

I can't follow the tracks because the condition of the footprints is poor.

I squashed a bug by accident

If I can enclose (1) these insects in a cage, I can study them.

→ **Write Ideas** On a separate sheet of paper, write about an animal you would like to study in the wild. Use the Spelling Review Words.
Responses will vary. (5)

DAY 5 — TEST

Say each underlined word, read the sentence, and repeat the word. Have students write only the underlined words.

Basic Words

1. Does the idea of a **vacation excite** you?
2. She felt **terrible** about the **accident**.
3. They built a fence to **enclose** the **vacant** lot.
4. The clothing **merchant** always wore **fashionable** outfits.
5. The **proverb** filled me with **emotion**.
6. They wanted to **preserve** the **natural** beauty of the place.
7. I like my stew to **consist** of broth, meat, **potato**, and onion.
8. It is not **possible** to add a **prefix** to the end of a word.
9. The **condition** of this house is so bad that it is not **suitable** for living in.
10. I **propose** that we **complete** this project.
11. She thought the play was quite **remarkable**, but I really found it **laughable**.
12. We must **continue** to **enforce** the law.
13. I **imagine** that job is very **dangerous**.
14. The doctor was **sensitive** to the couple's **concern**.
15. If you are a **resident**, you may use the laundry service on a **regular** basis.

Challenge Words

16. The police officer had to **confront** the **juvenile** about what he had done.
17. I bought a very **durable, reversible** jacket.
18. She is an **excellent, amateur** player.
19. After reading aloud the **preamble** to the new constitution, we will discuss the **enactment** of its various provisions.
20. The **extravagant** meal was enough to **astonish** us all.

Options SKILL REVIEW: Grammar

GRAMMAR

OBJECTIVES

Students review how to

- identify and write contractions with *not*
- identify double negatives and use negatives in sentences correctly
- identify prepositions and their objects
- identify prepositional phrases
- identify and use object pronouns as objects in prepositional phrases
- use pronouns as part of the compound object of a prepositional phrase

DAY 1 NEGATIVES

Review negatives and contractions with *not*, and display the examples.

- A negative is a word that means "no" or "not."

- You can combine some verbs with the word *not* to make contractions: *is not → isn't*.

- An apostrophe takes the place of the letter or letters dropped to shorten the word.

- Do not use double negatives in sentences: *We <u>haven't</u> found <u>no</u> turtles.* (incorrect) *We <u>haven't</u> found <u>any</u> turtles.* (correct)

Have students write contractions and correct double negatives.

- Assign **Practice Book** page 264.

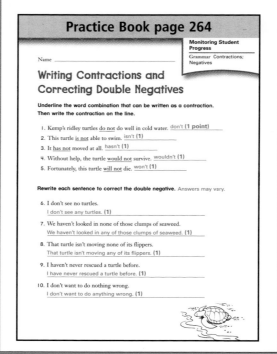

Practice Book page 264

Name _____

Monitoring Student Progress
Grammar Contractions; Negatives

Writing Contractions and Correcting Double Negatives

Underline the word combination that can be written as a contraction. Then write the contraction on the line.

1. Kemp's ridley turtles <u>do not</u> do well in cold water. don't **(1 point)**
2. This turtle <u>is not</u> able to swim. isn't **(1)**
3. It <u>has not</u> moved at all. hasn't **(1)**
4. Without help, the turtle <u>would not</u> survive. wouldn't **(1)**
5. Fortunately, this turtle <u>will not</u> die. won't **(1)**

Rewrite each sentence to correct the double negative. Answers may vary.

6. I don't see no turtles.
   I don't see any turtles. **(1)**
7. We haven't looked in none of those clumps of seaweed.
   We haven't looked in any of those clumps of seaweed. **(1)**
8. That turtle isn't moving none of its flippers.
   That turtle isn't moving any of its flippers. **(1)**
9. I haven't never rescued a turtle before.
   I have never rescued a turtle before. **(1)**
10. I don't want to do nothing wrong.
    I don't want to do anything wrong. **(1)**

DAY 2 PREPOSITIONS

Review prepositions.

- A preposition relates the noun or the pronoun that follows it to another word in the sentence.

- The object of the preposition is the noun or the pronoun that follows the preposition.

Identify prepositions and their objects.

- Display these sentences: *The director puts the turtle in a pool. The team from the aquarium arrives.*

- In the first sentence, underline *in* and circle *pool*. Explain that *in* is a preposition and *pool* is the object of that preposition.

- Point out that *in* relates the noun *pool* to the verb *puts*. It helps tell *where* the director puts the turtle.

- In the second sentence, underline *from* and circle *aquarium*. Explain that *from* is a preposition and *aquarium* is its object.

- Point out that *from* relates the noun *aquarium* to the noun *team*. It helps give information about the team.

Have students identify prepositions and their objects.

- Display these sentences: *One turtle swims on the table. The color of its blood is brownish red.*

- Have students identify the prepositions and their objects. (prepositions: *on, of*; objects: *table, blood*)

M40 **THEME 6: Animal Encounters**

GRAMMAR

DAY 3 — PREPOSITIONS

Review prepositional phrases.

A prepositional phrase is made up of a preposition, the object of the preposition, and all the words in between.

Identify prepositional phrases.

Display these sentences: *A tiger fell into a deep pit. The walls of the pit were steep.*

Underline *into a deep pit.* Explain that these words make up a prepositional phrase.

Point out that *into* is the preposition and *pit* is its object.

Underline *of the pit.* Explain that this is also a prepositional phrase.

Point out that *of* is the preposition and *pit* is its object.

Have students identify prepositional phrases.

Display these sentences: *A man peered over the side. The cries of the tiger had reached his ears.*

Have students identify the prepositional phrase in each sentence. *(over the side, of the tiger)*

DAY 4 — OBJECT PRONOUNS

Review object pronouns in prepositional phrases and display the examples.

- The object pronouns are *me, you, him, her, it, us,* and *them.*

- Use object pronouns as objects in prepositional phrases: *The tiger spoke to the man.* → *The tiger spoke to him.*

Have students choose object pronouns.

- Assign **Practice Book** page 265.

Practice Book page 265

Name _____

Choosing Pronouns

Underline the pronoun in parentheses that correctly completes each sentence.

1. After being saved by the man, the tiger circled around (him, he). (1 point)
2. I would have walked away from (him, he). (1)
3. A tiger would run after (I, me) once he was out. (1)
4. Tigers are hunters, and you cannot take chances with (they, them). (1)
5. Those animals are dangerous to (us, we). (1)
6. The tale is a warning for (me, I). (1)
7. My father has told it to (we, us). (1)
8. My cousin Noreen enjoys tales told by (he, him). (1)
9. My father asked about (her, she) last week. (1)
10. My aunt bought a book of folktales for (us, we). (1)

DAY 5 — OBJECT PRONOUNS

Review pronouns in prepositional phrases with compound objects.

- Use object pronouns in compound objects of a preposition.

- To decide whether to use a subject or an object pronoun in a compound, say the sentence aloud without the other part of the compound.

Identify correct pronoun forms in prepositional phrases with compound objects.

- Display these sentences: *I received a gift from her and him. They came to visit you and me.*

- Underline the preposition *from* in the first sentence.

- Underline *her* and *him.* Point out that these object forms are used after a preposition.

- Follow the same procedure with the pronoun *me* in the second sentence.

Have students choose correct pronoun forms.

- Display these pronoun forms: *I, me, she, her, him, me, we, us.*

- Display these sentences: *Rico will give the bloom to you and ___. He has buckets and sponges for Sue and ___. We must give these messages to Sue and ___.*

- Have students complete each sentence by choosing an appropriate pronoun from the list. (Answers will vary but must make sense in the sentence and be object forms.)

SKILL REVIEW:
Prompts for Writing

WRITING

OBJECTIVES

Students review how to
- write an opinion paragraph
- write a compare/contrast essay
- write an answer to an essay question
- write a summary
- write a persuasive essay

Opinion Paragraph

👤 Singles	🕐 30 minutes
Objective	Write an opinion paragraph.

The selections in Theme 6 discuss animals and their habitats. People often hold strong opinions about environmental issues, such as whether or not endangered animals should be protected. Writing an opinion paragraph is a good way to explain your own views about such an issue.

Choose a topic from this theme. Write an opinion paragraph about the topic that

- begins with a personal belief
- persuades others to see your point of view
- offers facts or reasons to support your opinion
- clearly shows your personal thoughts, feelings, and voice
- ends with a strong conclusion

Remember to avoid using two negatives within a single phrase.

Compare/Contrast Essay

👤 Singles	🕐 45 minutes
Objective	Write a compare/contrast essay.

The selections in this theme describe people who observe wildlife. Having read several selections, you have the knowledge to compare and contrast how wildlife observation is done for different animals.

Choose two animals from the theme. Write an essay to compare and contrast the methods used to observe each animal, as presented in the selections.

- State the topic at the beginning.
- Explain the similarities and differences between the two methods of observation.
- Organize your points in a way that makes sense.

Remember to streamline your writing by combining sentences with the same subject but different prepositional phrases.

An observer of golden lion tamarins and a photographer of grizzly bears have similar and different ways of watching.

Consider copying and laminating these activities for use in centers.

Answer to an Essay Question

👤 Singles	🕐 30 minutes
Objective	Write an answer to an essay question.

Sometimes you read stories such as *The Rabbit's Judgment* for enjoyment only. Other times you are also expected to answer questions about them. Tests often include essay questions, which require an answer that is longer than just a few sentences.

Write an essay in response to one of these questions:

- By what process are some sea turtles rescued? Explain each step in detail.

- What lesson do you think *The Rabbit's Judgment* teaches? Give a personal opinion and back it up with reasons and examples.

- What experiences have you had with a pet or animal? Write about one or more.

In your answer, be sure to restate what the question asks. Present your ideas in a way that makes sense and answers the question completely.

Remember to place prepositional phrases next to the words they modify.

Summary

👤 Singles	🕐 30 minutes
Objective	Write a summary.

After reading an interesting selection such as *Interrupted Journey* or *The Rabbit's Judgment,* readers may want to remember important information or events. Writing a summary is a good way to recall a selection or story for your personal use or to share it with another person.

Choose one selection from this theme to write a summary about. Make sure that your summary

- retells in a brief form what the selection is about

- describes a story's main characters and events, or a nonfiction selection's main ideas

- does not include minor events or details

Remember to paraphrase, or restate ideas in your own words, without changing the author's meaning.

Persuasive Essay

👤 Singles	🕐 60 minutes
Objective	Write a persuasive essay.

Most people find animals interesting and may even have strong opinions about issues having to do with animals. Sometimes people take their personal opinions a step further and try to persuade or convince others to take a certain action or adopt a certain point of view.

In *The Rabbit's Judgment,* characters express strong opinions about how humans treat and use nature. Do you agree or disagree with their point of view? Review the characters' arguments to develop your own opinion on the subject. Then write an essay to try to persuade or convince others to adopt your point of view. Make sure that your persuasive essay

- has a fast-paced, interest-grabbing opening

- states your purpose or goal in the introduction

- uses supporting facts and details to build your arguments

- ends with a convincing conclusion that restates your position and may call on the reader to take action

Remember to correct any run-on sentences.

Assessing Student Progress

Monitoring Student Progress

Preparing for Testing

Throughout the theme your students have had opportunities to read and think critically, connect and compare, and practice and apply new and reviewed skills and reading strategies.

Monitoring Student Progress

For Theme 6, *Animal Encounters,* students have read the paired selections—*Interrupted Journey* and *The Rabbit's Judgment*—and made connections between these and other selections in the theme. They have practiced strategies for writing an opinion essay, and they have reviewed all the tested skills taught in this theme, as well as some tested skills taught in earlier themes. Your students are now ready to have their progress formally assessed in both theme assessments and standardized tests.

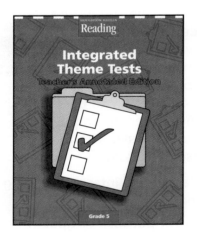

Testing Options

The **Integrated Theme Test** and the **Theme Skills Test** are formal group assessments used to evaluate student performance on theme objectives. In addition to administering one or both of these tests, you may wish to assess students' oral reading fluency.

Integrated Theme Test
- Assesses students' progress as readers and writers in a format that reflects instruction
- Integrates reading and writing skills: comprehension strategies and skills, word skills, spelling, grammar, and writing
- Includes authentic literary passages to test students' reading skills in context

Theme Skills Test
- May be used as a pretest or administered following the theme
- Assesses students' mastery of discrete reading and language arts skills taught in the theme: comprehension skills, word skills, spelling, grammar, writing, and information and study skills
- Consists of individual skill subtests, which can be administered separately

Fluency Assessment

Oral reading fluency is a useful measure of a student's development of rapid automatic word recognition. Students who are on level in Grade 5 should be able to read, accurately and with expression, an appropriate level text at the approximate rates shown in the table below.

Early Grade 5	Mid-Grade 5	Late Grade 5
106–132 words correct per minute	118–143 words correct per minute	128–151 words correct per minute

- You can use the **Leveled Reading Passages Assessment Kit** to assess fluency or a **Leveled Reader** from this theme at the appropriate level for each student

- For some students you may check their oral fluency rate three times during the year. If students are working below level, you might want to check their fluency rate more often. Students can also check their own fluency by timing themselves reading easier text.

- Consider decoding and comprehension, as well as reading rate, when evaluating students' reading development.

- For information on how to select appropriate text, administer fluency checks, and interpret results, see the **Teacher's Assessment Handbook** pages 25–28.

Technology

Managing Assessment

The *Learner Profile*® CD-ROM lets you record, manage, and report your assessment of student progress electronically.

You can

- record student progress on objectives in Theme 6

- add or import additional objectives, including your state standards, and track your students' progress against these

- record and manage results from the **Integrated Theme Test** and the **Theme Skills Test** for Theme 6, as well as results from other reading assessments

- organize information about student progress and generate a variety of student assessment reports

- use *Learner Profile to Go*® to record student progress throughout the day on a hand-held computer device and then upload the information to a desktop computer

Using Multiple Measures

In addition to the tests mentioned on page M44, multiple measures might include the following:

- Observation Checklist from this theme
- Persuasive Essay writing from the Reading-Writing Workshop
- Other writing, projects, or artwork
- One or more items selected by the student

Student progress is best evaluated through multiple measures. Multiple measures of assessment can be collected in a portfolio. The portfolio provides a record of student progress over time and can be useful when conferencing with the student, parents, or other educators.

*Turn the page to continue

You can use the results of theme assessments to determine individual students' needs for additional skill instruction and to modify instruction during the next theme. For more detail, see the test manuals or the **Teacher's Assessment Handbook**.

This chart shows Theme 6 resources for differentiating additional instruction.

Differentiating Instruction

Assessment Shows	Use These Resources	
Difficulty with Comprehension **Emphasize** Oral comprehension, strategy development, story comprehension, vocabulary development	• Get Set for Reading CD-ROM • Reteaching: Comprehension, *Teacher's Edition,* pp. R8; R10; R12 • Selection Summaries in *Teacher's Resource Blackline Masters,* pp. 41–43 • *Reader's Library Blackline Masters,* pp. 1F–36F	• *Extra Support Handbook,* pp. 206–207, 212–213; 216–217, 222–223; 226–227, 232–233
Difficulty with Word Skills Structural Analysis Phonics Vocabulary **Emphasize** Word skills, phonics, reading for fluency, phonemic awareness	• Get Set for Reading CD-ROM • Reteaching: Structural Analysis, *Teacher's Edition,* pp. R14; R16; R18 • *Extra Support Handbook,* pp. 204–205, 208–209; 214–215, 218–219; 224–225, 228–229	• *Handbook for English Language Learners,* pp. 208–209, 210, 212–213, 214, 216; 218–219, 220, 222–223, 224, 226; 228–229, 230, 232–233, 234, 236 • **Lexia Quick Phonics Assessment CD-ROM** • **Lexia Phonics CD-ROM: Intermediate Intervention**
Difficulty with Fluency **Emphasize** Reading and rereading of independent level text, vocabulary development	• Leveled Bibliography, *Teacher's Edition,* pp. 594E–594F • Below Level **Theme Paperback** • Below Level **Leveled Readers**	• Leveled Readers: Below Level lesson, *Teacher's Edition,* pp. 623O; 647O; 671O
Difficulty with Writing **Emphasize** Complete sentences, combining sentences, choosing exact words	• *Handbook for English Language Learners,* pp. 217; 227; 237 • Reteaching: Grammar Skills, *Teacher's Edition,* pp. R20–R25	• Improving Writing, *Teacher's Edition,* pp. 623J, 623L; 625E; 647J, 647L; 671J, 671L
Overall High Performance **Emphasize** Independent reading and writing, vocabulary development, critical thinking	• Challenge/Extension Activities: Comprehension, *Teacher's Edition,* pp. R9; R11; R13 • Challenge/Extension Activities: Vocabulary, *Teacher's Edition,* pp. R15; R17; R19 • Reading Assignment Cards, *Teacher's Resource Blackline Masters,* pp. 89–95	• Above Level **Theme Paperback** • Above Level **Leveled Readers** • Leveled Readers: Above Level lesson, *Teacher's Edition,* pp. 623Q; 647Q; 671Q • Challenge Activity Masters, *Challenge Handbook,* CH6–1 to CH6–6

Resources for Theme 6

Contents

Leveled Theme Paperbacks

Dolphin Adventure

Summary *In this nonfiction chapter book, the author recounts an amazing scuba diving experience. While diving off the coast of Florida, he removes a fishing hook from the back of a baby dolphin, at the apparent urging of the baby's parents.*

Vocabulary

current a mass of water in motion, *p. 10*

reef a strip of rock, sand, or coral that rises close to the surface of a body of water, *p. 10*

wound a cut or break in the skin or other body tissue, *p. 22*

hovered stayed in one place in air or water, *p. 23*

shaft the stem of a spear, arrow, or hook, *p. 23*

embedded fixed firmly in a surrounding substance, *p. 31*

Preparing to Read

Building Background Have students briefly tell what they know about scuba diving and dolphins. Tell students that this book is subtitled "A True Story" because the author is telling about his own adventure while scuba diving with dolphins. Remind students to use their reading strategies as they read the book.

Developing Key Vocabulary Students may use context to infer meanings for terms about diving equipment and dolphins' bodies, which are key to understanding the selection. Preview with students the meanings of the Key Vocabulary words listed at the left for the first two segments of the book, pages 7–21 and pages 22–37.

Previewing the Text

Dolphin Adventure may be read in its entirety or in three reading segments: chapters 1–3, pages 7–21; chapters 4–6, pages 22–37; and chapters 7 and 8, pages 38–47. To preview each segment, students may read the chapter titles and offer ideas about what is shown in each illustration.

Supporting the Reading

pages 7–21

- What words on pages 10 and 11 are names for diving equipment, and how do you figure out their meaning? (Students may note how they use context to understand *tank of compressed air, regulator, diving knife in a sheath, rubber wet suits, flippers,* and *masks*.)

- What gives the author his *deep sense of peace* when he dives? (He is far from the busy world above. He enjoys the silence and beauty of the colorful fish. The current pushes him along gently.)

- What are the most important events that have happened so far? (The author makes two dives off the coast of South Florida. Before he makes his second dive, he has a strange feeling that makes him want to dive in a different spot farther north. When he is underwater, he hears a clicking noise and sees three dolphins coming closer.)

pages 22–37

Do the three dolphins behave like most dolphins? Why or why not? (They behave differently. Dolphins don't usually approach people because people can hurt them. But these dolphins seem desperate because the baby is wounded, and they approach a human diver.)

How do the dolphins communicate with the author? (They look directly at him. They let the author touch them. The father dolphin pushes the author's arm up with his nose, as if to say, "Get to work.")

What do the parent dolphins want the author to do? Why? (They want the author to remove the fish hook from their baby's back. The wound is bleeding, and blood attracts sharks.)

pages 38–47

What happens while the author is holding his hand over the baby's wound? (Two bull sharks speed toward them to attack. The parent dolphins bump the sharks fiercely to send them away.)

Why can't the author get the dolphins out of his mind for the next couple of weeks? (Helping them gave him an unforgettable sense of happiness. He keeps thinking that they are still trying to communicate with him. He is worried about them and wonders whether the baby survived.)

How does the author know that he has seen the baby dolphin he helped? (He sees the scar on the baby's back.)

Responding

Have students summarize the main events of the book. Then ask them to find examples of communication between the author and the dolphins. Have them read those examples aloud and offer ideas about what the dolphins might be saying if they could speak.

The Tarantula in My Purse and 172 Other Wild Pets

Summary *In these nonfiction narratives, nature writer Jean Craighead George recalls the wild animals she and her children welcomed into their home. As she recounts the family's adventures, the author conveys her "enthusiasm for the ingenuity of nature."*

Vocabulary

innate inborn; possessed at birth, *p. 2*

migrate to move from one region to another at a set time of year, *p. 3*

instinct an inborn pattern of behavior shared by members of a species, *p. 5*

heredity the traits passed from parents to their young, *p. 46*

menagerie a collection of wild animals, *p. 51*

harass to torment; to carry out repeated attacks, *p. 74*

fledgling a young bird that has just grown the feathers it needs to fly, *p. 84*

Preparing to Read

Building Background Point out the words *wild pets* in the full book title. Ask students how a wild pet might differ from other pets and from tamed wild animals. Explain that this book will look at the wonderful role wild pets play in the author's life. Remind students to use their reading strategies as they read this book.

Developing Key Vocabulary Important terms related to animal behavior are defined in the context of the selection. Preview with students the meanings of the Key Vocabulary words listed at the left for each segment of the book, pages 1–79 and pages 80–134.

Previewing the Text

The Tarantula in My Purse may be read in its entirety or in two segments: the introduction ("The Genesis") through chapter 10, pages 1–79; and chapters 11–21, pages 80–134. To preview each segment, students may read the chapter titles and offer ideas about likely content.

Supporting the Reading

pages 1–79

- Why is the first chapter called *The Genesis*? (It is the author's introduction to the stories that follow. In it, she explains the genesis, or the origin, of her family's love of wild pets.)

- On page 9, the author says that *most scientists are taught not to read human emotions into animals, but sometimes they wonder about the truth of it.* What does she mean? (It isn't scientific to assume that animals act in certain ways for the same reasons that people do. There's no way to prove that animals feel happy or sad, for example. But when you get to know animals well, they often do seem to act like people.)

- What evidence does the author give to show that crows are vindictive? (The crow named New York tries to harm a child, possibly because the child hurt it. When the author captures New York in a towel, she senses that it will never forgive her. The crow expert Dr. Kalmbach has written about a pet crow's clever method of getting even for being disciplined.)

ages 80–134

What effect does watching Boay eat have on the girls in the Nancy Drew Club? (They are *riveted with horror and fascination*. One of the girls, Ellie, decides that Boay is much more exciting than Nancy Drew. The experience plays a role in inspiring Ellie to become an environmentalist.)

Why might the author have included the story of Twig's science experiment with white mice? (Answers will vary. Students should note the humor that comes from recognizing that natural events can be *revolting*.)

What happens to most of the wild pets that have lived with the author's family? (Since most are free to come and go, many eventually join others of their own kind—for example, skunks in the neighborhood or migrating birds. Some are taken to the wild and released. Some, such as the kestrel, disappear, possibly having come to harm. Others die.)

Responding

sk students to tell how they were able to follow the events and understand the author's main points. They may give examples of their use of he strategy Monitor/Clarify to make sense of the book's stories. Students hould then share their reactions to the book and to the household the uthor's children grew up in. Finally, have students summarize the key deas and events.

English Language Learners

Language Development

The book includes many bird-related terms, including *owlets, ducklings, hatchlings, gosling, fledgling, nestling, migrate, migration, migratory,* and *migrants.* Discuss the terms' meanings and usage. What categories can students create from this list?

■ **ABOVE LEVEL**

JIM BRANDENBURG
To the Top of the World
ADVENTURES WITH ARCTIC WOLVES

Reading

To the Top of the World: Adventures with Arctic Wolves

Summary *Text and photographs are combined in this first-person informational account by wildlife photographer Jim Brandenburg. He spends a summer on remote Ellesmere Island, photographing wolves and testing his courage in a treacherous and beautiful land.*

Vocabulary

perceptive having sharp insight, *p. 1*

dominant having the most influence or control, *p. 12*

submissive willing to submit or yield, *p. 12*

adaptation a physical or behavioral trait that helps an animal live in a particular environment, *p. 23*

ritual a set of actions that is faithfully followed, *p. 29*

exhilarating thrilling; causing happiness, *p. 30*

unprovoked not driven to take action, *p. 41*

Preparing to Read

Building Background Have students discuss what is likely to be found at *the top of the world,* and why visitors go there. Tell them they will read about a wildlife photographer's visit to an Arctic island. Remind students to use their reading strategies as they read this book.

Developing Key Vocabulary Important terms related to wolf packs are defined in context. Preview with students the meanings of the Key Vocabulary words listed at the left for each segment of the book, pages 1–22 and pages 23–44.

Previewing the Text

To the Top of the World may be read in its entirety or in two segments: chapters 1–3, pages 1–22; and chapters 4–7, pages 23–44. To preview each segment, students may read the chapter titles, look at the captioned photographs, and offer ideas about how the author took the photographs.

Supporting the Reading

pages 1–22

- From the author's description of the *ultimate photograph,* what can you say is generally true of wild animal photographs? (Most photographs do not come out as the photographer hoped because so many things can go wrong. In this case, the photographer takes dozens of shots of a *perfectly composed photograph,* but only one comes out the way he hoped.)

- Why don't the wolves act nervous when they see the author? (They live in such an isolated place that they've never learned to fear humans. He approaches them cautiously and doesn't get too close.)

- How does the author define *anthropomorphism* on page 21 and what is his opinion of it? (It is the *common practice of giving human characteristics and feelings to nonhumans.* The author believes in keeping a line between animals and people, but he also believes that animals have feelings even if people cannot observe or measure them scientifically.)

THEME PAPERBACKS

THEME PAPERBACKS

ages 23–44

How are Arctic wolves adapted to their environment? (They curl into tight balls to reduce their bodies' exposure to the cold. Their bodies are insulated with hair. They keep their white coats clean to better camouflage themselves in the snow. Their senses of smell, vision, and hearing are excellent not just for finding prey but also for communicating with one another.)

The author says that when wolves howl, they try to achieve discord. Why is this behavior called an *adaptation*? (The pack protects itself from other wolves by acting as if it has many members. With each voice howling a different note, listeners can be fooled into thinking the pack is very large.)

What is the *groveling* that the author mentions on page 34? (It is the cringing, begging, belly-crawling behavior of the lower-ranking wolves as they wait for the alpha pair to signal that the carcass can be shared.)

Responding

sk students how they were able to follow the events and understand the author's main points. They may give examples of their use of the Monitor/ larify strategy to make sense of the text. Students should then share their eactions to the book. Finally, have students summarize the key ideas and vents.

onus Have students review the captioned photographs, note any nguage that shows anthropomorphism of the wolves, and rewrite he captions in the neutral language of science.

English Language Learners

Language Development

Read aloud the account of the wolf hunt from the time *events took an abrupt turn* on page 32 to the point when *the calf fell and died* on page 34. Have students note vocabulary that conveys the fast pace and danger. (Examples: *stampede, frenzy, panic, trampled, thundering, fiercely, pursuit, wildly, split second*)

Making Generalizations

OBJECTIVES

- Recognize generalizations.
- Distinguish between generalizations and overgeneralizations.

Target Skill Trace

- Making Generalizations, pp. 623A–623B

Teach

Review generalizations: A **generalization** is a broad statement that is true about most of the items or people in a given category. A generalization also may be a broad rule that applies to several different examples. A generalization should be based on facts from sources that can be checked.

Use the following example to illustrate a generalization: *Most dogs are domesticated, or tame, animals.* Note that this statement is true of most dogs and can be checked in reliable sources.

An **overgeneralization** is a broad statement that does not follow from facts. An overgeneralization cannot be *verified,* or supported, by facts from reliable sources.

Use this example to illustrate the concept: *Toys made of plastic break easily.* Note that many toys made of plastic are well constructed and do not break easily. The statement cannot be verified, or supported, by reliable sources.

Practice

Use this sentence to illustrate the concept of a generalization: *Bears can be dangerous animals.*

Think Aloud *This is a broad statement. The writer is saying that bears can be dangerous. Bears are large, wild animals. They have big teeth and long, sharp claws. When they snarl, they look ferocious. Bears have been known to ransack campsites searching for food. This statement probably can be supported by facts from reliable sources. Therefore, it is a generalization.*

Use this sentence to model the concept of an overgeneralization: *Nature is too complex to ever be understood by human beings.*

Think Aloud *This is a broad statement. The writer is saying that we can never understand nature. It's true that nature is complex, but scientists are learning about and understanding more things about nature all the time. I don't think we can say that humans will never be able to understand nature. This statement cannot be supported by facts from reliable sources. Therefore, it is an overgeneralization.*

Apply

Direct students to the following sentence from the selection, on page 608: *Bears avoid fighting if at all possible.*

Have them repeat the process in the Practice section and decide whether the statement is a generalization or an overgeneralization. (This statement is a generalization.) Ask them to share their reasoning in a class discussion.

Ask students to look for generalizations and decide whether the broad statements can be supported by facts from reliable sources, as they read their **Leveled Readers** for this week. Have students complete the questions and activity on the Responding page.

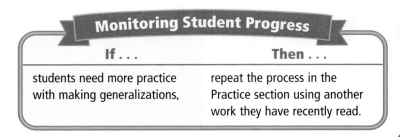

Monitoring Student Progress

If . . .	Then . . .
students need more practice with making generalizations,	repeat the process in the Practice section using another work they have recently read.

CHALLENGE/EXTENSION:
Making Generalizations

Picture This

Partner Activity Perhaps you've heard the saying "One picture is worth a thousand words." Hoshino's photographs reflect his love and respect for grizzly bears. With a partner, reexamine each picture. Find details in his writing that describe or explain the details in each photograph. Discuss words, phrases, and sentences you might add to the narrative. Then collaborate to write a sentence caption that summarizes the main idea in each illustration. Think in terms of generalizations that can be made about the images shown.

Write from the Grizzly's Point of View

Individual Activity Review those passages in the narrative in which Hoshino describes close encounters with "grizzlies." Imagine that you are the bear who is seeing Hoshino for the first time. Write a paragraph describing the bear's impressions and thoughts concerning this "strange-looking and unpredictable" creature. Try writing with humor. Remember to think in terms of sensory details, such as sight, sound, smell, and touch, to make your writing more vivid.

CHALLENGE

Look at the Size of That Bear!

Small Group Activity Work in groups to create a compare/contrast poster using reference materials such as encyclopedias, health texts, and nature magazines or books. You also might locate helpful websites on the Internet. Include a chart listing statistics, such as the average height, weight, etc., of adult male and female grizzly bears and mature humans. Add pictures or drawings of each species. Finally, collaborate to include a paragraph comparing differences in size. For example, if an average male adult grizzly weighs 1,000 pounds and an average male human weighs 200 pounds, the bear weighs five times as much as the human. You may also want to compare and contrast the diets and habitats of each species.

CHALLENGE / EXTENSION

Topic, Main Idea, and Details

OBJECTIVES

- Identify topics, main ideas, and details.
- Infer main ideas from details.

Target Skill Trace

- Topic, Main Idea, and Details, pp. 647A–647B

Teach

Review that the **topic** is the subject the author is writing about. The **main idea** is the most important idea that the writer wants readers to understand about the topic. **Supporting details** are pieces of information that explain or tell more about the main idea. Supporting details may include facts and examples.

Explain that in a longer piece of writing, one paragraph (or a group of paragraphs) may have a topic, a main idea, and supporting details that explain this main idea. Remind students that main ideas are often stated in headings or key sentences. However, sometimes readers must infer the main idea by summing up details and inferring the author's meaning.

Direct students to the first two paragraphs on page 631 of the selection. Use this passage to model the concept:

Think Aloud *The rain forest once was huge. Human beings cut down trees. A large city grew in the area. Now only 2 percent of the original rain forest is left. If I add these details together, I can infer the main idea of the paragraph. The main idea is that human development has destroyed the habitat of golden lion tamarins.*

Practice

Point out the topic of the entire selection: *the return of golden lion tamarins to the rain forest.* Discuss with students the main idea of the entire selection: *People are trying to save the golden lion tamarin from extinction.* Explain that students are going to focus on

passages that are individual paragraphs. Have them infer the main idea by summing up details in these paragraphs. You might include these excerpts:

paragraph 1 on page 633 (Main Idea: Zoo keepers are trying to prepare the tamarins for life in the wild.)

paragraph 2 on page 636 (Main Idea: The zoo-bred tamarins do not yet know how to find food on their own.)

paragraph 2 on page 638 (Main Idea: Observers must be prepared for emergencies as they track the tamarins.)

paragraph 3 on page 639 (Main Idea: Observers want to remain objective and not think of the tamarins as pets.)

Challenge students to infer the main idea in a two-paragraph passage. Use the last paragraph on page 640 and the first paragraph on page 641. (Main Idea: Over time, the observers force the tamarins to become more independent.)

Apply

Ask students to infer main ideas by summing up supporting details in paragraphs, as they read their **Leveled Readers** for this week. Have students complete the questions and activity on the Responding page.

Monitoring Student Progress

If . . .	Then . . .
students need more practice with topics, main idea, and details,	provide them with nonfiction works in which topics, main ideas, and details are clearly stated.

CHALLENGE/EXTENSION:
Topic, Main Idea, and Details

Take the Tamarins Home

Small Group Activity Work in small groups to map out routes that people use when they take golden lion tamarins from zoos to the reserve in Silva Jardim in Brazil. Review the major cities mentioned in the selection (Washington, D.C., Cologne, Germany, and Rio de Janeiro, Brazil). Use a copy of a world map as a reference. Gather resources, such as atlases, to which your group can refer for more detailed or easily read maps. Draw arrows indicating the departure points and the destination of airplanes carrying the tamarins.

Create an Illustrated Children's Story

Individual Activity Imagine that you write and illustrate books for beginning readers. Write a book about golden lion tamarins aimed at that audience. First, you should list details you will include about the monkeys. Then you should write a narrative. Remember to use straightforward sentences and vocabulary suited to the age and reading level of your audience. Next, you should draw colorful pictures that illustrate several important points that you make in your story. Finish your project by inserting each picture near the written passage it illustrates. Share your story with younger siblings or beginning readers in your school.

CHALLENGE

Save the Tamarins!

Partner Activity Imagine that you are members of the Golden Lion Tamarin Conservation Program. Your goal is to present a persuasive argument for saving these beautiful animals. Take turns stating and listing reasons why your mission is important to people and the environment. You also might state reasons why more people should become involved in the effort. Use the lists to write notes to which you can refer during an oral presentation. You and your partner might review each other's notes and make suggestions concerning organization of ideas and details.

Make an oral presentation to the class.

RETEACHING: Comprehension Skills

Drawing Conclusions

Teach

Review that readers draw conclusions when they use facts and details to reach an understanding about something that is not directly stated in the text.

Explain that readers draw conclusions to help them understand characters in a story. Direct students to pages 652 and 653. Model how readers can use details to draw conclusions and understand characters.

Think Aloud *On page 652, Sam describes what is happening in the mountains in September. He talks about the weather, the plant life, and the animals. He sounds happy when he describes them. Then he says that he felt wonderful. I can conclude that Sam likes being in the mountains in the fall.*

On page 653, Sam talks about gathering unusual bulbs, tubers, and roots. He eats a cricket, but he does not like it. He smokes fish and rabbits, digs wild onions, and races September for her crop. I can conclude that Sam knows how to survive in the woods by gathering wild plants, fishing, and hunting.

Practice

Work through events in the story to have students draw other conclusions about Sam's character by "adding up details." Examples might include

paragraphs 3–4 on page 654 (Sam makes clothing from hides and furs. Conclusion: He is handy.)

paragraphs 3–5 on page 656 (He uses imagination to solve problems when building a fireplace. Conclusion: He is resourceful.)

paragraph 3 on page 660 (Sam eats slightly wormy apples. Conclusion: He is not squeamish.)

paragraph 7—"note" on page 660 (Sam does not disturb Baron Weasel when he fiercely protects his food. Conclusion: Sam understands wild animals and is cautious around them.)

Apply

Have students find other examples of details on which they can base conclusions about Sam's character. Have them write a character study based on their conclusions. Tell them to support their conclusions about Sam with details from the story. They might use a word web to list traits they identify in Sam's character. Suggest that behind each trait they write the page number(s) on which supporting details can be found. They can refer to these pages, as necessary, when writing their character study. Afterward, have partners compare and contrast their work.

Ask students to draw conclusions about characters based on details as they read their **Leveled Readers** for this week. Have students complete the questions and activity on the Responding page.

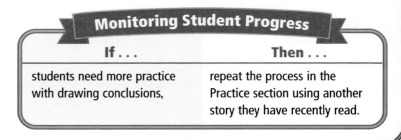

Monitoring Student Progress	
If . . .	Then . . .
students need more practice with drawing conclusions,	repeat the process in the Practice section using another story they have recently read.

CHALLENGE/EXTENSION: Drawing Conclusions

Observing Animals in My Neighborhood

Individual Activity Keep a journal about animals you observe. Note that animals can be found all around us no matter where we live. The animals that you observe can be domesticated (cats, dogs, hamsters, etc.) or wild (deer, rabbits, squirrels, and birds of all kinds). Animal life also includes insects, such as bees, wasps, crickets, and butterflies. Write your observations in your journal and compile the information in a chart.

Write About the Next Day

Individual Activity Imagine that you are Sam. Write a follow-up scene that could be added to the story. Note that on page 654, Sam wonders if he should go home for the winter. Review later scenes in the story. Remember some of the unpleasant incidents that occur. He wakes to find two raccoons have made a mess of his tree house and have eaten much of his food. A skunk sprays him, and the frightened hawk scratches his hand. What will he do? Write a scene in which Sam decides whether to stay on the mountain or return home for the winter. Explain his decision based on the traits Sam possesses.

CHALLENGE

I'd Like to Know...

Partner Activity Write five questions that you and your partner would like to ask Sam. Examples might include, "Why are you living alone in the mountains?" "How did you learn the things you know?" "How did you tame Frightful, the hawk?" You might frame most of your questions in a way that allows "Sam" to use details from the story when answering. Work with your partner to role-play an interview with Sam. Take turns asking questions and playing the role of Sam. If possible, tape-record your interview. Then you might share your interview with your classmates.

RETEACHING: Structural Analysis

Prefixes *com-*, *con-*, *en-*, *ex-*, *pre-*, *pro-*

OBJECTIVES

- Decode words with the prefixes *com-, con-, en-, ex-, pre-, pro-*.
- Identify the meaning of words with the prefixes *com-, con-, en-, ex-, pre-, pro-*.

Target Skill Trace

- Prefixes *com-, con-, en-, ex-, pre-, pro-,* pp. 623C–623D

Teach

Write *enjoy* on the board. Ask students to name things they enjoy doing and to define *enjoy*. Remind students that a prefix is a word part added to the beginning of a word. A prefix adds to or changes the meaning of a word. Write *en + joy*. Explain that the prefix *en-* means "to cause to be" or "to go into or onto." *Enjoy* means "to cause to be happy."

Write these sentences on the board. *Grizzly bears enjoy life. I watched as a mother and her club played tag.* Ask: How do bears enjoy life?

Write the following sentence on the board, underlining as shown: *It had been a pretty frightening experience.* Explain that *ex-* means "out, away from" or "not, without." Model decoding *experience*.

Think Aloud *In the words* explain *and* explore, ex- *is the first syllable so it probably is here. Many words end in -ence. That may be the last syllable. Could the word be* iks-PUR-ih-ens? *It doesn't sound right. I'll change the vowel sounds—*iks-PIR-ee-ens. *That works in the sentence.*

Practice

Explain the meaning of these prefixes and ask students to decode the underlined words.

(*com- con-:* together, with) Mother animals must keep <u>constant</u> watch over their babies.

(*pre-:* earlier, before, prior to) The mother bear <u>preceded</u> her cubs into the river.

(*pro-:* prior to, in front of) The mother bear <u>provides</u> a den against the freezing winter.

Apply

Have students use the practice words in original sentences.

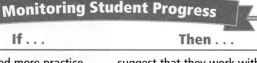

Monitoring Student Progress

If . . .	Then . . .
students need more practice with the prefixes *com-, con-, en-, ex-, pre-,* and *pro-,*	suggest that they work with the following words: *community, consume, consist, enlarge, expose, prevent, protrude.*

Using Context

Individual Activity You can use context, the words and sentences surrounding an unknown word, to figure out the meaning of an unknown word. By determining what you do know about the text, you can often figure out the unknown.

Write down this sentence: *When salmon are rare, grizzlies will hungrily <u>devour</u> every one they catch.* Answer the questions below to determine the meaning of *devour*.

1. Who or what is the sentence about?

2. What do you know about the salmon?

3. What do you know about the grizzlies?

4. Since the grizzlies are hungry, what will they probably do to any animal they catch?

5. What might be a meaning for *devour*?

Substitute *eat* for *devour* in the sentence and in the first paragraph on page 610 to check if this meaning is logical.

CHALLENGE

Vocabulary Expansion

Small Group Activity To expand your vocabulary about the sky, discuss the Milky Way and some of the constellations seen in the Northern Hemisphere, such as Ursa Major, Pegasus, Hydra, Cassiopeia, and Orion. Work in small groups to choose a constellation to research and report on.

Three-Syllable Words

OBJECTIVE

• Students decode words with three syllables.

Target Skill Trace

• Three-Syllable Words, pp. 647C–647D

Teach

Discuss with students when the word *unloaded* might be used: truck drivers unloaded packages, school bus drivers unloaded passengers, and so forth. Write this sentence on the board: *The tamarins are unloaded and carried into the woods.* Ask students to look for the base word in *unloaded* and then name and explain the ending. Next, review that the prefix *un-* means "opposite" or "not," and help students define *unloaded*.

Write this pair of sentences on the board:

When the tamarins begin to eat natural foods, the observers <u>reduce</u> the number of visits. The <u>reduction</u> in visits goes down slowly until all feeding is stopped.

Point out that since *reduce* and *reduction* have the same base word, students might expect to pronounce *reduction* as *re-DOOS-shuhn*, but adding the suffix had two results:

• dropping the *e* made the *c* sound like *k*
• the changed syllabication affected the pronunciation of the *u*

Use this sentence to model decoding *starvation*: *Alone, a newly reintroduced tamarin can die of <u>starvation</u>.*

Think Aloud *I see the word* starve. *The* a *before the suffix* -tion *could be pronounced* ah *or long* a. *I'll try long* a: star-VA-shuhn. *That sounds right.*

Practice

Have pairs of students use different strategies to decode the underlined words.

The nesting box is a <u>modified</u> picnic box.

Cages in the woods await the <u>immigrants</u>.

The tamarins are <u>accustomed</u> to the climate.

Apply

Encourage students to find other three-syllable words in the story. Have them make a list of the words and divide the words into syllables after they have identified any prefixes and suffixes.

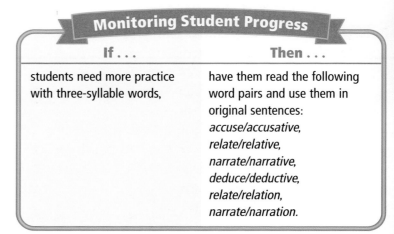

Monitoring Student Progress

If . . .	Then . . .
students need more practice with three-syllable words,	have them read the following word pairs and use them in original sentences: *accuse/accusative, relate/relative, narrate/narrative, deduce/deductive, relate/relation, narrate/narration.*

Place Names and Proper Adjectives

Individual Activity Think about the underlined word in this sentence: *Some tamarins are killed by Africanized, or "killer" bees.* Did you identify *Africa* as the base word? Brainstorm the names of the other continents and the proper adjectives associated with them. Use *South America* and *South American* in sentences that relate to *The Golden Lion Tamarin Comes Home.*

More Proper Nouns

Small Group Activity List the four cardinal directions. Note that the directions are not capitalized. Then name different sections of the U.S. After you list designations, such as the *North,* the *Southwest,* and so forth, notice that they are capitalized. Last, list titles, such as *Southerners, Easterners,* and so forth to name the people who live in these areas. As an alternative, you can do this activity as a word web.

CHALLENGE

Vocabulary Expansion

Partner Activity City names can be used to form additional proper nouns, such as New Yorkers, Bostonians, and Angelinos (for the people of Los Angeles). Compile a list of names for inhabitants of local communities. You may discover that proper nouns do not exist for the residents of some towns! If you wish to extend research to the international level, you may need to look in travel guides as the most efficient way of finding these proper nouns. A resident of Rio de Janeiro, by the way, is called a *Carioca,* which originally meant "white man's house" or "trading station" and then became the name of a dance.

RETEACHING

Word Endings *-ent, -ant, -able, -ible*

OBJECTIVES

- Identify the meaning of words with the suffixes *-ent, -ant, -able,* and *-ible.*
- Decode words with the suffixes *-ent, -ant, -able,* and *-ible.*

Target Skill Trace

- Word Endings *-ent, -ant, -able, -ible,* p. 671C

Teach

Ask students to name people or things that they can rely on. Then write this sentence on the board: *Living alone on the mountain had made me self-reliant.* Circle the *-ant* in *reliant* and write its meaning: "being in a certain condition" or "performing or causing a certain action." Discuss why the letter *i* might be a *y* in the base word. Change *reli* to *rely.* Help students define *self-reliant:* in the condition of relying on yourself. Then ask a volunteer to explain the strategy used. Point out that *-ent* and *-ant* have the same meaning.

Discuss where students might see *audio,* such as on a remote control, and the word's meaning. Then write this sentence: *An audible yelp announced the red fox.* Circle the *-ible.* Explain that *-ible* and *-able* mean "capable of" or "inclined to." Help students define *audible* as "capable of being heard."

Use this sentence to model how to decode *livable:* *I realized I had to make my tree livable during the cold winter.*

Think Aloud *I see the suffix -able. Liv looks like* live, *so* live *may be the base word. If so,* livable *would mean "capable of being lived in." Yes, that makes sense in the sentence.*

Practice

Ask students to decode the underlined words, using suffixes and base words.

> I did not go any closer to the <u>defiant</u> Baron.
>
> The flat stone could work. It was not <u>flexible</u>.
>
> It is <u>apparent</u> Frightful scares the squirrels.
>
> The fox thought the mess was <u>laughable</u>.

Apply

Have students define each of the underlined words that they decoded, using the context, base word, and suffix to help with meaning. Then have them use the practice words in original sentences.

Monitoring Student Progress

If . . .	Then . . .
students need more practice with the suffixes *-ent, -ant, -able,* and *-ible,*	suggest that they repeat the process used in the Practice and Apply sections with some of these words: *hesitant, irritant, occupant, assistant, defendant, observant, pollutant, chewable, likable, reliable, revivable, peaceable, imaginable, wearable, visible.*

Vocabulary Expansion

Partner Activity Sam, like everyone, needs food, clothing, and a place to live. Make a word web of the things that Sam used from his environment for food. Write *Food* on the center circle. Then make two more circles for the subcategories *From Plants* and *From Animals* before you add details from the reading. Look up the meaning of any unfamiliar word.

Many animals are mentioned in *My Side of the Mountain*. The author also describes how they move and the sounds they make. Make a chart of the animals and their corresponding movements and sounds. Include the animal sounds that Sam makes in the last paragraph of the story.

CHALLENGE

Slogans

Small Group Activity In the last paragraph of the story, Sam says that *might makes right*. Discuss what this expression means. Restate this expression in several ways, including using synonyms for *might* and *right*. One example might be *power gives control*.

CHALLENGE / EXTENSION

RETEACHING: Grammar

Contractions with *not*

OBJECTIVES

- Identify contractions with *not*.
- Form contractions with *not*.
- Write sentences using contractions with *not* correctly.

Target Skill Trace

- Contractions with *not*, p. 623I

Teach

Write the following sentences on the board, and ask students to choose the sentence that best describes their feelings about the story *The Grizzly Bear Family Book*:

> I liked the story, and I thought it was interesting. I did not like the story, and I didn't think it was interesting.

After students respond, underline the words *did not* and *didn't* in the second sentence. Ask students what they notice about the words. Lead them to recognize that *didn't* is a contraction that stands for the words *did not*.

Tell students that some verbs can be combined with the word *not* to make contractions. A *contraction* is a word formed by joining two words, making one shorter word. Review with students that an apostrophe (') takes the place of the letter or letters that are dropped to shorten the word.

Remind students that they know that *not* is not a verb. Therefore, it cannot be part of a verb phrase. The *n't* in a contraction is also not part of a verb or a verb phrase. Work with students to draw out the following points:

- You may use contractions when you talk with friends or when you write friendly letters.
- Do not use contractions in formal reports or business letters.

Practice

Model how to form a contraction from *is not* using this sentence: *It is not a sad event.*

Think Aloud *As I read this sentence, I notice the verb is* followed by the word *not. I know I can combine a verb with* not *to make a contraction. If I combine* is *with* not, *I form the contraction* isn't. *I'll check to see if this contraction works in the sentence.* It isn't a sad event. *That makes sense. The contraction* isn't *is a shortened form of the words* is not.

Have students use this thinking process to form contractions from these words: *have not, did not, cannot.*

Review by having students name some contractions with *not*. (Answers will vary.) Ask how an apostrophe is used in a contraction. (It takes the place of the letter or letters dropped to shorten the word.)

Apply

Have students write five interesting facts they learned about bears. Ask them to use at least three contractions with *not* in their sentences. Have students exchange papers, underline the contractions with *not* in each other's writing, and name the words that were used to make each one.

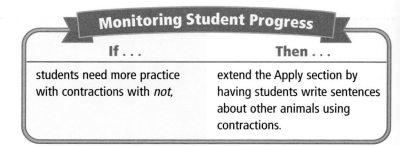

Monitoring Student Progress	
If . . .	**Then . . .**
students need more practice with contractions with *not*,	extend the Apply section by having students write sentences about other animals using contractions.

Negatives

OBJECTIVES

- Identify words that are negatives.
- Correct sentences that have double negatives.
- Use negatives correctly in sentences.

Target Skill Trace

- Negatives, p. 623J

Teach

Ask students to think about what they learned from the story *The Grizzly Bear Family Book*. Ask what advice they might give others about what to do if they see a grizzly bear in the wild. Display responses that include negatives. If necessary, add responses of your own. For example:

> <u>Never</u> bother a mother bear's cubs.
> <u>Don't</u> forget that bears might be in a berry patch.
> <u>No</u> animal in the wild is tame—especially a bear!

Underline the negatives in the sentences. Tell students that negatives are words that mean "no" or "not."

> She has <u>no</u> more berries.
> There are <u>none</u> in this area.

Tell students that they have already learned to form a contraction from a verb and *not*. These contractions are also negatives. The letters *n't* stand for *not*. The word *not* is an adverb.

> A mother <u>won't</u> abandon her cubs.
> She <u>couldn't</u> move quickly.

List the common negatives on a chart as shown, and have students use each word in a sentence.

Common Negatives

not	nobody	haven't
never	no one	wouldn't
nowhere	aren't	
nothing	doesn't	

Tell students that a sentence should have only one negative. Using double negatives in a sentence is usually incorrect.

INCORRECT: The park hasn't no cages.

CORRECT: The park has no cages. The park hasn't any cages.

INCORRECT: I haven't forgotten nothing.

CORRECT: I haven't forgotten anything. I have forgotten nothing.

Practice

Remind students that double negatives should not be used in sentences.

Have students identify the negatives in sentences on pages 610, 612, and 614.

Apply

Have students write a brief summary of the story. Ask them to use at least three negatives in their summary. Students can read aloud their summaries and have classmates identify the negatives.

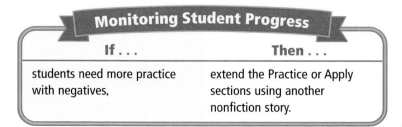

Monitoring Student Progress

If . . .	Then . . .
students need more practice with negatives,	extend the Practice or Apply sections using another nonfiction story.

RETEACHING: Grammar

Prepositions

> ### OBJECTIVES
> - Identify prepositions.
> - Identify objects of prepositions.
> - Use prepositions in original sentences.
>
> ### Target Skill Trace
> - Prepositions, p. 647I

Teach

Tell students that small words that we use all the time can make a big difference in meaning. Display these sentences.

> We walked *through* the tropical forest.
> We walked *near* the tropical forest.

Elicit from students that the words *through* and *near* show very different relationships between *walked* and *forest*. Explain that words that show relationships between other words are called prepositions.

Some Common Prepostions

about	for	on
above	from	out
across	in	over
before	into	to
behind	near	under
below	of	with

Tell students that a preposition relates some other word in the sentence to the noun or the pronoun that follows the preposition. The noun or the pronoun that follows a preposition is the *object* of the *preposition*. The object answers the question *whom* or *what* after the preposition.

A lizard ran under the <u>car</u>. (object of the preposition under*)*

I saw a turtle near the <u>pond</u>. (object of the preposition near*)*

A lizard ran under what?

I saw a turtle near what?

Practice

Have students look at the sentence on page 631 that begins, "The rain forest is alive …" Use the following Think Aloud to model how to identify prepositions.

Think Aloud *As I read this sentence, I see the word* with*. I think* with *is a preposition, but I'll check to make sure. I look at the words that follow* with *and ask: Do these words tell whom or what? The word* wildlife *tells* with *what. So* with *must be a preposition.*

Have students find four prepositions on page 631. Ask them to write the preposition and the object of the preposition.

Apply

Have students write four things that they learned about tamarins. Ask them to include a preposition in each statement. Then invite students to exchange papers and circle the prepositions in each other's writing.

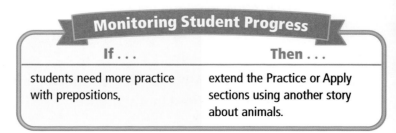

Monitoring Student Progress

If . . .	Then . . .
students need more practice with prepositions,	extend the Practice or Apply sections using another story about animals.

Prepositional Phrases

OBJECTIVES

- Identify prepositional phrases.
- Identify prepositional phrases with compound objects of the preposition.
- Use prepositional phrases in sentences.

Target Skill Trace

- Prepositional Phrases, p. 647J

Teach

Remind students that a preposition is always followed by an object. Tell them that a *prepositional phrase* is made up of a preposition, the object of the preposition, and all the words between them.

Have students describe the position of objects in the classroom. Record responses on the board and underline the prepositions. For example:

> The flag is <u>near</u> the window.
> The pencil sharpener is <u>on</u> the bookshelf.
> The dictionary is <u>above</u> the reading books.
> The map is <u>behind</u> the desk.

Ask students what kind of word is underlined in each sentence. (a preposition) Review that the object of a preposition is the noun or the pronoun that follows it. Then have students name the prepositional phrase in each sentence on the board. (near the window, on the bookshelf, above the reading books, behind the desk) Tell students that the object of the preposition can be a compound object.

> We looked carefully <u>at the trees and other plants</u>.

Demonstrate and discuss with students that a prepositional phrase can be at the beginning, in the middle, or at the end of a sentence.

> <u>At dawn</u> we began our walk.
> The map <u>of the area</u> was helpful.
> The path went <u>by tall trees and a large owl</u>.

Practice

Display the following sentences, and underline the prepositions. Have students name the entire prepositional phrase.

> The golden lion tamarin is named <u>for</u> its color and its mane. (for its color and its mane)
> It is found only <u>in</u> coastal rain forests. (in coastal rain forests)
> The tall trees <u>of</u> the rain forest offer the tamarin food. (of the rain forest)
> <u>Above</u> the tamarins fly owls that are predators. (Above the tamarins)
> Ocelots and feral dogs prowl <u>along</u> the ground. (along the ground)

Summarize by asking: How can you identify a prepositional phrase? (A prepositional phrase includes a preposition, its object, and all the words in between.)

Apply

Ask students to write a brief summary of *The Golden Lion Tamarin Comes Home*. Have them use prepositional phrases in their writing. Then have students read their summaries aloud. Ask listeners to identify the prepositional phrases they hear.

Monitoring Student Progress

If . . .	Then . . .
students need more practice with prepositional phrases,	extend the Practice or Apply sections using another story that students have read.

RETEACHING: Grammar

Object Pronouns in Prepositional Phrases

OBJECTIVES

- Identify object pronouns in prepositional phrases.
- Use prepositional phrases with object pronouns in sentences.

Target Skill Trace

- Object Pronouns in Prepositional Phrases, p. 671I

Teach

Have two volunteers go to the front of the class and read aloud their favorite part of *My Side of the Mountain* to each other. Then write sentences such as the following on the board, and underline the objects of the preposition.

> Mia read to <u>Arthur</u>.
> Arthur read to <u>Mia</u>.

Point out that each underlined name is the object of the preposition *to*. Remind students that they already have learned that the object of a preposition is the noun or the pronoun that follows the preposition. Tell them that when the object of the preposition is a pronoun, it must be an object pronoun. Remind students that a pronoun is a word that is used in place of a noun. Then ask students to substitute a pronoun for each underlined name on the board.

> Mia read to <u>him</u>.
> Arthur read to <u>her</u>.

Explain that the pronouns *him* and *her* are object pronouns. Emphasize that the only pronouns that can be used in a prepositional phrase are object pronouns.

Create a complete list of object pronouns with students.

> me   him   it
> you   her   us   them

Practice

Display the following sentences. Have students identify the prepositional phrase in each sentence that has an object pronoun.

> Frightful snagged crickets as Sam paddled <u>past her</u>.
> The creek seemed like an old friend <u>to him</u>.
> Sam dug clay for a fireplace and went home <u>with it</u>.
> He heard birds in the trees and smiled <u>at them</u>.

Caution students that people sometimes get confused when the pronoun is part of a compound object. Give them this tip: To see whether the pronoun is correct, remove the other object and check the pronoun alone.

> I gave a picture to <u>Tom</u> and <u>her</u>. I gave a picture to her.

Summarize by asking: What is a pronoun? (a word that is used in place of a noun) What kind of pronouns are used in prepositional phrases? (object pronouns) Which words are object pronouns? (*me, us, you, him, her, it, them*)

Apply

Ask students to write a brief summary of *My Side of the Mountain*. Have them use object pronouns in some of the prepositional phrases they write. Then have students read their summaries aloud. Ask listeners to identify the object pronouns they hear.

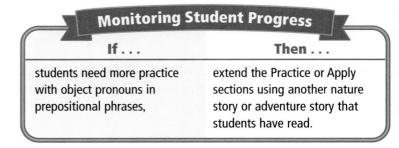

Monitoring Student Progress

If . . .	Then . . .
students need more practice with object pronouns in prepositional phrases,	extend the Practice or Apply sections using another nature story or adventure story that students have read.

Pronouns in Prepositional Phrases with Compound Objects

OBJECTIVES

- Identify pronouns in compound objects of a prepositional phrase.
- Distinguish the correct pronoun form to use in a compound object of the preposition.
- Write sentences using the correct pronoun form in a compound object of the preposition.

Target Skill Trace

- Pronouns in Prepositional Phrases with Compound Objects, p. 671J

Teach

Have students look at the "Meet the Author" section on page 650 and name the author and illustrator who are described. Then write the following sentence on the board. Underline the prepositional phrase. *This page tells about Jean Craighead George and Gary Aagaard.* Have students identify the object of the prepositional phrase. (Jean Craighead George, Gary Aagaard)

Point out that the object is compound. It refers to more than one person. Remind students that when a pronoun is used in a compound object of a preposition, it must be an object pronoun.

Ask them to substitute an object pronoun for one of the names in the sentence. (This page tells about Jean Craighead George and him. This page tells about her and Gary Aagaard.)

Display the following pairs of sentences. Have students choose the object pronoun that best completes each compound object.

Frightful was tethered to a tree as Sam filled his pouches. Squirrels ran away from Sam and _____. (she, her)

The Baron licked Sam's turtle-shell bowl. It was a tense moment for _____ and Sam. (him, he)

Animals visited Sam often. So Sam held a Halloween party for _____ and himself. (they, them)

Practice

Tell students if they are having a hard time deciding which pronoun to use in a compound object, they should say the sentence aloud without the other part of the compound object. For example, with the sentence *Squirrels ran away from Sam and _____ (she, her)*, they can say *Squirrels ran away from her.*

Have students write an object pronoun to complete the compound object in each of these pairs of sentences.

The wind blew the grass seed, and animals ate it.

The grass seed was harvested by _____ and the wind. (them)

Many animals joined Sam's party.

At first it was fun for the animals and _____. (him)

Sam and Frightful had lunch along the creek.

As they walked home, golden light fell upon Sam and _____. (her)

Summarize by asking: What can you do if you are having a hard time deciding which pronoun form to use in a compound object of a preposition? (Say the sentence aloud without the other part of the compound.)

Apply

Ask students to write a description of an outdoor trip they took with a friend or a family member. Have them use prepositional phrases with compound objects of the preposition in their sentences. Tell them to include object pronouns in the compound.

Monitoring Student Progress

If . . .	Then . . .
students need more practice with pronouns in prepositional phrases with compound objects,	extend the Practice or Apply sections using another story that students have read.

Word Cut-Ups

Cut out each word or word root. Match each part to the appropriate
prefix written on your index cards.

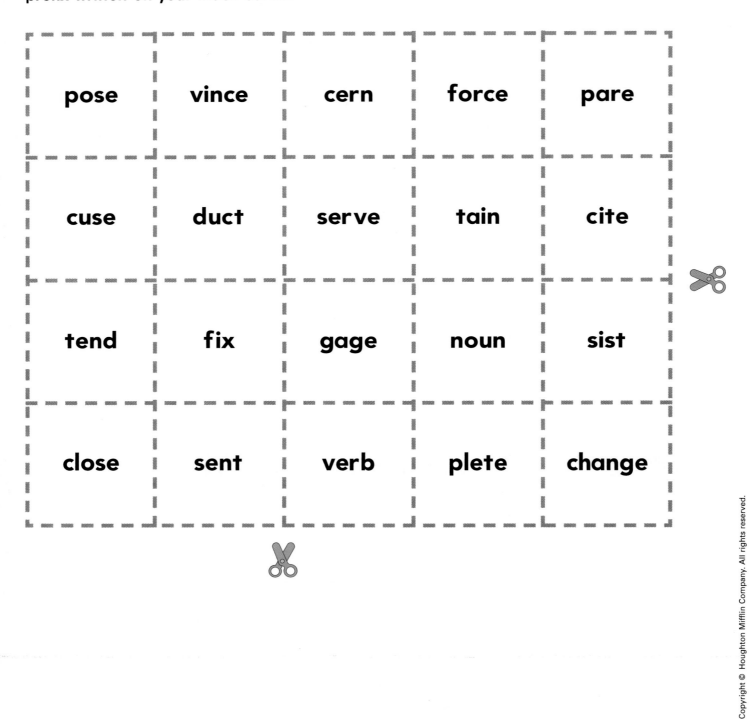

| pose | vince | cern | force | pare |
| close | sent | verb | plete | change |

contend, extend, pretend; prefix; engage;
pronoun; consist, exist; enclose, consent;
present; proverb; complete; exchange

compose, expose, propose; convince,
province; concern; enforce; compare,
prepare; excuse; conduct, product;
conserve, preserve; contain; excite;

Theme 6: **Animal Encounters**

Arctic Word Game

Key Vocabulary

abundant: more than enough; plentiful

aggressive: bold; ready and quick to fight

carcass: the dead body of an animal

caribou: a type of Arctic deer

dominance: the condition of having the most control

subservience: the state of being willing to yield to others' power

territory: an area inhabited by an animal or animal group and defended against intruders

tundra: a treeless Arctic region where the subsoil is permanently frozen and where only low shrubs, lichens, and mosses can grow

wariness: the state of being on one's guard

wilderness: any unsettled region in its natural state

Theme 6: **Animal Encounters**

Fish for Synonyms

**After each Key Vocabulary Word, write three synonyms from the list
below. Then use this page to help you make your deck for the "Go
Fish" game.**

Key Vocabulary Words

canopy _____	habitat _____
captive _____	humid _____
dilemma _____	observation _____
extinction _____	predators _____
genes _____	reintroduction _____

Synonyms

ceiling	hunters	resuming
cells	imprisoned	returning
destruction	jailed	roof
determiners	killers	slayers
difficulty	misty	study
environment	muggy	territory
extermination	noticing	top
held	obliteration	trouble
heredity	quandary	watching
home	repopulation	wet

environment, home, territory
misty, muggy, wet
noticing, study, watching
hunters, killers, slayers

ceiling, roof, top
held, imprisoned, jailed
difficulty, quandary, trouble
destruction, extermination, obliteration

Theme 6: **Animal Encounters**

Crossword Puzzle

Copy your finished crossword puzzle onto this page. Put the clues on the back of the page. Then trade puzzles with your partner.

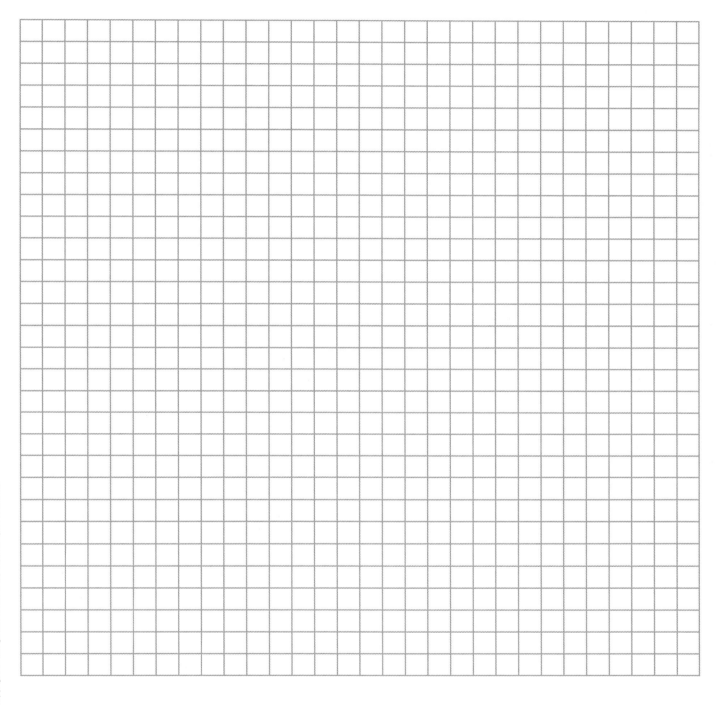

Theme 6: **Animal Encounters**

Writer _____   Listener _____

Writing Conference

What Should I Say?

In a writing conference, a writer reads a draft to a partner or a small group. A listener can help the writer by discussing the draft and asking questions such as these.

If you're thinking . . .

- I don't understand the goal.
- Why should I think that? Why should I do that?
- This reason is not very convincing.

You could say . . .

- What do you want your audience to think or do?
- Could you give me some more reasons to support your goal?
- Could you tell more about this reason, using facts and examples?

More Questions a Listener Might Ask

Read these questions before you listen. Take notes on the other side of this paper. Then discuss your thoughts with the writer.

1. What do you like about the writer's persuasive essay?

2. What is the writer's goal? What reasons does the writer give to support this goal? Retell what you heard.

3. What facts and examples make the writer's reasons clear?

4. Are there places where the writer needs to tell more? or tell less? Give examples.

Theme 6: **Animal Encounters**

TECHNOLOGY RESOURCES

American Melody
P.O. Box 270
Guilford, CT 06437
800-220-5557
www.americanmelody.com

Audio Bookshelf
174 Prescott Hill Road
Northport, ME 04849
800-234-1713
www.audiobookshelf.com

Baker & Taylor
100 Business Center Drive
Pittsburgh, PA 15205
800-775-2600
www.btal.com

BDD Audio/Random House
100 Hohn Road
Westminster, MD 21157
800-733-3000

Big Kids Productions
1606 Dywer Ave.
Austin, TX 78704
800-477-7811
www.bigkidsvideo.com

Books on Tape
P.O. Box 25122
Santa Ana, CA 92799
www.booksontape.com
800-541-5525

Broderbund Company
1 Martha's Way
Hiawatha, IA 52233
www.broderbund.com

Filmic Archives
The Cinema Center
Botsford, CT 06404
800-366-1920
www.filmicarchives.com

Great White Dog Picture Company
10 Toon Lane
Lee, NH 03824
800-397-7641
www.greatwhitedog.com

HarperAudio
10 E. 53rd St.
New York, NY 10022
800-242-7737
www.harperaudio.com

Houghton Mifflin Company
222 Berkeley St.
Boston, MA 02116
800-225-3362

Informed Democracy
P.O. Box 67
Santa Cruz, CA 95063
800-827-0949

JEF Films
143 Hickory Hill Circle
Osterville, MA 02655
508-428-7198

Kimbo Educational
P.O. Box 477
Long Branch, NJ 07740
800-631-2187
www.kimboed.com

Library Video Co.
P.O. Box 580
Wynnewood, PA 19096
800-843-3620
www.libraryvideo.com

Listening Library
P.O. Box 25122
Santa Ana, CA 92799
800-541-5525
www.listeninglibrary.com

Live Oak Media
P.O. Box 652
Pine Plains, NY 12567
800-788-1121
www.liveoakmedia.com

Media Basics
Lighthouse Square
P.O. Box 449
Guilford, CT 06437
800-542-2505
www.mediabasicsvideo.com

Microsoft Corp.
One Microsoft Way
Redmond, WA 98052
800-426-9400
www.microsoft.com

National Geographic School Publishing
P.O. Box 10597
Des Moines, IA 50340
800-368-2728
www.nationalgeographic.com

New Kid Home Video
P.O. Box 10443
Beverly Hills, CA 90213
800-309-2392
www.NewKidhomevideo.com

Puffin Books
345 Hudson Street
New York, NY 10014
800-233-7364

Rainbow Educational Media
4540 Preslyn Drive
Raleigh, NC 27616
800-331-4047
www.rainbowedumedia.com

Recorded Books
270 Skipjack Road
Prince Frederick, MD 20678
800-638-1304
www.recordedbooks.com

Sony Wonder
Dist. by Professional Media Service
19122 S. Vermont Ave.
Gardena, CA 90248
800-223-7672
www.sonywonder.com

Spoken Arts
195 South White Rock Road
Holmes, NY 12531
800-326-4090
www.spokenartsmedia.com

SRA Media
220 E. Danieldale Rd.
DeSoto, TX 75115
800-843-8855
www.sra4kids.com

Sunburst Technology
101 Castleton St.
Suite 201
Pleasantville, NY 10570
800-321-7511
www.sunburst.com

SVE & Churchill Media
6677 North Northwest Highway
Chicago, IL 60631
800-829-1900
www.svemedia.com

Tom Snyder Productions
80 Coolidge Hill Road
Watertown, MA 02472
800-342-0236
www.tomsnyder.com

Troll Communications
100 Corporate Drive
Mahwah, NJ 07430
800-526-5289
www.troll.com

Weston Woods
143 Main St.
Norwalk, CT 06851-1318
800-243-5020
www.scholastic.com/westonwoods

PRONUNCIATION GUIDE

In this book some unfamiliar or hard-to-pronounce words are followed by respellings to help you say the words correctly. Use the key below to find examples of various sounds and their respellings. Note that in the respelled word, the syllable in capital letters is the one receiving the most stress.

Dictionary letter or mark		Respelled as	Example	Respelled word
ă	(pat)	a	basket	BAS-kiht
ā	(pay)	ay	came	kaym
âr	(care)	air	share	shair
ä	(father)	ah	barter	BAHR-tur
ch	(church)	ch	channel	CHAN-uhl
ĕ	(pet)	eh	test	tehst
ē	(bee)	ee	heap	heep
g	(gag)	g	goulash	GOO-lahsh
ĭ	(pit)	ih	liver	LIHV-ur
ī	(pie, by)	y	alive	uh-LYV
		eye	island	EYE-luhnd
îr	(hear)	eer	year	yeer
j	(judge)	j	germ	jurm
k	(kick, cat, pique)	k	liquid	LIHK-wihd
ŏ	(pot)	ah	otter	AHT-ur
ō	(toe)	oh	solo	SOH-loh
ô	(caught, paw)	aw	always	AWL-wayz
ôr	(for)	or	normal	NOR-muhl
oi	(noise)	oy	boiling	BOYL-ihng
ŏŏ	(took)	u	pull, wool	pul, wul
ōō	(boot)	oo	bruise	brooz
ou	(out)	ow	pound	pownd
s	(sauce)	s	center	SEHN-tur
sh	(ship, dish)	sh	chagrin	shuh-GRIHN
ŭ	(cut)	uh	flood	fluhd
ûr	(urge, term, firm, word, heard)	ur	earth	urth
			bird	burd
z	(zebra, xylem)	z	cows	kowz
zh	(vision, pleasure, garage)	zh	decision	dih-SIHZH-uhn
ə	(about)	uh	around	uh-ROWND
	(item)	uh	broken	BROH-kuhn
	(edible)	uh	pencil	PEHN-suhl
	(gallop)	uh	connect	kuh-NEHKT
	(circus)	uh	focus	FOH-kuhs
ər	(butter)	ur	liter	LEE-tur

Glossary

Visit www.eduplace.com for *e • Glossary* and *e • Word Game*.

This glossary contains meanings and pronunciations for some of the words in this book. The Full Pronunciation Key shows how to pronounce each consonant and vowel in a special spelling. At the bottom of the glossary pages is a shortened form of the full key.

Full Pronunciation Key

Consonant Sounds

b	**bib**, ca**bb**age	kw	**ch**oir, **qu**ick
ch	**ch**ur**ch**, sti**tch**	l	**l**id, need**l**e, ta**ll**
d	**d**ee**d**, maile**d**, pu**ddl**e	m	a**m**, **m**an, du**mb**
f	**f**ast, fi**f**e, o**ff**, **ph**rase, rou**gh**	n	**n**o, su**dd**en
g	**g**a**g**, **g**et, fin**g**er	ng	thi**ng**, i**nk**
h	**h**at, **wh**o	p	**p**o**p**, ha**pp**y
hw	**wh**ich, **wh**ere	r	**r**oa**r**, **rh**yme
j	**j**u**dg**e, **g**em	s	mi**ss**, **s**au**ce**, **sc**ene, **s**ee
k	**c**at, **k**i**ck**, s**ch**ool	sh	**d**i**sh**, **sh**ip, **s**ugar, ti**ss**ue
		t	**t**igh**t**, s**t**o**pp**ed
		th	ba**th**, **th**in
		th	ba**th**e, **th**is
		v	ca**v**e, val**v**e, **v**ine
		w	**w**ith, **w**olf
		y	**y**es, **y**olk, on**i**on
		z	ro**s**e, **s**i**z**e, **x**ylophone, **z**ebra
		zh	gara**g**e, plea**s**ure, vi**s**ion

Vowel Sounds

ă	p**a**t, l**au**gh	ô	h**o**rrible, p**o**t	û	c**u**t, fl**oo**d, r**ou**gh, s**o**me
ā	**a**pe, **ai**d, p**ay**	ō	g**o**, r**ow**, t**oe**, th**ou**gh	û	c**i**rcle, f**u**r, h**ea**rd, t**er**m, t**ur**n, **ur**ge, w**or**d
â	**ai**r, c**a**re, w**ear**	ô	**a**ll, c**au**ght, f**o**r, p**aw**		
ä	f**a**ther, k**o**ala, y**ar**d	oi	b**oy**, n**oi**se, **oi**l		
ĕ	p**e**t, pl**ea**sure, **a**ny	ou	c**ow**, **ou**t	yōō	c**u**re
ē	b**e**, b**ee**, **ea**sy, p**ia**no	ōō	f**u**ll, b**oo**k, w**o**lf	yōō	**a**b**u**se, **u**se
ĭ	**i**f, p**i**t, b**u**sy	ōō	b**oo**t, r**u**de, fr**ui**t, fl**ew**	ə	**a**go, sil**e**nt, penc**i**l, lem**o**n, circ**u**s
ī	r**i**de, b**y**, p**ie**, h**igh**				
î	d**ear**, d**eer**, f**ier**ce, m**ere**				

Stress Marks

Primary Stress ´: bi·ol·o·gy [bī **ŏl´** ə jē]
Secondary Stress ´: bi·o·log·i·cal [bī´ ə **lŏj´** i kəl]

A

ab·o·li·tion·ist (ăb´ ə **lĭsh´** ə nĭst) *n.* A person who felt that slavery should be against the law. *Quakers and other **abolitionists** believed that owning slaves was wrong.*

a·bun·dant (ə **bŭn´** dənt) *adj.* More than enough; plentiful. *Fish and game were **abundant** along the coast.*

ac·com·pa·ni·ment (ə **kŭm´** pə nĭ mənt) *n.* A musical part, usually played on an instrument, that goes along with the performance of a singer or musician. *Victoria sang to the **accompaniment** of a guitar.*

ad·ven·ture (əd **vĕn´** chər) *n.* An unusual or exciting experience. *Greg thought that sailing to Africa would be a real **adventure**.*

ag·gres·sive (ə **grĕs´** ĭv) *adj.* Ready and quick to fight; bold. *The bear cub snarled in an **aggressive** way.*

am·a·teur (**ăm´** ə chər) *n.* Someone who performs a sport or other activity without being paid. *You must be an **amateur** to compete in high school sports.*

a·maz·ing·ly (ə **mā´** zĭng lē) *adv.* In a way that causes surprise or wonder. *The test questions were **amazingly** easy.*

ap·plause (ə **plôz´**) *n.* The clapping of hands to show approval. *Adam's speech was greeted with loud **applause**.*

ap·pren·tice (ə **prĕn´** tĭs) *n.* Someone who works for another person in order to learn a trade. *The blacksmith helped the **apprentice** learn how to use the tools.*

arm (ärm) *v.* To equip with weapons. *The rebels were **arming** themselves as the British troops approached the town.*

ar·ti·fi·cial (är´ tə **fĭsh´** əl) *adj.* Created by humans rather than occuring in nature. *The zookeepers built an **artificial** den for the lion to live in.*

ar·tis·tic (är **tĭs´** tĭk) *adj.* Showing imagination and skill in creating something beautiful. *The dancers gave an **artistic** performance.*

as·tro·naut (**ăs´** trə nôt) *n.* A person trained to fly in a spacecraft. *Neil Armstrong was the first **astronaut** to walk on the moon.*

at·tach·ment (ə **tăch´** mənt) *n.* A feeling of closeness and affection. *The two cousins have a strong **attachment** to one another.*

amateur
Amateur comes from the Latin word *amare*, which means "to love." Someone who is an amateur takes part in an activity for the love of it.

apprentice
Apprentice comes from the Latin word *apprehendere*, which means "to grasp." An apprentice is a learner who must grasp what to do in a profession.

astronaut
This word was created in 1929 by combining two ancient Greek word parts, *astro-* and *nautes*, which translate as "star sailor."

---

au·di·ence (**ô´** dē əns) *n.* People who gather to see and hear a performance. *The **audience** cheered loudly as the singer bowed.*

B

ban·dit (**băn´** dĭt) *n.* An outlaw, especially one who robs. *The **bandit** demanded that the passengers hand over their wallets.*

bluff (blŭf) *n.* A high cliff or bank. *From the top of the **bluff**, he could see the entire valley.*

braille (brāl) *n.* A system of writing that uses raised dots, for people who are visually impaired. *Angela ran her fingers over the **braille** letters on the page.*

C

cache (kăsh) *n.* A store of hidden goods. *The bear dug up the campers' **cache** of food.*

can·o·py (**kăn´** ə pē) *n.* The highest layer of a forest, formed by the treetops. *Many kinds of parrots and monkeys live in the dense **canopy** of the rain forest.*

cap·tive (**kăp´** tĭv) *n.* A prisoner. *The soldiers brought their **captives** back to the fort.* — *adj.* Captured; held against one's will. *The **captive** squirrel managed to escape from the trap.*

car·cass (**kär´** kəs) *n.* The dead body of an animal. *The wolves fed on the **carcass** of a deer.*

car·go (**kär´** gō) *n., pl.* **cargoes.** The freight carried by a ship or other vehicle. *The ship's **cargo** included molasses from the West Indies.*

car·i·bou (**kăr´** ə bōō) *n., pl.* **caribou.** A large deer found in northern North America, related to the reindeer. *The herd of **caribou** swam across the river.*

cau·tious (**kô´** shəs) *adj.* Careful; not taking chances. *It is best to be **cautious** when crossing a busy street.*

cel·e·bra·tion (sĕl´ ə **brā´** shən) *n.* A special activity that honors a person, event, or idea. *I invited ten friends to my birthday **celebration**.*

cin·der (**sĭn´** dər) *n.* A partly burned piece of coal or wood. *A pile of **cinders** lay at the bottom of the fire pit.*

claim (klām) *n.* A piece of land that someone reserves for ownership. *The settlers took a **claim** that bordered on the river.*

col·lide (kə **lĭd´**) *v.* To come together with forceful impact. *When warm and cold air masses **collide**, the weather becomes stormy.*

braille
Louis Braille (1809–1852) was a French inventor who lost his sight at the age of three and as a student of fifteen created the unique writing system that bears his name.

canopy
The Greek word *konopeion*, a bed with a netting to keep out mosquitoes, gave us the word for the covering created by treetops in a rain forest.

caribou
Caribou is the Canadian French version of a Native American word — the Micmac *khalibu*, which means "snow scraper."

D

col·o·ny (**kŏl´** ə nē) *n., pl.* **colonies** A territory ruled by or belonging to another country. *The thirteen **colonies** no longer wanted to be taxed by England.*

com·pete (kəm **pēt´**) *v.* To take part in a contest. *The runners hoped to **compete** in the Boston Marathon.*

con·cen·trate (**kŏn´** sən trāt´) *v.* To give full attention to. *It is difficult to **concentrate** on my book when the television is on.*

con·flict (**kŏn´** flĭkt´) *n.* A struggle; a war. *The United States had a second **conflict** with England in 1812.*

con·vinced (kən **vĭnsd´**) *adj.* Persuaded; certain. *They were **convinced** that the bridge was strong enough to carry their weight.*

cra·ter (**krā´** tər) *n.* A hollow bowl-shaped area at the mouth of a volcano. *The hikers peered down into the deep rocky **crater** below.*

crust (krŭst) *n.* The hard outer layer of the earth. *Cracks in the earth's **crust** help create volcanoes.*

cus·tom (**kŭs´** təm) *n.* Something that members of a group usually do. *One of the **customs** of people in the desert is to offer visitors refreshment and shade.*

de·bris (də **brē´**) *n.* The remains of something broken or destroyed; rubble. *The bulldozer pushed the **debris** into the corner of the lot.*

de·but (dā **byōō´**) *n.* First public performance. *The actor made his stage **debut** as Peter Pan.*

dec·o·rate (**dĕk´** ə rāt´) *v.* To make festive or beautiful. *We will **decorate** the room with flowers and streamers.*

dem·on·stra·tion (dĕm´ ən **strā´** shən) *n.* A showing and explanation of how something works. *The teacher gave a **demonstration** of how to operate a camera.*

de·scrip·tion (dĭ **skrĭp´** shən) *n.* A statement that uses words to tell about something. *Debbie wrote an exciting **description** of the game.*

de·tain (dĭ **tān´**) *v.* To delay; to hold back. *If you **detain** us much longer, we will miss the bus.*

de·ter·mi·na·tion (dĭ tûr´ mə **nā´** shən) *n.* Firmness in carrying out a decision. *The team's **determination** to do better showed in how well they played.*

dev·as·ta·tion (dĕv´ ə **stā´** shən) *n.* Destruction or ruin. *The floods brought **devastation** to much of the coast.*

crater

Glossary continued

dex·ter·i·ty (dĕk stĕr´ĭ tē) *n.* Skill in the use of the hands, body, or mind. *The juggler showed great **dexterity** in keeping the oranges in the air.*

di·a·ry (dī´ ə rē) *n., pl.* **diaries**. A daily record of a person's thoughts and experiences. *Every night Marta wrote about the day's events in her **diary**.*

dominance
The root of this word is the Latin word *domus*, meaning "house." The head of a household often had control, or dominance, over a large staff of people.

dic·ta·tor (dĭk´ tā tər) *n.* A ruler who has complete power over a country. *The **dictator** would not allow any citizens to travel outside the country.*

di·lem·ma (dĭ lĕm´ ə) *n.* A situation in which one has to choose between two or more difficult options. *Sara's **dilemma** was whether to wake up her father or try to figure out the problem herself.*

dim sum (dĭm´ sŏŏm´) *n.* A type of traditional Chinese meal where small portions of different foods are served one after another. *Many Chinese restaurants serve **dim sum** on Sunday mornings.*

dis·ap·point·ed (dĭs´ ə point´ əd) *adj.* Unhappy because of an unsatisfied hope or wish. *Tanya was **disappointed** when her team lost the game.*

dis·com·fort (dĭs kŭm´ fərt) *n.* A feeling of mild distress. *Noah always feels **discomfort** when people ask him about his famous brother.*

dim sum

dis·cour·aged (dĭ skûr´ ĭjd) *adj.* Not hopeful or enthusiastic. *Sam felt **discouraged** when he learned that he had not won a prize.*

dis·mayed (dĭs māad´) *adj.* Filled with sudden concern or distress. *They were **dismayed** to learn that the bus had left without them.*

dog guide (dôg´ gĭd) *n.* A dog especially trained to lead visually impaired people. *May's **dog guide** waited until it was safe to cross the street.*

dom·i·nance (dŏm´ ə nəns) *n.* The greatest control within a group. *Wolves compete for **dominance** in the pack.*

dread (drĕd) *n.* Great fear. *The panther's roar filled the villagers with **dread**.*

drill (drĭl) *v.* To perform training exercises. *The soldiers were **drilling** all morning.*

du·o (dŏŏ´ ō) *n.* Two people performing together. *The sisters performed in the show as a singing **duo**.*

E

earth·quake (ûrth´ kwāk´) *n.* A trembling or shaking of the ground caused by sudden movements in rock below the earth's surface. *The **earthquake** caused buildings to topple.*

ă rat / ā pay / â care / ä father / ĕ pet / ē be / ĭ pit / ī pie / î fierce / ŏ pot / ō go / ô paw, for / oi oil / ŏŏ book

678

el·e·ment (ĕl´ ə mənt) *n.* A basic part of a whole. *Spirals, spins, and jumps are **elements** of a figure skating program.*

em·bar·rassed (ĕm băr´ əsd) *adj.* Made to feel self-conscious and ill at ease. *Josh felt **embarrassed** when he realized he had called her by the wrong name.*

en·cour·age (ĕn kûr´ ĭj) *v.* To give support to; to inspire. *Hal's parents **encouraged** him to become a skater.*

en·slave·ment (ĕn slāv´ mənt) *n.* The process by which one person becomes the property of another. *After years of **enslavement** by cruel owners, the men were set free.*

e·rup·tion (ĭ rŭp´ shən) *n.* A volcanic explosion or large flow of lava. *The newspaper showed photos of the **eruption** of a volcano in Nicaragua.*

ex·cite·ment (ĭk sīt´ mənt) *n.* A stirred-up feeling. *The fire caused a lot of **excitement** in our neighborhood.*

ex·per·i·ence (ĭk spîr´ ē əns) *n.* An event that someone takes part in or lives through. *Camping was a new **experience** for the children.*

ex·press (ĭk sprĕs´) *adj.* Fast, direct, and often nonstop. ***Express** services promise overnight deliveries.*

ex·tend·ed (ĭk stĕn´ dĭd) *adj.* Including more; broadened. *Your **extended** family includes your aunts, uncles, and cousins.*

ex·tinc·tion (ĭk stĭngk´ shən) *n.* The condition of having died out. *No one knows for sure what caused the **extinction** of the dinosaurs.*

F

fash·ion (făsh´ ən) *v.* To give a form or shape to; to make. *Ralph was able to **fashion** a waterproof cape from a large plastic bag.*

fault (fôlt) *n.* A break in a rock mass caused by a shifting of the earth's crust. *An active **fault** runs through the center of our town.*

fer·tile (fûr´ tl) *adj.* Rich in material needed to grow healthy plants. *Wheat and corn grew well in the prairie's **fertile** soil.*

fes·tive (fĕs´ tĭv) *adj.* Joyful; merry. *The party guests were in a **festive** mood.*

fierce (fîrs) *adj.* Intense; ferocious. *The lion gave a **fierce** roar.*

for·ty-five re·cord (fôr´ tē fīv´ rĕk´ ərd) *n.* A small phonograph record that is played at forty-five revolutions per minute. *The **forty-five record** has one song on each side.*

eruption

fierce
The Latin word *ferus* ("wild and savage") is the origin of the words *ferocious* and *fierce*.

funnel cloud

fran·tic (frăn´ tĭk) *adj.* Very upset, as from fear or worry. *When she couldn't find her backpack anywhere, Julie became **frantic**.*

fright·ened (frīt´ nd) *adj.* Scared, alarmed. *Billy was **frightened** as he stepped out on the diving board.*

fun·nel cloud (fŭn´ əl kloud´) *n.* A storm cloud that is wide at the top and narrow at the bottom, often becoming a tornado. *Whenever the settlers saw **funnel clouds**, they hurried toward storm shelters.*

G

gene (jēn) *n.* A tiny part of a plant or animal cell that determines a characteristic passed on to the next generation. *Lucy has blue eyes like her parents because of their **genes**.*

H

hab·i·tat (hăb´ ĭ tăt´) *n.* The type of environment where an animal or plant naturally lives and grows. *Sloths and jaguars live in the rain forest **habitat**.*

harsh (härsh) *adj.* Demanding and severe; unpleasant. *Winter is a **harsh** season for most animals.*

har·vest (här´ vĭst) *v.* To gather a crop. *The workers were **harvesting** apples.*

heif·er (hĕf´ ər) *n.* A young cow that has not yet had a calf. *Sally's cow has been winning blue ribbons since it was a **heifer**.*

herd (hûrd) *n.* A group of animals of a single kind. *A **herd** of wild horses galloped across the plain.*

her·i·tage (hĕr´ ĭ tĭj) *n.* Traditions, practices, and beliefs passed down from earlier generations. *Yinglan celebrates her Chinese **heritage** in her choice of music, clothes, and food.*

home·stead (hōm´ stĕd´) *n.* A piece of land given to settlers for farming and building a home. *The Andersens' **homestead** lay near Blackberry Creek.*

hon·or (ŏn´ ər) *v.* To show respect for; to accept. *They will **honor** their mother's request to dress up for Thanksgiving dinner.*

hu·mid (hyŏŏ´ mĭd) *adj.* Containing a large amount of water vapor; damp, sticky. *The air is often **humid** before a storm.*

I

im·mi·grant (ĭm´ ĭ grənt) *n.* A person who moves to a new country. *Many **immigrants** from Norway made their homes on the Great Plains.*

ă rat / ā pay / â care / ä father / ĕ pet / ē be / ĭ pit / ī pie / î fierce / ŏ pot / ō go / ô paw, for / oi oil / ŏŏ book

680

im·mo·bile (ĭ mō´ bəl) *adj.* Fixed in one place; unable to move. *He stood **immobile** against the cliff face as the hikers passed by.*

im·pact (ĭm´ păkt´) *n.* The striking of one object against another. *The **impact** of the bike hitting the fence knocked the flowerpots to the ground.*

im·press (ĭm prĕs´) *v.* To have a strong, favorable effect on someone's feelings. *His piano playing **impressed** the audience.*

in·flu·en·tial (ĭn´ flŏŏ ĕn´ shəl) *adj.* Having the power to affect events or sway opinions. *The **influential** Women's League brought the problem to the mayor's attention.*

in·her·it (ĭn hĕr´ ĭt) *v.* To receive something from a parent or ancestor. *They **inherited** their mother's talent for music.*

in·stinct (ĭn´ stĭngkt´) *n.* An inner feeling or way of behaving that is automatic, not learned. *A newly hatched sea turtle's **instinct** is to crawl toward the water.*

in·tense (ĭn tĕns´) *adj.* Very strong; focused. *Patrice put in hours of **intense** study to get ready for the test.*

J

jag·ged (jăg´ ĭd) *adj.* Having a ragged or pointed edge or outline. *Jamal cut his hand on a **jagged** piece of tin.*

jar (jär) *v.* To bump or cause to shake from impact. *By **jarring** Matthew, I caused him to drop the ball.*

jolt (jōlt) *n.* A sudden jerk or bump. *When the car went over the speed bump, the passengers got quite a **jolt**.*

judge (jŭj) *n.* A person who decides who wins a contest. *The **judges** awarded first prize to my grandfather's pumpkin pie.*

just (jŭst) *adj.* Honorable and fair. *It is **just** to listen to both sides of an argument.*

K

kin (kĭn) *n.* Relatives; family. *Your father's cousins are your **kin**, too.*

L

launch (lônch) *v.* To forcefully send upward. *A powerful blast **launches** the rocket into the sky.*

la·va (lä´ və) *n.* Hot melted rock that flows from a volcano. *As the **lava** moved down the hillside, it set fire to the trees in its path.*

lava
People from Naples, Italy, near Mt. Vesuvius, used the Italian word *lava*, meaning "a stream caused suddenly by rain" for the molten rock that flowed down the volcano. It became an English word in 1750.

lay·out (lā´ out´) *n.* The way something is arranged. *The* **layout** *of the office building confuses visitors.*

lib·er·ty (lĭb´ ər tē) *n.* Freedom from the control of others; independence. *The colonists won their* **liberty** *from England.*

light·ning (līt´ nĭng) *n.* The flash of light when electricity builds up in storm clouds. *A bolt of* **lightning** *lit up the night sky.*

lime·light (līm´ līt´) *n.* The center of public attention. *Ana's performance in the play brought her into the* **limelight***.*

limelight
In the 1800s, theaters used limelights, made by burning the mineral lime. That bright stage light came to stand for the attention of the public.

M

mag·ma (măg´ ma) *n.* Molten rock underneath the earth's surface. **Magma** *boiled up through cracks deep inside the mountain.*

mare (mâr) *n.* A female horse. *Some of the* **mares** *were followed by their colts.*

mas·ter (măs´ tər) *v.* To become expert in a skill or art. *Ramón* **mastered** *the violin through years of practice.*

ma·ture (mə tyŏŏr´) *adj.* Fully grown or mentally developed. *A* **mature** *dog is calmer than a puppy.*

mem·o·rize (měm´ ə rīz´) *v.* To learn by completely remembering. *The hikers are* **memorizing** *the landmarks along their route.*

mustang
This word for a wild horse came from the Mexican Spanish word *mestengo,* which means "stray animal."

mi·gra·tion (mī grā´ shən) *n.* A movement of animals to a different habitat, especially in response to the change of seasons. *Scientists have mapped the spring* **migration** *of the whales.*

mill (mĭl) *v.* To move around in confusion. *The impatient crowd* **milled** *in front of the theater doors.*

mis·sion (mĭsh´ ən) *n.* An operation that attempts to achieve certain goals or carry out specific tasks. *The astronauts'* **mission** *included bringing back samples of moon rocks.*

mol·ten (mōl´ tən) *adj.* Made liquid by heat. *The* **molten** *lava glowed red-orange.*

mus·tang (mŭs´ tăng) *n.* A wild horse of the plains of western North America. *Joe could not ride as fast as the herd of* **mustangs***.*

N

no·ble (nō´ bəl) *adj.* Showing greatness of character by unselfish behavior. *It was* **noble** *of Karen to share her prize money with her teammates.*

no·to·ri·ous (nō tôr´ ē əs) *adj.* Well known for something bad. *Billy the Kid was a* **notorious** *outlaw.*

å **rat** / ā **pay** / â **care** / ä **father** / ĕ **pet** / ē **be** / ĭ **pit** / ī **pie** / î **fierce** / ŏ **pot** / ō **go** / ô **paw, for** / oi **oil** / ŏŏ **book**

682

O

o·be·di·ence (ō bē´ dē əns) *n.* Willingness to follow orders. *Mr. Yee expects* **obedience** *from his crew.*

ob·ser·va·tion (ŏb´ zür vā´ shən) *n.* The act of paying careful attention. *You can learn a lot about nature through* **observation***.*

ob·sta·cle (ŏb´ stə kəl) *n.* A thing that stands in one's way. *The horse had to jump over such* **obstacles** *as bushes and fences.*

op·er·a (ŏp´ ə rə) *n.* A form of theater in which the dialogue is sung to musical accompaniment. *The actors in the* **opera** *wore beautiful costumes.*

op·pose (ə pōz´) *v.* To be against something or someone. *The neighbors* **oppose** *the plan to turn the park into an office building.*

or·bit (ôr´ bĭt) *n.* The path of a spacecraft around the earth. *Shannon Lucid spent six months in* **orbit** *aboard the spacecraft Mir.*

o·ver·take (ō´ vər tāk´) *v.* To catch up with. *If we continue at this pace, we will* **overtake** *Billie's group.*

P

pan·to·mime (păn´ tə mīm´) *n.* The use of movements and facial expressions instead of words to convey meaning. *Jean used* **pantomime** *to show us how she caught the fish.*

Pa·tri·ot (pā´ trē ət) *n.* A colonist who was against British rule in the time of the Revolutionary War. *Patrick Henry spoke as a* **Patriot** *when he said "Give me liberty or give me death!"*

peer (pîr) *v.* To look at with concentration. *Mom* **peered** *at Paul suspiciously as he told his story.*

pi·o·neer (pī´ ə nîr´) *adj.* Describing a person who is first or among the first to settle in a region. *Our town was settled by three* **pioneer** *families in the 1800s.*

prai·rie (prâr´ ē) *n.* A large area of flat or rolling grassland. *The treeless* **prairie** *stretched for miles in all directions.*

pred·a·tor (prĕd´ ə tər) *n.* An animal that hunts other animals for food. *Small lizards must always be on the alert for hungry* **predators***.*

pres·en·ta·tion (prĕz´ ən tā´ shən) *n.* Performance. *Although the actor knew his lines, his* **presentation** *was flat.*

pioneer
This word comes from the French word *peonier,* meaning "foot soldier." Those who marched into unknown territory were often soldiers on an expedition.

ŏŏ **boot** / ou **out** / ŭ **cut** / û **fur** / hw **which** / th **thin** / *th* **this** / zh **vision** / ə **ago, silent, pencil, lemon, circus**

683

pres·sure (prĕsh´ ər) *n.* A strong influence or force. *Sandra felt* **pressure** *to finish the book over the weekend.*

pri·va·teer (prī´ və tîr´) *n.* A privately owned ship that is ordered by the government to attack enemy ships during a war. *The* **privateers** *captured several merchant ships without firing a shot.*

pro·gram (prō´ grăm´) *n.* In figure skating, the routine that one performs in front of judges or an audience. *The young skater spent hours getting his* **program** *ready for the competition.*

prose (prōz) *n.* Ordinary spoken or written language, in contrast to poetry. *Most fiction and nonfiction books are written in* **prose***.*

R

raid (rād) *n.* A sudden attack, often with the goal of taking property. *The men brought back horses after their* **raid** *on their neighbors' village.*

ra·vine (rə vēn´) *n.* A narrow, deep valley, usually formed by the flow of water. *A small stream trickled at the bottom of the* **ravine***.*

reb·el (rĕb´ əl) *n.* A person who opposes or defies the government in power. *The* **rebels** *refused to obey King George's laws.*

ravine

ref·u·gee (rĕf´ yŏŏ jē´) *n.* A person who flees to find protection from danger. *As the fighting in the hills grew worse,* **refugees** *streamed into the city.*

re·hear·sal (rĭ hûr´ səl) *n.* A session of practicing for a public performance. *The cast needed one more* **rehearsal** *before the play opened.*

re·in·tro·duc·tion (rē´ ĭn trə dŭk´ shən) *n.* The process of returning animals to their native habitats. *The zoo's tamarins are doing well since their* **reintroduction** *into the rain forest.*

re·ject (rĭ jĕkt´) *v.* To refuse to accept. *The magazine* **rejected** *her poem.*

re·luc·tant (rĭ lŭk´ tənt) *adj.* Unwilling to take an action. *Emily was* **reluctant** *to get out of the swimming pool.*

re·morse (rĭ môrs´) *n.* A feeling of regret or guilt for having done something wrong. *Jennie felt* **remorse** *for the trouble she had caused her sister.*

rep·u·ta·tion (rĕp´ yə tā´ shən) *n.* What others think about someone's character, behavior, and abilities. *Alex had a* **reputation** *for getting along well with everyone.*

re·quired (rĭ kwīrd´) *adj.* Needed. *Kayla has all of the training* **required** *for this job.*

å **rat** / ā **pay** / â **care** / ä **father** / ĕ **pet** / ē **be** / ĭ **pit** / ī **pie** / î **fierce** / ŏ **pot** / ō **go** / ô **paw, for** / oi **oil** / ŏŏ **book**

684

re·spect (rĭ spĕkt´) *n.* A feeling of admiration and approval. *Mr. Garcia won the* **respect** *of all his students.*

re·us·a·ble (rē yŏŏz´ ə bəl) *adj.* Able to be used again. *April's family never throws away* **reusable** *paper bags.*

rev·o·lu·tion·ar·y (rĕv´ ə lŏŏ´ shə nĕr´ ē) *adj.* Connected with complete change. *The American colonists fought for their independence from England during the* **Revolutionary** *War.*

rhyth·mic (rĭth´ mĭk) *adj.* Having a noticeable beat with a pattern to it. *It is easy to dance to* **rhythmic** *music.*

ro·tate (rō´ tāt) *v.* To turn around on a center or axis. *It takes twenty-four hours for the earth to* **rotate** *once.*

rug·ged (rŭg´ ĭd) *adj.* Having a very rough and uneven surface. *The valley was surrounded by* **rugged** *mountains.*

S

sat·el·lite (săt´ l īt´) *n.* A human-made device that orbits a planet. *A weather* **satellite** *sends weather photos and data back to earth.*

sen·try (sĕn´ trē) *n., pl.,* **sentries**. A guard who is posted at a spot to keep watch. *Two* **sentries** *guarded the gates of the city.*

se·vere (sə vîr´) *adj.* Serious or extreme in nature. **Severe** *thunderstorms caused flooding in parts of the Midwest.*

shud·der (shŭd´ ər) *v.* To suddenly shake, vibrate, or quiver. *The house* **shuddered** *every time a heavy truck drove by.*

siz·zling (sĭz´ lĭng) *adj.* Crackling or hissing with intense heat. *The tree trunk was* **sizzling** *after the lightning bolt hit it.*

skir·mish (skûr´ mĭsh) *n.* A small, short fight; a minor battle. *The soldiers galloped away after a brief* **skirmish** *with the rebels.*

skit·ter (skĭt´ ər) *v.* To move lightly and quickly, especially with many changes of direction. *The mice* **skittered** *across the floor.*

skit·tish (skĭt´ ĭsh) *adj.* Nervous and jumpy. *The cat was* **skittish** *during the thunderstorm.*

snoop (snŏŏp) *n.* Someone who tries to find out about other people's doings in a sneaky way. *Maria's brother is such a* **snoop** *that she must keep her diary locked.*

sod (sŏd) *n.* A chunk of grass and soil held together by matted roots. *Settlers built houses out of blocks of* **sod** *because wood was scarce.*

satellite
In the Middle Ages the French used the word *satellite* to refer to an attendant who waits upon an important person. That same idea is in the modern meaning of a small device circling around a planet.

ŏŏ **boot** / ou **out** / ŭ **cut** / û **fur** / hw **which** / th **thin** / *th* **this** / zh **vision** / ə **ago, silent, pencil, lemon, circus**

685

Glossary   G3

sombrero
The name of the broad-brimmed hat that shades the wearer's eyes came from the Spanish word for shade, *sombra.*

shuttle
Shuttle started out as an Old English word, *scytel,* meaning "dart." It came to mean a weaving device that carried thread back and forth, and from that, a vehicle going back and forth over a short route.

som·bre·ro (sŏm **brâr**′ ō) *n.* A tall hat with a wide brim, worn in Mexico and the American Southwest. *The farmers wore* ***sombreros*** *to shade their eyes from the sun.*

space shut·tle (spās **shŭt**′ l) *n.* A reusable spacecraft that is launched like a rocket and can be landed like a plane. *The* ***space shuttle*** *landed safely after a seven-day flight.*

space·craft (**spās**′ krăft′) *n.* A vehicle designed for travel beyond the earth's atmosphere. *The* ***spacecraft*** *carried astronauts to the moon.*

spe·cial·ist (**spĕsh**′ ə lĭst) *n.* Someone who is an expert in a particular field. *A pediatrician is a medical* ***specialist*** *who treats only children.*

spec·ta·tor (**spĕk**′ tā′ tər) *n.* A person who watches an event or performance. *The* ***spectators*** *cheered when Jessie hit a home run.*

splen·did (**splĕn**′ dĭd) *adj.* Excellent. *The actor gave a* ***splendid*** *performance.*

stal·lion (**stăl**′ yən) *n.* An adult male horse. *Lizzie rode a black* ***stallion*** *at the horse show.*

stam·i·na (**stăm**′ ə nə) *n.* The strength needed to keep doing something tiring or difficult. *A young child lacks the* ***stamina*** *for a ten-mile hike.*

store·house (**stôr**′ hous′) *n.* A place or building where supplies are stored for future use. *The settlers'* ***storehouse*** *contained dried fruit and hams.*

sub·mit (səb **mĭt**′) *v.* To offer one's work to someone for their judgment or approval. *She* ***submitted*** *an article to the student newspaper.*

sub·ser·vi·ence (səb **sûr**′ vē əns) *n.* Willingness to give in to others' power. *Letting the tail droop is a sign of* ***subservience*** *in a wolf.*

sum·mit (**sŭm**′ ĭt) *n.* The top of a mountain. *Carolyn and I cheered when we finally reached the* ***summit*** *of Mount Rainier.*

sur·viv·al (sər **vī**′ vəl) *n.* The preservation or continuation of one's life. *Quick thinking is often necessary for* ***survival*** *in the wilderness.*

sus·pect (sə **spĕkt**′) *v.* To believe without being sure; to imagine. *Scott* ***suspects*** *that we are planning a surprise party for him.*

T

tack (tăk) *v.* To change the course of a boat. *The sailing ship was* ***tacking*** *in order to return to the harbor.*

ă rat / ā pay / â care / ä father / ĕ pet / ē be / ĭ pit / ī pie / î fierce / ŏ pot / ō go / ô paw, for / oi oil / ŏŏ book

tal·ent (**tăl**′ ənt) *n.* A natural ability to do something well. *She has a* ***talent*** *for playing the violin.*

tax (tăks) *n.* Money that people must pay in order to support a government. *England insisted that the colonists pay* ***taxes*** *on tea, stamps, and many other items.*

tech·ni·cal (**tĕk**′ nĭ kəl) *adj.* Showing basic knowledge of a complex task. *The acrobat performed the triple somersault with great* ***technical*** *skill.*

ter·ri·fy (**tĕr**′ ə fī′) *v.* To fill with overpowering fear. *The angry bear* ***terrified*** *the campers.*

ter·ri·to·ry (**tĕr**′ ĭ tôr′ ē) *n., pl.* **territories.** An area inhabited by an animal or animal group and defended against intruders. *The mountain lion hunted within its own* ***territory.***

To·ry (**tôr**′ ē) *n., pl.* **Tories.** An American who sided with the British during the American Revolution. *As the British troops departed, most of the city's* ***Tories*** *followed.*

tor·na·do (tôr **nā**′ dō) *n.* A violent, whirling wind in a funnel-shaped cloud that can cause great destruction. *Many* ***tornadoes*** *form in Kansas and Oklahoma.*

tra·di·tion (trə **dĭsh**′ ən) *n.* The passing down of customs and beliefs from one generation to the next. *There is a long* ***tradition*** *of helping others in our family.*

train·ing (**trā**′ nĭng) *n.* The process of learning how to behave or perform. *Guide dogs must go through a long period of* ***training*** *before they can help people.*

trans·form (trăns **fôrm**′) *v.* To change greatly in appearance or form. *The make-up* ***transformed*** *the actor into the character of an old man.*

tun·dra (**tŭn**′ drə) *n.* A treeless Arctic region where very few plants can grow. *Large plants cannot put down roots in the frozen subsoil of the* ***tundra.***

U

un·der·stand (ŭn′ dər **stănd**′) *v.* To get the meaning of. *After the teacher explained it again, Ivan could* ***understand*** *the problem.*

un·du·lat·ing (**ŭn**′ jə lāt′ ĭng) *adj.* Moving in waves or with a smooth, wavy motion. *The* ***undulating*** *water raised and lowered the rowboat.*

un·sure (ŭn **shŏŏr**′) *adj.* Not certain; having doubts. *She was* ***unsure*** *of whether to bring her umbrella.*

tornado
Tornadoes were unknown and unnamed in Britain, so Americans borrowed and adapted the Spanish word *tronada,* meaning "thunderstorm."

tradition
Our word for the passing down of customs from one generation to another comes from the Latin verb *tradere,* which means "to hand down."

undulate
The Latin word for a wave, *unda,* contributes the sense of rising and falling in *undulate.*

ŏŏ boot / ou out / ŭ cut / û fur / hw which / th thin / *th* this / zh vision / ə ago, silent, pencil, lemon, circus

wilderness

up·heav·al (ŭp **hē**′ vəl) *n.* A lifting or upward movement of the earth's crust. *The mountain range was created by a great* ***upheaval.***

ur·gent·ly (**ûr**′ jənt lē) *adv.* In a way that calls for immediate action. *The team* ***urgently*** *needs someone to take Kate's place.*

V

vol·un·teer (vŏl′ ən **tîr**′) *v.* To offer to do something of one's own free will, usually without being paid. *He* ***volunteered*** *to make the posters for the show.*

W

war·i·ness (**wâr**′ ē nĭs) *n.* Extreme caution. *Wild animals show* ***wariness*** *with people they don't know.*

weight·less·ness (**wāt**′ lĭs nĭs) *n.* The condition of experiencing little or no pull of gravity. *Astronauts experience* ***weightlessness*** *in outer space.*

wil·der·ness (**wĭl**′ dər nĭs) *n.* A region in its natural state, unsettled by human beings. *Grizzly bears live in the Alaskan* ***wilderness.***

wound (wo͞ond) *n.* Injury in which the skin is cut or broken. *The soldier's* ***wounds*** *were not serious.*

ă rat / ā pay / â care / ä father / ĕ pet / ē be / ĭ pit / ī pie / î fierce / ŏ pot / ō go / ô paw, for / oi oil / ŏŏ book

Acknowledgments

Main Literature Selections

And Then What Happened, Paul Revere? by Jean Fritz, illustrated by Margot Tomes. Text copyright © 1973 by Jean Fritz. Illustrations copyright © 1973 by Margot Tomes. Reprinted by permission of the Putnam & Grosset Group, a division of Penguin Putnam Inc.

Black Cowboy, Wild Horses: A True Story, by Julius Lester, illustrated by Jerry Pinkney. Text copyright © 1998 by Julius Lester. Illustrations copyright © 1998 by Jerry Pinkney. Reprinted by permission of Dial Books for Young Readers, a division of Penguin Putnam Inc.

Selection from *Blizzard!,* by Jim Murphy, published by Scholastic Press, a division of Scholastic Inc. Copyright © 2000 by Jim Murphy. Reprinted by permission of Scholastic Inc.

A Boy Called Slow: The True Story of Sitting Bull, by Joseph Bruchac, illustrated by Rocco Baviera. Text copyright © 1994 by Joseph Bruchac. Illustrations copyright © 1994 by Rocco Baviera. Reprinted by permission of the Putnam Grosset Group, a division of Penguin Putnam Inc.

Selection from *Dear Mr. Henshaw,* by Beverly Cleary, illustrated by Paul O. Zelinsky. Text copyright © 1983 by Beverly Cleary. Reprinted by permission of HarperCollins Publishers.

Selection from *Earthquake Terror,* by Peg Kehret. Copyright © 1996 by Peg Kehret. Reprinted by permission of Dutton Children's Books, a division of Penguin Putnam Inc.

Selection from *Elena,* by Diane Stanley. Copyright © 1996 by Diane Stanley. Reprinted by permission of Hyperion Books for Children.

Eye of the Storm: Chasing Storms with Warren Faidley, by Stephen Kramer, photographs by Warren Faidley. Text copyright © 1997 by Stephen Kramer. Photographs copyright © 1997 by Warren Faidley. Reprinted by permission of G. P. Putnam's Sons, a division of Penguin Putnam Inc.

Selection from *The Fear Place,* by Phyllis Reynolds Naylor. Copyright © 1994 by Phyllis Reynolds Naylor. Reprinted by permission of Atheneum Books for Young Readers, an imprint of Simon & Schuster Children's Publishing Division. Cover copyright © 1994 by Doron Ben Ami. Reprinted by permission of the author and illustrator.

The Golden Lion Tamarin Comes Home by George Ancona. Copyright © 1994 by George Ancona, except photographs of frog, snake and sloth by James M. Dietz and map by Isabel Ancona. All rights reserved. Reprinted with permission of Simon & Schuster Books for Young Readers, an imprint of Simon & Schuster Children's Publishing Division.

The Grizzly Bear Family Book, by Michio Hoshino, translated by Karen Collier-Taylor. Copyright © 1992 by Michio Hoshino. Reprinted by permission of North-South Books Inc., New York. All rights reserved.

Selection from *Iditarod Dream,* by Ted Wood. Copyright © 1996 by Ted Wood. Reprinted by arrangement with Walker & Co.

Selection from *Interrupted Journey,* by Kathryn Lasky, photographs by Christopher Knight. Text copyright © 2001 by Kathryn Lasky. Photographs copyright © 2001 by Christopher Knight. Reproduced by permission of Candlewick Press Inc., Cambridge, MA.

"James Forten" from *Now Is Your Time: The African-American Struggle for Freedom,* by Walter Dean Myers. Copyright © 1991 by Walter Dean Myers. Reprinted by permission of HarperCollins Publishers.

Selection from *Journey to Nowhere,* by Mary Jane Auch. Copyright © 1997 by Mary Jane Auch. Jacket illustration copyright © 1997 by Bob Crofut. Cover and excerpt reprinted by permission of Henry Holt and Company, LLC.

Katie's Trunk, by Ann Turner, illustrated by Ron Himler. Text copyright © 1992 by Ann Turner. Illustrations copyright © 1992 by Ron Himler. All rights reserved. Reprinted by permission of Simon & Schuster Books for Young Readers, an imprint of Simon & Schuster Children's Publishing Division.

"La Bamba" from *Baseball in April and Other Stories,* by Gary Soto. Copyright © 1990 by Gary Soto. Reprinted by permission of Harcourt Inc. The song "La Bamba" adaptation and arrangement by Ritchie Valens © 1958 Picture Our Music (Renewed). All rights for U.S.A. administered by EMI Longitude Music (BMI). All rights for the World except U.S.A. administered by Warner-Tamerlane Publishing Corp. All rights reserved. Reprinted by permission of Warner Bros. Publications U.S. Inc.

Mae Jemison: Space Scientist, by Gail Sakurai. Copyright © 1995 by Gail Sakurai. Reprinted by permission of Childrens Press Inc., a division of Grolier Publishing.

Selection from *Mariah Keeps Cool,* by Mildred Pitts Walter, illustrated by Pat Cummings. Text copyright © 1990 by Mildred Pitts Walter. Cover illustration copyright © 1990 by Pat Cummings. Reprinted by permission of Simon & Schuster Books for Young Readers, an imprint of Simon & Schuster Children's Publishing Division.

"Mary Redmond, John Darragh, and Dicey Langston: Spies" from *We Were There, Too!: Young People in U.S. History,* by Phillip Hoose. Copyright © 2001 by Phillip Hoose. Reprinted by permission of Farrar, Straus and Giroux, LLC.

Selection from *Me, Mop, and the Moondance Kid,* by Walter Dean Myers. Copyright © 1988 by Walter Dean Myers. Used by permission of Random House Children's Books, a division of Random House, Inc.

Selection from *Michelle Kwan: Heart of a Champion, An Autobiography.* Copyright © 1997 by Michelle Kwan Corp. Reprinted by permission of Scholastic Inc. and Momentum Partners Inc.

Mom's Best Friend, by Sally Hobart Alexander, photographs by George Ancona. Text copyright © 1992 by Sally Hobart Alexander. Photographs copyright © 1992 by George Ancona. Text reprinted by permission of the Author and Bookstop Literary Agency. Photographs reprinted by permission of the Photographer.

Selection from *My Side of the Mountain,* by Jean Craighead George. Copyright © 1959 by Jean Craighead George. Reprinted by permission of Dutton Children's Books, a division of Penguin Putnam Inc.

Selection from *Night of the Twisters,* by Ivy Ruckman. Text copyright © 1984 by Ivy Ruckman. Reprinted by

Cumulative Index

oldface page references indicate formal strategy and skill instruction.

schedules, TE2: **229H**
tables, TE1: **105H**
timelines, TE1: *87, R8;* TE2: *208,* **229H**
Venn diagram, TE2: *229H*

Graphic organizers

author's viewpoint chart, TE3: *262, 265, 271, 278, 279, 285A*

category chart, TE1: *83C, 84, 85, 90, 98, 99, 105A;* TE2: *149, 181AA*

cause/effect chart, TE3: *292, 298, 302, 309A, M9, M16, M22;* TE4: *399*

character development chart, TE5: *547A, 547B*

charts, TE1: *31, 81A, 105A, 105M;* TE2: *159R, 177, R9*

classification chart, TE1: *97*

clusters, TE1: *53B*

comparison chart, TE4: *R7;* TE5: *466B, 470, 477, 484, 485,* **569D;** TE6: *623, 623M*

conclusion chart, TE6: *650, 665,* **671A, 671B, M9, M14, M22**

connotation chart, TE4: *437G*

definition circle, TE2: *181M*

details chart, TE1: *37;* TE4: *368, 367C, 376, 378, 384, 385, 391A, R5*

details list, TE5: *481*

diagrams, TE1: *61;* TE5: *515, 543*

event map, TE1: *28, 34, 44, 45*

fact and opinion chart, TE2: *138, 141, 142, 143, 150, 151, 157B;* TE6: *613*

family relationships chart, TE5: *575*

folktale chart, TE1: *103, 105*

fun fact cards, TE2: *R13*

generalization chart, TE6: *602,* **623A,** *609, 617*

inferences chart, TE4: *416, 415C, 424, 425, 430, 431, 437A, R9*

judgments chart, TE5: *522, 530, 531, 540, 541, M9, M15, M22*

K-W-L chart, TE1: *48, 51;* TE2: *204;* TE3: **312,** *313, 320, 321, 326, 327;* TE5: **498,** *507, 512, 513;* TE6: *644*

log book, TE1: *71*

main idea chart, TE1: *95;* TE2: *209C, 210, 215, 222, 223, 229A*

mind map of mixed emotions, TE4: *381*

note cards, TE5: *566, 569*

outline frame, TE4: *388*

plot map, TE4: *442, 450, 458, 461A*

population chart/graph, TE5: *R36*

predictions chart, TE2: *184, 185, 200, 201, 207A, M9, M16, M26*

problem-solution chart, TE4: *344, 350, 351, 356, 357, 363A;* TE5: **519O;** TE6: *633*

schedules, TE1: *71*

selection map, TE1: *56, 57, 81A*

sequence charts, TE1: *95, M9, M16, M24;* TE2: *147, 213;* TE5: *571J, 576, 589*

story map, TE1: *43;* TE2: *162, 170, 171, 174, 175, 181B, R10;* TE3: *295;* TE4: *355;* TE5: *533, 547BB, 550, 556, 559, 562, 569A, R14*

summary log, TE1: *75;* TE3: *322;* TE6: *638*

tall tale chart, TE1: *107J*

timeline, TE1: *R8*

topic, main idea, and details chart, TE1: *89;* TE6: *628, 635, 641,* **647A**

Venn diagram, TE2: *229H, 232;* TE4: *354, 394, 393C, 394, 400, 401, 403, 406, 407, 413A, M9, M16, M19, M22, M25;* TE5: *479, 545*

word webs, TE1: *23J, 51J, 51M, R19;* TE2: *181M, R21;* TE3: *285M, R19;* TE4: *437M, R2;* TE5: *519M, 547J, 547M;* TE6: *625T, 671M*

Graphophonemic/graphophonic cues. *See* Phonics.

Guided reading. *See* Reading modes.

Handwriting, TE1: *53G;* TE2: *159G;* TE3: *289G;* TE4: *365G;* TE5: *495G;* TE6: *625G*

Home-Community Connection. *See* Home/Community Connections Book.

Home-School Connection. *See* Home/Community Connections Book.

Homework. *See* Home/Community Connections Book.

Illustrators of Anthology selections

Aagaard, Gary, TE6: *651*

Adams, Mike, TE1: *M10*

Baviera, Rocco, TE5: *485*

Bennett, Nneka, TE4: *344*

Boatwright, Phil, TE1: *45, 114*

Carpenter, Nancy, TE4: *431*

Colón, Raúl, TE5: *563*

Fuller, Stephen, TE2: *M19*

Heo, Yumi, TE6: *M18*

Himler, Ron, TE3: *292*

Jenkins, Leonard, TE3: *312*

de Kiefte, Kees, TE4: *407*

Lee, Paul, TE2: *184*

Lorraine, Walter, TE1: *125*

Mitchell, Melanie, TE4: *M10*

Mordan, C.B., TE3: *M19*

Ortega, José, TE2: *162*

Peet, Bill, TE5: *582*

Pinkney, Jerry, TE5: *22*

Spearing, Craig, TE1: *119*

Spector, Joel, TE3: *M10*

Spender, Nick, TE5: *M10*

Tomes, Margot, TE3: *279*

Van Allsburg, Chris, TE1: *110*

Illustrator's craft

characterization, TE3: *284*

layout and design, TE4: *412*

photographs and captions, TE4: *390*

picture details, TE3: *284, 308*

point of view, TE3: *308*

setting, TE3: *284*

Independent and recreational reading

suggestions for, TE1: *23E–23F, 51B, 51O–51R, 81B, 81O–81R, 105B, 105O–105R, R2–R3, R4–R5, R6–R7;* TE2: *130E–130F, 157B, 181B, 207B, 229B, R2–R3, R4–R5, R6–R7;* TE3: *254E–254F, 285B, 285O–285R, 309B, 309O–309R, 333B, 333O–333R, R2–R3, R4–R5, R6–R7;* TE4: *336E–336F, 363B, 363O–363R, 391B, 391O–391R, 413B, 413O–413R, 437B, 437O–437R, R2–R3, R4–R5, R6–R7;* TE5: *491B, 491O–491R, 519B, 519O–519R, 547B, 547O–547R, 569B, 569O–569R, R2–R3, R4–R5, R6–R7;* TE6: *594E–594F, 623B, 623O–623R, 647B, 647O–647R, 671B, 671O–671R, R2–R3, R4–R5, R6–R7*

See also Reading modes.

Independent writing

suggestions for, TE1: *51L, 81L, 105L;* TE2: *157L, 181L, 209L, 229L;* TE3: *285L, 309L, 333L;* TE4: *363L, 391L, 413L, 437L;* TE5: *491L, 519L, 547L, 569L;* TE6: *623L, 647L, 671L*

See also Language Center; Teacher's Resource Blackline Masters.

Individual needs, meeting. *See* Reaching All Learners.

Inferences, making

about author's craft, TE1: *92, 98, 105, 116, 120;* TE2: *166, 174, 192, 198, 238, 242;* TE3: *274, 294, 325, 326;* TE4: *370, 372, 374, 378, 382, 385, 396, 416, 418, 437, M15, M22, 460;* TE5: *504, 526, 540, 552, 560, 562, 586, 590;* TE6: *606, 614, 623, 630, 638*

about characters' actions and feelings, TE1: *31, 44, 60, 62, 70, 72, 74, 76, 88, 103, 105, M20;* TE2: *140, 142, 144, 152, 166, 174, 175, 185, 188, 191, 193, 194, 201, 216, 218, 222, 236, M16, M22, 248, 250;* TE3: *272, 280, 285, 294, 302, 309, 326, M10, M16, M17;* TE4: *348, 350, 353, 356, 357, 363, 370, 384, 386, 396, 397, 398, 402, 406, 417, 423, 428, 432, 437A–437B, M10, M20, M32, 444, 452, 454,456, R14–R15;* TE5: *472, 476, 478, 480, 486, 506, 508, 512, 519, 528, 532, 536, 538, 542, 554, 556, 562, 563, 564, M10, M18, M19, 576, 578, 584;* TE6: *608, 634, 635, 640, 647, 652, 654, 656, 665, 666, 671, M10*

by drawing conclusions, TE1: *38, 40, 51, 86, 94, 100, 105, 122, M14;* TE2: *140, 142, 144, 152, 176, 198, 207, 215, 229;* TE3: *264, 266, 268, 272, 285;* TE4: *344, 348, 351, 353, 356, 357, 376, 386, 397, 432, 444, 437A–437B, M17, M33, R8–R9, R16–R17;* TE5: *500, 510, 514, 519, 526, 563, M10, M14, M19, M22, 576, 580, 592*

from text organization, TE1: *81, 89;* TE2:

226–229
See also Comprehension skills, cause and effect; Comprehension skills, generalizations, making.

Inflected forms. *See* Structural analysis.

Information skills
adjusting reading rate/method of reading, TE3: ***333H***
applications and forms, completing, TE6: ***671H***
atlas, using an, TE1: ***129H***
bias and assumption, TE4: ***413H***
categorization, TE6: *668–671*
checks for accuracy in other sources, TE2: *157D, 157H*
collecting data, TE1: *51, 81;* TE2: *157H, 207, R13;* TE6: *M12*
comparing different sources, TE1: *51, 51H, 105H;* TE2: *157H*
comparing information in different forms: primary and secondary, TE3: ***309H***
comparing information in various media, TE3: ***333H***
dictionaries, using different, TE2: ***253H***
finding and evaluating information, TE2: *138,* ***157H;*** TE4: ***413H,*** *M6;* TE5: *462J, 495C*
generating questions, TE2: *207*
graphic aids: maps, globes, charts, tables, and graphs, using, TE1: ***105H, 129H;*** TE6: ***623H***
index, using, TE2: ***207H***
Internet, using the, TE2: ***157H,*** *229*
interviewing, TE1: *M27;* TE2: *207;* TE4: ***437H,*** *R37;* TE5: *547*
investigation, TE2: *177, 207*
library, using, TE5: *466B, 518, 593H*
locating information, TE2: *207, 207H*
media, evaluating effects of, TE6: ***647H***
multiple sources to locate information, using, TE3: *285,* ***285H***
note taking, TE4: ***363H***
paraphrasing and synthesizing, TE4: ***391H***
parts of a book, using, TE2: *207H*
presenting information, TE1: *51, 51H, 81, 81BB, 101*
print and electronic card catalogs, using, TE1: ***81H***
print and electronic reference sources, using, TE1: ***51H;*** TE2: *181, 229, 253H;* TE4: *363, 391*
scanning for information, TE2: ***204–207***
selecting the appropriate reference source, TE2: ***181H,*** *207*
summarizing graphically, TE2: ***229H;*** TE6: *638*
video and audio resources, finding, TE4: ***461H***
See also Reference and study skills.

Informational selection, structure of. *See* Comprehension skills, text organization.

Interviewing. *See* Speaking; Reference and study skills, reference resources.

Journal, TE1: *29, 47, 53A, 57, 77, 85, 101, 111;* TE2: *139, 153, 163, 177, 185, 203, 211, 225, 235;* TE3: *263, 281, 293, 313, 329;* TE4: *345, 359, 369, 387, 395, 409, 417, 433,* ***437K–437L,*** *440, 443, M43;* TE5: *471, 487, 491M, 499, 515, 523, 543, 551, 564, 565, 574, 582, 591;* TE6: *603, 619, 629, 643, 651, 667*

Judgments, making. *See* Comprehension skills.

Knowledge, activating prior. *See* Background, building.

K-W-L strategy. *See* Graphic organizers.

Language and usage. *See* Grammar and usage.

Language Center, TE1: *51M–51N, 81M–81N, 105M–105N, 129M–129N;* TE2: *157M–157N, 181M–181N, 207M–207N, 229M–229N, 253M–253N;* TE3: *285M–285N, 309M–309N, 333M–333N;* TE4: *363M–363N, 391M–391N, 413M–413N, 437M–437N;* TE5: *491M–491N, 519M–519N, 547M–547N, 569M–569N;* TE6: *623M–623N, 647M–647N, 671M–671N*

Language concepts and skills
active verbs, TE2: *152*
archaic language, TE3: *307*
borrowed words: words from other languages, TE2: ***253G***
British English, TE2: *157F*
categories, TE2: *253M*
colorful language, TE2: *152*
conversational language, TE2: *138–151*
descriptive language, TE1: *62, 66;* TE2: *152;* TE3: *314*
figurative language. *See* Literary devices.
formal and informal language, TE2: *229K;* TE4: *363N, 423;* TE5: *593M*
idioms/expressions, TE2: *142, 168, 220, R3;* TE4: *448*
informal language, TE2: *140*
jargon, TE5: ***547F***
poetic. *See* Poetic devices.
primary language activities. *See* English Language Learners.
sensory language, TE1: *52, 53, 53B,* ***53C;*** TE6: *622, 630*
slang, TE2: *140;* TE4: *M12*
Spanish words, TE2: *170, 253G;* TE5: *552*
superlatives, TE2: *165*
word play: jokes, puns, riddles, TE1: *40;* TE4: *360, 361, 443*
See also Vocabulary, building.

Language games, TE1: *23J, 51F, 51M, 81F, 81M, 105F, 105M, 129M, R26–R29;* TE2: *157F, 181F, 181M, 181N, 207F, 207M, 229F, 229M, 229N, 253M, R21, R23;* TE3: *285F, 285M, 309F, 309M, 333D, 333M, 333N;* TE4: *363F, 363M, 391 391M, 413F, 413M, 437F, 437M, 461M, R32–R35* TE5: *491M, 519M, 547M, 569M, R34, R35;* TE6: *623M, 647M, 671M, R27–R29*

Language mechanics. *See* Mechanics, language.

Learning styles, activities employing alternate modalities to meet individual, TE1: *46, 47, 56, 76, 77, 84, 100, 101;* TE2: *138, 152, 153, 177, 203, 225;* TE3: *280, 281, 292, 304–305, 312, 328–329;* TE4: *358, 359, 386, 387, 408, 409, 432, 433;* TE5: *486, 487, 514, 515, 542, 543, 564, 565, 592, 593;* TE6: *618, 619, 642, 643, 666, 667. See also* Extra Support Handbook; Reaching All Learners.

Lesson plans
daily, TE1: *25A–25B, 53M–53N, 81W–81X, 107E–107F, M4–M5;* TE2: *133A–133B, 159M–159N, 181W–181X, 207W–207X, M4–M5, 231E–231F;* TE3: *257A–257B, 289M–289N, 309W–309X, M4–M5;* TE4: *339A–339B, 365M–365N, 391W–3991X, 413W–413X, M4–M5, 439E–439F;* TE5: *465A–465B, 495M–495N, 519W–519X, 547W–547X, 571E–571F;* TE6: *597A–597B, 625M–625N, 647W–648X, M4–M5*
Managing Flexible Groups, TE1: *25C–25D, 53O–53P, 81Y–81Z;* TE2: *133C–133D, 159O–159P, 181Y–181Z, 207Y–207Z, 231G–231H;* TE3: *257C–257D, 289O–289P, 309Y–309Z;* TE4: *339C–339D, 365O–365P, 391Y–391Z, 413Y–413Z, 439G–439H;* TE5: *465A–465B, 495O–495P, 519Y–519Z, 547Y–547Z, M4–M5, 571G–571H;* TE6: *597C–597D, 625O–625P, 647Y–647Z*

Lessons, specific
comprehension, TE1: ***51A–51B, 81A–81B, 105A–105B, 129A–129B;*** TE2: ***157A–157B, 181A–181B, 207A–207B, 229A–229B, 253A–253B;*** TE3: ***285A–285B, 309A–309B, 333A–333B;*** TE4: ***363A–363B, 391A–391B, 413A–413B, 437A–437B,*** TE5: ***491A–491B, 519A–519B, 547A-547B, 569A-569B, 593A–593B;*** TE6: ***623A–623B, 647A–647B, 671A–671B***
decoding, TE1: ***51C–51D, 81C–81D, 105C–105D, 129C–129D;*** TE2: ***157C–157D, 181C–181D, 207C–207D, 229C, 253C–253D;*** TE3: ***285C–285D, 309C–309D, 333C–333D;*** TE4: ***363C–363D, 391C–391D, 413C–413D, 437C–437D, 461C–461D;*** TE5: ***491C–491D, 519C–519D, 547C–547D,***

Library, using. *See* Information skills; Reference and study skills.

Limited English proficient students. *See* English Language Learners.

Linking literature. *See* Connections; Cross-Curricular activities; Links, content area.

Links, content area
art, TE4: *410–413;* TE5: *488–491*
careers, TE1: *78–81;* TE5: *544–547;* TE6: *668–671*
health and safety, TE4: *388–391*
literature, TE1: *102–105*
music, TE2: *178–181;* TE3: *282–285*
poetry, TE4: *434–437;* TE6: *620–623*
primary sources, TE3: *306–309*
science, TE1: *48–51;* TE2: *226–229*
social studies, TE2: *154–157, 204–207;* TE3: *306–309, 330–333;* TE4: *360–363;* TE5: *516–519, 566–569*
technology, TE2: *178–181;* TE6: *644–647*

Listening
assessing, TE1: *25G, 53S, 81CC, 107K;* TE2: *135A, 159S, 181CC;* TE3: *259A, 289S, 309CC;* TE4: *341B, 365T, 391V, 413V;* TE5: *467A, 495S, 519CC, 547CC, 571K;* TE6: *599B, 625T, 647DD*
connecting/comparing, TE1: *25H, 53T, 81DD, 107L;* TE2: *135B, 159T, 181DD;* TE3: *259B, 289T, 309DD;* TE4: *341C, 365T, 391V, 413V,*

439L; TE5: *467B, 495T, 519DD, 547DD, 571L;* TE6: *599B, 625T, 647DD*
for details, TE1: *81CC, 81DD;* TE3: *259A, 259B, 289S, 289T, 309CC, 309DD;* TE4: *341A, 341B, 365S, 365T, 391CC, 391DD, 413CC, 413V, 439L;* TE5: *491N;* TE6: *625S, 625T*
for information, TE1: *25G–25H, R13;* TE3: *309CC, 309DD;* TE6: *599A–599B, 625S–625T, 647CC–647DD*
for main idea, TE2: *R15;* TE5: *491N*
for pleasure/enjoyment, TE1: *25G–25H, 53S–53T, 81CC–81DD, 107J, 107K–107L;* TE2: *135A–135B, 159S–159T, 181CC–181DD, 207CC–207DD, 231K–231L;* TE3: *254J, 259A–259B, 289S–289T, 309CC–309DD;* TE4: *341A–341B, 365S–365T, 391CC–391DD, 413CC–413DD, 439K–439L;* TE5: *467A–467B, 495S–495T, 519CC–519DD, 547CC–547DD, 571K–571L, R15*
for tone and expression, TE1: *25G*
guidelines
for asking clarifying questions, TE5: *519N, 593N*
for asking for help, TE5: *519N*
for avoiding interruptions, TE1: *51N*
for careful, attentive listening, TE1: *51N, 105N;* TE3: *259A, 289S, 309CC;* TE5: *491N, 519N*
for demonstrating appropriate listening behaviors, TE3: *259A–259B, 289S–289T, 309CC–309DD;* TE4: *363N, 391N, 413N, 437N, 461N*
for establishing listening purpose, TE3: *289S, 309CC*
for interviewing, TE4: *437H*
for listening to directions, TE6: *647N*
for taking notes, TE5: *593N*
for taking a telephone message, TE4: *413N*
in a writing conference. *See* Reading-Writing Workshop, conferencing.
personal response to, TE1: *25H, 53T, 81DD, 107L;* TE2: *135B, 159T, 181DD, 207DD, 231L;* TE3: *259B, 281, 289T, 309DD;* TE4: *341B, 365T, 391DD, 413DD, 439L;* TE5: *467B, 495T, 519DD, 547DD, 571L;* TE6: *599B, 625T, 647DD*
prior knowledge for, TE1: *25G, 53S, 81CC, 107K;* TE2: *135A, 159S, 181CC, 207CC, 231K;* TE3: *259A, 289S, 309CC;* TE4: *341A, 365S, 391CC, 413CC, 439L;* TE5: *467A, 495S, 519CC, 547CC, 571K;* TE6: *599A, 625S, 647CC*
purpose
to analyze and evaluate. *See* Literature, analyzing; evaluating.
to assess/evaluate, TE2: *135B*
to determine author's viewpoint, TE3: *R9*
to evaluate author, TE1: *81CC*
to follow directions, TE3: ***309CC–309DD**, R13*
to identify high, low, near, far, soft, and loud sounds, *177*
to reinforce/extend learning through use of technology, *153, 177, 203, 223*

to retell a story, TE1: *33, 45*
to think aloud. *See* Modeling, think aloud.
to visualize. *See* Visualizing.
to write from dictation, TE3: *285E, 309E, 333E;* TE4: *363F, 391F, 413F, 437F*
to a news report, TE2: *R15*
to a poem, TE2: *231K–231L, 253N;* TE3: *254J*
to a read aloud. *See* Reading modes.
to a speech, TE2: *R9*
to a story, TE2: *159S–159T, 181CC–181DD*
to an announcement, TE2: *181N*
to an audiotape, TE3: *R9*
to an oral presentation, TE5: *593N*
to creative dramatics. *See* Creative dramatics.
to interviews, TE2: *207*
to literature discussion. *See* Responding to literature.
to music, TE2: *R11*
to oral presentation. *See* Speaking activities.
to oral presentation. *See* Speaking, oral report
to oral reading. *See* Reading modes; Rereading
to poetry, TE4: *434–437*
to recognize bias, TE4: *413H*
to take notes and summarize, TE5: *491N*

Listening comprehension
author's viewpoint, TE3: ***259A–259B**, R9*
categorize and classify, TE1: ***81CC–81DD***
cause and effect, TE3: ***289S–289T***
compare and contrast, TE4: ***391CC–391DD***
drawing conclusions, TE5: ***467A–467B;*** TE6: ***647CC–647DD***
fact and opinion, TE2: ***135A–135B***
following directions, TE3: ***309CC–309DD***
making generalizations, TE6: ***599A–599B***
making inferences, TE4: ***413CC–413DD***
making judgments, TE5: ***519CC–519DD***
noting details, TE4: ***365S–365T***
predicting outcomes, TE2: ***135A–135B***
problem solving, TE4: ***341A–341B***
propaganda, TE5: ***495S–495T***
sequence of events, TE1: ***25G–25H***
story structure, TE2: ***159S–159T;*** TE5: ***547CC–547DD***
text organization, TE1: ***53S–53T***
topic, main idea, and details, TE2: ***207CC–207DD;*** TE6: ***625S–625T***
understanding autobiography, ***571K–571L***
understanding plays, TE4: ***439K–439L, 461A–461B***
understanding poetry, TE2: ***231K–231L***
understanding tall tales, TE1: ***107K–107L***

Literacy, expanding. *See* Skills links.

Literary analysis
change story elements, TE2: *181A–181B*
classic literature, TE1: *102–105;* TE3: *259A–259B;* TE6: *620–623*
common themes, TE1: *25G, 25H, 46, 51, 54, 76, 82, 100;* TE2: *136, 160, 182, 202, 207, 224;* TE3: *259B, 260, 289T, 290, 304, 309, 309DD*

Main idea and supporting details, identifying. See Comprehension skills, topic/main idea/supporting details.

Management. See Teaching and Management.

Managing
assessment. See Assessment, planning for.
instruction. See Classroom Management.
program materials. See Teaching and management.

Managing flexible groups. See Lesson plans.

Maps, using. See Graphic information, interpreting.

Mathematics activities. See Cross-curricular activities.

Meaning, constructing from text. See Comprehension skills; Decoding skills; Language concepts and skills; Phonics; Strategies, reading.

Monitoring comprehension. *See* Strategies, reading.

Morphemes. *See* Decoding skills.

Morphology. *See* Decoding skills; Phonics.

Multi-age classroom. *See* Combination classroom.

Multicultural activities/information
African-American participation in the American Revolution, TE3: *310, 322*
art of origami, TE4: *410–413*
arts, crafts, and traditions of students' cultures, TE4: *411*
Chinese characters, TE4: *394–407*
Chinese culture and customs, TE4: *392, 393, 409*
cultural celebrations, TE5: *569*
cultural concepts of time as circular, TE2: *180*
early Hawaiians, TE1: *85*
Hawaiian Volcanoes, TE1: *92*
Latin music, TE4: *R3*
Latino people, TE4: *436–437*
life in Trinidad, TE4: *R6–R7*
monarchies, countries with, TE4: *444*
multi-ethnic neighborhood, TE4: *R2–R3*
myths and legends about nature, TE1: *59*
Native American art, TE5: *467A–467B, 488–491*
Roman belief in Vulcan, TE1: *85*
storytelling customs, TE2: *207O*

Narrative text, TE1: *28–44, 102–105*; TE2: *138–150, 163–175, 182, 185–201, 210–222*; TE3: *263–278, 293–303, 306–309, 313–327*; TE4: *344–357, 368–385, 394–407, 416–431, 442–459*; TE5: *470–484, 555–562, 574–577, 578–581, 582–587, 588–591*; TE6: *651–665*

National Test Correlation. *See* Assessment, planning for.

Newsletters. *See* Home/Community Connections book.

Nonfiction. *See* Literary genres; Selections in Anthology.

Notes
from a lecture or speech, TE1: M6; TE5: 547, 59
from written sources, TE1: M45; TE4: 363H, 391N; TE3: 254J, 289R, 309AA, 309BB, M6; TE5: 491N, 495B, 547BB, 566–569, 571J; TE6: 598B, 625Q, 647AA, 647BB
organizing, TE3: 289R
speaking from, TE3: 285N
taking, TE1: 53Q, 53R, 107J; TE2: 130I, 134A, 181AA, 207AA, 207BB; TE4: M24

Nouns. *See* Speech, parts of.

Oral composition. *See* Speaking.

Oral language development. *See* Listening; Speaking.

Oral presentations. *See* Speaking.

Oral reading. *See* Reading modes; Rereading.

Oral reading fluency. *See* Fluency.

Oral reports. *See* Speaking.

Oral summary. *See* Summarizing.

Paired learning. *See* Classroom management partners.

Parent conferences. *See* Home/Community Connections book.

Parent involvement. *See* Home/Community Connections book; Teacher's Resource Blackline Masters.

Parts of a book. *See* Reference and study ski

Peer conferences. *See* Reading-Writing Workshop: conferencing.

Peer evaluation. *See* Cooperative learning activities; Reading-Writing Workshop, conferencin

Peer interaction. *See* Cooperative learning activities.

Personal response. *See* Responding to literatu

Phonics
consonants
alternations, TE6: **647D**
clusters *str, rch, mpr, mpl*, TE4: *363C,* **363D**, *363M*
digraphs, TE5: **569D**, *569N*
digraphs, voiced and silent final, TE3: **309D**

Index I13

-*able*, TE2: *164*

-*ent*, -*ant*, -*able*, and -*ible*, TE6: **671C,** *671M, M35, R18*

-*er*, TE3: *319*

-*ful*, TE5: *R1*; TE6: *647M*

-*ion*, TE1: *105N*; TE5: **491C,** *593N, M34, R17*

-*ive*, -*ic*, TE1: *105N*; TE2: **229C,** *229N, M39,* **253C,** *253M, R22*

-*less*, TE3: *301*; TE5: *503, 593C, R17*

-*ly*, -*ness*, -*ment*, -*ful*, -*less*, TE1: *57*; TE2: *185*; TE4: *397*, **437C,** *437N, M35, R24*; TE5: *537, R17*

-*ment* and -*ward*, TE5: *593C, R17*

-*ness*, TE5: *523, R17*

-*or*, -*ure*, TE1: *105N*

-*ous*, TE2: *185*, **207C, 207N, 253C,** *253M, M39, R20*

-*sion*, TE1: *85*

-*tion*, TE1: *64*

-*ward*, TE2: **207C,** *207N,* **253C,** *253M, M39, R20*; TE5: *593C, R17*

syllables

multi-syllabic words, TE1: *64*, **81C, 81N,** *M36, R16*; TE2: *157C–157D, 181C–181D, 207C–207D, 211, 218, 229C*; TE4: *363C, 363D, 391C, 413C, 437C*

patterns VCV, VCCV, VCCCV, TE3: **309C,** *M34, R16*; TE5: *471,* **547C,** *547N,* **M35,** *R20*; TE6: *647M*

stressed and unstressed, TE5: **519C,** *519N, M34, R18*

three-syllable words, TE6: **647C,** *647M, M34, R16*

VV, TE4: **391C, 461C,** *461M, M34, R20*

VCCCV, TE4: **363C, 461C,** *461M, M34, R18*

word roots

Greek root *phot*, TE1: *81J*

ped, TE4: *461M*

side, TE3: *333C*

spec, spect, opt, TE2: **181C,** *M38, R18*

struct and *rupt*, TE1: **105C,** *105N, M37, R18*

vis and *vid*, TE1: **129C,** *129M*

See also Decoding skills; Vocabulary, building; Vocabulary, selection;

Student self-assessment. *See* Assessment, planning for; Self-assessment.

Study skills. *See* Reference and study skills.

Study strategies. *See* Reference and study skills.

Suffixes. *See* Structural analysis.

Summaries, reading selection

Reader's Library, TE6: *R2, R4, R6*

Summarizing

oral summaries, TE1: *25B, 34, 35, 44, 45, 54, 68, 69, 74, 75, 91, 98, 99, R3, R5, R7*; TE2: *142, 143, 150, 151, 162, 169, 170, 171, 175, 177, 181, 181A, 195, 201, 222, 223*; TE3: *259B, 271, 278, 279, 289T, 298, 299, 302, 303, 320,* *321, 326, 328, 330*; TE4: *350, 351, 356, 357, 379, 384, 385, 391, 401, 406, 407, 424, 425, 430, 431, 450, 458*; TE5: *477, 484, 485, 491N, 531, 535, 540, 541, 562, 569, R4, R5*; TE6: *609, 617, 635, 641, 659, 665, R3, R5, R7*

written summaries, TE2: *181*, **181K–181L,** *229H, R15*; TE4: *376, 391*; TE5: *M43*; TE6: *R23*

Syntactic cues. *See* Structural analysis.

Syntax. *See* Decoding, context clues.

Teacher-guided reading. *See* Reading modes.

Teacher Read Aloud

autobiography

"Thrilled" by Avi, TE5: *571K–571L*

biography

"Barbara Jordan: A Powerful Voice for America," TE2: *207CC–DD*

historical fiction

"Sleds on Boston Common: A Story From the American Revolution" by Louise Borden, TE3: *289S–289T*

"Samuel Adams 'The Father of American Independence'" by Dennis Brindell Fradin, TE3: *259A–259B*

narrative nonfiction

"Dakota Dugout" by Ann Turner, TE5: *519CC–519DD*

"The Wreck of the E.S. Newman" from *Cricket* by Ruth Ewers, TE1: *25G–25H*

nonfiction

"Flag Facts," by Fran Hodgkins, TE3: *309CC–309DD*

"Generations Together" by Gabriel Davis, TE4: *365S–365T*

"Giving Wildlife a Second Chance" by Connie Goldsmith, TE6: *647CC–647DD*

"Intown Animals" by Carolyn J. Gard, TE6: *599A–599B*

"Nunavut" from *Faces* magazine, TE6: *625S–625T*

play

"Job Interview, The" by Robert Mauro, TE4: *439K–439L*

poem

"Poetry" by Edwin A. Hoey, TE2: *231K–231L*

science articles and features

"Making Waves!" from *Contact Kids* by Gail Skroback Hennessey, TE1: *81CC–81DD*

"Hurricanes: Weather at Its Wildest" by Fran Hodgkins, TE1: *53S–53T*

social studies article

"Gold Rush, The" by Dayton Duncan, TE5: *495S–495T*

sports article

"Baseball's Hero with a Heart" by Kitty

Colton, TE2: *135A–135B*

story

"Anna Meyer: A Wartime Chance to Play Ball" by Phillip Hoose, TE4: *413CC–413DD*

"Art of the Needle and Loom" by Kay Wood, TE5: *467A–467B*

"Darning Needle, The" by Eric A. Kimmel, TE5: *547CC–547DD*

"Digby Perkins's Secret Code" by Fran Hodgkins, TE4: *341A–341B*

"Getting Even with Glover," TE4: *391CC–391DD*

"Just One of the Guys" by Donna Gamache from *Cricket Magazine*, TE2: *159S–159T*

"Little Coaching, A" by Noah Edelson from *Chicken Soup for the Preteen Soul*, TE2: *181CC–181DD*

tall tale

"Bess Call" retold by Kevin Supples, TE1: *107K–107L*

Teaching across the curriculum. *See* Content areas, reading in the; Cross-curricular activities; Links, content area.

Teaching and management

managing assessment, TE1: *23K–23L*; TE2: *130K–130L*; TE3: *254K–254L*; TE4: *336K–336L*; TE5: *462K–462L*; TE6: *594M–594N*

managing instruction, TE1: *23G–23H*; TE2: *130G–130H*; TE3: *254G–254H*; TE4: *336G–336H*; TE5: *462G–462H*; TE6: *594G–594H*

managing program materials, TE1: *24A–24D, 53I–53L, 81S–81V, M1–M3, 107A–107D*; TE2: *131A–132B, 159I–159L, 181U–181X, 207S–207V, 231A–231D, M1–M3*; TE3: *255A–256B, 289I–289L, 309S–309V, M1–M3*; TE4: *337A–338B, 365I–365L, 391S–391V, 413S–413V*; TE5: *463A–464B, 495I–495L, 519S–519V, 547S–547V, 571A–571D, M1–M3*; TE6: *595A–596B, 625I–625L, M1–M3*

parent conferences. *See* Home/Community Connections Book.

special needs of students, meeting. *See* Reaching All Learners.

Technology resources, TE6: *R30*

address list, TE1: *R31*; TE2: *R38*; TE3: *R30*; TE4: *R40*; TE5: *R39*; TE6: *R32*

Internet, TE1: *45, 47, 56, 77, 99, 101*; TE2: *151, 153, 177, 203, 223*; TE3: *279, 281, 292, 305, 312, 329*; TE4: *359, 387, 409, 433*; TE5: *485, 487, 498, 495C, 515, 522, 543, 565*; TE6: *619, 643, 667*

Test Prep, TE1: *28, 51B, 56, 81B, 84, 105B, 129B*; TE2: *157B, 162, 181B, 184, 207B, 210, 229B, 253B*; TE3: *262, 285B, 292, 309B, 312, 333B*; TE4: *344, 363B, 368, 391B, 394, 413B, 416, 437B, 442, 461B*; TE5: *470, 491B, 498, 519B, 522, 547B, 550, 569B, 574, 593B*; TE6: *602, 623B, 628, 647B, 650, 671B*